LEARNING TO WRITE DIFFERENTLY

Beginning Writers and Word Processing

Language and Educational Processes

Judith Green, *Series Editor*
University of California at Santa Barbara

LEARNING TO WRITE DIFFERENTLY

Beginning Writers and Word Processing

Marilyn Cochran-Smith
Cynthia L. Paris
Jessica L. Kahn

 ABLEX PUBLISHING CORPORATION
NORWOOD, NEW JERSEY

11/94

23080244

Library of Congress Cataloging-in-Publication Data

Cochran-Smith, Marilyn, 1951–
    Learning to write differently : beginning writers and word
processing / Marilyn Cochran-Smith, Cynthia L. Paris, Jessica L.
Kahn.
        p.   cm.—(Language and educational processes)
    Includes bibliographical references and index.
    ISBN 0-89391-761-3.—ISBN 0-89391-762-1 (pbk.)
    1. English language—Composition and exercises—Computer-assisted
instruction.   2. Word processing in education.   I. Paris, Cynthia
L.   II. Kahn, Jessica L.   III. Title.   IV. Series.
LB1576.7.C63 1991
372.6'23044—dc20   91-1998
                                                                CIP

Ablex Publishing Corporation
355 Chestnut Street
Norwood, New Jersey 07648

This book is for T.T., M.A., N.B., M.D., K.L., and M.S. with appreciation and deep respect.
—MCS, CLP, JLK

Table of Contents

List of Figures

Preface to the Series

LANGUAGE AND EDUCATIONAL PROCESSES

This series of volumes provides a forum for the exploration of how language in use influences and is influenced by educational processes. The volumes in this series reflect the diverse theories, methods, and findings about the roles and functions of language in educational processes. The common theme across these volumes is an understanding of the central role that language plays in education. Of particular concern is the need to make visible the often invisible influences of language on what and how students learn or fail to learn from participating in various educational processes throughout their lives.

Education and language are viewed as diverse and situated processes. Thus, to understand the role and function of language in the education of individuals and social groups, we must understand how language functions in and across various educational situations—in the home, in pre-kindergarten through high school, in college, in the workplace, and in post-graduate and professional education.

Scholars working on the nexus of language and education from the perspective of sociolinguistics, psycholinguistics, ethnomethodology, ethnography of communication, literary theory, sociology of language, cognitive psychology, linguistics and related areas are invited to submit monographs and edited collections of original papers to the series editor for review by the editorial board.

Judith L. Green
University of California, Santa Barbara

Associate Editor:
Ginger Weade
University of Florida

xiii

chapter 1
Understanding Writing and Word Processing: Tools, Tasks, and Teaching Cultures

Learning to write with computers and learning to teach writing with computers are qualitatively different experiences from learning with paper and pencil. As we describe in the chapters that follow, this argument is based on a study of elementary classrooms in which young children used word processing as one of their writing tools. We found that teachers who used word processing taught writing differently from the ways they taught it with paper and pencil. Although initially they used word processing to bolster their ongoing programs, over time they altered the learning contexts of their classrooms and even came to understand children's writing in new ways. When teachers introduced word processing, they also set up new procedures, especially new ways to provide assistance for beginning writers. The concurrent introduction of a new tool and a new form of writing assistance significantly altered the participation structures of writing instruction. Consequently, as our title phrase emphasizes, young children who learned to write with word processing had an experience that was significantly different from their experience learning to write with paper and pencil. They had the opportunity to work closely with adults to use a writing tool whose production and revision capacities are revolutionary in the history of writing. As a pedagogical tool, word processing precludes a narrow concentration on aesthetics and temporarily removes the difficulties of print production that often preoccupy young writers. Working with adults to use word processing provided opportunities for beginners to shift their efforts from inscribing, recopying, and correcting to encoding, informing, and editing. Our title phrase also emphasizes that the tool of word processing was utilized in ways that varied considerably from setting to setting, and that these ways interacted with the cultures of teaching and school, people, conditions of learning, and teachers' and children's goals over time. In a very real sense, then, the life worlds of various classrooms established different conditions for learning and hence different opportunities for teachers and children to learn to write with the tool of word processing. As we demonstrate throughout this book, understanding word processing and writing requires careful attention to the dynamic interrelationships of tools, tasks, and teaching cultures.

LEARNING TO WRITE IN RETROSPECT

For several years, three of us worked together to explore the interrelationships of tools, tasks, and teaching cultures by documenting what happened when 5- to 10-year-old beginning writers and their teachers had the opportunity to use word processing for classroom writing. As a point of information, we should confess that each of us is an ardent user of word processing, committed to composing directly at the keyboard and inclined to announce that she is no longer able to write anything longer than a paragraph without benefit of machinery. On the other hand, none of us is a technophile, and only one would venture to claim the title *computer expert*. Our work together was not prompted by a passion to find more ways for teachers to use computers in their classrooms, nor was it motivated by a desire to demonstrate that teachers using computers could teach children better and faster than teachers using other materials or methods. Rather, as researchers, we were driven by a need to know more about the ways the computer, as a writing tool, might interact with and shape children's as well as teachers' opportunities to learn about, demonstrate, and use writing in early elementary classrooms.

During the 5-year course of data collection and analysis, our close observations of teachers and children elicited many memories of our own early writing experiences. We discovered that our experiences were remarkably similar and that they represented the largely "traditional" approach of the individual child learning to write with the tools of paper and pencil by copying from an expert model. For this reason, we have chosen to begin this book, not with a description of the current world of learning to write, but with a reconstruction of what was "normal" for all three of us. Our hope is that, by creating a picture of writing in classrooms before computers, we will both provide a point of departure for the exploration of writing with the tool of word processing and raise questions about what is involved in learning to write in school settings.

Each of us started going to school in the 1950s. Each was taught to write with tools that obviously did not include word processing and in classrooms that clearly did not encourage collaboration and experimentation. The commonality in our early writing lives is reflected below in the experiences recalled by the senior author. These are used to introduce and frame the questions addressed in this volume.

In September of 1956, just before I started first grade, I went to Woolworth's Five-and-Ten with my mother to buy a 29-cent red pencil box. It was an inch wide, less than half an inch tall, and 10 inches long. The cardboard case had a picture of a school bus on it and a tray that slid in and out like a matchbox. The tray was divided in half vertically to make two skinny compartments and had a third compartment about an inch square at one end. Woolworth's also offered a 99-cent pencil box. It had an outer case that wrapped around the tray and closed with a real snap, and it had two drawers already filled with school supplies—pencils and pens and strange items like plastic protractors and metal compasses that I had never seen before but was willing to take on faith I needed for school.

I looked fleetingly at the fancy boxes, but I understood that we had come for the no-frills version and that the pricier boxes were for big kids. And anyway I loved my one-drawer pencil box. It was new, it was red, and it told everybody that I was old enough to go to school. But I loved even more the things my mother bought to put inside it. Number-two yellow pencils with pearly pink erasers at the ends fit perfectly into the long, skinny compartments in the tray, and a fat pink eraser that smelled faintly of rubber and looked like a just-opened piece of bubble gum took its place in the little square compartment at the end of the box. These items announced to the world that I was not simply going to school . . . I was going to write! I intended to create wonderful stories with my yellow pencils and use my pink eraser, rounded corners first, when I changed my mind about an ending or a character's name. I would write on blue-lined white paper, smooth to the touch, with three holes and a red line down the side margin, the kind I had seen my high school babysitter use to write notes to her boyfriend.

Writing in Miss Dagg's class was not what I had imagined. Each first grader received a flat metal box with eight school-brand crayons that were more wax than color and one fat green pencil with no eraser. Miss Dagg Scotch-taped red and white name labels to the crayon boxes and around our pencils, and we were cautioned to guard them carefully because we wouldn't be getting new ones for a long time. After a week the tape began to fray, and from then on the pencils felt scratchy and slightly sticky whenever we picked them up. Those fat green utensils, which Miss Dagg assured us were specially designed "first-grade pencils," were obviously not number-two—the lead inside them was softer, darker, and thicker. Even if we had been allowed to use erasers, the dark lines we made when we clenched the stems with stiff, sweaty fingers could not have been erased without ripping holes out of the paper, which, I soon learned, was not milky white with a glossy surface, but Band-Aid gray with a decidedly dull finish. The only accurate part of my writing dream was that first-grade paper had blue lines, but it also had lots of odd marks and bumps in it, created by not fully processed bits of paper pulp that somehow made their way into the finished product.

My beautiful red pencil box held slick number-two pencils and a precious pink eraser that I was not allowed to use. I could carry the box back and forth to school if I wished, but the pencils and eraser were not to be visible on my desk during writing time. After a few days, like most of my new first grade friends, I chose to leave my pencil box at home.

Fat first-grade pencils and bumpy first-grade paper were not used to write stories. In first grade we practiced our names; we practiced making rows and rows of sticks and balls because, Miss Dagg taught us, they were the two shapes out of which all other manuscript letters were formed; and we practiced printing the letters of the alphabet one at a time until we covered entire pages with each of them. Some of us learned to draw the letters accurately, staying on the lines and measuring the amount of space to leave between with a damp index finger laid to the right of each word. Some of us learned quickly that first graders did not erase or cross out, did not talk to their neighbors, and did not ask for additional pieces of paper so that they could start over. But some of us didn't. Some of us never learned to draw the letters properly, and some of us insisted on leaving our seats in search of help (or distraction). Long after Thanksgiving some papers still had smudges, heavy write-overs, and jagged rips at the spots where we tried in vain to rub out mistakes with spit-moistened fingers. Miss Dagg was patient and kind to all. Day after day she reminded us that we learned better in our own seats. And she encouraged the smudgers and rippers to keep on trying, acknowledging that writing was very difficult, and silently letting us know that some children, sadly enough, might never get it right.

When most of us had mastered the individual letter forms, we began to practice them in combination. We copied strings of words and later whole sentences out of the Palmer Method handwriting booklet in the same careful fashion we had learned to use for copying individual letters from the blackboard. Two years later, when Miss Greist taught us cursive writing in third grade, we followed the same approach. We learned first to make rockers, ovals, humps, and loops across the third-grade paper, which had somewhat narrower lines but no fewer bumps than first-grade pages. After we learned to combine the basic cursive strokes to form individual letters, we copied daily sentences out of the handwriting booklet: "Haste makes waste," allowed us to practice cursive "a's," "e's," and "s's" while, "A stitch in time saves nine," forced us to concentrate on "i's" and "t's." It took most of the year to make our way through the booklet of maxims and practice words that foregrounded each letter and cursive stroke, but when June came, most of us had accomplished the task.

By fourth grade, our teachers paid little attention to writing, occasionally pointing out seldom used and slightly odd upper-case forms like "Q," which was to be made like a loopy "2," or improperly connected lower-case cursive letters, especially "v's" and "b's," which had tricky little half-rockers at their ends, and, if omitted, left a "v" looking more like an "r" or half an "n" and left a "b" looking exactly like an "l." Third and fourth graders were allowed to use yellow number-two pencils, and by then most of us had learned to erase neatly enough so that our papers were still acceptable to the teacher even if we had made some mistakes along the way. But right after Christmas in fourth grade, the rules suddenly shifted. Miss Lonsway announced that our handed-in work for every subject except math was to be completed in ink. We were allowed to use ballpoint pens, even though our teacher assured us, somewhat wistfully, that former classes had faced the much more difficult task of dipping fountain pens into ink wells that had sat in the holes carved out of the top of each desk. We eyed the empty ink well holes with relief and rushed to purchase our first ballpoint pens.

Unfortunately, pens were not the grown-up treat we had anticipated. They often leaked or clogged up, so that our papers were dotted with unwanted blobs of blue, and, worst of all, they were filled with a brand of ink that was stubbornly permanent. We rushed out again to purchase coarse grey ink erasers and typing erasers with stiff green bristles on the ends to sweep away the rubbery remains of errors. But ink erasers never really worked right: they simply wouldn't eradicate ballpoint pen ink, they wore rough tell-tale spots on the white paper to which we had finally graduated, and eventually, if we rubbed hard enough to really remove an error, they wore through the paper completely. White-out, surely invented before 1960, was not known to us.

We had made it to fourth grade, but we found ourselves living by rules that were pretty much the same as those of the first graders who labored with green eraser-less pencils: Do it right the first time, work slowly enough to avoid errors, stay in your seat and do your own work, don't change your mind, and, at all costs, don't make any mistakes so big that you have to start again and copy it over.

This retrospective account emphasizes that learning to write is not a process wherein an isolated individual puts pencil to paper at a discrete point in time. Rather it is a process embedded in the life world of the individual in and out of school, an enterprise that interacts with the writer's dreams and fears, the cultures of learning and teaching, the people who construct learning environments, and the writing tools available. As young children learn to write, the tools they use, the tasks they are assigned to complete, and the ways they interact with adults shape their theories and practices of writing and the ways they understand the nature and functions of writing in the world. As teachers plan for writing instruction, the tools they offer, the tasks they design, and the learning contexts they construct with children interact with the cultures of their classrooms and shape their understandings of writing.

As our reconstruction makes clear, the heavy, eraser-less pencils of the 1950s emphasized that accuracy of letter formation, carefully drawn characters, and error-free initial production were what mattered most about writing. The routine task of copying words and sentences pre-selected for their physical features made it clear that precise penmanship was an end in itself and not a means to the ends of expression and communication. Writing programs that called for daily demonstrations of correct letter formation and pencil maneuvering indicated that the teacher's role was that of expert, modeling adult skill and later providing information about the degree to which children had accurately imitated the model. Generic writing lessons that revolved around multiple repetitions of the same strokes, letters, and word forms made it clear to teachers that perfection was the goal of writing instruction, and the patience that some teachers demonstrated during writing lessons (which surely consoled many frustrated but grateful children) did not controvert that goal. Eraser-less pencils, and, later, unerasable ballpoint pens used to approximate Palmer perfection, shaped the ways we learned to understand the activity of writing in the 1950s. Although most of us eventually learned to act on the world through pencil and pen, those tools undoubtedly also acted on us as we worked to understand the world. Thus, as Weizenbaum (1976) has suggested is true of the machines of man (sic), our writing tools are not simply devices which we use to accomplish writing tasks, but are also "pedagogical instruments" that help us understand the world and subsequently act on the world based on our understanding.

Because learning to write is an ongoing process, it is constantly influenced by changes in tools and cultures. Learning to write in the computer age of the 1980s and 1990s is a process that is considerably different from learning to write in the 1950s when we went to school. The writing tools of the 1980s and 1990s still include pencils and pens, and in some schools, first graders are still handed fat eraser-less pencils as their first school writing tools. Teachers in many places are still expected to demonstrate cŏrrect handwriting strokes and evaluate children's progress according to how closely they correspond to the model. But today almost every elementary school in America also has a computer (U.S. Office of Technology Assessment, 1988), and in some of these, beginning writers are offered the opportunity to use word processing as one of their earliest tools. Writing tasks have also changed during the last three decades. In many schools beginning writers are invited to dictate their own stories, invent their own spellings, and read their own texts instead of copying canned sentences with no attention to meaning. Teachers in some schools confer with children about their writing, arrange for peers to meet together to respond to one another's work, and encourage children to progress through multiple drafts. As a writing tool, word processing has the potential to support the goals of many current writing programs, because it facilitates the production, physical manipulation, and revision of text without necessitating the tasks of rewriting and recopying. Accordingly it has been claimed in several quarters of the educational community that word processing offers one of the most promising uses of microcomputers for elementary school literacy instruction (Cochran-Smith, Kahn, & Paris, 1986; Daiute, 1985a; Edelsky, 1984; Smith, 1986).

Looking at writing retrospectively raises important questions about looking at writing currently: What does it mean to write with a tool that makes a different kind of inscribing and revising possible? What messages about writers and writing are embodied in the tool of word processing and in the tasks it makes possible? How is this tool interpreted by elementary school teachers? How do they introduce and teach it? Do they incorporate word processing into existing learning structures, or does it prompt the construction of new ones? In what settings do young children have opportunities to write with word processing? Which tasks are they invited or assigned to complete? What kinds of texts do they create? With whom do they have a chance to work with word processing? How are they assisted? In a fundamental sense, each of these issues is part of the larger question addressed in this book—how using word processing as a writing tool interacts with the cultures of teaching and learning in different elementary classrooms.

LEARNING TO WRITE DIFFERENTLY

This volume addresses some of the unanswered questions of teachers, teacher educators, and researchers about the role of word processing as a tool for elementary school writing. Specifically, the book focuses on the children and teachers in five classrooms who were observed and interviewed over a 2-year period. We highlight how teachers interpreted and chose to use the open-ended tool of word processing, as well as how children learned about writing as they learned to use word processing. Particularly, the volume provides insights into the differences among teachers and children as writers, learners, and users of word processing across grade levels and within the social and organizational contexts of a working-class, public elementary school. The volume also builds an analytic framework for thinking about and talking about teachers, students, and technology over time. The framework begins with a set of questions which we argue are the most productive ones to ask about beginning writers and word processing. The questions are followed by a set of concepts that capture the interrelationships of classroom culture, teachers' interpretations and uses of technology, and students' theories and practices of writing.

The book argues that, over time, both teachers and children *learned to write differently* with word processing—that is, working with word processing shaped the ways teachers thought about teaching and learning writing, and also shaped the ways beginning writers understood and practiced the activity. Teachers initially interpreted the tool of word processing in ways that supported their goals for their students' language and literacy development. The teachers shaped the tool to fit their ongoing instructional programs, which, although quite different from one another, had in common the conventional writing tools of paper and pencil. Over time, however, the tool also shaped the teachers—eventually they restructured some of the social processes of their classrooms and developed some new ways for seeing and thinking about children as writers. These changes gave children opportunities to learn to write that were qualitatively different from those previously available.

In parallel fashion, beginning writers learned that word processing did not work like the writing tools they commonly used. Using a new tool shaped the children's theories of writing by enabling teachers to demonstrate that the activity need not center on penmanship, first-round precision, and error-free production. Eventually, as they worked with their teachers with the tool of word processing as well as other writing tools, beginning writers' altered theories of writing shaped their writing practices. The current volume explores in detail the ways that working with word processing interacted with the social processes of classrooms to shape participants' theories and practices of writing. It offers an expanded image of the ways teachers constructed writing curricula that included word processing, and it reveals an interactive, long-term relationship between the writing contexts teachers and children construct, on the one hand, and the capacities and requirements of the tool of word processing, on the other.

For the 2-year data collection phase of our project, teachers were invited to work with word processing in their classrooms in whatever ways they saw fit. Our project prescribed no curriculum and imposed no requirement about what children had to produce with word processing. Yet, as the volume demonstrates, teachers at all grade levels, kindergarten through fourth, introduced and taught word processing as part of their writing programs, and children at all age levels, 5 through 10 years, regularly used word processing as one of the tools for writing. These practices continued following completion of the study. By almost any standards of program implementation or technology innovation, this would be considered a successful implementation effort. But we were interested in questions of interpretation, not success or failure. We found that teachers by no means simply "implemented" word processing into "the writing curriculum." Rather they interpreted and adapted it to their own evolving reading/writing programs, which varied considerably from classroom to classroom despite common school district requirements, and they found ways for word processing to serve their goals for children's literacy and social development. These ways were connected to, and indeed embedded within, the wider cultures of the school and the school district as well as the teachers' assumptions and values about schools, teaching and teachers' roles in curriculum matters, literacy learning, and the technology of word processing itself.

Eventually, using the tool of word processing shaped the ways teachers chose to structure some of the contexts for writing instruction and, hence, the learning opportunities ultimately available to the children in their classrooms. Word processing was radically different from the marking tools to which beginning writers were accustomed. Unlike paper and pencil, it managed for them some of the problems of print production and foregrounded for them certain conventions of written language. When they worked with teachers using word processing, beginning writers were not bound by the limitations of their own fine-motor coordination and penmanship skills and therefore had the opportunity to compose without having to deal with some of the problems of print production. By the same token, when children were free of some of the burdens of print production, more of their language competence was made visible to teachers who could both respond to children's writing as it unfolded and instruct directly about writing strategies and word-processing procedures. With the support of the word-processing tool and within social situations that made it possible for children and teachers to interact around language in new ways, many children eventually shifted the focus of their attention from penmanship and neatness to letter–sound relationships in encoding, content and organization, and final editing. As they worked with teachers to use the tool of word processing, beginning writers modified their theories of writing, which, in turn, made it possible for them to take advantage of some of the features of word processing to carry out new writing strategies.

This volume makes it clear that word processing, in and of itself, did not make children write better, prompt them to revise more, or teach them new writing strategies. Rather, teachers and children working together with word processing often constructed social contexts within which children had opportunities to learn new writing strategies, new ways to think about strategies they already had, and ways to execute those strategies efficiently with the tool of word processing. Teachers came to see beginners' writing differently too—first, they often had the opportunity to see written language skills that had been masked when children were bound by the limits of paper; and second, they could see some of young writers' operational theories of writing more clearly and provide more continual responsiveness. Because word processing made the execution of some writing strategies easy, children were often more willing to carry them out than they were with paper and pencil. Further, because beginning writers often worked jointly with adults when they used word processing, they were able to produce texts that were more linguistically and substantively sophisticated than the texts they could produce alone. The physical arrangements of the word processing tool made it possible for adults to see explicitly some of the children's internal writing practices and subsequently enter into production of text with them more effectively and appropriately.

The many examples in this book reveal that word processing was not just a writing tool, but was indeed a "pedagogical instrument" that shaped the ways teachers and children constructed learning contexts for writing that in turn shaped children's theories and practices of writing. Our research offers evidence that word processing has the potential to be a particularly useful tool in the growth and development of beginning writers and is one of the most promising uses of computer technology for elementary school literacy instruction.

Learning to Write Differently also builds an analytic framework for understanding and studying teachers' and children's writing with word processing over time. The framework is intended to capture the interrelationships over time of classroom culture, teachers' interpretations and decisions, and uses of word processing, *as well as* altered classroom culture, teachers' interpretations and decisions, and uses of word processing. We emphasize that implementing word processing is a process of evolution, and that culture, interpretations, and decisions about word processing, the social interactions of teachers and children around word processing and writing, and learners' thinking processes are dynamic and spiralling, rather than static features of "implementation." The aim of the framework is to make visible the dynamic interrelationships of all of these.

EARLY WRITING AND WORD PROCESSING: TERMS FOR INVESTIGATION

Readers of this volume will find three terms helpful in reading and interpreting the findings presented: the notion of *beginning writers*, the notion of adult *coaches* who worked with beginning writers to produce text with the tool of word processing, and the notion of *word processing events* or individual occasions on which word processing was used to produce text in the classroom setting. These notions emerged over the lengthy course of this study both from a sense of perspectives that seemed to be missing from the substantial literature on word processing and writing, and from our observations. The three terms help to structure the volume and provide both an entry into, and an exit from, the extensive research literature already available on word processing and writing. In concert, the terms suggest that both teachers and children are important in investigations of word processing, as are the tools they use and the social contexts within which they teach and learn word processing. A perspective of this sort depends almost entirely on analytic interpretation of closely observed adults and children working and writing together. This is not the common perspective in the word processing and writing literature, but it is one which we believe holds the most promise for investigating the tools and tasks of early writing as they interact with the social processes of the classroom.

Beginning Writers

In this book we use the term *beginning writer* to refer to elementary school children, 5 to 10 years of age, who were in kindergarten, first, second, third, or fourth grade at the time of the study. *Beginning writer* distinguishes the children we studied from two other groups who, as Chapter 2 makes clear, are often referred to in the literature—those who are in a state of "emergent literacy" and those who are characterized as "inexperienced writers." The term *emergent literacy* (Clay, 1966) has come to mean what children know about reading and writing before they come to school and before they begin to have formal instruction in these areas (Farr, 1985). The focus of emergent literacy research— the significant written language development that occurs informally in homes and communities—generally stops when the child reaches the age of 5 or 6 and begins to attend school (Teale & Sulzby, 1986). Although there are many ways in which the children in our study may be thought of as *emergent* writers (that is, writers whose knowledge and skills are in the process of emerging), we have chosen not to use this term in order to emphasize that our children were at a period of literacy development when they were building on the knowledge and skills they brought to school with them through formal regular school instruction.

Many beginning writers are concerned about issues of production—letter formation, spatial orientation, paginal restrictions, invented or standard spellings—and often have not yet developed the fine motor skill or knowledge of language needed to control the production of print. The 5- to 10-year-old children in our study spanned a wide range in their awareness of and information about print, their physical abilities to produce print with conventional marking tools, and their knowledge of standard orthography. Although some kindergarten and first grade children began the school year unable to write their own names, most could recognize them, and many children knew the letters in their names as well as some additional letters of the alphabet. These children were just starting to develop their formal knowledge about the conventions and functions of printed language. Children in the middle of the age span of the study, roughly those who were 7 and 8 years old, varied greatly in the extent of their knowledge and skill about language, some still at "primer level" according to school records and others at grade level or beyond. These children seemed to be in the process of developing writing fluency. The oldest children we observed, those who were 9 and 10 years of age, were for the most part at the very last stages of what might be considered "beginning writing." These children had developed basic fluency and were generally able to produce in print those sentences and phrases they could produce orally. Although many of them were beginning to address some issues of revision, audience, and purpose in writing, they were still not at a point of complete automaticity in writing—that is, they hesitated frequently to consider or ask for help with spellings, punctuation, and sentence forms. We use the term *beginning writer* throughout this volume to refer to children within this age and ability span.

We have also chosen not to utilize the term *inexperienced writers* to describe the children in our study, although this term is one that is widely used in the writing and word processing literature. Our analysis of the literature, reviewed in the following chapter, indicates that the terms experienced and inexperienced have been applied in a relative rather than an absolute way, often to differentiate among the varying writing abilities of the subjects in a given study rather than to differentiate across studies groups of writers with similar writing skills or concerns. Hence in some studies average or slightly below average college writers are referred to as inexperienced to distinguish them from college students who have well-developed writing and revising skills, while in other studies high school or junior high school writers are divided into groups with the same labels. As we point out later in this volume, all of the writers in our study were, in a very real sense, inexperienced writers, regardless of their progress and abilities relative to one another or to older children. But the term *inexperienced writer* implies a deficit and tends to call attention to what children are unable to do. *Beginning writer*, on the other hand, suggests an early point in a course of development. It is the latter view of young writers that we wish to emphasize in this volume.

Our study highlights beginning writers across the full range of those whom we would describe with the term, 5- to 10-year-old children in kindergarten through fourth grade, who wrestled with issues of print production when they wrote. An emphasis on beginning writers stands in contrast to much of the word processing and writing research, which has focused on older children, adolescents, and young adult writers. The cross-grade design of the study provides a developmental perspective that is needed in word-processing research.

Coaches and Coaching

In our analysis of adults and children working together with word processing, we often refer to adults as *coaches*. Coaches were teachers in the five classrooms where we observed, teacher-assistants or parent volunteers in the classrooms, and sometimes, ourselves, as researchers who had been requested by teachers to assist children as we observed them working with word processing. When we use the term *coach*, we signify a particular role that an adult played in relation to a beginning writer during a word processing event. We distinguish the adult role of coach and the activity of coaching from the broader role of teacher and the more encompassing activity of teaching, although the larger activity of teaching includes coaching among its many complex roles.

When an adult is referred to in this volume as a coach, it signifies that the adult was collaborating with a child during a word processing event, helping the child with word-processing procedures, writing strategies, or, in most instances, both of these, rather than offering the child direct instruction. The participation structures created during coaching situations were not the same as the participation structures of conventional instruction wherein teachers provide information, initiate questions, receive responses from students, and provide evaluation about those responses. Rather, during coached word-processing events, coaches coaxed, supported, and filled in the gaps that seemed to exist between the individual beginning writer and the text he or she was attempting to create. Although there was usually no preselected lesson plan for coached writing events and no specific skill that these events were designed to teach, many coached word-processing events were structured by the nature of the writing task the child had been assigned or selected. During these events the coach moved with the child as the text unfolded, judging the child's knowledge, answering the child's questions, and providing needed information. At times the coach carried the burden for most of the word-processing event, doing most of the composing, typing, and reading of the text. At other times the beginning writer directed the event, composing and typing his or her own text and asking the coach for the assistance needed in order to complete the task.

The concept of coaching used throughout this volume is derived from Vygotsky's (1978) notion of the ways children eventually internalize intellectual moves by first interacting with adults in social situations where those moves are displayed externally. When they acted as coaches, the adults we observed reacted and responded to children's writing as it unfolded, and also provided direct information about both writing strategies and word processing procedures. Often, coaches were able to take advantage of the features of word processing to help beginning writers function at a level of text production that was more advanced than they could have achieved independently.

Although a number of studies of word processing and writing have focused on children in classroom settings, few have looked at teachers or analyzed teachers' roles—as coaches or otherwise—in the deployment of word processing technology in the classroom. The research reported in this book provides a dual focus— on teachers as well as children, and, of course, on their work together.

Word-Processing Events

A *literacy event* has been defined as an occasion during which a piece of writing is integral to participants' interactions and interpretations (Heath, 1983) and as an action sequence in which the production or comprehension of print plays a significant role (Anderson & Stokes, 1984). Like the speech events (Hymes, 1972) from which they are derived, literacy events are assumed to be structured according to certain rules for occurrence and participation and assumed to function in a variety of ways for various community or cultural groups. We are suggesting here that a *word-processing event* is best understood as a particular brand of literacy event in which word processing is central to participants' interactions and in which one or more persons use computer word processing to create or modify a piece of writing and/or to read, respond to, or otherwise use a piece of writing created with word processing.

The word-processing events we observed varied considerably according to the ways the technological possibilities and restrictions of computer hardware and software combined with the social interactions constructed by individual teachers and children. In all five classrooms we observed, word-processing events functioned in more than one way. For example, teachers used word processing to produce room decorations, labels, instructions, and classroom rules for posting. Some teachers used word processing to create worksheets and to keep instructional and evaluative records, anecdotal notes, class lists, letters to parents, movie orders, and test question files. In some classes children were permitted to take spelling tests or create math word problems using word processing, while in others children could correspond informally with one another by writing notes on the word processor, make directories of each others' names and phone numbers, list team members, and so on.

Although other functions of word processing occurred, the major function of word-processing events in all five classes, and the function which is the focus of this volume, was writing practice or writing instruction, although we do not limit this function to those activities relegated to the block of time in the daily schedule labeled writing or language arts. Rather, many of the teachers included as part of their overall writing programs the children's creation of stories, reports, and articles related to the science, social studies, and reading curricula as well. We are including all of these as part of the category of writing instruction and practice. By instruction and practice, we mean occasions on which teachers invited or assigned children to plan, compose, revise, or edit text; experiment with written language; publish words, sentences, stories, and essays; or read pieces composed with word processing on a prior occasion.

RESEARCH FRAMEWORK

The study reported in this volume is based on the premise that classrooms are interactive and communicative environments that teachers and children together construct and reconstruct (Erickson, 1986; Florio-Ruane, 1987; Hymes, 1974). Both teaching and learning are taken to be highly complex, context-specific activities. Central to this perspective is the assumption that language functions as a social context for learning, and, at the same time, that social context influences language use and learning (Bloome & Green, 1984; Cochran-Smith, 1984; Green, 1983; Green & Weade, 1987). To understand the learning processes that occur in given classrooms, then, it is assumed that researchers must study the dynamic interplay of social contexts and learners' thinking (Emihovich & Miller, 1988; Genishi, 1988) and attempt to make visible the intricate and shifting stitches that weave together social task structures and academic task structures (Evertson & Green, 1986; Weade & Evertson, 1988;), or what Erickson (1982) has called "taught cognitive learning."

The meaning perspectives of teachers, children, and school administrators are taken to be central and intrinsic to teaching and learning processes. It is assumed that, to seek to understand one classroom activity or one part of the academic curriculum, it is also necessary to understand the social structure as well as other parts of the curriculum, their relationships to one another, and their relationships to participants' and researchers' own frames of interpretation (Paris, in press). Underlying this study is a sociocognitive view of literacy—that is, a view of literacy as a social and cultural phenomenon as well as a cognitive one, something that exists between people and connects individuals to a range of experiences and points in time (Schieffelin & Cochran-Smith, 1984), as well as something that occurs in people's heads. It is assumed that children learn and develop the skills of literacy by actively trying to use those skills in order to communicate (Edelsky, Draper, & Smith, 1983; Goodman, 1986; Harste, Woodward, & Burke, 1984), and it is assumed that literacy development is a gradual process of getting better at communicating through print.

This volume, *Learning to Write Differently*, attempts to capture the dynamic relationship of beginning writers' theories and practices of writing as they interacted with the social processes of their classrooms, especially the notions of writing demonstrated and negotiated in the conversations that supported word-processing events. A research framework of this sort highlights the fact that beginning writers' experiences with word processing are both nested within, and built out of, the language and social interactions constructed in classrooms.

The methods for the study reported in this volume are theoretically grounded in the above assumptions. Our work both assumes and argues that an ethnographic perspective provides the most useful information about children and teachers using word processing for teaching and learning writing. Such a perspective allows us to see the teaching and learning of word processing within the complexity of teaching cultures. The notion *teaching culture* includes the character of the community in which the school and school district are located and the values that operate in that community. It allows us to see the web of relationships of teachers, principals, and school district administrators and the formal and informal requirements and policies in force. And it makes visible the assumptions and perceptions of individual teachers about teaching and learning, the nature of language, and literacy acquisition and development; the ways these assumptions were translated into curricular and instructional decisions; the specific needs and abilities of children in particular situations; and the personal and professional identities, goals, strengths, and concerns of individual teachers. Further because of the relatively long time frame involved—a 2-year observation period—the ethnographic perspective permits a view of the ways in which teachers' and children's work with word processing changed and developed.

Data were collected over a 2-year period in the classrooms of five teachers in a working-class community school in a small urban school district located on the edge of a much larger northeastern city. In Year One of the study, one class each of kindergarten, second, and fourth grade were included, and in Year Two the new classes of the original three teachers plus one new class each of first and third grades were included. Each classroom in the study had the use of a small number of IBM Personal Computers. Children used "Bank Street Writer" software, which was, at the time the study began in 1984, one of the few word processing packages especially designed for use by children and compatible with IBM hardware. Information about computer hardware and word processing, as well as research site, data collection, and data analysis, are provided in the Appendix.

A number of ethnographic methods were used for data collection, and the major database of the study was comprised of five parts: (a) annotated transcriptions of field notes, audio-recordings of individual word-processing events, and narrative profiles of individual children using word processing; (b) narrative descriptions from field notes of classroom activities and the organization of writing and word-processing programs; (c) transcriptions of audiorecordings of interviews with individual teachers and children; (d) transcriptions of audiorecordings of monthly group meetings; and (e) collection of children's writing produced with word processing and, in some cases, with paper and pencil. Standard methods of qualitative data analysis were employed. These included review of the corpus of field notes, audio tapes, and documents, identification of typical and discrepant instances by the methods of analytic induction and triangulation, and content analysis of interview and group meetings. The reader of this volume who is interested in research methodology is advised to turn now to the Appendix for extensive information about the design of the study. All readers, however, need to know something about the context of the study. This information is provided in the section that follows.

SCHOOL CULTURE AS RESEARCH CONTEXT

Five teachers at Summit Grove Elementary School, the largest elementary school in the West Brook School District, allowed us to observe in their classrooms over a 2-year period as they learned to use word processing as a tool for teaching writing to young children. These five teachers were close professional colleagues, and Summit Grove was a school where individual professional development and innovation were emphasized. At the same time, however, West Brook was a school district with a new and growing emphasis on standard procedures and curriculum uniformity. Inner school culture, with its focus on individualism and innovation, was at odds with outer school district culture, which emphasized standardization. School culture, school district culture, and the conflict between the two were invisible, but critical, aspects of the context in which we planned and conducted our research. (See Paris, 1989a, in press, for extensive analysis of school and school district culture.) Teaching cultures and the clashes that existed between them help to account for the substantial differences in the ways five teachers chose to teach and use word processing and ultimately for the kinds of learning opportunities they made available to the beginning writers in their classrooms. School and school district culture did not function simply as backdrop, location, or site for our work. Rather, as our discussion in the next six chapters demonstrates, classroom cultures and the teaching and learning that occurred within them were deeply embedded within school and school district cultures. Hence these made up the research "context" in the richest sense of the word—the meanings, attitudes, beliefs, values, practices, and history of participants.

When we began our observations at Summit Grove Elementary, West Brook School District was engaged in a major program of curriculum revision and standardization. Prior to this time, individual teachers had been responsible for selecting their own teaching materials and, to some extent, curriculum topics. Under the school district's new curriculum policy, however, the varied and individualized curricula that teachers had constructed for their students were being replaced by a uniform curriculum, and the process of adopting and adapting to the new standardized curriculum engaged much of the attention and energy of teachers and administrators. Two curriculum policy decisions directly influenced teachers' work with word processing. First, the administration decided not to mandate a unified computer curriculum, although it continued to encourage computer use. In the absence of district guidelines and pupil outcome requirements, teachers were free to use computers in ways they found most appropriate or not to use them at all. The absence of school district requirements concerning the use of computers in the curriculum also allowed teachers relative freedom to select the word-processing skills they would teach and how and when they would teach them.

Second, the school district adopted a "process approach" to teaching writing, which defined the framework within which the teachers learned to use word processing in their classes. In the elementary schools, "process writing" meant that teachers were to teach children a five-step procedure for writing—brainstorming and prewriting, drafting, revising, editing, and publishing or sharing writing with an audience. Children were encouraged to draft freely, to focus on content rather than form, and in the earliest grades to invent their own spellings.

Policies concerning writing and computers broadly defined the limits within which teachers and children could teach and learn to write with word processing, yet even the mandated writing curriculum did not have a direct and linear relationship to the teaching and learning that took place in classrooms. All five teachers we observed adapted the standardized writing program. Some believed that the existence of a mandated curriculum denied their expertise by the implication that their current practices were inferior to, and in need of replacement by, a uniform program. Others felt that a mandated curriculum denied teachers' individuality by overlooking their unique interests and expertise and at the same time denied the individual differences in children. Although they complied with curriculum mandates at the surface level, many West Brook teachers quietly adapted or overlooked parts of the mandated curriculum in order to meet the needs of their individual students. This was so in part because the district administration could not, in fact, enforce its curriculum mandates. As a "loosely coupled system" (Weick, 1976), the school district, like any large institution, made curriculum policies at quite a distance from the site at which they were to be carried out. Consequently it was possible for teachers to alter continuously what was given them to teach rather than carry out mandates as stated.

In contrast to the curriculum mandates and standardization of the West Brook School District, Summit Grove Elementary provided a context in which collegial relationships were nurtured, individual variation was valued, and curriculum innovation was encouraged in an atmosphere of mutual trust. Open-plan, shared-classroom spaces encouraged ongoing communication among and between grade level teams, and a history of strong personal ties among staff members provided a nurturing climate. Collegiality grew out of shared classrooms, shared histories, personal relationships, and collaborative efforts in planning. To be a good colleague was to be considerate of other teachers' needs and wishes (often especially important in a setting in which up to three teachers might share the same open space), and to share one's resources and expertise with colleagues. As we point out in Chapter 3, the centrality of the role of colleague led teachers to see their work with word processing, not only from the perspective of their own needs and goals in their own classrooms, but also in terms of their colleagues' needs. The decisions teachers made about how to use word processing enhanced rather than jeopardized these important collegial roles and relationships.

Compatible with a school culture that emphasized collegiality and community, there was a shared history at Summit Grove of respect for individual variation and innovation. Teachers' curriculum projects were valued as expressions of their individuality, as contributions to the pool of expertise available to colleagues, and as a means of distinguishing their school from other elementary schools in the district. Some Summit Grove teachers had begun exploring computer use in their classrooms with machines and software purchased by the Home and School Association well before the school district began systematically investing in computers. Most of them had considered and rejected the available drill and practice software on the basis that it did not support their curricula. At the time our study began, a number of teachers were exploring alternative ways to utilize computers. It is significant that word processing was made available to them at a time in the school's history when both interest in computer use and dissatisfaction with drill and practice were considerable. This development also converged with Summit Grove's school-wide emphasis on language development, West Brook's district-wide mandate that all teachers adopt a process approach to teaching writing, and Summit Grove faculty's desire to continue to distinguish themselves as individuals and as a staff.

Summit Grove's history of innovation and interpersonal cohesion can be understood as a result of the tension between an outer culture of increasing standardization and an inner culture of shared values and assumptions about teachers' relationships to curriculum, roles in curriculum change, and ongoing learning opportunities. Underlying the supportive school culture in which the teachers learned to use word processing and planned ways to incorporate word processing into their teaching of writing was the school's history of close and stable faculty relationships and prior experiences with curriculum innovation. Past and present school and school-district curriculum policies, the faculty's shared values, and their assumptions about teachers' roles in curriculum development and implementation shaped the deployment of word processing in each classroom.

HOW TO READ THIS BOOK

The six chapters that follow document how word processing, as a writing tool, shaped the ways teachers thought about teaching writing as well as the ways beginning writers practiced and understood the activity. Each chapter functions in two ways: (a) it contributes an argument toward the thesis that teachers and children eventually learned to write differently when they worked with word processing; and (b) it provides one or more concepts toward an analytic framework that captures the interactive relationships of classroom cultures, teachers' interpretations and uses of word processing, and beginning writers' theories and practices of writing.

Chapter 2 describes how and where this study fits into current knowledge of the relationships of writing and word processing. We examine the research and pedagogical literature in these areas: professional writers' assessments of word processing as a composing tool; the effects of word processing on students' composing processes; the effects of word processing on students' written products; the effects of word processing on students' attitudes; students' abilities to master keyboarding and word processing operations; and the relationships of word processing, classroom social organization, and teachers' goals. The chapter is organized around five propositions, or tentative conclusions, constructed from evidence across individual studies and methods in each of these areas, which identify what we know and need to know about beginning writers and word processing. These suggest unanswered, but potentially productive, questions and begin to build a perspective for investigating the tools and tasks of early writing as they interact with the social processes of the classroom.

Chapter 3 describes the ways that five teachers introduced and used word processing in their classrooms over a 2-year period. Portraits of individual teachers emphasize the diverse ways teachers chose to use word processing and make it clear that each teacher's decisions were embedded in her understanding of her place in the culture of the school as well as her individual educational values and her ongoing practices. We argue in Chapter 3 that the influences of teaching cultures and the uses teachers made of word processing were interdependent, evolving and compounded over time. Thus teaching cultures and word processing conjointly determined both what opportunities were available to children to learn about word processing and writing and how those opportunities came into being. Chapter 3 constructs a framework for analyzing and understanding teachers' deployment of word processing as a spiraling process of goals, beliefs, and instructional practices mediated through interpretations and decisions about word processing. This framework sets the uses of word processing within the culture of each classroom and the larger contexts of the school and school district and permits examination of the interrelationships of evolving uses of word processing and teaching culture.

Chapters 4 and 5 analyze the ways that 5- to-10-year-old children learned to write with a tool that was radically different from the paper and pencil tool to which they were accustomed and which contained the raw capacity to alter radically their composing strategies. Chapter 4 identifies the features of word processing that children learned, the difficulties they encountered, and the ways they incorporated word processing into their prior and emerging writing strategies. It provides evidence that, unlike professional and other experienced writers, beginning writers generally did not use the most powerful features of word processing to reorganize and reconceive their writing. Through analysis of word processing episodes that were productive and unproductive for children, Chapter 5 explores the conditions under which word processing was an effective writing tool for beginners. We describe coached word-processing events wherein adults and beginning writers working together created texts that were more linguistically and substantively developed than those beginners could have created alone. We make the case that word processing functioned effectively when writing tasks and social learning contexts were structured in ways that enabled the individual child to take advantage of specific capabilities of word processing. We also point out, however, that this kind of structuring is not always possible and not always desirable.

Together, Chapters 4 and 5 build the case that writing with word processing, which foregrounded certain features of written language and often occurred with the assistance of adult coaches, provided unusual opportunities for children to learn both procedural and propositional knowledge about written language. These two chapters also contribute the analytic framework for word-processing event analysis according to the dimensions of task, tool, skills of beginning writer, and learning/teaching processes. The ways that these four features converge and dynamically interact provides a way of understanding particular word processing events that are productive or unproductive.

Chapter 6 provides a close look at one beginning writer over a 2-year period. This chapter demonstrates that writing with word processing was a powerful experience for the child, allowing him to break certain connections that had hampered his writing and enabling him to forge new connections that facilitated his writing. In Chapter 6 we make the case that the child's development as a writer over the course of a 2-year period can be understood as the outcome of the dynamic interrelationship of his evolving theories of writing, on the one hand, and the ways he practiced writing with word processing and paper and pencil, on the other. But both of these can be understood only in terms of the ways they were embedded within, and interacted with, the social processes of the classroom, especially the notions of writing demonstrated and negotiated during word processing sessions.

Throughout *Learning to Write Differently*, we make connections and interconnections that allow us to discern the individual, developmental, and social differences and similarities that emerged over a 2-year period in the ways teachers and children dealt with word processing. Chapter 7 discusses implications for the teaching, research, and school policy communities. For the teaching community, the study provides an interpretation of word processing events and the classroom contexts that surrounded and supported them. The study sheds light on the ways five teachers acted on their implicit assumptions about teaching and learning. As such, it offers information that can influence the practical theories of classroom teachers and teacher educators as they plan for and think about events of this kind. For the research community, the volume provides not only an in-depth analysis of word processing in five classrooms, but also a way of looking at children's and teachers' experiences with word processing that is in keeping with the perspectives of both classroom-based ethnography and teaching as a sociolinguistic process. Long-term observations help to tease out patterns of behavior that explain, from teachers' and children's perspectives, the meanings of teaching and learning with word processing in various classrooms. For the community of school policy makers, this volume suggests that staff development programs in classrom computer use ought to include opportunities for teachers to consider how new technology can serve current practice as well as how it can shape new practices.

chapter 2
Beginning Writers and Word Processing: What We Know and Need to Know

Since 1982 investigators from a variety of disciplines and with different goals in mind have explored the roles and potential benefits of word processing. The bulk of the literature has examined the effects of word processing on the composing processes and products of adolescent and college level writers. In this chapter we begin to develop a perspective for examining the tools and tasks of early writing as they interact with the social processes of elementary classrooms by constructing a set of propositions, or tentative conclusions, developed from evidence across individual studies and methods. To do so, we draw from the literature on word processing and writing for all age groups, consider the claims of teachers and writers as well as empirical researchers, and examine many different kinds of evidence. The extraction of propositions from a diverse and extensive body of literature provides: (a) a schema for understanding and categorizing what is known and still needs to be known about word processing and young writers, (b) a framework for probing the significant theoretical and substantive issues underlying the findings, and (c) a point of departure for discussing the most provocative themes and questions that emerge from many fields of study.

The chapter is organized around five major propositions. The extent of the discussion around each proposition reflects its relative emphasis in the literature. The five propositions, summarized in Figure 2.1, encompass these areas: (a) the effects of word processing on students' composing processes, (b) the effects of word processing on students' written products, (c) the effects of word processing on students' attitudes, (d) students' abilities to master keyboarding and systems skills, and (e) interrelationships of word processing, the social organization of classrooms, and teachers' goals. The sources from which propositions were derived include the largely impressionistic comments of writers and innovative practitioners who, very early on, experimented with implementing word processing into the writing curriculum. They also include the single-classroom results of researchers who observed individuals and groups of children using word processing, as well as the findings of large-scale correlational and observational studies conducted in classrooms or computer laboratories.

The findings in the literature on word processing, as well as the questions and assumptions that underlie these findings, are complex and varied. They defy global generalization and require, instead, careful consideration of nuances in terminology, research methods, and pedagogical contexts. Further, as we show in the pages that follow, the tool of word processing itself is a variable device, interpreted in specific contexts in diverse ways and for varying purposes. Although we know a great deal about the potential impacts of word processing on young children's writing, we know much less about the ways the technology is

Figure 2.1
Teachers, Children, and Word Processing: What We Know

Proposition 1.0: In classroom or computer laboratory situations, using word processing affects the composing processes of student writers.

1.1   When they use word processing instead of paper and pencil, student writers often make a greater gross number of revisions.

1.2   When they use word processing instead of paper and pencil, student writers often increase the number of surface-level revisions and error corrections made, but word processing does not, in and of itself, increase the number of meaning-level revisions.

1.3   Without instructional intervention, student writers tend to assimilate the capabilities of word processing to their own models of composing and to their already-learned revision strategies.

1.4   The effects of word processing are interactively related to the skills and strategies of the individual writer: without instructional intervention, word processing is used more effectively by writers who have well-developed writing and revising skills than by those who do not have such skills.

1.5   Students who use word processing accompanied by instruction in the form of computer prompting revise their writing more effectively (that is, with increased meaning-level revisions) than do either those who use word processing alone or those who use paper and pencil.

Figure 2.1
(Continued)

1.6 Word processing with computer prompting is more effective for students who do not have well-developed writing and revising skills than it is for those who do have such skills.

1.7 When it is accompanied by instructional intervention that invites students to view their writing as a meaning-making activity, word processing facilitates the creation of fluid texts and increases meaning-level revisions.

Proposition 2.0:   When students use word processing in classroom or computer laboratory situations, the quality and quantity of their written products is affected.

2.1 When they write with word processing in classroom or computer laboratory situations (and once they have developed basic keyboarding familiarity), many students produce slightly longer texts than they do with paper and pencil.

2.2 When they work with word processing in classroom or computer laboratory situations, many students produce a greater quantity of writing and/or spend more time writing than they do with paper and pencil.

2.3 When they work with word processing in classroom or computer laboratory situations, students often produce neater, more error-free written products than they do with paper and pencil.

2.4 Using word processing, in and of itself, generally does not improve overall quality of writing.

Proposition 3.0:   Student writers respond positively to the use of word processing for writing.

Proposition 4.0:   Student writers are able to master keyboarding and word processing strategies for use in age-appropriate writing activities.

4.1 When students begin to use word processing, there is an initial learning period, the length of which is dependent in part on the prior typing and writing experiences of the student.

Figure 2.1
(Continued)

Proposition 5.0: The ways that word processing is used for writing in individual classrooms, the social organization of classroom learning environments, and the goals and strategies of individual teachers are interactively related.

5.1 Part of the impact of word processing technology in the classroom is explained by individual teachers' interpretations, which change over time depending on teachers' goals, the social organizations of their classrooms, and children's developing skills.

5.2 Word processing technology is used differently for writing depending on the ways individual teachers organize their classrooms for learning and the ways they structure their writing programs.

5.3 The logistical and physical requirements of using word processing equipment make writing public and often prompt new social arrangements, especially collaboration.

actually implemented and used in classroom situations over time. The research we report in the remainder of this volume offers insights in some of the least explored areas.

WORD PROCESSING AND STUDENT WRITING: THE BURGEONING INTEREST OF THE 1980s

In her study of the cultural impact of computers, Turkle (1984) points out that even at the end of the 1970s, intense involvement with computer technology was largely limited to the subcultures of computer programmers and those members of the scientific community who were exploring the realms of artificial intelligence. By the mid-1980s, however, involvement with computers had become a popular phenomenon, and our culture had become one in which everyone was invited and even required to interact with the technology. Within this climate of intensifying and widespread public involvement with computers, there was a tremendous upsurge in the number of computers available for classroom use at all levels. In 1981, for example, fewer than one school in five had a computer. Today almost all do (U.S. Congress Office of Technology Report, 1988), and it is not unusual for elementary schools to have one computer per grade level and, in many cases, per classroom. Although they diminished by the end of the decade, enormous enthusiasm and optimism heralded the introduction of micro-computers into the elementary school curriculum in the early and mid 1980's (Laboratory of Comparative Human Cognition, 1989).

During this time period, legions of adults who wrote profesionally—staff and freelance writers, researchers, journalists, educators, publicists—made the conversion from pencil and typewriter to computerized word processing. For the most part, professional writers found that word processing was a highly effective writing tool, and some were eager to describe their experiences and speculate about the benefits of word processing for others. Zinsser (1983) wrote a full-length monograph about his experiences learning to write with a word processor, and others wrote briefer essays that appeared in popular as well as academic publications (e.g., Fallows, 1982; McKenzie, 1984; Moran, 1983; Murray, 1985; Stillman, 1985). The self-reflective commentaries of professional writers revealed their authors' ingenuous fascination with their own experiences as both writers and beginners at word processing. While they learned to compose with word processing, the authors thought about themselves as learners and writers and attempted to discover whether or not the technology of the computer would accommodate, interfere with, or change their work in desirable ways.

The public accounts of professional writers provided interesting metacognitive glimpses—windows into some of the insights of those who spent a good deal of time both writing and thinking about writing. They touched on what was involved in the conversion from competent composing with pencil or typewriter to composing with word processing, a topic which, during the early part of the decade, was of widespread interest to other writers but also especially interesting to educators and classroom researchers. The writers expressed initial concerns about overcoming the "humanist's bias" (Zinsser, 1983, p. 21) against computer technology in general, adjusting to the abstract "paperless-ness" of word processing, and learning to delay editing impulses while discovering what they had to say through a speedily produced first draft. They commented on the advantages of the impermanent and easily revisable text of the computer screen, ways of adjusting to the word processor's light keyboard touch and rapid speed, and the thrill of emancipation from recopying, retyping, cutting, and pasting. The verdict in the commentaries of the professionals was unequivocal enthusiasm—word processing was a boon for writers! Zinsser in fact concluded, "The word processor will help you to achieve three cardinal goals of good writing—clarity, simplicity, and humanity—if you make it your servant and not your master" (p. 112). Stillman (1985), both writer and teacher of writing, echoed the same sentiment, claiming that with word processing the writer "begins to see a little more clearly what's going on inside, down where the subject is as [word processing begins] to close, if only by a meager inch, the gap between thought and word" (p. 28). From the general enthusiasm of the late 1970s and early 1980s, a research agenda on word processing, writing, and classrooms began to emerge.

AN EMERGING RESEARCH AGENDA

There were two implicit arguments in the public commentaries of those newly converted to word processing and, less explicitly, in the general interest in the technology that was burgeoning at the turn of the decade. First, as was clear to almost everyone who had tried out the technology, word processing had the capacity to make easier and speedier the production, revision, and editing of text and could, therefore, change the ways total writing time was allocated to these activities. Second, many writers were claiming that using word processing made it more likely that they would treat their developing texts as impermanent and would, therefore, write in order to discover and shape what they had to say. The first of these arguments was for convenience, time-saving, and relief from the physical constraints of writing. It hinged on the idea that writers could use the tool of word processing to do more easily what they would normally have to do with typewriter, paper and pencil, or scissors and paste. The second, however, was an argument in favor of a tool that could help change the nature of composing processes themselves. It was not for ease and speed, but for a qualitatively different kind of writing that would support speculative thought and discourage premature closure on divergent ideas. It was the implicit causal link between these two premises that made the word processing case so seductive to the educational community: *because* of the speed and ease with which one could produce and revise text, the argument went, word processing would let writers keep their writing tentative and exploratory while they discovered and refined the intricacies of what they wanted to say. The final and generally unstated step in this line of reasoning was both simple and obvious—word processing was a tool that would help writers write better.

The enthusiasm of the early part of the decade—both the unwritten excitement of countless educational researchers, teachers, and writers who converted to word processing as well as the published commentaries of professional writers—implied obvious and nontrivial advantages for student writers who were given opportunities to use the new tool. But the same enthusiasm also helped to raise questions about the potential uses of word processing for school instruction. In what ways were inexperienced student writers (of any age, but especially young children who were beginners at the task of writing) like and not like experienced adult writers who possessed already-established and effective writing strategies? Could student writers, who were in the process of learning and developing writing strategies, simultaneously learn to manage the technological operations of word processing? Could schools manage to make word processing technology available to student writers, and if so, to which students and for what purposes? Out of the tension between provocative questions and unmitigated enthusiasm, a research agenda for student writing and word processing emerged.

- What aspects of the mechanical strategies of keyboarding and word processing are student writers able to learn? Under what conditions? Within what time periods?

- What advantages and disadvantages does word processing offer to beginning and inexperienced writers? How do these compare with the advantages it offers to experienced writers?
- How does writing with word processing affect students' composing processes? Does it make revision easier for them? Do students revise, edit, reread, or plan more, less, or differently when they use word processing?
- Does word processing qualitatively change students' composing processes? If so, in what ways does composing change? Does word processing bring writing closer to spoken language and thought? How does this happen?
- Do students like writing with word processing? Under what conditions? For what reasons?
- When they use word processing, do students produce better quality writing? How does this happen? Under what conditions?
- Does word processing encourage students to play with language, experiment more in their writing, and write initial drafts to discover what their ideas are? In what ways? Under what conditions? For which writers?

Most of these questions focused on the potential effects word processing would have on the composing processes, the written products, and the attitudes of student writers—essentially the outcomes of writing with word processing. At the same time, however, some researchers also raised questions about students' uses of word processing within, and in relation to, school and classroom settings. They began to explore the interrelationships of word processing, classroom learning contexts, and the social and organizational structures of schools, curriculum, and educational goals. These questions also became part of the research agenda of the 1980s.

- How is word processing used in classrooms over time? Does implementation of word processing vary across classrooms and schools? In what ways? What are the factors that affect implementation?
- How do the tools and tasks of writing with word processing interact with the social processes of classrooms?
- Does using word processing and other computer software change the curriculum, the organization of learning, or the patterns of classroom interaction? In what ways? Are these desirable?
- What are the relationships of word processing, teachers' goals, the social organizations of classrooms, and the learning opportunities available to students? How are these played out in various classroom and school settings?
- What are the relationships of word processing and the social and organizational structures of schools, school systems, and school communities?

Although there is less research that addresses the second group of questions, the growing body of literature in this area is particularly rich. All of the literature that is related to uses of word processing in elementary classrooms is included in this review. We begin with the largest body of research, which has explored the effects of word processing on student writers' composing processes.

THE EFFECTS OF WORD PROCESSING
ON STUDENTS' COMPOSING PROCESSES

In the last two decades there has been a major shift away from analysis of written products and toward examination of both the processes writers use and the relationships between composing processes and written products (Applebee, 1981; Emig, 1971; Flower & Hayes, 1981; Graves, 1975; Scardamalia, Bereiter, & Goelman, 1982). Research on word processing and writing is in keeping with this shift. The largest number of studies in this area has examined the composing processes of students who use word processing for writing, with the major emphasis on the occurrence of revision. At a very general level, as Proposition 1 suggests, the literature indicates that using word processing affects composing processes.

> Proposition 1.0: In classroom or computer laboratory settings, using word processing affects the composing processes of student writers.

Most of the research in this area has focused on the numbers and kinds of revisions writers make when using word processing, the kinds of writers who use word processing most effectively, and the instructional interventions that encourage revision with word processing. The discussion that follows points out that, when students write with word processing, they often increase the gross number of revisions made. It also argues, however, that, while word processing offers writers the raw capacity for extensive and easy revisions of all kinds, it does not lead to increased revision that improves overall writing quality unless instructional intervention also occurs.

Numbers of Revisions Made by Writers Using Word Processing

There are mixed results in the research that explores the effects of word processing on numbers of revision. Some studies indicate significant increases in revisions made with word processing, while others indicate that there is little or no difference in number of revisions. It is possible to sort out these discrepancies by clarifying what counts as revision in various studies and applying the notion *gross number of revisions* across studies. Gross number is used to represent the total occurrence of all kinds of changes to text at all points of composing, including changes at the point of initial production of print as well as immediate or delayed correction of minor typographical errors.

If gross number of changes is the only criterion, then there is both informal and empirical evidence across studies to indicate that using word processing increases the number of revisions made by adults and college student writers (Andrews, 1985; Bean, 1983; Collier, 1983; King, Birnbaum, & Wagen, 1985; Lutz, 1987; Zurek, 1985), as well as middle- and high-school writers (Bradley, 1982; Butler-Nalin, 1985; Engberg, 1983a,b; Martinez, 1985a). Although there are few studies that examine the number of revisions made by elementary school children using word processing, there is some evidence that working with word processing may increase the gross number of revisions made by children as well. For example, teachers report that using word processing encouraged fourth graders to revise (Boudrot, 1984), children using a talking version of word processing edited more than they had with paper and pencil (Borgh & Dickson, 1986), and young children who dictated stories to their teacher at a word processor made more suggestions for changes than they did when they dictated paper-and-pencil stories (Barber, 1982; Bradley, 1982). Thus we propose Proposition 1.1 as follows.

> Proposition 1.1:   When they write with word processing, students often make a greater gross number of revisions to their writing than they do with paper and pencil.

The problem with this proposition is that gross number of revisions is a relatively meaningless representation of a writer's composing and revising practices at the word processor. Anyone who has worked at a computer keyboard knows that it is virtually impossible to avoid making numerous easily correctable, word-level errors. This is true for speedy touch-typists, practiced hunt-and-peckers, and newcomers to the keyboard, which means that part of the reason writers make more changes when they use word processing is that they make more mistakes in keypress selection as they produce text. This is not to suggest that typing skill and keyboarding rhythms, which are discussed in a later section, are unimportant factors in writing with word processing. They are important and doubly so where young children are concerned. But the point here is that corrections to trivial typographical errors have little to do with the qualities of revision that are generally praised in the writing literature—attention to conceptual issues, such as the emerging substance and organization of a piece, or, for younger writers, attention to production and content issues, such as encoding or topic consistency. When every textual change, including typographical error correction, is counted as an instance of revision when writers use word processing, then it is likely that these increases are at least partially artifacts of keyboarding itself and not evidence of qualitatively different modes of composing.

Several researchers, however, have reached conclusions that are contradictory to those stated above. For example, when Hawisher (1987) compared the paper-and-pencil writing and revising of college freshmen with their writing and revising using word processing, she found that paper-and-pencil writers made more revisions than their counterparts who used word processing. Similarly, Kurth (1987) found no significant differences in the number or kinds of revisions made by high school students when using word processing and using paper and pencil. The discrepancies between these findings and those mentioned above are not explained by differences in what counted as revision, but by differences in the points at which revisions were counted. In both the Hawisher and Kurth studies, researchers tallied revisions by comparing hard copies of writers' initial drafts (i.e., the drafts completed at the end of the first and second sittings) with their final drafts.

Unlike the research cited above, which counted all changes in texts at all points of composing as instances of revision, the latter studies do not capture, and hence do not count as revision, the in-process changes writers made in the act of composing first drafts. When researchers fail to count revisions made at what Britton (1970) calls "the point of utterance" (or, with written texts, the point of initial text production), they are probably failing to capture a significant aspect of composing with word processing. The importance of revisions of this sort is implied in the claims of the professional writers cited earlier, who assert that "point of utterance" modifications in language, order, and emphasis are what made composing with word processing unique. Support for this interpretation is found in interviews with adults who composed with paper and pencil and then composed similar pieces with word processing (Lutz, 1987). They reported marked differences in approaches: they were willing to plan less and let their texts "evolve" when they used word processing, but they engaged in a more planful kind of "drafting" with paper and pencil. Studies that explore revision with word processing by examining only those changes made from one hard-copy draft to the next may be throwing out the baby with the bath water. Since hard copies do not retain changes made as the draft is created, revision counts are not contaminated by typographical changes that are artifacts of word processing itself. But they also fail to account for all other kinds of revisions to the evolving text. Excluding all revisions made as a text is initially shaped may be tantamount to excluding the very aspect of writing with word processing that makes it unusual.

Variations in the ways researchers define and quantify revisions and subsequently construe their data raise many questions. They make interpretation across studies somewhat tricky. Underlying some of the problems is the fact that many of the features of writing that have been studied in the previous writing literature—number of drafts produced, changes made from first to final drafts, strategies used at various stages of composing—may be more artifacts of paper and pencil writing than they are features of writing as a general process. Some of the features of composing with hard-surface marking tools may not carry over to composing with the tool of word processing. Writing with word processing blurs the distinctions between earlier and later drafts and between various writing strategies. More research is needed that explores kinds and numbers of revisions in relation to different chronological points in composing and the ways that composing may differ under different conditions.

A second concern raised by the research that simply counts instances of revision is the simplicity of the underlying premise "more is better." We know that good writers have effective revision strategies: in general, the effective writer is able to monitor his or her emerging text by being tentative and alternating between the roles of reader and writer. It is erroneous to conclude from this characterization of good writers, however, that more revising is equal to better writing. There are two faulty assumptions embedded in the premise: (a) the observable activity of revising text is evidence of the nonobservable state of tentativeness and self-monitoring; (b) more revising is indicative of more self-monitoring and hence can be equated with better writing. These assumptions are faulty in several ways. They tend to treat revision as an end rather than a means to good writing. As we know, the goal of instructional programs in writing is not revision, but effective writing in a variety of forms and for different purposes some of which are well served by frequent revision and some of which are not. Hawisher (1987) is one of the few researchers who makes the critical connection by counting revisions, measuring quality, and relating the two. At another level, these assumptions tend to equate the external and explicit act of revision with the internal and implicit act of self-conscious rethinking. This cannot be assumed. In fact, there is evidence that some writers who use word processing learn simply to tinker with their texts and attend endlessly to superficial changes rather than substantive ones (Grow, 1988; Lutz, 1987).

When the equation, more revision is better writing, is coupled with revision counts that include even minor typographical error correction, research results are confounded. If conclusions are not teased apart and examined carefully, it is easy to reach conclusions based on faulty reasoning such as that found in a recent volume on teaching writing with word processing (Knapp, 1986). Citing Butler-Nalin's (in Knapp, 1985) finding that seventh and eighth graders made three times as many changes in their writing when they used word processing as they did when they used paper and pencil, Knapp concluded that "even without the direct supervision of a teacher" students are "more likely to watch the meaning evolve as they write" and "more willing to correct errors and attempt all levels of revisions" (pp. 6, 7). Conclusions like Knapp's are problematic. While there is often a correlation between using word processing and gross numbers of changes made, we cannot conclude from this finding that there is a similar correlation between using word processing and taking advantage of the malleability of word-processed texts to take risks with writing and to make significant meaning-level revisions.

In an effort to address this problem and refine findings about word processing and extent of revision, a number of researchers have investigated whether and under what conditions word processing encourages risk taking and experimentation in writing. These researchers have examined the kinds of changes made by writers using word processing, the kinds of writers who do and do not make changes, and other factors that prompt writers to revise when using word processing. These are discussed in the sections that follow.

Kinds of Revisions Made by Writers Using Word Processing

As the preceding discussion suggests, one way to elaborate the finding that using word processing increases gross number of revisions is to distinguish the kinds of revisions that writers make. A number of studies do so by differentiating between microstructural changes and more significant alterations at the level of meaning, content, organization, tone, point of view, and so on. Generally these studies demonstrate that using word processing increases the former but not the latter. This finding forms Proposition 1.2.

> Proposition 1.2:   When they use word processing, student writers often make more surface-level revisions and error corrections, but, unless instructional intervention occurs, they do not make more meaning-level revisions.

For example, Harris (1985) distinguished between microstructural changes and what she called "significant modifications" in content and organization, only the latter of which she counted as revision. Based on this distinction, Harris found that word processing did not increase the revisions made by college writers. Similarly, in case studies of five college writers, Bridwell, Sirc, and Brooke (1985) found that using word processing increased surface level changes and concerns about formatting issues for all writers, but only some students expanded revision units when using word processing, while others cut down on these. Lutz (1987) found that experienced adult writers using word processing made five times as many changes as they did when they wrote with paper and pencil, but their changes were at lower linguistic levels and involved smaller chunks of writing.

Grow (1988) cautioned that adults using word processing often "substitute writing for thinking" by repeatedly editing small sections of what they have already written instead of rethinking ideas, sentences, and so on. On the surface, Hawisher's (1987) findings again seem contradictory: College students made more meaning-preserving changes when they used paper/pencil or typewriter than they did when they used the computer, while both groups made about the same number of meaning-level revisions. As indicated previously, however, Hawisher's study looked only at between-draft changes and consequently did not capture any of the word processing group's composing changes as they worked. It is likely that many surface-level as well as meaning-level changes were lost.

This interpretation is supported by the fact that Hawisher's word processing group created slightly better quality first drafts than did pen and typewriter users.

More importantly, however, it may also be the case that composing with word processing makes writing/rewriting entirely fluid and hence obscures the notions of "first draft" and "successive drafts" to such an extent that analyzing changes between first and final versions is not a meaningful comparison. The discussion that follows indicates that the difference between making primarily surface-level corrections and making both surface and meaning-level modifications is dependent in part on the already-established skills, habits, styles, and past experiences of individual writers rather than on features inherent in word processing itself.

Kinds of Writers Who Use Word Processing Effectively

In addition to the research that has categorized the kinds of revisions writers make when using word processing, some research has investigated the kinds of writers who do and do not adjust to word processing and learn to take advantage of its capacities. This literature indicates that writers tend to use word processing to revise in ways they already know. It also suggests that, without intervention, more skilled or more experienced writers revise more successfully with word processing than do less experienced writers. Thus we construct a third proposition about the effects of using word processing on student writers' composing processes.

> Proposition 1.3:   Without instructional intervention, student writers tend to assimilate the capabilities of word processing to their own models of composing and to their already-learned revision strategies.

Research that supports this proposition indicates that word processing was used least successfully by both college writers (Collier, 1983) and high school writers (Herrmann, 1987) who were marginal students and/or had the weakest writing skills. Success with word processing depended on students' willingness to exchange traditional composing tools for word processing and their abilities to adapt their normal composing strategies to the word processing program (Selfe, 1985). Similarly, although Pufahl (1986) found that word processing was often effective with basic college writers, he concluded that word processing itself did not induce students to make changes in their work. Rather, students' prior knowledge of how to use the computer, and their knowledge of what they needed to do as writers, lead them to revise. Like Pufahl, Bridwell and colleagues (Bridwell et al., 1985; Bridwell-Bowles, Johnson, & Brehe, 1987; Bridwell & Ross, 1984) suggest that effectiveness with word processing depends on inter-relationships among several factors: writing tasks, features of word processing, and especially, individual styles and strategies of writers themselves.

Variations among the preadolescent and early adolescent writers who use word processing successfully are along the same lines as variations among high-school and college student writers. Writers used word processing to revise in the ways they already knew, and better writers revised more effectively. Kane (1983), for example, concluded that junior high school writers assimilated word processing to their own already-established (but often linear and sequential) models of composing. Wolf (1985) found that, although both 11- to 12-year-old and 13- to 15-year-old writers did line editing with word processing, only the older students also revised larger chunks of texts and realized the connections between text parts. Pearson and Wilkinson (1986) ventured at the conclusion of their report that 12- and 13-year-old writers seemed to "compose more boldly" with word processing. They also concluded, however, that word processing itself was not a prerequisite for revision, but was rather a catalyst for individual students who were at a "point of readiness to develop further in their writing."

MacArthur (1988) rightly points out that the appropriate conclusion from this kind of research is that students tend to revise with word processing in the ways they already know with paper and pencil rather than that experienced writers are more successful at writing with word processing than are less experienced writers. This conclusion is supported by two other studies (Evans, 1986; Flinn, 1985) conducted in upper-level elementary classrooms. Evans compared the uses of word processing for writing by fifth and sixth graders in what she called a "process" writing class and a "skills" writing class. She found that, in the skills class, children wrote more after word processing was introduced than they had before it was introduced, but that they did not edit more. In contrast, the quantity of children's writing in the process class did not increase when word processing was introduced, but children did do more editing of their writing. Evans concluded that these variations had more to do with what the children had been doing with writing before the computer became available than they did with features of word processing in and of itself. "Process class" writers did not produce more once they had access to word processing because they were already writing extensively. By the same token, however, because word processing made it easier to do, they did do more editing of the kinds they had been taught with paper and pencil. "Skills class" writers, on the other hand, did do more writing with word processing because they had done little writing before the teacher invited them to use the computer to write. However, editing by the children in the skills class did not increase because they had not been taught how to edit.

Similarly, over the course of nine months, Flinn (1985) compared the writing of sixth graders in four classes, two of which used word processing for writing and two of which did not. On a structured revision task, children who had had word-processing experience received higher scores than did those who had written with paper and pencil. Flinn points out, however, that both groups tended to revise "the kinds of problems" their teachers had previously taught them.

This literature makes it clear that there is a relationship between the strength and already-established writing and revising skills of the writer and his or her ability to utilize the capacities of word processing. Generally, because they have well-developed revising skills, experienced writers tend to utilize the capacities of word processing to support revision more effectively than inexperienced writers do. Taken together, these findings lend support for Proposition 1.4 as follows.

> Proposition 1.4:   The effects of word processing are interactively related to the skills and strategies of the individual writer; consequently, without instructional intervention, word processing is used more effectively by writers who have well-developed writing and revising skills than by those who do not have such skills.

This body of work indicates that stronger writers, with a greater repertoire of skills at creating and manipulating text, are able to take more advantage of these capacities than are writers with fewer or weaker skills. There is some contradictory evidence that indicates that weak writers show significant improvement when writing with word processing, especially writers considered to be low achievers (Daiute, 1986; Dalton & Hannafin, 1987; McAllister & Louth, 1988), learning disabled (Morocco, 1987), or having communication disorders (Rosegrant, 1984). In each of these cases, however, the opportunity to write with word processing was coupled with instruction in writing and revising, which in many cases took the form of close individual work with a teacher. The presence or absence of instruction and the nature of the learning context appear to be differentiating factors in the uses writers make of the capacities of word processing. These issues are discussed in the following section.

In a sense all beginning writers are, by definition, "weak" writers: they do not have the well-developed composing and revising strategies of either professional adult writers or skillful student writers. Instead their inscribing, encoding, and composing strategies are in the process of emerging and developing. Furthermore, children usually do not have the keyboarding and/or typing skills that are assumed, or at least not at issue, in many of the studies of high school and college writers. If the major contribution of word processing is that it allows writers to deploy more efficiently and with greater ease the composing strategies they have already mastered, then it follows that word processing could be expected to play an important role in the elementary classroom. It could provide opportunities for beginning writers to practice their revising skills, but word processing could not be expected to have the a central role in initiating new strategies, as some technology advocates have claimed.

We have only a few examinations of the types of revisions beginning writers make when they use word processing for writing. Barber (1982) found that using word processing to record language experience stories with groups of first graders prompted them to revise and edit more "naturally," including trying out several alternative spellings of individual words. We also know very little about the kinds of beginning writers who benefit most from opportunities to write with word processing. An 8-week observational study of fourth graders (Broderick & Trushell, 1985) indicated that children initially used word processing to carry out their paper-and-pencil strategies, primarily focusing on producing flawless texts. However, as time went on, these students learned to delay corrections to the end of the process and began to use more sophisticated revision and editing strategies.

In a 6-week study of word processing and writing/revising experiences in a first grade class, Phenix and Hannan (1984) found that word processing was a successful experience for four of the six children upon whom they focused. For many of the children in the classroom, teachers observed that word processing helped increase the length, fluency, and literary quality of writing. Phenix and Hannan's brief account stresses the benefits of word processing as a function of the skills, abilities, and needs of the individual child as well as the social setting of the classroom. For example, a child who was a good reader and an enthusiastic writer learned with word processing to write longer pieces. But close examination indicated that increased length was the result of the child's adding many irrelevant parts to his pieces in order to extend his turn at the machine. At the same time another child who was an excessive reviser with paper and pencil was freed to create imperfect drafts at the word processor. Teacher-researcher Seltzer (1986) also found that, although word processing seemed to help all of the children in her kindergarten class, they used word processing in different ways depending on their skills and needs as writers.

These results are in keeping with those of the studies that have focused on adults' and adolescents' uses of word processing for writing. They indicate that word processing in and of itself does not lead writers to better revision strategies, although it often allows writers to make more revisions of the kinds they have already learned and its effects interact with the styles and strategies of the individual writer. (The relationship of word processing, writing, and social context, which is touched upon here, is dealt with specifically in the discussion of Proposition 5.) Because word processing allows writers to make more revisions of the kinds they have already learned, using it often makes for a larger number of corrected surface errors and hence more error-free products. In addition in cases where writers have already developed sophisticated revision skills, greater application of those skills yields more refined products. (See the discussion of quality of written products under Proposition 2.3.) However, the students with whom we are most concerned in the study reported in this volume are beginning writers who generally do not have well-developed, effective revision strategies. In order to assess the effectiveness of word processing for writing with young children, therefore, we need especially to examine the kind of instruction that accompanies the deployment of word processing.

Word Processing, Instructional Intervention, and Revising

One of the conclusions that can be drawn from the literature discussed above is that word processing makes available to writers what Wolf (1985) calls the "raw capacity" for large scale as well as small scale revision. As we have seen, however, raw capacity for revision neither causes nor teaches writers how to use that capacity. For the educational community, then, the central question is how to take pedagogical advantage of this capacity—in other words, how to intervene instructionally to enable student writers to use the capacities of word processing effectively. Researchers have explored both technological and human instructional interventions.

Computer Technology as Instructional Intervention. Several researchers have explored the use of computer technology itself as instructional intervention during students' use of word processing (Daiute, 1983a,b; 1984, 1985b, 1986; Daiute & Kruidenier, n.d.; Woodruff, Bereiter, & Scardamalia, 1981-1982) These researchers focus on the instructional roles that computer assisted instruction can play through a combined word processing/automatic prompting program. Their research reveals that prompting may be an effective instructional approach, perhaps especially for writers without well-developed writing and revising skills. From this work we derived the following proposition.

Proposition 1.5:   Using word processing accompanied by instruction in the form of computer prompting may help students produce higher quality writing.

Although their prompting programs are not widely used or known, the work of Woodruff and colleagues and Daiute and colleagues is instructive because of what it reveals about instructional intervention. The studies of these two groups begin with the premise that word processing frees writers to think more about their writing by relieving much of the physical burden of writing. Their research on technological interventions builds several interlocking arguments on this premise: (a) As they write, experienced writers engage in an inner, self-monitoring dialogue. (b) A way to help young writers improve their writing is to provide them with models of experienced writers' internal revision processes. (c) Computer prompts that ask explicitly some of the questions experienced writers presumably ask themselves provide writers with a model of revision and, hence, facilitate their writing. (d) Computer facilitation allows writers to approach their task with higher level strategies than they would be able to use independently.

In several early studies, Woodruff, Bereiter, and Scardamalia (1981-1982) explored these premises by comparing the opinion essays of sixth and eighth graders produced using paper and pencil with those produced using word processing with prompting. Woodruff and colleagues found that students did not produce higher quality work with any of the three prompting programs they tested. In one case the help provided in the prompting program was too easily assimilated to a low level, "what-next" composing strategy. In the other cases, the programs appeared to be either too intrusive for writers or too late in offering help after students had written. Discussion by these researchers identifies strategies for revising the software. As they point out, however, the most important finding of their first study was that students as young as sixth grade were able to interact with a computer while a composition was developing. Their second study suggests that it is possible for a prompting program to influence high-level composing strategies, since the effects noted by raters involved choice of arguments and overall approach. Finally, the researchers point out that students both enjoyed working interactively with the computer and believed that they could produce better texts using the word processing/prompting program. Researchers also comment that the help students received appeared to be worthwhile, since such a large portion of time was spent asking for help and interacting with the program.

Daiute and colleagues compared the writing of junior and senior high-school students who used word processing with prompting to the writing of those who used paper and pencil and those who used word processing without prompting. Daiute and colleagues concentrated on students who used word processing with prompting. They concluded that these students were stimulated to revise (Daiute, 1983, 1985a); revised more and more closely than they did with paper and pencil (Daiute, 1985); and made more gross revisions, more kinds of revisions, more revisions within texts, and achieved a better balance of revision within and at the ends of texts than they did using word processing alone (Daiute, 1984, 1986; Daiute & Kruidenier, n.d.). Daiute also found that although they corrected more errors and added more words at the ends of texts, junior high school students using word processing alone (that is, without a prompting program) actually wrote shorter drafts and made fewer revisions than they did using paper and pencil (Daiute, 1986). Similarly, in preliminary analysis of students' writing produced with word processing plus "Writer's Assistant" and other "dynamic supports" for writing, Levin, Boruta, and Vasconcellos (1983) found that writing increased in quality and quantity with the support of computer prompts.

Daiute (1986) suggests that the literature in this area indicates that word processing may be most successful when used in conjunction with cognitive and instructional aids that help students develop revision strategies. This is an important finding that tends to confirm the conclusion that using word processing in and of itself does not increase revision. Daiute and colleagues also conclude, however, that word processing with prompting is most effective for poorer writers and least effective for better writers; and, probably most importantly, that better writers do benefit from using word processing without a prompting program (Daiute, 1986). These findings are in keeping with the research cited above on interrelationships of effective writing, students' already-established revising skills, and the instructional interventions and aids provided to them.

It is possible that the most important insight provided by this work has to do with the nature of the instruction that accompanies students' uses of word processing rather than with its form as a computer prompting program. In the computer prompting studies as in much of the work on classroom instruction with word processing (discussed below), the intention is to provide instruction that helps student writers develop more and more sophisticated cognitive composing strategies. Woodruff, Bereiter, and Scardamalia use the term *procedural facilitation* to mean assistance that reduces the cognitive demands of writing while allowing the writer to control lower level aspects of the text (e.g., spelling, mechanics) and high-level aspects (e.g., abstract structural planning, organization). In their work, some of which involves word processing and some of which does not, they explore ways to intervene into the composing process to facilitate the procedural strategies used by student writers. Their work suggests that a central area that ought to be explored in the word-processing and writing research is the way in which various kinds of procedural assistance can be offered to young writers using word processing. A number of recent studies and teacher accounts provide information about the ways teachers use word processing to support the teaching of writing and to facilitate their students' work. These are discussed below.

Instructional Intervention in Classrooms. A number of university-based researchers as well as teacher-researchers have examined various instructional strategies used as teachers work with students using word processing. This body of work indicates that, when word processing is used as part of an instructional program that fosters self-consciousness about writing, it can facilitate the creation of meaning-centered, fluid texts. Proposition 1.6 captures this relationship.

> Proposition 1.6: When it is accompanied by instruction that invites students to view writing as a meaning-making activity, using word processing can facilitate the production of discovery-centered texts and increase meaning-level revisions.

Morocco (1987) studied teachers using word processing for writing instruction with mainstreamed, learning disabled fourth graders in a resource room setting over a 2-year period. She found that procedural instruction aimed at developing generative structures and frameworks throughout the writing process was more effective in enabling children to complete drafts and develop ideas than were substantive or direct skills instruction. Teachers subsequently learned to increase procedural instruction and to offer oral prompts to help children think like writers. Morocco and Neuman (1986) point out that word processing had an impact for learning disabled children on two levels—it made easier the entering and erasing of text and also gave teachers greater access to what children were doing by making their needs for procedural prompts more visible. Rosegrant's (1984) report of work with children with communications disorders provides similar insights about the ways adults can interact with children at the word processing screen to provide support for literacy development.

In quite different ways Woodruff and Daiute, on the one hand, as well as Morocco and Rosegrant on the other, all investigate ways to teach writing with word processing. In each case they try to provide prompts that presumably parallel internal models of composing and, hence, make explicit to students some of what is known and done implicitly by experienced writers. An interesting difference in their work is that a word-processing-with-prompting program is accommodative of the needs and abilities of individual writers only within certain preestablished limits. In contrast, a teacher using word processing for writing instruction is limited only by his or her own insights and abilities within the learning context. Barrett and Paradis (1988) make a related point in their discussion of teaching writing in an "online" university classroom: they propose that the significance of their experimental writing program, which used the technology of electronic networks, was that a teacher, not a programmer, directed the educational process by calling up educational software packages as needed by individual students. In an unrelated study of first and second graders' writing with word processing, Porter and Sherwood (1987) altered the design of their study after they concluded that the effects of word processing itself could not be sorted out from the instruction provided by teachers, aides, and researchers.

It is important to interpret the research on instructional interventions with word processing in light of the previous findings that writers use word processing to make the kinds of changes they already know how to make and that the effectiveness of word processing for writing depends on the skills of individual writers. When combined, these findings suggest that one of the richest areas for continued investigation is writing instruction provided by teachers in classroom situations.

The question most often explored in this area is whether or not using word processing as part of writing instruction stimulates students to write as a process of exploration and discovery. Hubbard (1985) asserts that the word processor "crystallizes in silicon" a useful separation between generative and critical activities in writing (a separation originally recommended by Peter Elbow). Because changes can be made so easily with word processing, this line of thinking goes, writers can take risks as they generate text and hold their critical powers in check until later. Sudol (1985) suggests that using word processing allows a different principle of revision to operate: writers can generate and weigh many alternatives to their texts before they actually delete any of them. Catano (1985) suggests the term *the fluid text* to describe the dynamic relationship of the writer and his or her emerging material. In his year-long study of two adult novelists using word processing for writing, he concluded that, because word processing supports the fluidity of text for as long a time as possible, it is uniquely suited to help writers make meaning and find connections as they write.

The argument underlying these three claims is very similar to the claims made by the professional writers cited earlier. It is precisely this argument for the creation of the fluid text that is explicitly or implicitly at the heart of many of the studies of the effects of teaching writing with word processing. At this point we know that word processing *can* facilitate the fluid text. However the critical pedagogical question is: *Does* using word processing to teach writing create the fluid text for student writers? That is: *Does* it help them explore, experiment, and take risks as they write to make meaning?

We have already pointed out that student writers tend to assimilate word processing to their own models of composing, which are, in many cases, linear and sequential. Harris (1985), who specifically concluded that there was no evidence of increased experimentation in the composing of college students who used word processing, also speculated that, because of difficulties locating and rereading text on the computer screen, word processing might even hinder recursion, or the fluid movement from one part of a text to another or from one composing strategy to another. On the other hand, a number of studies, conducted primarily by teacher-researchers in their own classrooms (Barber, 1982; Crist, 1984; Evans, 1985; Gula, 1982; Lindemann & Willert, 1986; Martinez, 1985a; McAllister, 1985; Piper, 1983-1984; Riel, 1985; Smye, 1984; Womble, 1985) or by researchers in teaching situations (Pearson & Wilkinson, 1986; Pufahl, 1986), conclude that teaching with word processing does enhance students' writing processes by encouraging experimentation and risk taking. Schwartz (1982) also suggests that college freshmen were more receptive to conferencing suggestions that they try out alternatives when they used word processing because they could so easily change their texts.

The discrepancy in these findings is explained by the fact that those who found that word processing enhanced experimentation in writing were exploring its use *in conjunction with* their explorations of strategies for writing instruction. That is, as they introduced and taught word processing, they were also teaching strategies for thinking and rethinking about their students' own writing. Underlying their accounts is an argument, either explicit or implicit, for the interrelationships of instructional strategies for writing, the exploratory nature of students' writing processes, and the capacities that word processing makes available.

Smye (1984) and McAllister (1985), for example, found that college students elaborated their ideas, "messed around" with more features of their writing, and debated alternative versions of their writing when they used word processing for various exercises and peer exchanges in small groups. Along similar lines, Crist (1984) used word processing with high school students to demonstrate sentence combining strategies and discuss writing style and alternatives for overused words. Gula (1982) found that using word processing helped improve both the writing quality of his twelfth-grade students and the level of his own teaching suggestions and expectations for them. Teacher-researcher Womble (1985) centered her classroom study of word processing around dialogue journals and discussions with students about their changing writing practices. She noted increasing fluency and more meaningful revising in the writing of all three high school students upon whom she focused. Evans (1985) coupled the introduction of word processing in a high school senior literature class with peer and teacher conferences. Pearson and Wilkinson (1986) did not intentionally explore variations in instruction but discovered that the authenticity of the writing tasks they constructed and the dynamics of social situations they set up had more influence on students' motivation to take risks with their writing than did word processing itself. Willer (1984) found that small groups of sixth graders used word processing to compose collaborative stories in a way that was "distinctly nonlinear." Piper (1983, 1983-1984) taught fifth graders through sentence combining activities on the word processor and then helped them expand this strategy to their original stories. Riel (1985) found that third and fourth graders who participated in a "newswire" network of communication improved their reporting, writing, and editing skills as they wrote and rewrote their stories for actual audiences and submitted them to a cooperative editorial board.

Each of these examples involves the use of word processing in combination with instructional activities that invite students to think about their own writing strategies and view writing as an unfolding, recursive process. Most of them, including peer or teacher-student conferences, work in small groups, and discussion of alternative versions of texts could have been done in some related version without word processing. What is important to note, however, is that, in each case, the unique capabilities of word processing were used to support the goals of the writing teacher, and in each case, the teacher's goal was to improve writing by increasing students' self-consciousness about their composing strategies. This supports Crist's assertion that "English teachers must look at the computer as a tool to be used" (p. 78). However it only partly supports his conclusion that "word processing can change the way student writers look at the page before them" (p. 80). The body of research discussed here suggests that the more accurate conclusion is that *teachers* often change the way student writers look at the page before them by helping them harness the raw capacities of word processing to enhance their creation of fluid, meaning-making texts.

Word Processing and Other Composing Processes

In addition to the literature that has explored the effects of word processing on revising, there has been some exploration of other composing processes. For example, a number of studies conclude that word processing allows easy and speedy "publishing," or multiple copy production, of students' writing (Bickel,

1985; Evans, 1986) and that word processing encourages the production of more drafts (Engberg, 1983a, b; Pufahl, 1986; Womble, 1985). Others conclude that using word processing can prompt students more frequently and/or more closely to read and reread their emerging texts (Daiute & Kruidenier, nd; Phenix & Hannan, 1984). Piazza and Riggs (1984) suggest that kindergarteners who are allowed to experiment at the keyboard actively explore language in ways that parallel their oral explorations of speech as well as ways that are computer specific.

An especially interesting line of recent work has focused on word processing and planning. This work is based on the findings of earlier writing research that indicates that effective writers plan more in general and plan more at higher conceptual levels than less effective writers do. Both Bridwell-Bowles, Johnson, and Brehe (1987) and Haas and Hayes (1986), however, found that, when college students used word processing, they did less planning than they did when they wrote with paper and pencil. Haas's (1989) recent study compared the effects of word processing, pencil and paper, and a combination of the two on the planning processes of experienced writers and college writers. Based on analysis of think-aloud protocols, Haas found that those who used word processing alone planned significantly less, and did less conceptual planning and significantly more local and sequential planning, than they did when they used paper and pencil alone. Haas speculates that, in light of the fact that the length of composing periods was comparable across the three conditions, it is possible that writers using word processing made up for their lack of planning in other ways, such as more thorough or more frequent rereading of texts.

One way to think about the results of the literature on word processing and planning or other composing processes is in light of the possibility we raised earlier that, with word processing, stages and strategies commonly identified as parts of composing are not so distinct as they may be when writers use paper and pencil. With word processing the boundaries between planning and composing, for example, may be considerably more fluid than they are with paper and pencil. This would certainly be in keeping with the comments of adult writers (e.g., Lutz, 1987) that they are more willing, when using word processing, to allow their pieces to evolve. Similarly, the boundaries between one draft and another often blur when writers write with word processing. Unfortunately, this blurring is often not acknowledged in various research designs, and the notion of *draft* is operationalized as the end of a single sitting at the computer, at which point the writer prints out in hard-copy form what he or she has accomplished up to that point. This makes for an implicit equation of draft, which previously has been used in the writing literature to imply a kind of cognitive activity, and termination of time period available to sit at the computer keyboard. The action of printing out because of time restrictions may or may not be equivalent to a writer's decision that he or she has concluded a working version of a text.

Finally some recent literature has explored the ways college students use word processing to evaluate and correct their writing. Haas (1987) found that students used printouts of their writing produced with word processing to proofread, check formatting, read, and reorganize, especially when writing tasks were longer, less familiar, or "knowledge forming." Online correction and evaluation, on the other hand, was used for shorter, more familiar writing tasks.

Issues surrounding the effects of word processing on various composing strategies need to be further untangled as the word processing and writing research continues. Many of the questions explored in the literature on word processing and composing processes are not appropriate to explorations of the uses young children make of word processing. Production, rather than revising, tends to be the preoccupation of beginning writers. This suggests that research is needed in order to explore the ways beginners produce text with word processing and the ways the tool functions for them. Unfortunately, very little of the literature has looked at what beginning writers actually do when they use word processing. A few studies have explored young children's uses of word processing in relation to the social organization of classroom learning contexts; this literature is examined in the discussion around Proposition 5.

Summary: Word Processing and Composing Processes

The above synthesis indicates that using word processing for writing does affect the composing processes of student writers. However, the effect is a complex one that is mediated by many other interrelated factors about which we need to know a great deal more. As Propositions 1.5 and 1.6 point out, the effects of word processing interact with the preexisting skills and strategies of individual writers. We have some global indications that the distinction is between "weak/strong" or "inexperienced/experienced" writers. But we need a great deal more information about the particular kinds of problem-solving and writing skills writers have or do not have, and the particular ways in which these influence the effectiveness of word processing for writing. We also know that the effects of word processing are intertwined with the kinds of instructional interventions that occur with the introduction of word processing into the curriculum and with the nature of individual writing tasks that are assigned. We need to know more about the nature of these interrelationships, and we need many examples that demonstrate how these relationships are played out in various classroom or computer laboratory situations. It is necessary that we have both insider and outsider perspectives on the nature of the interrelationships of classroom instruction and word-processing effects. That is, we need both the perspectives of teacher-researchers who systematically and intentionally inquire about the uses and effects of word processing in their own classrooms and the perspectives of outside researchers who bring more traditional university-based research perspectives to the task. (See Cazden, 1989, and Cochran-Smith and Lytle, 1990, for discussions of teacher research in relation to more traditional approaches to research on teaching.)

We have the least information about the effects of using word processing on the writing of elementary-school-age children, especially beginning writers roughly ages 5 through 10. This is a particularly important group because it is precisely this group of children who are in the process of developing as writers and who are always, by a certain definition, "weak writers." Since the literature suggests that there is an important relationship between the skills and abilities of individual writers and the usefulness of word processing to individual writers, it is especially important to explore the effects of word processing on the composing processes and written products of this group.

THE EFFECTS OF WORD PROCESSING ON STUDENTS' WRITTEN PRODUCTS

The literature indicates that using word processing in classroom or computer laboratory situations affects both the quality and the quantity of students' written products. We argue below that, although writing with word processing often produces slightly longer and more error-free texts, we need to consider these findings in light of the mediating factors of teachers' and students' keyboarding and systems familiarity, allocation of writing time, changing classroom organizations for learning, length of time of word-processing implementation, and students' attitudes. Proposition 2.0 provides a general statement of the processes to be discussed within the section that follows.

> Proposition 2.0: When students use word processing in classroom or computer laboratory situations, the quality and quantity of their written products are affected.

Quantity of Texts Produced with Word Processing

Two related measures of quantity have been assessed—the length of individual texts or overall quantity of writing produced, and the total time devoted to writing by students using word processing. A number of studies indicate that writers using word processing produce slightly longer texts than they do with paper and pencil (Bradley, 1982; Bridwell-Bowles et al., 1987; Broderick & Trushell, 1985; Collier, 1983; Hawisher, 1987; Kane, 1983). Hence, Proposition 2.1 can be added.

> Proposition 2.1: When they write with word processing in classroom or computer laboratory situations (and once they have developed basic keyboard familiarity), many students produce slightly longer texts than they do when they write with paper and pencil.

In a review of primarily unpublished papers and dissertations on word processing and writing, Hawisher (1988) points out that increased length of texts is one of the few textual features most researchers agree on. In Daiute's (1984, 1985b, 1986) series of studies mentioned previously, however, the writing of junior high-school students who used word processing for writing was compared with the writing of those who used paper and pencil, as well as with the writing of those who used a computer prompting program coupled with word processing. Contrary to the conclusions of the researchers above, Daiute found that the writing produced with word processing alone, and with word processing with prompting, was shorter than the writing produced with paper and pencil. Part of the explanation for this finding was the students' lack of typing skill and speed. This same factor may also account for Kurth's (1987) discrepant finding that there was no difference in the length of writing produced by junior high school students and high school sophomores who used word processing as compared with those who used paper and pencil. The constraining factor in the use of word processing in Kurth's study was that the word processing treatment groups received only one hour of computer instruction and were not encouraged to learn additional features of the system, since the focus of the course was writing and not computers.

We know that students' keyboard familiarity and text production speed increase over time (Cochran-Smith, Kahn, & Paris, 1986, 1988; Kahn & Freyd, 1990a,b), and we know that the ways students and teachers use word processing in classrooms change significantly over time (Cochran-Smith, Kahn, & Paris, 1990; Paris, in press). Thus very limited time periods for word processing instruction and use confound the results of some of the research on text length. The general body of work suggests that conclusions about length of texts produced with word processing need to be formulated over relatively long periods of time in light of writers' keyboarding skills and overall length of time that particular writers have worked with word processing.

Time spent writing with word processing is a factor that has also been explored in the quantity studies. A number of studies indicate that, either by actual word/page counts or by teacher reports, student writers of a variety of ages write more often, stay with writing tasks for longer periods, and produce a greater overall quantity of writing when using word processing (Bickel, 1985; Boudrot, 1984; Broderick & Trushell, 1985; Evans, 1985; O'Brien, 1984; Phenix & Hannan, 1984; Watt, 1983; Womble, 1985). This finding is reflected in Proposition 2.2.

Proposition 2.2:   When they write with word processing in classroom or computer laboratory situations, many students produce a greater quantity of writing and/or spend more time writing than they do when they write with paper and pencil.

Evans (1986) provides an interesting interpretation of this literature, pointing out that the effect of word processing on quantity of writing may be related more to the nature of ongoing writing programs and the quantity of writing students were producing before they started using word processing than it is to some absolute effect of word processing itself. Two other qualifying issues are relevant. First, implicit in some of the research in this area is the equation of quantity of writing with quality of writing. Clearly, longer pieces are not necessarily better pieces. Indeed, some children (Kane, 1983; Daiute, 1984; Phenix & Hannan, 1984) as well as adults (Grow, 1988) who use word processing revise their pieces by simply adding on to the end of what they have, whether appropriate and effective for the particular piece of writing or not. As we have argued, it is problematic when writing and word-processing research seems to imply that length of text, like gross number of revisions, is itself an end of writing instruction rather than a feature of writing that mediates and is mediated by many other considerations.

Second, teachers who include word processing as part of their instructional programs in writing, and/or researchers who set up writing opportunities in computer laboratories, often structure these writing contexts in ways that are qualitatively and quantitatively different from the ways that paper-and-pencil writing situations are structured in classrooms. The former contexts often allow for, invite, or require students to give both more and different kinds of time and attention to writing, resulting in a situation where increased quantity of writing is an effect that is both once removed from the technology of word processing itself and deeply embedded within the context of the writing situation. The reciprocal relationship between the social organization of the classroom and the effects and uses of computer technology within the classroom is significant. This relationship is analyzed in greater detail in the discussion following Proposition 5. Finally, increased quantity of writing with word processing is probably in large part explained as an effect that is mediated by positive student attitude toward writing and word processing (see Proposition 3 below) and/or by changes in the ways writers allocate their total time for writing among various writing activities, rather than by technological features inherent in word processing itself.

Quality of Texts Produced with Word Processing

Although the effect of word processing on quality of writing is considered by some to be the quintessential question, the results of research in this area are mixed. In addition, it is likely that definitive conclusions about the effects of word processing on quality of writing are simply not possible. *Quality of writing* is a complex and slippery notion, especially as it applies across age and developmental levels. Factors that mediate quality, such as time available to spend on various aspects of writing, are often not considered. Finally, the interconnectedness of instructional intervention and the technology of word processing itself are difficult to sort out in ways that cut across the highly context-specific activity of teaching. Despite these qualifications, there is some evidence across groups of writers that using word processing can help produce more attractive texts with fewer errors. This work leads to the construction of Proposition 2.3.

Proposition 2.3:   When they write with word processing, students often produce neater, more error-free texts than they do with paper and pencil.

Bridwell et al. (1985) found that college students who used word processing were more concerned with the formatting of their writing and produced neater products. Similarly, youngsters in sixth grade who used word processing for writing made fewer errors and fewer new errors when moving from one draft to the next, and corrected a greater percentage of errors than they did when using paper and pencil (Levin, Riel, Rowe, & Boruta, 1985). And seventh graders corrected more errors when using a word-processing-with-prompting program (Daiute, 1984). We have already discussed some of the problems of implicit equations between quality and revision or quality and length. The case holds here as well—quality does not equal neatness nor flawlessness.

A number of other studies have examined the effects of word processing on overall quality of writing with mixed results. Once again, the interrelationships of various factors are almost impossible to sort out across studies. Generally, however, there is little evidence that using word processing, in and of itself, improves the quality of students' writing whether at the college or early adolescent levels. This finding is reflected in Proposition 2.4.

Proposition 2.4:   Using word processing, in and of itself, generally does not improve overall quality of writing.

Most of the research on quality of writing has concentrated on college or adolescent writers. In an early case study of several college writers, for example, Collier (1983) found that students manipulated more text and revised more with word processing, but the quality of their writing generally did not improve. Similarly low-skills college writers wrote longer pieces, used some sophisticated revision strategies, and had an easier time revising when they used word processing. They also made more errors in standard usage than did those who used paper and pencil, however, and the writing of both word processing users and paper-and-pencil users improved overall when they worked with tutors and peers (King et al., 1985).

Further, Hawisher (1987) found that able college freshmen who received word-processing and revising instruction over a semester produced essays of about the same overall quality whether they used word processing or paper and pencil. Hawisher's study is unusual in its attention to number of revisions and kinds of revision in addition to overall quality. As we have pointed out, the correlational links between these aspects of the writing process are often implied but seldom examined empirically. Two of Hawisher's findings are especially noteworthy: (a) there was a significant negative correlation between the number of meaning-preserving revisions and improvement in overall writing quality from first to final drafts; and (b), conversely, there was a significant positive correlation between number of meaning-changing revisions and improvement in overall writing quality in first to final drafts. This finding suggests that conceptual or organizational changes that alter the meaning of a piece may account more for overall improvement in writing quality than changes that retain the meaning and alter the surface structure. Coupling this finding with the fact that users of word processing tend to revise microstructural rather than macrostructural features of their writing (Bridwell et al., 1985; Harris, 1985; Lutz, 1987), we can raise serious questions about the effects of using word processing on overall quality of writing. Most importantly, these findings suggest serious implications for the kinds of writing and revising instruction students receive, along with the instruction they receive in word-processing techniques.

The factor of instruction helps to explain two sets of findings that are contrary to Hawisher's conclusion that paper-and-pencil users and word-processing users produced writing of about the same overall quality. McAllister and Louth (1988) found that basic college writers who received computer-assisted composition instruction over two semesters and then wrote sample paragraphs significantly increased the quality of their revisions in test paragraphs as compared with the revisions of a control paper and pencil group who had the same instruction. Similarly O'Brien and Pizzini (1986) concluded that advanced high school students who used word processing produced better scientific abstracts than did their counterparts who wrote with paper and pencil. Part of the discrepancy between the findings of Hawisher, on the one hand, and McAllister and Louth and O'Brien and Pizzini, on the other, may be explained by the fact that, in the latter studies, groups of writers in the treatment conditions received writing instruction of some sort at the same time as they received word processing instruction. This fact makes it clear that examination of the kinds of writing instruction students receive along with opportunities to use word processing is critical.

A second point is also important. Neither McAllister and Louth nor O'Brien and Pizzini discuss the limitations of generalizing to the quality of other kinds of writing the results achieved when students write only paragraphs or abstracts. It has been suggested that word processing may actually hinder recursion in writing because of the difficulty locating and rereading sections of texts longer than a screenful (Haas & Hayes, 1986; Harris, 1985) and that working only with word processing is difficult in knowledge-forming tasks (Haas, 1987). Similarly, it has been noted that writers using word processing often fail to have an overview of their writing or an accurate sense of the whole (Grow, 1988). In light of these cautions, it seems appropriate to wonder what relevance the results obtained from written products in the form of paragraphs or abstracts have for the production of longer written genres.

The results of research on the quality of writing produced with word processing by younger adolescents, generally sixth grade through ninth grade, are consistent with the mixed results reported above. Quality of writing of junior high-school students who used word processing without a prompting intervention generally did not improve (Daiute, 1984), although the quality of writing of another group of junior high-school students who used word processing with a prompting program was somewhat longer and judged higher by raters who consistently associated length with quality (Daiute, 1986). The attitudes toward writing of another group of sixth graders improved significantly with word processing, but the quality of their writing did not (Woodruff et al., 1981-82). Similarly, junior high-school students who used word processing within a holistic writing program over the course of a year generally did not write better than their counterparts in a control group who used paper and pencil (Dalton & Hannafin, 1987). However, sixth graders who had had word-processing experience received generally higher scores on a structured revision task than did those who had not, but both groups tended to revise the writing problems about which they had been instructed by their teachers (Flinn, 1985). This body of work tends to confirm the general finding that using word processing in and of itself does not produce better quality writing.

There is almost no research on the overall quality of writing produced with word processing by younger children under the age of about 11 or 12. Only one study addresses this issue. Third, fourth, and fifth graders who used word processing along with a supporting planning and message network system improved significantly from pre- to posttests of expository writing, although some control groups did as well (Bruce & Rubin, 1984).

There are many difficulties in trying to synthesize across studies the research on writing quality and word processing. Variations in conditions are considerable. It is clear that word processing interacts with many other variables in classroom and even in laboratory situations. Pearson and Wilkinson (1986), for example, point out that, although word processing seemed to facilitate adolescents' motivation to improve their writing, the greatest influences were group dynamics, the social situation, and students' differential interest in various writing tasks. Finally, as we pointed out in the discussion of revision and instructional intervention, word processing and instructional intervention are often completely bound up with one another, and the effects of one are impossible to separate out from the effects of the other. In Hawisher's (1987) study, for example, all students were instructed in revising and word-processing strategies but later produced some essays with word processing and some with paper and pencil. It is difficult to know, therefore, whether or not students learned certain composing and revising strategies on the word processor and later transferred them to their paper-and-pencil writing as well. This interpretation is supported by other research (e.g., Womble, 1985) that suggests that strategies learned with word processing do carry over to paper-and-pencil writing.

There are two central problems with research on word processing and quality. First, it is unlikely that we can separate out the effects of word processing from the effects of other interrelated variables. And second, it is not at all clear that questions about quality are the most useful questions to ask. Even in experimental studies that find word processing to be the one major factor that accounts for differences in quality of writing (e.g., McAllister & Louth, 1988), different teachers are often involved and the social settings of classrooms vary. Indeed we know from years of ethnographic and other observational research that teachers do not teach in a "manner exactly parallel" to one another, and that differences across classrooms are not trivial. (See, especially, syntheses of interpretive research in Erickson, 1986; classroom observation in Evertson & Green, 1986; and multiple perspective analysis in Green & Harker, 1988.) In word-processing and writing research, as in much of the research on more general instructional strategies in classrooms, the "control group" comparison simply does not pertain (Porter & Sherwood, 1987), and serious difficulties are encountered when word processing is treated as an independent variable (Amarel, 1983; Hawkins & Sheingold, 1986). An argument for multiple perspectives, made in greater detail in the discussion following Proposition 5, suggests that we need to look closely in individual classrooms over time to investigate the ways that factors such as time allocation, teaching interventions, and quantity of writing interact with and mediate overall quality.

Summary: Word Processing and Written Products

Proposition 2 and its modifying subpropositions indicate clearly that writing quality is tied up with nature of instruction and with writing contexts. As is the case with the effects of word processing on composing processes, there is much that we still do not know about the effects of word processing on students' written products. We know very little about the writing produced by young children who have access to word processing, and about the ways that the factors of time, attitude, instructional intervention, and classroom social organization mediate the quality and quantity of written products. Some of what we do know in these areas is discussed under Propositions 3, 4, and 5 below, which examine students' attitudes, keyboard mastery, and the social organizations of classrooms that incorporate word processing into writing instruction.

THE EFFECTS OF WORD PROCESSING ON STUDENTS' ATTITUDES

In informal interviews as well as written surveys, student writers and/or their teachers at elementary through college levels report that they like using word processing and have generally positive attitudes toward writing with word processing (Bridwell et al., 1985; Daiute & Kruidenier, n.d.; Haas & Hayes, 1986; Harris, 1985; Kahn, 1988; Levin et al., 1985; O'Brien, 1984; Piper, 1983, 1983-84; Pufahl, 1986; Skublkowski & Elder, 1987; Smye, 1984; Willer, 1984; Woodruff et al., 1981-82). This finding is captured in Proposition 3.

Proposition 3:   Student writers have positive attitudes toward using word processing for writing.

Many researchers and teachers consider this result particularly significant. Riel (1985), for example, argues that improved attitude toward writing on and off the computer was the single most striking change observed in her study of third and fourth graders who used word processing as part of a communications network. Positive attitudes are not the case when students work with computers in any and all ways. If this were the case, it would be easy to suggest that novelty or some other feature of computer technology itself accounts for word processing's overwhelming appeal to student writers. However, as indicated by Griswold's (1984) finding that computer-assisted math drill and practice accounted for significant variations in attitudes about self-responsibility and self-confidence but not for attitudes toward school or math itself, this is not the case. The nearly universal positive student responses to writing with word processing are noteworthy.

In addition to broadly positive attitudes toward writing with word processing, students often report that they believe their writing improves with word processing (Bridwell et al., 1985; Bridwell & Ross, 1984; Feldman, 1985; Palmer, Dowd, & James, 1984), they feel more relaxed with word processing because they have more opportunities to reconsider their texts (Collier, 1983; Feldman, 1985), and they are proud of the polished look of their writing (Bickel, 1985; Lindemann & Willert, 1986). In early work in his laboratory, Papert (1980) reported that students who had totally rejected writing became intensely involved with word processing and rapidly improved their writing. This is not to suggest that every single writer likes working with word processing for all writing tasks or prefers it to paper and pencil, and indeed some students do not elect to use word processing (Evans, 1986; Porter, 1986). But in the overwhelming majority of cases, teachers and students alike report that word processing is very positively received.

Probably the most salient explanation for positive attitudes toward word processing is the most obvious one: it is less physically demanding of writers, and it takes the recopying/retyping penalty out of the production of final drafts and the cutting-and-pasting penalty out of revision and refinement of texts. Teachers and researchers also speculate that students like word processing because they feel powerful when they control the technology, are less intimidated as writers because a machine rather than a person is the first "audience" for their efforts, and are impressed by the professional-looking results of their products. The most important reason to consider student attitudes toward writing with word processing is its potentially powerful mediating effect on allocation of time spent on writing, willingness to revise and edit, and quantity of texts produced. As we have argued repeatedly, it is the interrelationship of these factors that is the most interesting and probably most important consideration in research on word processing and writing.

KEYBOARDING AND SYSTEM SKILLS

The argument for the value of word processing for students' writing is contingent upon the fact that they can master the technology of word processing relatively easily and quickly, including both the various word processing system commands and the typewriter keyboard. There is a great deal of controversy about the latter. Some insist that even young children must be taught touch-typing skills in order to use the capabilities of word processing effectively (Kisner, 1984). Others, pointing out that journalists and computer programmers often use some version of a two-finger hunt-and-peck system with remarkable speed and efficiency, argue instead for keyboard familiarity rather than touch-typing skill (Kahn & Freyd, 1990a, 1990b). (See Hoot, 1988, and Koenke, 1987, for discussions of the keyboarding controversy and relevant research in this area). Interestingly, however, neither informal classroom reports nor formal studies of word processing and writing describe serious difficulties when students use word processing for writing (Clements, 1987). These findings suggest an additional proposition.

> Proposition 4.0:   Student writers are able to master keyboarding and word processing strategies for use in age-appropriate writing activities.

When difficulties with keyboarding are mentioned (Collier, 1983; Haas & Hayes, 1986), they can often be explained as a function of inefficient or particularly slow word processing equipment, now largely outdated, rather than of students' difficulties mastering the technology. On the contrary, there is evidence that writers as young as fourth graders, as well as their college level counterparts, learn word-processing commands fairly easily, have minor keyboarding problems, and are remarkably unintimidated by the machinery (Bradley, 1982; Broderick & Trushell, 1985; Evans, 1985; Kane, 1983; Kurth, 1987; Piper, 1983, 1983-1984; Willer, 1984; Zurek, 1985).

Examination across studies, however, indicates that, more significant than the conclusion that students are capable of managing the computer, is the finding that it takes time for students to learn word processing and to become familiar with the keyboard if they cannot already type. This finding indicates the need for Proposition 4.1.

Proposition 4.1:   When students begin to use word processing, there is an initial keyboarding/systems learning period, the length of which is dependent in part on the prior typing and writing experiences of the student.

In a preliminary analysis of the study of word processing in the early elementary grades that is the focus of this volume (Cochran-Smith et al., 1986), we pointed out explicitly that all writers seemed to need a period of time for mastering word processing before they could also use it for writing:

> There is a learning period, for adults as well as children, during which attention must be focused on learning to word process, frequently at the expense of writing . . . Children need time simply to learn word processing skills, without the added burden of a writing task. [For example] second graders [with no word processing familiarity] generally took an hour to compose their first pieces at the computer. This was so because children were trying to do both word processing and writing. The writing we saw at the beginning of the year in fourth grade was done primarily on paper, and computer time was used for transcribing [which separated the tasks of writing and word processing]. By contrast, another group of second graders who began word processing were given mini-lessons in word processing. When they went to the computer [later] to work on their own writing, they had fewer struggles with word processing. We see [the necessity of] a learning period in which the main effort is mastery of the word processor. (p. 6)

Based on these observations, we suggested that it was probably not productive for teachers to expect students to use word processing to create the fluid text before they had developed basic familiarity with word-processing commands and the typewriter keyboard. This seems particularly true for elementary-school-age students who generally do not have prior typing skills. For instance, Morocco (1987) found that fourth grade learning-disabled children needed to develop both word-processing and beginning keyboarding skills through regular, brief opportunities to practice and receive feedback in small increments. Porter (1986) also found that it took time and perseverance for first and second graders to develop keyboarding skills. Finally, Flinn (1985) concluded that using word processing caused a temporary loss of writing fluency for sixth-grade students. Even in studies with older writers who generally had more typing and writing skills, writers used abstract and difficult word processing commands only over time (Daiute, 1985b) and needed to focus on word-processing instruction early and separately from writing instruction (Bridwell & Ross, 1984).

The length of the learning period is probably directly related to the extent of the writer's prior typing skills and awareness of his or her own composing and revising skills. For experienced adult writers/typists such as the professionals discussed previously it is relatively easy (and indeed exciting) to learn the commands of word processing and to see ways in which one may use the capacities of word processing to implement already-practiced composing and revising strategies. Over time, however, even experienced writers discover ways to facilitate their composing strategies with word processing, and, for very experienced writers, the capacities of word processing may interact with writing skills to make the process qualitatively different.

For young children who have neither well-developed writing strategies nor efficient typing skills, the learning period may indeed be much lengthier than it is for older more experienced writers. The literature does not tell us much in this area. We need more information about the length of the learning period for various groups of children and how these vary across grades and age levels. In addition we need information about how teachers accommodate the need for a learning period and offer instruction in word-processing skills. We need to know some of the basics that young children need to get started with word processing and what teachers can reasonably expect young writers to do. It is particularly important that we have studies that examine these questions over the long term. Otherwise, researchers may unintentionally draw conclusions about the potential usefulness (or not) of word processing for elementary-school-age children which are artifacts of the learning period rather than accurate findings about writing processes.

WORD PROCESSING, CLASSROOM ORGANIZATION, AND TEACHERS' GOALS

A small but growing body of research has begun to explore the ways that word processing is introduced and used in individual classroom situations. This research indicates generally that both intra- and interclassroom variations occur and that differences are related to teachers' goals as well as to the social organization of the classroom learning environment. These findings lead to the identification of Proposition 5.0.

> Proposition 5.0: The ways that word processing is used for writing in individual classrooms, the social organization of classroom learning environments, and the goals and strategies of individual teachers are interactively related.

In an early ETS study of the use of PLATO mathematics and reading software in elementary classrooms, Swinton, Amarel, and Morgan (1978) found that there were huge variations from classroom to classroom in the amounts of time children spent actually working at computers using the software provided by the project, even though all teachers were volunteers and were keenly interested in the programs. Commenting on this finding, Amarel (1983) emphasized that teachers make ongoing decisions about computer implementations based on their individual instructional values and their assessments of the utility of computers in meeting their aims over time. She argued that, in planning for and assessing computer implementation programs, we have underestimated the "coercive power of the classroom environment" (p. 261), and she claimed that we needed to acknowledge the individual teacher as an enormous factor in the degree and kind of implementation that occurs.

In a 5-year study of the impacts of software (Logo, prototype mathematics and science software, and database management software) on the organization of learning in classrooms, Sheingold and Hawkins reached the related conclusion that the computer itself was not "a treatment" in the classroom, but rather a technological device with the potential for many different uses depending on the individual teacher's interpretation (Hawkins & Sheingold, 1986; Sheingold, Hawkins, & Char, 1984). Sheingold and Hawkins argued that research about computer implementation needed to acknowledge the classroom as a social context within which computers were used in a variety of ways.

> Neither cognitive nor social impacts can be considered independently of the functions the technology serves and of its meaning for those who use it. *That* the technology can have a particular impact on classrooms does not necessarily mean that it *will*. Effective research must examine how the use and meaning of technology are shaped in classrooms over long periods of time. (Hawkins & Sheingold, 1986, p. 42)

Salomon and Gardner (1986) make a similar case in their discussion of what research on computers and education can learn from research on television and education. They argue that computers, like television, are not single, undifferentiated "treatments" whose effects on children can easily be measured; rather they claim that researchers should expect variations in usage and experiences with computers and use holistic as well as experimental paradigms to explore the field.

Four recent studies of computers in school settings confirm and refine the notion that the introduction and use of word processing is interrelated with the social and organizational contexts of elementary classrooms. C.P. Olson (1988) examined general computer implementation in six diverse school sites, grades three through eight, over a 2-year period. Through rich descriptions of individual classrooms and teachers, he identified both successful and unsuccessful implementation efforts and located computer implementation within the culture of schools and classrooms. His analysis emphasizes that, although the particular cultures of school communities mediated computer usage, they did not cause them. Rather, the complex interplay of the cognitive styles of teachers, the organization and emphases of their curriculum, classroom relationships, and the learning environments teachers created for and with children had a dramatic impact on differences in outcomes. In a similar but unrelated study, J. Olson (1988) contrasted "schoolworlds" and "microworlds" by documenting eight cases of middle- and high-school teachers and students using computer technology. Olson discovered that computers had instrumental as well as "expressive" purposes, or uses teachers made of computers to express something about themselves as teachers (e.g., that they were aware of, and knowledgeable about, current teaching methods). Expressive uses often accounted for the ways teachers used computers, ways which were otherwise inconsistent with their general goals and practices. Olson argues that computers themselves do not create learning contexts, or microworlds, apart from the schoolworlds within which teachers interpret and use them.

Genishi (1988, 1989) also explored the social contexts of computer implementation in relation to the complex decision-making processes of individual teachers. Genishi, however, concentrated on the microworlds created by various children in their interactions around Logo activities in public kindergarten and first grade classrooms. She found that individual children constructed microworlds, or individual social contexts within which computers were used, primarily through talk with peers and teachers. In some cases these contexts controverted the intentions of teachers or software designers. Genishi's work points out that teachers as well as students interpret and construct their experiences with computers. It also emphasizes that the success or failure of computer implementation can only be understood in terms of the match or mismatch that occurs between teachers', children's, and software's goals and their complex interrelationships in classrooms. Mehan (1989) studied four elementary classrooms where microcomputers were introduced, observing changes in classroom organization, teacher-student relationships, and curriculum over the course of a year. He found that teachers fit microcomputers into their already-established classroom organizational structures, seldom modifying spatial and temporal arrangements. But he also found that new participation structures and new functional learning environments developed, which were used to support both old and new classroom goals. Mehan concludes that it is not the features of computer technology itself that account for how computers are used in classrooms, but what people choose to do with them.

These four studies locate the deployment of technology squarely within the social systems of classrooms and make it clear that uses of computers are social and cultural as well as technical practices. They emphasize that when we examine word processing as a tool for the elementary classroom, we must account for the existing cultures of classrooms and schools as well as teachers' and students' interpretations of the usefulness of the technology for their ongoing instructional programs. They also make it clear that different ways of using the same technology will be the rule rater than the exception in classroom studies.

An interesting parallel to the finding that individual teachers have a significant (albeit in some cases, unexpected and, in many cases, unacknowledged) impact on the implementation of technology in classrooms is that teachers themselves want to have a voice in the process of making decisions about the ways computers can best serve the curriculum. Teachers wish to be consulted, and they want the opportunity to find their own effective strategies for deploying the raw capacities of technology rather than being regarded as the recipients of others' decisions or the implementors of others' designs (Paris, in press). In an interesting nationwide survey recently conducted by the Educational Technology Center at Harvard (Wiske et al., 1987), teachers were asked how and why they used computers, what kinds of training and support were available, the effects computers had on them and their students, and the influences the teachers had on how the technology was used. Wiske and colleagues concluded that: (a) teachers were as likely to use computers for open-ended activities as they were to use it for drill and practice; (b) teachers' decisions were influenced by their beliefs about the educational potential of computers, external pressures and opportunities, and access to resources; and (c) teachers wanted more computer time and training tailored to their own interests and needs. Especially clear in the ETC survey are teachers' own calls for a voice in the decision-making process: "Let the demand and use for computers come from the ones who actually do the teaching" (p. 27), and "Teachers must not be cut out of the decision-making loop; they should be centrally involved in decisions regarding software and the integration of computers into the curriculum" (p. 70).

If we work from the view that computer technology is what Amarel (1983), following Papert (1980), has called a "Protean tool" that can be used in a variety of ways, then it becomes apparent that interpretation by the individual teacher is in and of itself a part of the impact of word processing technology on learning settings. If we work from the view that teaching is a highly complex, context-specific activity, and that differences across classrooms, schools, and school systems are not trivial (Cochran-Smith & Lytle, 1990), then we must also acknowledge that research is probably not going to lead to global generalizations about children's word processing and writing . How word processing "most effectively" can be used in classrooms is not likely to be understood apart from the ways individual teachers work within particular instructional contexts. How word processing affects the quality, quantity, or processes of children's writing is not likely to be understood apart from the ways these are embedded within, and mediated by, the individual social situation (see also Cochran-Smith et al., 1988; Kahn, 1988; Paris, in press).

The line of research in word processing and writing that seems most promising in this area is that which investigates the whys and hows of individual teachers' interpretations of the raw capacities of word processing over relatively long periods of time and within the contexts of specific classrooms and schools. This line of research includes information about ways children respond to, as well as influence, their teachers' interpretations of the potential uses of word processing. Across cases, it is likely that patterns will emerge in the ways teachers deploy computer technology and reason about its deployment, the ways children learn to use word processing within particular learning environments, and the ways these change and interact over time. Patterns of this kind can offer valuable information to members of the educational community, including teachers, who make decisions about how to utilize computer technology in elementary classrooms. Studies that have begun to address these relationships indicate that classroom contexts, teachers' goals, and children's word-processing and writing practices are intricately interdependent. These describe some of the specific ways these relationships are played out in particular classrooms.

Teachers' Interpretations of Word Processing

Like the impact of other kinds of computer technology, an important part of the impact of word processing technology in classrooms is particular teachers' interpretations of it. This concern suggests the need for Proposition 5.1.

> Proposition 5.1:   Part of the impact of word processing technology in the classroom is the individual teacher's interpretation of it, which changes over time depending on the teacher's goals, the social organization of classrooms, and students' developing skills.

Bruce and Rubin (1984) refer to word processing as "teacher dependent software." In classrooms across the country, they found that teachers' instructional philosophies were a more important influence on how "QUILL" software (a word processing plus electronic message system) was used than was the software itself. Similarly we have demonstrated elsewhere (Cochran-Smith et al., 1988) both that five elementary school teachers introduced word processing to children in ways that varied considerably from one another, and that these ways changed dramatically over the course of two years. Porter and Sherwood (1987) found at the end of the first of a 2-year study that it was impossible to sort out the impact of the teacher's instructional strategies, the research assistant's interactions with the children at the word processor, and the use of word processing technology itself on children's writing and attitudes. Similarly, two teachers who used word processing over a year to teach writing to sixth graders reported that they set up and organized word processing in their classrooms in ways that were quite different (Palmer et al., 1984).

In a report for the Alaska State Department of Education (Parson, 1985), a group of teachers who had had common training in both "process writing" and word processing emphasized the diverse ways they used word processing in their classrooms to meet the needs of individual students and in keeping with their own curricular emphases. This point is made dramatically in Lafrenz and Friedman's (1989) response to a computer symposium that appeared in a major journal. They assert that technology itself does not and will not transform education, even though it offers teachers possibilities for educating children "more interactively, [and] with more attention to cognitive differences and our nation's problems of educational equity" (p. 224). Rather, they emphatically point out that educational change is far more complex and will require extensive teacher training and systemic support.

It is clear from many studies and commentaries that the ways teachers use word processing in their classrooms vary considerably. Thus, the need for Proposition 5.2.

> Proposition 5.2:   Word-processing technology is used differently for writing, depending on the ways individual teachers organize their classrooms for learning and the ways they structure their writing programs.

In the discussions following Propositions 1 and 2 on the effects of word processing on students' writing processes and written products, we identified certain trends in the effects word processing has on writing. However, as our analysis in these previous sections makes clear, these results are not at all contradictory to the conclusion put forward in Proposition 5.2. Repeatedly, the effects research indicates that the answer to the bottom-line question, "Do students write better with word processing?" is, "It depends." The effects literature indicated that "it depends," among other things, on:

- Already-established writing and revising strategies of the writer
- Prior keyboarding and computer experiences of the writer
- Instructional interventions (whether human or technological) that accompany the introduction of word processing
- Particular definitions of *good writing, writing improvement*, and *revising/editing* that operate within a given study

Research that explores the interrelationships of teacher interpretations, classroom contexts, and children's writing with word processing begins to reveal some of the dimensions according to which results vary as well as some of the additional reasons for variation. This literature indicates that "it also depends" on:

- Ongoing classroom writing program, including the tools writers use and the tasks they select or are assigned
- Access teachers allow and/or encourage to computer equipment and expertise
- Individual teachers' goals and instructional strategies for the writing program and the reading/language arts/English program generally
- Social organization and learning contexts available in individual classrooms
- Particular school, school system, and school community

Cazden, Michaels, and Bruce (Bruce, Michaels, & Watson-Gegeo, 1985; Cazden, Michaels, & Watson-Gegeo, 1984; Michaels, 1985; Michaels & Bruce, 1989; Rubin & Bruce, 1984, 1986) conducted one of the few early studies of word processing used over time and in relation to the social context of classrooms by focusing on sixth graders' uses of QUILL software. The notion *writing system* was developed as a way of explaining the many variations between two sixth-grade writing programs, even though each was labeled a *process writing* class. The writing system in any given classroom includes the ways teachers organize for writing, their goals, the amounts and kinds of writing they assign and expect students to complete, the ways they allow and encourage access to computer equipment and expertise, and the provisions they make for responses to writing. Michaels and Bruce (1989) found that many aspects of a process approach to writing that one would expect to encourage emphasis on process—teacher–student conferences, use of word processing as a writing tool, and holistically scored writing tests—actually encouraged emphasis on final products as well. Michaels and colleagues found that the writing systems constructed by the teachers in each classroom had to be understood as independent variables upon which ways of using word processing as well as many other aspects of classroom learning depended, and that using word processing technology itself was not an independent variable in affecting classroom life and organization for learning (Cazden et al., 1984; Michaels, 1985; Michaels & Bruce, 1989).

It is clear from this work both that word processing cannot be regarded as an instructional "treatment" that can be implemented and then measured at different points in time in order to assess its effects, and, further, that process writing can not be regarded as "the context" into which word processing is inserted. The fact that the culture of learning in classrooms influences the uses of word processing rather than that the computer itself has a unilateral and invariant effect on life in classrooms is hardly surprising. It is in keeping with the accumulating body of ethnographic research on teaching and classrooms that indicates that the meaning of any particular classroom event—here, writing with word processing—is embedded within the layers of context in which it occurs and the webs of significance of its participants (Cochran-Smith, 1984; Erickson, 1986; Heath, 1983). Individual classroom environments are nested within the larger cultures of schools, school systems, and communities. For example, Sheingold, Kane, and Endreweit (1983) found significant variation in computer implementation in the schools of three different communities according to each community's goals, needs, and ways of operating, as did C.P. Olson (1988) in the work cited earlier. We have little research on the deployment of word processing for writing that analyzes relationships between computer implementation and context beyond the classroom.

Word Processing and Classroom Interaction

We argue in the above discussion that word processing does not have a unilateral effect on classroom life. However, it is also clear from a number of studies of word processing in classrooms that, like more general computer use that invites student interaction, use of word processing has the potential to prompt new social arrangements in the writing classroom. Thus, the need for one final proposition is clear.

Proposition 5.3:   The logistical and physical requirements of using word processing equipment make writing public and often prompt new social arrangements, especially collaboration.

Bruce et al. (1985) found that the public nature of the computer screen prompted more social interactions during writing among sixth grade students who tended to comment on and respond to one another's writing as they passed by, waited in line, or moved about the room. They argue that increased social interaction around writing encouraged the students to attend more self-consciously to audience as they wrote. Levin and Boruta (1983; Levin, Riel, Rowe, & Boruta, 1985) found that collaborative writing activities such as newspapers, message systems, and interactive writing systems were especially effective with word processing, and that sixth graders who had worked with word processing for a year collaborated more. In a first/second grade classroom, Dickinson (1986) found that the teacher eventually allowed and encouraged collaborative writing at the computer. This arrangement for writing fostered more talk about planning, writing, and responding than did the less frequent collaborative writing that occurred with paper and pencil. Even in classroom situations where there is one computer to share among a large number of students, collaborative small group writing projects have been effective (Tobin & Tobin, 1985). In a study of young children's uses of Logo software rather than word processing, Emihovich (1989) also explored the importance of children's collaborations. She concluded that 4- to 6-year old children's collaborations to solve Logo problems were precursors to their later independent metacognitive development in comprehension.

Heap (1989a, b) analyzed first-grade pairs of writers and helpers who used word processing to write stories over a 3-week period. Working from an ethnomethodological perspective, Heap studied the children's collaborative writing episodes from a situated perspective that attempted to account for the production requirements facing the participants. He analyzed the social organization of writing collaboration as the interrelationship of participants' rights and responsibilities and their strategies for composing, inputting, and arranging. Heap found that writing at the computer was constructed out of the children's interactions—essentially, "writing was talk" (1989b, p. 269). Heap's work makes a major contribution to the body of research in this area. Most importantly it points out that research on computer uses in classrooms cannot focus primarily or only on the "context-independent" features of computer equipment and software selections, but that instead it must examine the ways computers are deployed for specific tasks and within specific social learning environments.

Similarly in high school classes (Herrmann, 1987), college writing courses (Skublkowski & Elder, 1987), and even in professional situations (Arms, 1984) where collaboration is less likely to occur regularly, writers tended to collaborate when they used word processing, and word processing supported the notion of a community of writers. This work on word processing is in keeping with related Logo research that indicates that working with Logo facilitates peer interaction in support of social problem solving (Clements & Nastasi, 1988). As Johnson, Johnson, and Stanne (1986) have pointed out, however, placing students in groups for work at computers may not be enough. Their experimental research on eighth-grade students using a geography simulation indicated that computer-assisted and cooperative-learning situations led to greater achievement, problem solving, and computer skill than did computer-assisted and competitive and individualistic learning situations. Their results suggest that we need to look closely at the whole learning environment when investigating uses of word processing for writing.

The above findings are related to our earlier discussion of Hawkins and Sheingold's (1986) exploration of the effects of microcomputers on the organization of learning in classrooms. Hawkins and Sheingold found that use of Logo, math and science software, and database management software changed the learning interactions in elementary and middle school classrooms in two ways. Students collaborated more on computer activities than they did with other classroom activities (and teachers encouraged collaboration more), and when children were working in small groups, teachers were hesitant to intervene and were freed of continual management of large-group, whole-class activities. Hawkins and Sheingold speculate that, "when examined in the long run, the nature of learning interactions in classrooms may change dramatically" (p. 50). They point out that computer technology has the potential to shape the organization of classroom learning in profound ways. More importantly, they also point out that capacity is not reality, and that, if changes in the social organization of classrooms do occur with the use of computer technology, they will occur gradually.

Summary: Word Processing, Classroom Organization, and Teachers' Goals

There is an interactive relationship between the ways that word processing is used for writing in individual classrooms, the social organization of classrooms, and the instructional long and short-range goals of individual teachers. This means that it may be inappropriate to think of either social organization or uses of word processing as independent or dependent variables in word processing and writing research, but instead more appropriate to consider both as nonsymmetrical but interdependent and interactive variables. In other words, the way word processing (or other computer technology) is deployed in the individual classroom is dependent on the learning organization of the classroom, which, in reciprocal fashion, can also be shaped and changed by the capacities of computer technology to accommodate new patterns of social organization and interaction.

What is most needed are additional studies that attempt to consider this complexity of elements and the interplay of relevant factors over time and within various learning contexts. We need to consider not only outcomes of using word processing for writing with students at many levels, but also the factors that affect these outcomes. Most importantly, perhaps, is research that investigates how teachers in various settings and with various goals in mind interpret computer technology over relatively long periods of time and the consequent influences on students' opportunities to learn. When research is short-term, we may well be unwittingly examining only the first in a series of many stages, or mistaking what Hawkins and Sheingold (1986) have called "the beginning of a story" (p. 41) for its denouement.

Finally, we need research on word processing and writing that examines *both* writing and social context instead of one or the other, which has made for the current dichotomy between these two. On the one hand, the effects research has tended to explore predominantly what writers of varying ages and abilities do with word processing and has ignored in large part classroom and school context, the strategies of individual teachers, changes that have occurred over time, and the ways word processing is integrated or not integrated into the writing curriculum. On the other hand, the few studies that have considered the relationships of word processing and classroom organization have not paid enough attention to the written products that students actually produce with word processing, the ways their writing processes change or develop over time, or the ways teachers interact with students as they use word processing. Consequently we have little information about, say, revising with word processing in relation to a particular kind of classroom learning environment and a specific set of instructional goals. We need to have this kind of information in many individual classroom settings in order to get a sense of the dimensions according to which writing with word processing varies, and the factors that influence teachers' instructional decisions.

CONCLUSIONS: WHAT WE KNOW AND NEED TO KNOW

In this chapter we have represented what is known and still needs to be known about word processing and writing from both the research and the pedagogical literature, and we have identified a complex set of issues that surrounds this knowledge. We argue that five major propositions, modified in most cases by a set of subpropositions, cut across individual studies and research methods and synthesize a wide-ranging field of inquiry.

As each major section reveals, we know the least about young children's uses of word processing. Literature about emergent writers (roughly ages 0–5 years) using word processing is virtually nonexistent, and there is very little on beginning writers, their slightly older brothers and sisters (roughly ages 5–10) who participate in formal literacy instruction in school. While it is easy to dismiss the former group as simply too young to handle a keyboard for typing (although we are not convinced that this is the case), the latter group is particularly important. Beginning writers are involved in the process of becoming literate. When they write, there is often concern about issues of production—remembering letter shapes, forming them properly, aligning them correctly on a page, locating them in the proper direction, leaving adequate amounts of space, erasing errors, spelling correctly, fixing mistakes, inserting omitted words and lines, remembering proper punctuation, and so on. Since some of these are problems that word processing automatically manages, word processing obviously has potential to be a particularly useful writing tool for this age group.

Because the concerns and issues of beginning writers, on the one hand, and preadolescent, adolescent, and adult writers, on the other hand, are very different, the pertinent questions about word processing and beginning writers are different from those explored in most of the literature. Research on beginning writers and word processing functions as much to figure out what the important questions are as to determine their answers.

The literature clearly indicates that the effectiveness of word processing for writing "depends" on several important factors. The literature suggests that teachers' goals, the social organizations of classrooms, and the features of word processing interact in some important ways, but we know very little about what those ways are, what they look like at various grade levels, and how they are played out over relatively long periods of time in individual classrooms. The literature suggests that instructional intervention is important, that the effectiveness of word processing for writing depends on the nature of instruction that accompanies its implementation. We need to know more about the kinds of instruction teachers provide when they teach writing with word processing to beginning writers, and we need to know how this instruction changes over time.

Further, the small body of literature on classroom social organization and word processing suggests that using computer technology often prompts new social arrangements, especially collaboration among writers. We need to know more about the nature of collaboration with word processing, more about the ways beginners collaborate with other beginners and the ways they collaborate with adults. Especially we want to know what they write when they work together and what they look like as writers and users of word processing. We need research that looks at both the social organization of the classroom as it interacts with the use of technology and the actual writing beginners produce when they write with word processing.

Research of the kind called for here is long-term, located within the contexts of actual elementary school classrooms (rather than in school-based or outside-school computer labs), and qualitative. The intent of such research is not to measure the effects of word processing on the writing of beginners or to provide answers to the questions raised by the research on adult writers as they apply to young children. Rather, the intent is to find out what the relevant questions are when teachers use word processing for writing with beginners and to provide a general sense of what teachers as well as young writers do when they have the opportunity to use a powerful writing tool.

The study reported in the following five chapters of *Learning to Write Differently* was designed with some of these unanswered questions in mind. We do not claim to have found all the answers about teachers, beginning writers, and word processing, but we believe that we have identified many of the significant questions. Our volume suggests that questions about the effects of word processing on the quality, quantity, and processes of beginners' writing do not have definitive answers, nor do they prove to be particularly productive questions. How word processing is used effectively and ineffectively in five elementary classrooms can not be understood apart from the ways individual teachers and beginning writers construct particular instructional contexts. How word processing affects the quality, quantity, or processes of writing by beginners can not be understood apart from the ways these are embedded within, and mediated by, individual social situations.

We demonstrate throughout this book that questions about the quality and quantity of writing produced with word processing are not the right questions to ask about the experiences of beginning writers who do not have well-developed writing or keyboarding skills and for whom issues of fluency are still critical. To consider the usefulness of word processing as a writing tool for beginners, we looked beyond the correlations usually explored with older writers: the production of lengthier texts, the commission of fewer errors, the occurrence of more revisions, the creation of a larger number of drafts, the improvement of attitudes, and so on. Instead we asked whether or not teachers and children learned to write differently when they worked with word processing. We closely examined how teachers interpreted and chose to deploy the tool of word processing, as well as how children learned about writing as they learned to use word processing. We explored the ways working with word processing interacted with the social processes of five classrooms to shape participants' theories and practices of writing. And we analyzed the interactive, long-term relationship between the writing contexts teachers and children constructed, on the one hand, and the capacities and requirements of the tool of word processing on the other. In Chapters 3, 4, 5, and 6, we offer these analyses.

chapter 3
Classroom Culture
and Word Processing:
Five Teachers' Interpretations

When computers were brought into the schools a decade ago, it was predicted that the processes and outcomes of teaching and learning would be radically altered. Naysayers warned that computers would have dire effects, diminishing teachers' roles to insignificance and isolating children from contact with their peers and their teachers (Davy, 1984; Sloan, 1984; Turkle, 1984). In contrast, enthusiasts promised that computers would liberate teachers from mundane teaching tasks, create more time for important teaching responsibilities, and provide new learning opportunities for children (Papert, 1980; Snyder & Palmer, 1986; Walker, 1983). In short, on both sides of the issue, it was assumed that computers were powerful forces that would alter classroom life dramatically.

The research of the last decade has indicated that computers can indeed affect classroom culture—it is well documented, for example, that interactions among children and between teachers and children have been increased or altered when computers were introduced (Bruce et al., 1985; Dickinson, 1986; J. Olson, 1986). However, the research has also made it clear that the influence of computers on teaching and learning is neither uniform (Hawkins & Sheingold, 1986) nor predictable (Amarel, 1983) across classrooms and schools. The uses teachers choose to make of computers, and consequently the learning opportunities available to children (Carrol, 1963; Schmidt & Buchmann, 1963) vary significantly from classroom to classroom. On the other hand, there is also evidence that computers not only influence classroom culture, but are in fact influenced by the culture that already exists in classrooms and schools (J. Olson, 1986; Michaels, 1985) as well as by individual teachers' values and instructional goals (Amarel, 1983; Hawkins & Sheingold, 1986; Michaels, 1985; Sheingold et al., 1984).

In the classrooms we observed, we too found that word processing was both influenced by the existing classroom culture and altered the existing culture. We also found, however, that a linear conception of the influence of each upon the other does not accurately or fully represent what actually transpires in classrooms over time. Rather we found that altered classroom culture shaped subsequent uses of word processing. Hence classroom culture and the uses teachers made of word processing were, in fact, interdependent, evolving and compounded over time. Like the bank account in which yesterday's interest becomes part of today's principal when interest is calculated, word processing use that altered the

Figure 3.1
Interrelationships of Classroom Culture
and Word-Processing Use Over Time

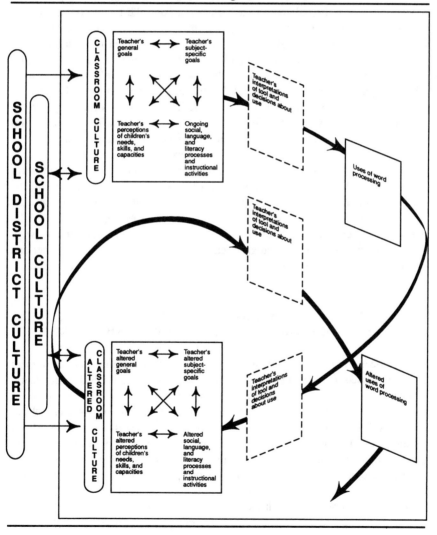

classroom culture at one point in time became part of that culture, which then shaped later uses of word processing. Classroom culture and the uses of word processing conjointly determined both what opportunities were available to children to learn about word processing and writing and how those opportunities came into being. In this way an interactive relationship between classroom culture and the ways children learned to write evolved over time.

In this chapter, we examine the introduction and evolving uses of word processing within the preexisting and altered cultures of five elementary classrooms. In doing so, we develop a framework for analyzing and understanding teachers' deployment of word processing. This framework sets the uses of word processing within the cultures of each classroom and the larger contexts of the school and school district. In the pages that follow, we consider first the influence of school and classroom cultures on the uses teachers and students made of word processing. Then we examine the interrelationships of evolving uses of word processing and evolving classroom cultures. We demonstrate that, with word processing, teachers and children learned to write differently—that is, the roles of *teacher* and *learner* were altered, time was allocated differently within the class day, children participated in writing in different ways, and children's skills and understandings were made visible to teachers in ways that had not previously been visible. In short, teachers' goals, the social and language processes of their classrooms, and teachers' perceptions of children's capacities and the capabilities and limitations of word processing, were altered with the implementation of word processing. Figure 3.1 illustrates the dynamic process by which classroom cultures and uses of word processing (as mediated by teachers' perceptions of children and of word processing) shaped and were shaped by one another. Once altered, each continued to influence the other and continued to shape the learning opportunities available in each classroom.

CLASSROOM CULTURES
AND THE INTRODUCTION OF WORD PROCESSING

Word processing differs significantly from most other materials and equipment commonly used in elementary classrooms. Unlike other materials that are clearly designated as either tools or content, word processing can be considered as both a subject to be taught and a tool to be applied to other learning tasks (J. Olson, 1988). Although the teachers we observed acknowledged that there was a body of knowledge to learn about word processing, only on a few occasions was word processing actually considered "content" in its own right. Rather, children and teachers deemphasized "learning *about* word processing" and instead emphasized "using word processing *for* . . ." various writing tasks.

With its potential for multiple applications, word processing differs from other teaching materials in a second way. For most teaching tools, there is a limited and predetermined range of uses—a thermometer, for example, is used for recording temperature. Although the tasks for which it might be employed may vary, the function it serves is the same. The computer, on the other hand, has been described as a "Protean tool" (Papert, 1980; Amarel, 1983), an "interpretable device" (Sheingold et al., 1984) and even a technological "ink-blot" (Simon, cited in Amarel, 1983) onto which we project uses that express our own individual assumptions and goals. Papert first used the myth of Proteus as a way to think about computers in an early discussion:

> The computer is the Proteus of machines. Its essence is its universality, its power to simulate. Because it can take on a thousand forms and can serve a thousand functions, it can appeal to a thousand tastes. (p. viii)

Word processing, as tool software, is as Protean and interpretable as are computers more generally. Our observations across classrooms indicated that the "raw capacity" (Wolf, 1985) of word processing permitted multiple interpretations by teachers. For example, the word-processing skills each teacher chose to introduce, and the ways each teacher used word processing for writing instruction, varied significantly. Although some of the differences were related to the ages of the children they taught, the most interesting differences in deployment appeared to grow out of the cultures of the school and of individual classrooms. Teachers' uses of word processing reflected their individual responses to the tensions between a school district culture in which curriculum standardization was valued, on the other hand, and a school culture in which innovation, collegiality and individuality were encouraged and supported on the other (Paris, 1989a, in press). Similarly, the uses individual teachers made of word processing were shaped by the cultures of their own classrooms, their general goals for the children they taught, and their specific goals and purposes for introducing word processing into the curriculum.

Each teacher's individual and evolving uses of word processing can be understood as the dynamic interplay of decisions (Berliner, 1986; Schmidt, Porter, Floden, Freeman, & Schwille, 1987; Schwille et al., 1983) made in response to the dilemmas posed by the introduction of a new pedagogical tool within a specific classroom and school culture. These decisions can be framed as responses to four teacher tasks: (a) *teaching word processing skills* to children, (b) *providing assistance* to children as they work with word processing, (c) *allocating space and time* to word processing and managing individual children's access to the word processor, and (d) *assigning or allowing tasks* to be completed at the word processor. These four tasks, and the ways teachers responded to them, were implicit in teachers' discussions of their work, journal entries, and informal communications. Together they provide a way of looking at each teacher's initial and evolving use of word processing in her classroom. Furthermore, when these decisions are considered in relation to the school and class-

Figure 3.2
Teachers' Decision Points in Implementing Word Processing

---

1. **TEACHING WORD PROCESSING SKILLS TO CHILDREN**

   Questions:
   What word processing skills should be taught?
   How should instruction be paced and sequenced?
   How should the children be grouped?
   What methods of instruction should be used?

2. **PROVIDING ASSISTANCE TO CHILDREN AS THEY WORK**

   Questions:
   Do children need assistance when they work with word processing?
   Who should assist children working at the word processor?

3. **ALLOCATING SPACE AND TIME TO WORD PROCESSING AND MANAG-
   ING INDIVIDUAL CHILDREN'S ACCESS**

   Questions:
   Where should the computers be located?
   When should the computers be used?
   Who should use the computers at which times?
   How much time should be made available to individual writers?

4. **TASKS COMPLETED WITH WORD PROCESSING**

   Questions:
   How do tasks relate to the content goals of the school district?
   How do tasks relate to content goals of the teacher?
   How do tasks relate to ongoing classroom routines and management
       practices?

---

room contexts in which they were made, they provide a conceptual frame for understanding why and how each teacher's uses of word processing developed over time.

In Figure 3.2 we elaborate on these four teacher tasks by listing questions that teachers addressed about how to teach children to use word processing and how to incorporate word processing into their teaching of writing: (a) which word processing skills should be taught to children, including the order and pace of instruction, how to group children for instruction, and which instructional methods to use; (b) what kind of assistance to provide as children used word processing, including whether children needed assistance, who should provide it, and when it should be provided; (c) how to place and time word-processing equipment and access, in relation to issues of size, noise, environmental conditions necessary, and relative scarcity of machines; and, (d) which tasks should be completed with word processing in relation to existing goals and ongoing practices.

The numerical listing of decisions points in Figure 3.2 is not intended to suggest that teachers addressed these issues sequentially. On the contrary, priorities differed for each teacher. Individual teachers' goals and values, their ongoing classroom practices, and their roles within and responses to the school culture led each one to foreground certain issues and questions for deeper or more immediate consideration. Further, teachers rarely answered any of these questions with finality. Instead they continuously revised their decisions as children changed, their own knowledge of teaching with word processing grew, and the cultures of their classrooms were altered. Wide variation in teachers' decisions reflected individual responses to the expectations and procedures of wider school contexts and the cultures of their own classrooms, as characterized by their ongoing practices and goals for their children and themselves.

In the following pages we introduce each of the five teachers in whose classrooms we observed over a 2-year period. We begin with analysis of the initial word-processing instruction organized by three teachers who joined our project during its first year and hence were part of the study for two full years— Tina Santori, fourth-grade teacher; Margaret Price, second-grade teacher; and Bev Winston, who taught kindergarten. This analysis is followed by examination of the introductions to word processing of two additional teachers who joined the project during its second year—Barbara Gold, whose experiences in the first grade were similar to Bev's in kindergarten, and Debby Perrone, a third-grade teacher who was relatively new to Summit Grove School. Following discussion of the ways each of these teachers introduced word processing to their classes, we revisit each of the five teachers to examine the dynamic interplay of their evolving uses of word processing and their evolving classroom cultures.

Tina Santori

Tina Santori's class was located in the middle of a long open-space room that housed three fourth grade classes. Only teachers' desks and low shelves separated the three teaching areas. Although each class functioned separately for reading/language arts and math instruction, Tina and the teachers of the other two classes shared responsibility for planning and teaching some combined classes in literature, science, social studies, and health, as well as conducting daily meetings of the nearly 90 children who shared the area. The front of Tina's space, which comprised the middle third of the room, was the natural meeting place for the full group. Behind the meeting area, she provided tables where her children worked independently, and a couch and pillow area where she met with small groups for instruction and book discussions.

In all three teaching areas, bulletin boards and posters welcomed children back to school, assigned responsibility for classroom tasks, and communicated energy and excitement about the coming school year. Technology was clearly important in Tina's classroom: video recording and playback equipment shared with other teachers was stored there, and the first two of four computers and printers that were eventually assigned to Tina's room as part of the equipment of the project were added to the one that was already in her classroom. Tina clustered the computers together near a front corner of her classroom area, so that children could assist each other as they worked. A name chart listed the rotation schedule of 20-minute turns that would assure each child's equal access to the computers, and a kitchen timer was used to regulate turns.

Visitors to Tina's classroom found her leading small groups in their reading of a novel or folk tale, conducting conferences with individual children as they edited and revised their writing, or coaching a small group which was dramatizing a story they had read or written. Children worked independently on projects related to literature or searched in reference books for the information they needed to respond to the weekly question in their Think Tank Journals. Writing played a central role in Tina's curriculum. Children wrote across subject areas and for many different audiences—they distributed a fourth-grade newspaper, composed stories for children in the primary grades, entered local and national reading and writing contests, and wrote books for their classroom library. Publishing and binding the books were major events in Tina's room, celebrated with a twice-yearly "Writer's Tea" for students and parents.

In Tina's classroom, taking initiative and being responsible for one's own work and belongings were highly valued—children who wandered around aimlessly or repeatedly misplaced materials interfered with everyone's work in this busy three-space classroom. Consequently, independence, problem solving, and responsibility were qualities that Tina Santori worked to develop in her students each year. Her fourth graders were expected to seek answers to their own questions, solve social problems, complete classroom housekeeping chores, submit completed homework assignments, and remember materials for special classes and lunch time without constant reminders from the teacher. The decisions Tina made about teaching word processing reflected this aspect of her classroom culture. In a meeting of researchers and teachers early in the first year of the project, Tina stated that her goals for introducing word processing included each child's independence as a software user, a sense of ownership of the technology, pride, accomplishment in mastery of technology, and consequently a heightened self-image and sense of worth. With word processing as with many other classroom activities, then, Tina emphasized mastery, independence, and problem solving.

Not only were Tina's word-processing goals and the practices she designed to meet them consistent with the culture of her classroom, they were also consistent with her role in the wider school culture. J. Olson's (1988) distinction between *instrumental* and *expressive* uses of computers in schools is helpful here. He suggests that instrumental uses are those in which computers are instruments for the teacher's achievement of an instructional goal, while expressive uses are those in which computers are used to express something about the teacher herself. Tina's uses of word processing were both instrumental and expressive. By preparing her children to be proficient in word processing, she maintained a well-organized classroom and promoted the writing skills of drafting, revising, and editing which were essential for children to be successful in her demanding and independent language arts curriculum (instrumental uses). But she also conveyed important messages about who she was as a teacher, curriculum leader, and colleague in the ways she deployed word processing (expressive uses).

As a teacher, Tina was widely regarded as innovative and effective and was valued for her individual curriculum knowledge and the expertise she brought to the school. Summit Grove was a school where respect and support for individuality among staff members were valued. Individual variation in personality, teaching style, and particularly curriculum expertise were valued for what they contributed to the quality of the school's programs. These took on added significance, since administrators at the school district level were working toward increased standardization of curriculum. Tina had long been recognized by her colleagues and principal as a curriculum and instructional leader in the school. For example, she had been among the first to experiment with process approaches to writing and had led faculty workshops on writing and bookbinding. She had also been instrumental in introducing computing into her school and responsible for teaching most of the staff to use the hardware and software.

As a colleague, a role which was highly valued in the culture of Summit Grove School, a teacher was expected, not only to plan activities that did not interfere with those of her teammates in open-space classrooms, but also to share freely both materials and expertise. Tina measured her decisions about the placement and scheduled use of the word processors against her teammates' ongoing practices. As she always did with new materials and ideas, she made plans to share both hardware and software with her colleagues and to teach her own students to be tutors for the 60-some other fourth graders who shared the area. When our study began, Tina was teaching small groups of colleagues to use word processing on her own time and on her own initiative. Because she gave assistance willingly and effectively, teachers throughout the school looked to Tina for help selecting software, fixing equipment, replacing printer ribbons and paper, initializing disks, and setting up new equipment. Tina provided guidance in how to introduce new software as well as how to integrate word processing and other software into the curriculum. She also sought out teachers who were not yet using computers and encouraged their first efforts.

Tina's decisions about word processing instruction reflected not only the instrumental goals of maintaining the smooth functioning of her classroom and teaching of process writing, but also her role in the school culture as curriculum leader and provider of technical and instructional support. Tina's introduction of word processing consisted of a series of carefully planned lessons designed to lead the children to mastery of basic operations and require minimal adult assistance freeing Tina to meet the demands of an active three-space classroom and support her colleagues as well.

[Ms. Santori calls her language arts class of 24 children to the floor in front of a large video monitor. To the left of the monitor is a laminated enlargement of the IBM keyboard on an easel. Each child is given a smaller laminated reproduction of the keyboard. To the right are the computers. Ms. Santori has trained the video camera on the monitor of the closest computer and its image is projected on the large video screen. She stands at the computer and demonstrates the first of the skills and understandings that she feels the children will need to master the software and hardware. She embeds the introduction of these skills in the task of typing in a draft of a story about an imaginary creature that she had composed with the class in a lesson conducted earlier that morning on the stages of the writing process. She engages the children in thinking with her as she works.]

Ms. Santori:	I'm typing in the letters.
	My name is getty-o
	Oh, I made a mistake. I wanted a capital G. Okay, now what do I do? Okay, there are two things you can do to erase. But there are no keys on your card (laminated keyboard) that say 'erase'. Do you know what you can do?
Child (calling out):	I know what one of them is.
Ms. Santori:	What is it?
Child:	Um, backspace? Right there. [Points to the key on his small keyboard.]
Ms. Santori:	Right. This erases. Good for you. Okay, where is it on the chart?
Child:	Right there . [Points to chart.]
Ms. Santori:	Right here. Okay, this key will erase. [Circles the key in red on the chart.] And what else? There's one other thing that erases for you.
Child:	Clear.
Ms. Santori:	No. Good try, though. That makes sense that 'clear' would erase.
Child:	Tab lock?
Ms. Santori:	No.

Child: Delete?

Ms. Santori: Delete. This thing right here erases. [Circles the delete key
                       on the large keyboard and draws a line connecting the two
                       keys.]

[She erases her error and continues to type in her text, demonstrating the use of the
return key and the cursor movement keys. As she types in the text, she demonstrates how to find the text screen and the edit screen, how to delete errors with the
backspace key and the delete key, how to move the cursor through the text, and the
use of the return key. Each time she presses keys other than the letter keys, she
points out the location of that key on the large keyboard chart, circles it with a
marker, and tells the children to 'press' that key on their keyboard reproductions.
She concludes the lesson by explaining the turn-taking system on the chart and tells
the children what their writing task will be when they come to the word processor.]

In subsequent lessons, these skills were reviewed and additional skills added.
Students were reminded to watch carefully because they would be expected to
figure out what to do on their own at the computer. Tina encouraged her students
to think first and then ask for help from the child working at the adjacent
computer.

   Tina connected the initial word processing lesson to her initial writing lessons, which demonstrated that writing was a process of drafting, revising, and
editing. The thumbprint stories which the children were assigned to create with
word processing were to be shared eventually with the younger children in one of
the special education classes in the school. Over a period of 6 to 8 weeks, each of
Tina's students came to the computer for an individual first session and either
drafted a story about a thumb-print creature or typed in the paper-and-pencil draft
of that story, which had been composed during the time that had elapsed between
the introductory computer lesson and the child's first allocated turn to use the
word processor. Because initial levels of computer experience varied from child
to child, and because different amounts of time passed between introductory
lesson and first turn, children needed widely varying amounts of assistance.

   Learning to use word processing in Tina's classroom was based on her initial
demonstration of selected procedures to the large group, followed by the individual child's practice of the skills as they were embedded within the writing
assignment. This procedure reflected Tina's view that good teaching involved
"taking specific steps one at a time" and that learning was best accomplished
through individual practice. Her theories of teaching and learning and her
decisions about the deployment of word processing were also based in part on her
own experiences as a learner (Schmidt et al., 1987). As a learner, Tina had
commented that she preferred to "get the basics" and then learn on her own. For
example, when familiarizing herself with the hardware and software used in our
study, she had elected not to work with a colleague or researcher, but preferred to
explore and practice on her own. She described her learning in this way:

I really wanted to be on it [the computer] myself. I really didn't want this other person, you know. They were slowing me down. . . . I would rather turn to a person at another computer and say, 'How do you do this?' and then get right back [to work].

Tina found that working with others while she learned to use technology "slowed her down," and she felt that, like her, her students would prefer not to work in pairs. She arranged instead for children to work individually, and she provided mechanisms for them to seek help on an as-needed basis and then quickly continue with their own work.

Tina's decisions were embedded in both the existing culture of her classroom and her roles and responsibilities in the wider school culture. In her busy three-space classroom, clearly established routines and student responsibility and independence permitted smooth management. These critical features of classroom culture shaped, not only the goals she set for her students, but also the content she chose to teach. The skills she selected were those that would permit her students to take full control of the system and allow her to attend to her many other classroom responsibilities and remain available to assist her colleagues as needed. Further, Tina initially chose to incorporate the teaching of word processing into the teaching of writing.

Just as Tina's way of introducing word processing grew out of the culture of her classroom and of the wider school, so too did the ways of each of the other teachers. The contrasts, however, are striking. In the following section, we meet Margaret Price, second grade teacher. She taught a different set of word-processing skills in her introductory lesson and embedded word processing in a very different task. Margaret's decisions reflected ongoing practice in her own classroom as well as her role in the culture of the school.

Margaret Price

Like Tina's fourth grade, Margaret's second grade was also housed in a shared three-space classroom where three teaching areas were separated by tall cupboards and movable bulletin boards. Each area, however, functioned as a self-contained classroom. Two walls of Margaret's teaching space had windows where she had built shelves and hung hooks for her many plants. Live plants and displays of harvest vegetables hinted at the integrated science, social studies, and writing activities (baking bread, making dried apple dolls, and writing directions for rooting sweet potatoes) that would follow during the year.

Margaret and her colleagues who shared the space combined their children to form nine ability-level reading groups that cut across classes, and carefully coordinated their schedules to assure that noisy activities in one space did not interfere with quiet activities in another. Children moved quietly as a group to their reading/language arts teacher and remained with her for most of the morning. The dominant character of the culture of Margaret's classroom was calm and order. Children were given explicit directions for organizing and storing their work and for moving from place to place. Instruction featured careful teacher direction. When children were not working with Margaret in small reading groups, they independently completed carefully structured seat-work activities at their desks. The activity in these classrooms was so calm and orderly that a visitor might fail to realize that 80-some second graders shared one large open space.

Margaret's goals for her students included, not only that they develop a "love for reading," "awareness of and joy in observing and participating in the world around them," and "respect and tolerance for others," but also that they develop "working relationships with others that will contribute to a harmonious class-room atmosphere." Her expectations of the children were clear and consistent. Even the most difficult groups experienced success in Margaret's room and learned to move through her classroom routines in an orderly fashion. For this reason, she had earned the respect of her colleagues as a teacher who could be counted on to succeed with even the most challenging children.

Although Margaret invested a great deal of attention to maintaining well-ordered and effective routines within her classroom, the greatest threats to her carefully organized routine came from outside. During the two years of our computer project, West Brook School District had introduced a new writing curriculum, a new basal reading series, and a formal handwriting program. Each altered element of the curriculum threatened to disrupt the carefully coordinated instruction Margaret had developed over the years. For example, Margaret had designed science, writing, and social studies activities that built upon or prepared her students for stories in their reading books. When the school district replaced the reading books, Margaret had to begin again the work of integrating and coordinating instruction. At about the same time, the school district mandated the exact number of minutes of instruction that were to be devoted to each curriculum area. This meant that the total amount of instructional time left to the discretion of the teacher was sharply curtailed. Margaret responded by integrat-ing instruction from different curriculum areas as she had all along but "double-counting" the time by recording it on the tally for each relevant curriculum area. In this way, she maintained the time she needed to develop the rich science and social studies activities on which she and her children thrived. For one mandated curriculum change after another, Margaret overlapped, adapted, and altered where necessary to maintain the integrity of her carefully organized program.

Margaret's goals for word processing were primarily instrumental (J. Olson, 1988). She confessed with a smile on many occasions that she did not "love computers" the way Tina Santori did, nor did her role in the school depend on her success or failure in using word processing. But Margaret was more willing to experiment with computer use than the other teachers at her grade level. She had used a computer previously to provide extra skill practice for some children, but expressed little enthusiasm. Word processing, on the other hand, offered something that she valued as a teacher—a tool that might, in her words, "make writing and editing a less tedious chore" and make writing "more exciting" for her students. It was to this end that she planned for instruction and use of word processing.

Margaret's initial word processing activity took place on the first day of school. She noted in her journal:

> Children were very interested in the computer the first day of school—so I decided to try using it with the whole group . . . Disaster—20 children could not see the screen or printer or wait for a turn.

Margaret's lesson was designed to introduce the capabilities of word processing for entering and editing texts. Her goal was to allow the children to "see what the computer could do." Her introduction to word processing was embedded in a first-day-of-school routine in which each child shared something about summer vacation as fieldnotes revealed.

> Miss Price sits at a small chair in front of the computer. Her 21 children are seated on the floor around her. When the children are settled, she begins. Her calm voice and measured pace reinforce her message to the children: this is a tool for work, not a toy to be played with. It is to be treated with care. She calls the children's attention to the fact that each key makes something happen on the screen. Miss Price demonstrates as she types and then erases her own name.
>
> Then one, by one, children are called to stand beside her at the computer and dictate a sentence or two about their summer vacations. Miss Price types in their sentences, pausing to explain the use of the space bar and the shift key. Particular emphasis is placed on the capability of word processing to easily correct errors. Interest is running high. Children rise to their knees, stretching their necks and whispering as they attempt to get a better look at the keyboard and the screen. In their eagerness for turns, others begin to wiggle and talk among themselves.
>
> (Margaret did not want to continue the dictation as planned—the children who were dictating simply had too much to say, and the eagerness of the others made waiting for turns difficult.) After five children have had a chance to dictate their sentences, Miss Price demonstrates the procedure for printing out text. The group focuses on Miss Price.
>
> Holding the printed page of the five children's dictation, Miss Price explains to the group that she will cut this apart into sentence strips so that they can paste their sentences on paper, illustrate their sentences, and then all of the sheets will be bound into a book about summer vacations. She assures the children who have not yet had turns that they will work the following day with Ms. Carlisle, an elementary education student from the university who helps in her class three days a week.
>
> The next morning, while Miss Price conducts the full class, Ms. Carlisle takes children one at a time to the computer and types their dictated sentences.

Although Margaret pronounced this lesson a "disaster," she accomplished her goal of demonstrating some of the most useful capabilities of word processing for beginning writers, and in the process she generated enthusiasm for writing with a new tool. After the initial full-group lesson, she arranged for coaches to provide word-processing instruction. Individual children or pairs of children were assigned to be coached and instructed by an adult at the computer while Margaret Price met with her reading groups. In order to avoid the problem of children being called to reading group while they were engaged at the computer, she assigned children from one reading group at a time to complete writing tasks with word processing that others were doing with pencil and paper. Each child could work with the adult coach until his or her task was complete, and no child missed a reading group. With coaching, each child learned the word-processing skills required to successfully complete the assigned tasks.

Margaret's decisions about how to provide instruction in entering and editing text, how to provide assistance to children as they worked, and how time would be allotted for children to complete word processing tasks allowed her to maintain her established teaching routine. The integrity of her classroom culture, and her identity in the school as a teacher who surely and carefully led children to success, were maintained.

Bev Winston

At the other end of the hall that housed Margaret Price's class was Bev Winston's kindergarten classroom. It, too, had been built to accommodate three classes. Bev's room, however, was divided by permanent partitions that absorbed much of the sound from the two classes on either side. Like Tina Santori and Margaret Price, Bev Winston and her teammates planned their daily schedules together, so that active, noisy activities coincided—all conducted free play at the same time, and the three groups met together in Bev's room for singing.

Within a structure that accommodated the needs of her colleagues, Bev scheduled her own class time flexibly in response to the children's and her own needs. For most of the 20 years or so that she had taught kindergarten in West Brook School District, Bev had designed her own kindergarten curriculum that reflected the children's developmental needs and built on her own strengths and interests, including music, poetry, and fairy tales. Gradually, however, time for free play, singing, and literature was being eaten up by district-mandated materials for handwriting and workbooks for reading and math. What had once been a developmental kindergarten program planned around children's social, emotional, physical, and cognitive needs was being transformed by district requirements, and the "trickle-down" from the primary curriculum, into an academic kindergarten.

Tina Santori and Margaret Price had to respond to school district mandates just as Bev Winston did, but the changes mandated for the kindergarten curriculum were even more dramatic. Although not without stress, the ongoing cultures of Tina's and Margaret's classrooms stretched to accommodate new curriculum requirements, and their fundamental teaching practices and goals remained relatively stable. In contrast, Bev Winston's deployment of word processing was shaped by a rapidly changing classroom culture and by classroom routines and teaching practices that were in revision. Only her goals for the children remained the same—that each child be happy, enjoy learning in school, and approach new experiences with confidence. Bev assessed the merit of instruction in word processing against her personal goals for the children, and she shaped her practices in the context of shifting classroom routines and a school district culture moving increasingly toward an academic kindergarten with a standardized curriculum.

Bev perceived her role as a kindergarten teacher as different from the roles of teachers "in the grades." In meetings of researchers and the teachers who were part of the computer project, Bev routinely set her experiences apart from the others' in discussions of scheduling, sharing classroom space, and especially teaching writing. When there was discussion of the time required to read children's writing folders or writing files on disk, Bev commented, "These concerns are more for their levels . . . I don't have the problems they do." When describing the evolution of her writing program, Bev compared the experiences of kindergarteners who wrote very brief texts to those of older children who worked on texts during more than one sitting. In doing so, she set kindergarten apart from the grades:

> We don't have to go through the process that Tina and Margaret do. For instance, they're typing something and we get instant results. They're not really going back to change it yet . . . to revise.

Her colleagues shared her perception. Discussion of practice was often interspersed with comments like "But kindergarten is different" and "But not your kids, right, Bev?" that set her experiences apart from her colleagues'. They implicitly afforded her freedom to explore word processing slowly, and explicitly supported her decision to approach word processing with caution.

Bev's approach to introducing word processing paralleled her approach to introducing the district-mandated curriculum. She adopted an attitude of experimentation and spent a great deal of time watching to "see what (the children) would do with it." Initially, she planned to use the word processor to record sentences dictated at the beginning of each class day, just as she used the chalk board. In addition, she planned to allow the children to "play" at the word processors during their free choice time in much the ways that they freely explored other classroom materials such as blocks or paints. Bev's allocation of time for word processing and the tasks she set allowed her to avoid introducing yet another separate activity into an already crowded curriculum. They also gave Bev the opportunity to observe the children's responses to the new technology in the context of activities that were familiar to her. Bev placed the computers on long, low kindergarten tables near the shelves of manipulative materials, puzzles, and blocks. This was a social area of the room where interactions among children working at the computers and in adjacent areas were possible.

Bev introduced word processing during the orientation days that preceded their first full day of school, thereby communicating her expectation that it would be an important part of their daily activities in kindergarten. Seven children and their parents came to the classroom on each of several designated days. In past years Bev had spoken to the parents at one end of the classroom while the children used puzzles and small toys at the other. This year, however, while Bev talked to the parents, the children could choose the computer as well as the usual selection of manipulatives. Mary Huston, an education student assigned to help in Bev's class two days a week, was instructed to oversee the computer activity.

[While Mrs. Winston addresses the group of parents seated in the small chairs at the children's long work tables, the children explore the materials set out for them on a floor area nearby. Some are tentative and quiet; others participate with enthusiasm. When all finally appear comfortable, Ms. Huston moves to the chair in front of the computer. She addresses her comments to the children working nearest her.]

Ms. Huston:	Do you know what this is?
Denise:	[Responds but it is not clear what she said]
Ms. Huston:	We can do all kinds of fun things with this. Denise, what is the first letter of your name?
Denise:	'D.' [Ms. Huston types Denise's full name. Denise is now standing beside her and Meghan has joined her.]
Ms. Huston:	Let's make that disappear. [Using the delete key, she erases 'Denise' from the screen.] Did Denise disappear? [Denise and Meghan look doubtful and shake their heads "no." Ms. Huston then asks Denise what her last name is then, checking the proper spelling on her name tag, she types Denise's full name. Both girls carefully watch her fingers and the screen.]
Ms. Huston:	Where's Meghan? What's the first letter in your name?
Meghan:	'M' [Ms. Huston types Meghan's first name, then pauses to show Meghan how to use the space bar to move the cursor then finishes typing Meghan's last name. Denise has lost interest and asks permission to leave. Gemma

	joins Ms. Huston and Meghan and her name is typed as well. When all three names are complete, Ms. Huston begins the print procedure.]
Ms. Huston:	Meghan, go over there [pointing to the printer. As sounds come from the printer Meghan and Gemma go to watch.]
Ms. Huston:	What's coming out?
Meghan and Gemma:	Names.

[The girls sound unimpressed as Ms. Huston explains how everything she typed on the screen was printed out on the paper. The girls go back to the manipulatives, leaving the printout behind. Children continue to explore the computer with Ms. Huston's help, and eventually alone. After the parents have gone, Mrs. Winston calls the children together as she will at the beginning of every class day. Following a tour of the classroom and the school, she gathers the children around the computer. Ms. Huston asks each child to tell about something they did in kindergarten that morning while she types each one. Some of the children watch the screen, some watch her hands as she rapidly strikes the keys. Most, however lose interest and look around the room. When all sentences have been typed, Ms. Huston takes the group to stand in front of the printer as it produces a copy of the entire collection of sentences for each child to take home. All are fascinated as the paper comes "spitting out" of the printer.]

Jung Ho:	Dededededededede . . . (Imitating the sound of the printer).
All of the children:	(Giggling) Dededededede . . .
Denise:	(Giggling) It's almost down to the floor!
Gemma and Meghan:	Look at it!

Bev's introduction of word processing to her kindergarten children reflected her caution and concern over the imposition of the kindergarten writing curriculum. She wrote to us in an early journal entry:

I'm not sure at this time how [using word processing] will apply to the kindergarten in the first few months of school.

She watched her children closely as they experimented with the word processors and participated in group dictation sessions like the one Ms. Huston conducted on their first day of school. She watched her children's responses to writing instruction as she introduced it for the first time, and measured what she observed against her goals. She made changes in her practices wherever she believed they were warranted.

Responding to pressures from the school district to alter radically her curriculum, Bev Winston took a "wait and see what they do with it" approach to introducing both writing and word processing. Reflecting the ongoing culture of her classroom and the goals she always held for her children, she adapted two preexisting classroom practices—group dictation and individual exploration—to introduce word processing.

At the beginning of the second year of the study, two additional teachers joined the computer project—Barbara Gold, a veteran first-grade teacher; and Debby Perrone, who, with three years of experience, was the youngest and newest faculty member in the school. Like the others, they brought their own goals, histories of instructional practice, and responses to changes in the school district and the task of integrating word processing into their teaching. Their task differed from the others', however, in that they had the benefit of the experiences of the three original teachers, the opportunity to take the computers home with them over the summer to familiarize themselves with the hardware and software, and the advantage of having some children in their classes who had gained computer experience in Bev Winston's or Margaret Price's classes the year before.

Barbara Gold

Barbara Gold's first grade was located in a self-contained classroom on the first floor. Children's desks, compactly arranged face to face in three short columns, occupied only a small portion of the room. Surrounding them were shelves of learning games and a floor area and tables on which to use them. One low shelf was tightly packed with children's literature, another held the children's art supplies. An easel with tempera paints and large pieces of newsprint stood beside the long low tables where Barbara placed her two computers and printers.

The hand-lettered name cards taped to each child's desk revealed the multicultural character of Barbara's class. *Sung Ho, Christos, Joel, Marcus, Padmini, Alexandra, Heather, Huan, Melinda, Ho Sook*, and the others, printed in perfect two-inch letters, were ready to be traced with fingers, decorated surreptitiously with crayons, and proudly carried to friends at the computer who typed their names. Barbara had a long history of success in working with children with limited language proficiency. Consequently, the majority of children placed in her classes were those who had been identified by their former teachers as delayed in language development or children for whom English was a second language. In most cases, children came to Barbara's class having already experienced academic difficulties and failure.

For Barbara, children's success and self-concept were the most important goals. Her language arts program was based on a language experience approach in which children discussed, dictated, and eventually composed their own texts about experiences in and beyond the classroom. Children were expected to express their thoughts in complete sentences, and were given many opportunities to practice this skill orally and in writing. In the beginning of the year, many activities were designed to help children learn that the words they spoke could be represented in print.

Barbara's curriculum differed considerably from West Brook's standardized curriculum. She examined the new writing curriculum and the new basal reading materials carefully and then drew these conclusions:

> I don't feel, practically, that they work [with my children]. Even though my kids are only coming from kindergarten, they come with a lot of conceptions about what they can and cannot do. I just have some real questions [about the standardized curriculum for] my kids who have started to read with some degree of frustration. And the reason that I disagree is that I just don't look for ways to keep that frustration process going. I look for ways to help them feel successful. So it seems to me that some of the things that they're asking me to do are defeating the very purposes of what I'm trying to do.

Not willing to compromise her goals, yet knowing that she had to conform to some extent to the goals of the school district, Barbara created a curriculum that served both. Careful not to call administrative attention to her work, she engaged in a form of quiet resistance to West Brook's curriculum mandates (Paris, 1989b, in press). In a discussion of teaching writing skills and process, she explained:

> How I approached it was not the same as how they would have approached it. . . . I made my own rules. And as far as the book the other language arts classes would use, I did not [use it]. It was not appropriate. But I think that we covered [the skills] in our own way. We still talked about capital letters and we still talked about periods and all the things that you're supposed to cover in first grade.

In her initial plans for using word processing in her classroom, Barbara emphasized that the ways she used word processing would be consistent with her ongoing practice.

> [The ways I will use word processing will] have very much have to do with the same kinds of things I have done in the past—language experience and all that—[to help the children] make the association between the spoken word and the written word.

Later in the school year, she explained further.

> The way that we use [word processing] fits into the whole program. . . . I don't do things with it that don't really seem appropriate to me and my program.

Underlying Barbara's goals and ongoing practice was her knowledge of content, pedagogy, children in general, and her children in particular. Her understanding of the connection between positive self-concept and learning was the basis for several important decisions about how her children would learn to use word processing and what kinds of tasks they would do. In her own words, she was always "look(ing) for ways to make them feel successful," to "feel good about themselves" and feel they were "a part of" the literate population of the school. She explained further:

> Self-esteem is a real important ingredient in my room. I want them to succeed and feel good about it regardless of whether they're writing a letter for an entire word, or a beginning and ending sound, or an entire word.

Consequently, Barbara devised procedures and assignments that enabled children to experience success in even their earliest efforts to write at the word processor.

Barbara introduced the children to word processing on the first day of school. The lesson was designed to explain what the computer could do and how it should be cared for. However, embedded in the lesson were other important messages as well. Barbara wanted her children to feel special, because they would be able to use computers all year whereas other children in other classrooms used them only for several weeks. Furthermore, she wanted the children to understand that writing—with word processor or pencil—was a way to preserve important ideas, and that every one of them had ideas that were worthy of being saved in print. The lesson was also a vehicle for the more fundamental idea—that each child was indeed valued and capable—an idea that would pervade her curriculum and her interactions with children throughout the year.

Barbara gathered the children on the floor in front of the computers. Although the school year was only a few hours old, Barbara addressed each child by name.

[Mrs. Gold opens discussion about the computer by asking the children to think back to their classrooms last year and remember if there were computers there. One by one, she invites the children to respond. Some had used a computer that was rolled into the room for short periods of time before it was moved to another classroom. Several had not had a computer in their classroom at all. Only those children who had been in Mrs. Winston's class the previous year had access to a computer all year.]

Mrs. Gold: Well, do you know what? We are really lucky. We are special. How many computers do we have?

Children: Two.

Mrs. Gold: We get to keep these computers for the. . . [There is a pause, then the children chime in with her] whole year! Isn't that neat?

[Children grin and glow and sit up very tall as she talks to them about the awesome responsibility of caring for these wonderful machines that have been entrusted to them. She lowers her voice to a hush and leans very close to them as she speaks.

She cautions against pounding on keys, or spilling snacks on keyboards, in a manner that suggests that she is conveying special and secret wisdom. Joel breaks the hushed and serious tone by interjecting that he has a computer at home and that he plays games on it. Mrs. Gold follows his lead and moves onto her next topic.]

Mrs. Gold: I'm going to talk about that right now as a matter of fact! What do you do on a computer?

Child: Play games!

Mrs. Gold: Yes, does anybody know what [else] you can do with it? Do you know what you can do with them, Joel?

Joel: You type.

Mrs. Gold: You can type, you're right. This is the keyboard [holding it up for the children to see]. Type what?

Teddy: Writing!

Mrs. Gold: Ah, writing! What does that mean, 'writing'?

Teddy: School.

Heather: Words.

Mrs. Gold: Ah, words. Writing is words . . . [She describes with enthusiasm how the computer has the capability of recording many, many words, and that it can print them on paper as well.]

Teddy: [In a voice that indicates that he is making an important pronouncement] Writing is learning.

[Children are beginning to inch toward the computers and printer as Mrs. Gold responds to Teddy's pronouncement.]

Mrs. Gold: True, true. . . . Oh, I can see that you want to see all about the computers. I'll tell you what. Everybody stand up wherever you are. Let's take a look at the computers. Come over real close and then when you've had a super good look, then you can go sit down.

[Children peer closely at the machines, some reaching out to touch, then drawing their hands back as Mrs. Gold gently reminds them that they will not be touching any keys just now. When all are seated again, she continues.]

Mrs. Gold: Somebody said—and they were so smart—that writing is words. And if you put a bunch of words together, that's a sentence. Who can raise their hand and tell me in a sentence what you did over the summer?

Padmini: I went swimming.

Mrs. Gold: You went swimming. Did someone do something else during the summer?

Heather: I went to my aunt's house and had a cookout.

Mrs. Gold: Terrific! [She takes several more examples before introducing the next task.] OK, now I want you to be super good listeners. I want to show you that we can put your words for your sentences on the computer. I want to show you your writing. Here's what we're going to do. Ms. Paris (researcher) and Mrs. Gold are both going to sit at a computer and we're going to let you—one at a time—come up and tell us what you did over the summer.

[Children are called in groups of four to come to a computer. Within ten minutes every child has dictated a sentence, then lined up at the door to go outdoors. Later in the day, Mrs. Gold prints each child's sentence out on a single page to be illustrated the next day and bound into a book.]

In her introductory activity, Barbara Gold began to develop the themes that the children were special, worthy of trust, and that each child had something of value to contribute. These would undergird her work with them throughout the year. Not only did her existing goals and the ongoing culture of her classroom shape her introduction of word processing, but she also used the introductory activity to help transmit that culture to her children. Her decision to embed her introduction of word processing in a language experience activity of sentence dictation reflected her ongoing practice, her continuing commitment to respond to the needs of the children entrusted to her by her colleagues, and her breach with the skills-based school district language arts curriculum.

Debby Perrone

Debby Perrone, the youngest and newest faculty member at Summit Grove, had joined the third grade teaching team just a year before she joined the computer project. She shared a three-space classroom with two veteran teachers who had well-established procedures in place before Debby arrived. Although actually beginning her fourth year of teaching, Debby was still a "new teacher" in the minds of many of her colleagues, and she referred to herself as "the new kid on the block." But Debby had plans to shed that image. Because sharing expertise was highly valued in the culture of Summit Grove, Debby was eager to learn to use word processing, not only to enhance her teaching, but also to gain knowledge and skill that she could share with her colleagues. In doing so, she could establish herself as a respected member of the faculty. Word processing, then, had both expressive and instrumental purposes for Debby.

The culture of Debby's classroom was best characterized as one which placed the children—as learners, teachers, and writers—at the center of productive and enthusiastic activity. A visitor to Debby's room always needed to pause and look carefully to find her, usually seated on the floor with a small group of children or in a child-sized chair pulled up next to the desk of a child with whom she was working. The decisions Debby made about instructing children in word-processing skills and providing them with assistance as they worked reflected her emphasis on children as teachers and teacher as a fellow learner. Debby declared that one of her greatest joys was seeing her children take responsibility for their own learning. She described what she called her "basic philosophy of teaching":

> I'm a firm believer in the teacher not being the instructor in the classroom all the time. That's probably the basic premise of my teaching . . . Teachers just need to create an environment where children can learn in any way they can, and just simply be a moderator.

To this end, she decorated the computer area with posters outlining basic word-processing procedures that would enable children to perform most basic word-processing functions without her assistance, and planned for children to work in pairs to provide help as needed. In her own description of her ongoing teaching practices, she commented. "I do a lot with small groups and I love to watch the children teach one another." This was particularly true of her writing instruction.

The walls of Debby's classroom were covered with computer-generated banners and posters that described the steps of the writing process and prominently displayed children's completed stories and books. Debby valued writing, and among her goals for the children were that they come to value it as well and consider themselves successful writers. Above all, writing had to be a meaningful activity for them. Inseparable from her writing goals was her larger goal that children actively participate in teaching as well as learning. Children routinely worked together to brainstorm ideas prior to writing, read and respond to each other's writing, and help each other edit their work.

During her first full year of teaching third grade, Debby had adhered fairly closely to West Brook's required reading curriculum. She was, in her own words, "weaving her way through the year, right up to the end." But several years before, she had experienced what she referred to as "a different way to teach" while employed as a substitute in Tina Santori's classroom.

> She was doing novels and fairy tales and folk tales and she wasn't using the basal at all, and that's all I had learned in my undergrad training, how to open a manual and teach from it. So I continued with her program as best I could. I got a whole different feel for teaching from your own material as opposed to all these manuals.

Debby was in the process of applying this approach to her own teaching of writing.

Her decisions about how to introduce word processing reflected her goals for her children, the role she sought in the school culture, and her firmly held beliefs about the teaching of writing. For example, she rejected the suggestion in the school district curriculum guide that all steps of the writing process be taught before assigning the first writing project. She based her decision on her conviction that to do so would have no meaning for the children, and that the writing process was more appropriately taught in the context of the children's writing projects. Similarly, she abandoned her initial plans to introduce word processing skills through a series of lessons and exercises before permitting the children to compose their own texts with the word processors. The evolution of her thinking and her practice are recorded below in her own words in journal entries written over a 5-week period. An exceptionally reflective and articulate teacher who took great pleasure in writing, Debby's journal provides valuable insight into the process of making word processing curriculum.

September 5
I have made up my mind that I will introduce [the computer] to the whole class using the large [cardboard] keyboards I have made for the kids. We will practice manually at our desks before I take them to the computer. . . . After a week of mini-lessons I have prepared in which each of the children will practice typing their name, a short sentence, etc., we will be ready to use the computer for our own writing.

September 18
I am really excited! I got the chance to start with the computer! The kids seem real excited. . . . I told them that they would all get a chance to work on the machines as much as we could possibly fit in. I also stressed to the kids that since there are only 2 machines a lot of cooperation is needed from them. They all seemed willing to be cooperative. . . .

Let's see, what did I cover so far? I gave out the "paper keyboards" [like those used in Tina Santori's lessons] . . . We searched the keyboards to make sure all 26 letters were there. . . . We looked at the special keys—the shift key and the space bar. I then put about 10 words on the board and the kids came up to the rug with their own [laminated] keyboards and we typed them in together very slowly. .

Most of them followed along right with me. Some were faster and some slower. The biggest problem I found was that some of the kids were bored! I asked them to bear with the rest of us. They seemed to cooperate pretty well. The kids who were bored were the ones who already "know" the keys or so they think. The whole lesson took 30 minutes. It was a bit too long looking back on it now. . . . So I reflected back later in the day and decided that I did not want them to become expert typists, but I do think it will be beneficial to them to know some of the keys.

The next day I only spent 10 minutes and it went much smoother. The kids all practiced some new words I had put on the board and when they had finished they could go back to their seats and start their other work. . . . The ones who were bored on the first day are now working on being the first ones to leave the rug after 10 words, and they usually are! Friday we are going to the machines! We're all excited. . . . I'm using the kids who know these keys as my first computer experts! . . .There are 12 of them, so I'm pairing them up with the ones who don't know. They will go to the computer together for a while. They are wearing their ['Computer Expert'] badges proudly!

In addition to Debby's reflection on her practice and revision of her initial teaching decisions following her lessons, she routinely revised her decisions in the midst of her teaching. For example, in the lesson described above, she observed that her children were having difficulty using the appropriate fingers to type each key. She revised her expectations on the spot, telling them that instead of attempting to use the designated fingers for each key, they should concentrate on using at least two fingers on each hand.

September 23
The children have finally gotten to the computer! Each and every one of them has had the thrill of typing their name in [to produce a class list for each to take home]. Again I am experiencing a little frustration dealing with the fact that some of them are ready to roll and others are not. . . . The ones who [are] want to go and write stories! The ones who [are not] need a little extra time until they are caught up. Not that it is necessary that all of them spend the same amount [of time] on the machines throughout the year, but I wanted to get them all at the same place as quickly as possible. It is not going to work! OH WELL. . .
    Plan B—The computer experts will be shown as a separate group how to save and retrieve . . . They will continue to work with the kids they have been assigned to for a time. The only problem with that is that it has been difficult for me to continue with my daily routine of reading groups since the pairs that have been established do not mesh with my reading groups. In other words, it is impossible for me to conduct any reading group while the kids are working on the machines. So computer time, for now, will be done as a separate area.

Debby's decision to pair children to provide assistance to those who needed it led to considerably more disruption to her reading groups than this entry indicates. But she valued children helping children so highly that she tolerated the disruption.

(September 23, continued)
    I am, however, going to let the [expert] computer kids start putting in their stories since they know what to do. They will be at the computer both helping [their partners seated at the computer next to them] and producing work of their own on a disk. Lessons they will help the beginners with will be as simple as:
    1. typing a simple sentence
    2. typing a short poem
    3. typing a short letter.
    The experts will begin to type in our first writing project for the year which will be a project involving 1 to 1 interviews with each other. Here, the expert will interview at the computer and type his information directly in. The beginners will continue to use paper for this project. The next project will involve all of them at the computer.

October 2
I've had a major change of thought! So what else is new? I found out that the beginner computer kids were extremely bored with typing in stuff that was not meaningful to them. And seeing their expert pal type in his or her own story really bugged them. So, they are now also typing in their first story. . . . They seem a lot slower, but their pals are real nice at coaching them through.

Each couple is going to remain a couple until I feel that they can break away and work on their own. I feel very strongly about the kids learning from one another. It is extremely effective. . .

We are working on our . . . funny stories about someone else in our class. Convenient for me, the kids are working with their [computer] partners. Some kids have done their actual interviews at the computer, others have typed in their rough drafts and others will do their editing [on the computer].

Debby's decisions about how to teach word processing skills reflected her emphasis on cooperation, peer coaching, and meaningful instruction.

Being a teacher with knowledge and skill to share was an important goal that Debby held for her children as well as for herself as an accepted member of the faculty. Consequently, she made certain that every child in the class achieved the status of "computer expert" and arranged for her children to teach the children in two other third-grade classes to use word processing and to work with a class of kindergarten children to help them produce a book. Like Tina Santori, who had also arranged for her children to teach the other fourth graders, Debby Perrone's decisions about word processing supported her existing classroom goals and practices and reflected the role she was shaping for herself within the faculty. The same practices in the hands of two different teachers reflected their different roles within the school culture—one as computer expert, the other as new teacher—and two different sets of goals and ongoing classroom practices.

Summary: Teachers' Decisions and School and Classroom Culture

The pedagogical decisions made by each teacher about the purposes of word processing and the methods of introducing children to word processing skills varied widely. Striking examples are their different responses to the dilemma of how to structure a first lesson. Grouping of children ranged from full class to small group, lessons ranged in duration from 10 minutes or so to over a half hour, the skills taught varied widely, and the methods of instruction differed as well.

The wide variation in teachers' answers to the questions of implementation outlined in Figure 3.2 reflected each teacher's responses to a school district culture where teacher discretion was being supplanted by a mandated standardized curriculum. Decisions also reflected a school culture in which individuality and colleagueship were highly valued. The influences of the school culture, the culture of the school district, the culture of each classroom, and each teacher's role within these cultures were interrelated. Tina continued to serve as computer consultant for her colleagues. Margaret Price and Barbara Gold preserved the individuality of their own curricula and teaching practices. Bev Winston's approach to word processing mirrored her responses to mandated changes in the kindergarten curriculum. Debby Perrone's initial word-processing instruction reflected an ongoing classroom culture where peer teaching was highly valued, but it also reflected her desire to alter her role in the school from "new kid" to respected colleague.

Variation in the teachers' decisions about instruction in word processing can also be attributed to the goals against which each the teacher judged classroom practice. For example, at one of our first group meetings, the teachers discussed the relative merits of different methods of introducing word processing to a class. Barbara interrupted a disagreement to point out that the ways word processing was introduced in each classroom reflected each teacher's very different goals.

> But . . . your goals were different. What you wanted (referring to Margaret Price) the kids to have was very different than what you wanted (referring to Tina Santori). You know, you, Tina, wanted to give the kids some familiarity with the keyboards so they could go off, handle it, be equipped to [work independently]. Whereas, you (Margaret) wanted them to, in a more general way, [see] this general capability of the machine. You were going to show them what it could do. . . . You know, you both were going to get to the same spot, but how you went about it was very different just because you are you and how you were going to approach the computer [differed].

Barbara's analysis was insightful. Tina thoroughly enjoyed exploring and mastering all aspects of the word-processing system and saw word processing as exciting content as well as a potentially powerful tool for children to use in their writing. As Barbara suggested, Tina's goals were to help children master the computer system so that they could be confident, competent, and independent users. Margaret, on the other hand, saw word processing as a tool to "make writing and editing a less tedious chore for the children." She sought to learn, and then to teach, "the least number of functions that must be mastered to write, edit, and print." Her goal in her introductory lesson was for the children to become aware of the capabilities of word processing that would make writing easier for them.

Furthermore each teacher initially used word processing not only in service of her existing goals, but also to maintain and enrich her ongoing practices. Favored teaching methods, management procedures, and classroom organization all were reflected in the teachers' initial answers to the decision questions in Figure 3.2.

Striking differences can be seen in teachers' responses to the same dilemma. For example, both Margaret and Debby faced the questions of how to allocate time and how to provide instruction and assistance without taking children's time and attention away from reading groups. Margaret's decision to have coaches work with children at the computers allowed her to maintain her ongoing practice of structuring language arts instruction around her time with reading groups and also to provide adult instruction and supervision at the word processors without disrupting ongoing practice. Debby, whose classroom culture included peer teaching and less adherence to a planned language arts schedule, devised a solution to the same problem that maintained her ongoing practice and in fact provided her with additional opportunities to work toward her goal of sharing instructional responsibility with her children.

Based on the descriptions provided here, it is possible to conclude, as Cuban (1986) did about the introduction of earlier educational technologies, that introducing word processing brought little innovation or change of real value into the five classrooms we observed. Although the presence of the computers and the concomitant demands on teachers' attention, schedule, and spatial organization of the classroom altered the surface structure of practice (Bussis, Chitenden, & Amarel, 1977), they primarily accommodated rather than disrupted established classroom procedures and goals. Hence, it might be said that word processing simply allowed teachers to do more of what they were already doing without substantially altering the instruction they provided.

However, this conclusion is neither accurate nor complete. It overlooks teachers' long history of embracing changes when those changes support their underlying goals and assumptions (Cuban, 1986), and it does not take into account the passage of time or the evolutionary nature of change. Weizenbaum's (1976) now classic observation about tool use in general and computer use in particular makes the point clearly.

> To say that the computer was initially used mainly to do things pretty much as they had always been done, except to do them more rapidly or, by some criteria, more efficiently, is not to distinguish it from other tools. (p. 32)

Initial uses of a new technology often mirror the practice that preceded it, and only later do new and more imaginative uses evolve. Our data make clear that the classroom cultures that so powerfully influenced teachers' initial interpretations and uses of word processing were themselves altered over time by the very presence of word processing. In the following section, we examine the ways in which word processing affected the cultures of the classrooms into which it was introduced, and how, in fact, routine practice was altered as each teacher's answers to the decision questions outlined in Figure 3.2 evolved over time.

CLASSROOM CULTURES
AND WORD PROCESSING OVER TIME

The deployment of word processing reflected\each teacher's responses to the culture of the school and to the goals and ongoing practices that characterized the culture of her own classroom. Each teacher interpreted the potential and limitations of word processing in terms of her ongoing practice and established goals. Margaret Price thought of word processing as an efficient editing tool, Barbara Gold saw it as a tool to allow children to experience success, Bev Winston saw it as a material for children to explore, Debby Perrone considered word processing as yet another occasion for children to teach children, and Tina Santori viewed it as a tool to make writing more efficient and an important new technology for children to master. We have seen that the teachers interpreted word processing expressively as well as instrumentally. Their expressive interpretations, which reflected their roles in the wider culture of the school or the school district, remained essentially unchanged over time. However, their instrumental interpretations, which reflected the evolving culture of each teacher's classroom, shifted over time.

Although word processing use was initially shaped by the classroom culture, once it was introduced, it also contributed to the shape of that culture. Over time, using word processing challenged some established routines such as the allocation of time for writing. It also called into question teachers' expectations about children's writing abilities and led to the creation of social contexts for learning to write that differed significantly from traditional classroom practice. In no case did the mere presence of word processing "cause" these qualitative changes in practice, but as Clark and Salomon suggest (1986), the technology provided a context in which change could evolve.

The ways and extent to which word processing shaped classroom culture depended on practices already in place and the unique conditions that existed in each classroom prior to the introduction of word processing. For example, the public nature of the computer screen (Bruce et al., 1985; Weir, 1989) invites children to respond to and critique each other's writing, whether they are working at an adjacent computer or simply passing by. Its effect frequently is to encourage interaction among children while they compose, revise, and edit. In a classroom culture where writing is conducted as a solitary activity, then, we could expect the public nature of word processing to alter the social context surrounding writing in significant ways. If, on the other hand, the children in a classroom routinely read and respond to each other's writing throughout the writing process, the public nature of the computer screen would not so much alter the learning context as enhance or extend an already existing feature. Consequently, although word processing contributes to changes in classroom cultures, the nature and extent of those changes are not uniform across classrooms. Rather, potential effects are confounded by what is already there.

The influences of word processing and classroom culture on one another are not direct. Classroom culture does not simply determine word processing use, nor does the nature of word processing as content to be learned or a tool to write with directly alter the classroom culture. The effects of each are mediated by the individual teacher's interpretations of the potential of word processing as a pedagogical tool, her observations of children using word processing, and her critical judgments about what she observed and measured against her goals. Tina summarized the ongoing cycle of questioning, observing, evaluating, and adapting that characterized the teachers' work in all curriculum areas in her comments:

> We're always judging our work. We look at ourselves all the time—[at] our previous work. We're constantly saying, 'Are we doing our jobs?'

Each of the five teachers whom we observed looked on their work with word processing with the same critical eye they brought to other areas of their curriculum. Evolution of practice as mediated by critical reflection was documented in Debby's journal entries that we looked at above.

The interacting relationship of classroom culture and word processing implementation was a dynamic rather than a static one. Classroom practice, and even the teacher's goals from which it emerged, moved forward through the mechanism of reflection, evaluation, and adaptation (Paris, 1989a, in press). The introduction of word processing foregrounded some aspects of existing practice and tested them against an altered reality. For example, the allocation of time for writing with word processing presented a problem that did not exist when children wrote with paper and pencil. There were sufficient papers and pencils available for all children to work on writing assignments at the same time. With a limited number of word processors available, however, this was not possible, and different arrangements for providing time for writing were required. Similarly, the taken-for-granted social contexts in which children traditionally learned to write—a full class of children sitting alone at their desks with pencil and paper as the teacher circulated among them, offering assistance—were called into question. Even teachers' assessments of children's writing abilities were reevaluated in light of their writing with word processing.

What transpired was an evolution of classroom cultures that also helped to shape different ways in which children learned to write. In the sections that follow, we revisit each of the five teachers and sketch the evolution of their practices, beginning with Margaret Price, whose practices changed considerably, and concluding with Tina Santori. The development of each teacher's practice is summarized in a figure that contains many, although not all, of the major events, routines and procedures that the teacher used in her work with word processing. The figures can be read in several ways. First, they can be read from left to right, as a chronological account of each teacher's work with word processing over time. Second, the evolution of a teacher's answers to the decision questions in Figure 3.2 can be followed by tracing a single line horizontally from its beginning to end. A continuous line represents a practice or category of practices that remained in use over the time period indicated, while a broken line represents sporadic use, and a short line with endpoint marked indicates a practice that was abandoned or replaced by another. Finally, the figures can be read from top to bottom to produce a snapshot of a teacher's work with word processing at a single point in time. A snapshot of this sort has been chosen to represent a point in time that best characterizes the context in which children learned to write with word processing in each classroom.

Margaret Price

Margaret Price's evolving use of word processing can be described as a kind of winnowing. Although strategies for instruction and assistance proliferated at first, by the second year of the project, only the most promising practices remained. Figures 3.3a and 3.3b provide an overview of some of the practices that were devised and tested over the two years. The evolution of Margaret's practice paralleled her own increasing sophistication and ease with word-processing. During the two years, she moved from orchestrating word-processing instruction provided by an adult coach to taking full responsibility for word processing instruction on her own. Further, using word processing in the writing program eventually altered Margaret's expectations of her children and consequently influenced the content and pacing of the writing instruction she provided and the tasks she assigned.

   Teaching Word-Processing Skills. Over two years of working with word processing, Margaret Price's methods of instruction in word-processing skills changed dramatically. In the first year, instruction was provided to her second graders primarily by Ms. Carlisle, an education student from the university, or by Mrs. Kahn, the researcher who was often asked to assist children as she observed. Skills were taught to individual children as they watched an adult type their dictation and, later, as they completed writing assignments (see Figure 3.3a). When capitalization, spacing and erasing were necessary in the context of children's compositions, these procedures were taught or reviewed. (Children's interactions with adult coaches are described in detail in Chapters 4 and 5.) On several occasions more sophisticated procedures such as "REPLACE" were taught in the same way. For both dictation and working on texts of their own construction, Margaret often arranged to have pairs of children observe each other dictate or edit at the word processor. She explained her rationale:

> Well, then they see it twice. I did that on purpose so that they could see SAVE, PRINT, and RETURN and [everything] twice.

This proved to be an effective means of teaching and reviewing basic word processing skills. However, looking back on her first year of work with word processing, Margaret commented:

> If I hadn't had Ms. Carlisle two days a week and Jessica (the researcher), I wouldn't be teaching word processing at all.

With little "love" for computers and a well established reading group routine that occupied her attention throughout the language arts period, there seemed to Margaret to be no alternative to incidental teaching of word processing skills by assistants. But after a year of work with word processing, she was not satisfied with the children learning word processing in this manner. She sought an approach to the development of word processing skills that would be consistent with her more orderly instructional practices. One aspect of her more systematic approach, noted in a brief journal entry, was the introduction of word processing "mechanics before writing process this year." Furthermore, Margaret decided that she herself would provide direct instruction in basic word processing skills to each reading group.

In early October of the second year, Margaret brought each of her reading groups to the word processor for a brief introduction. In the first lesson, the children were introduced to the parts of the computer and their functions, the shift key, the space bar and how to print text. Margaret demonstrated these skills as she typed in her name. Then children typed their own names, and she directed one child through the procedure to print a copy of the list of names for each child while the others looked on. The second lesson, although different in content, was similar in format. Later in the fall, she took pairs of children to the word processor for instruction in editing. She entered one child's text, and then together Margaret and the two children searched for and corrected errors. In the context of this task, she reviewed cursor movement and the use of the delete key.

Providing Assistance. Given the demands on Margaret's time during the language arts period, and the need to minimize disruption of her classroom routine, she initially arranged for children to use word processing only when adult coaches were available to oversee their work. It was anticipated that children who encountered difficulty with the mechanics of word processing could turn to the coach for help rather than interrupt Margaret's work with a reading group. Following a group meeting where we discussed Tina Santori's plan to train and certify "computer experts" to assist their peers, Margaret decided to train a child who had shown particular skill to assist his classmates.

Coaching was not the only source of support available to the children. The tasks that Margaret devised to be completed with word processing provided internal supports as well. It had always been her practice to design writing tasks

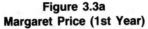

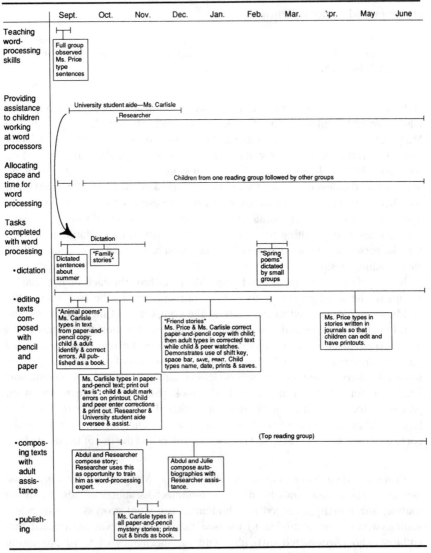

that could be completed at children's desks without teacher assistance, and she designed word-processing tasks in similar ways. For example, pairs of children were required to write a summary of a story they had just read, using their reading book as both a source of information and a "dictionary" of sorts in which they could find the spelling of words they were most likely to need. With a

Figure 3.3b
Margaret Price (2nd Year)

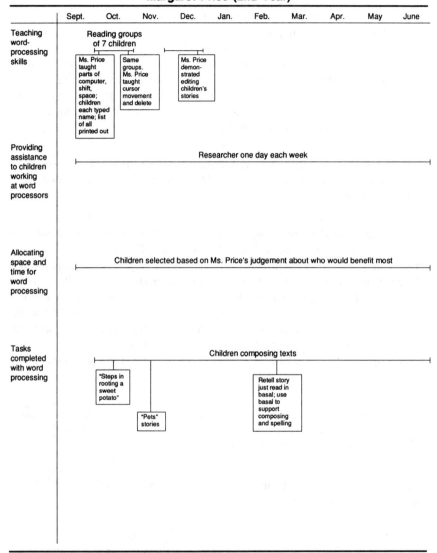

	Sept.	Oct.	Nov.	Dec.	Jan.	Feb.	Mar.	Apr.	May	June

Teaching word-processing skills

Reading groups of 7 children

Ms. Price taught parts of computer, shift, space; children each typed name; list of all printed out

Same groups. Ms. Price taught cursor movement and delete

Ms. Price demonstrated editing children's stories

Providing assistance to children working at word processors

Researcher one day each week

Allocating space and time for word processing

Children selected based on Ms. Price's judgement about who would benefit most

Tasks completed with word processing

Children composing texts

"Steps in rooting a sweet potato"

"Pets" stories

Retell story just read in basal; use basal to support composing and spelling

peer and reading book for support, children were unlikely to disrupt ongoing classroom routines with requests for help.

Allocating Time. Arrangements for computer turn-taking and scheduling raise questions of equity. Should all children have the same experiences with computers, with the same frequency and for the same duration? Margaret's procedures over two years reflected not only the evolution of her thinking about these matters, but also the shifting conditions in which she taught.

In both years of the project, children from one reading group completed writing tasks with the word processor, followed by children from another reading group. In the first year, this procedure resulted in children's having approximately equal amounts of time working with word processing although the tasks they completed there varied from more dictation for the "low" reading group to more composing of their own texts for the "high" reading group. In the second year, however, Margaret was less concerned about each child having an equal number of opportunities to use word processing.

> I don't worry as much about how many turns each kid gets. I'm no longer trying to keep track and making sure that everybody gets an equal turn. I just don't think that's important. . .. Whoever happens to be ready to write, writes.

Two changes in Margaret's ongoing practice in the second year altered her decisions about how often and in what ways to allocate time to use word processing. First, the introduction of the new basal reading series required that she develop ways to integrate the new reading material with her writing assignments and other subjects areas as she had done in the past. Second, the children assigned to her class, it was generally agreed, were "less mature" than the previous year's class—many were less able readers and writers, and many had been difficult to manage in past years. Margaret discussed the effects of these two changes on her allocation of time for word processing in the second year of the study.

> I'm not doing as much. A lot of this is because of the new reading series and because of the type of class that I have this year. It's kind of difficult. So I'm not doing as much and I don't feel bad about it.

Furthermore, she decided to allot time at the word processors to those whom she believed would benefit most.

> Some [children] I have to watch more carefully because they could be destructive and those children don't use it much. And the others that are better behaved and more capable on it use it more.

Word processing time was now allotted based on Margaret's judgement of a child's ability to benefit from its use.

In both years, Margaret allowed children to remain at the word processor until they had completed their tasks. When thinking about Tina's procedure for turn-taking, Margaret commented, "I like closure. If two children are sitting there writing their stories, then they [stay] there." For her the record-keeping involved in a system that interrupted a child's writing before he or she could complete a task was too cumbersome. She preferred the simplicity of finishing each task started, just as children would an assignment completed at their desks.

Word Processing Tasks. Finally, over the course of her first two years of work with word processing, Margaret altered her assessment of her children's abilities to identify and correct errors independently in their texts. Prior to working with word processing, she had no evidence that her second graders were capable of finding and correcting their own spelling and punctuation errors. What she saw instead were children reluctant to correct or perhaps even to acknowledge errors that required them to laboriously recopy entire texts. In her first year of work with word processing, she described what she had come to expect of the children.

> You see, they really don't [change their writing] that much. At that age they are happy with what they wrote down first and they don't want to change it.

When the children edited with word processing, however, Margaret found they were both willing and able to find and correct their errors. Using word processing made visible to Margaret the children's ability to find their own errors and edit their own work. Consequently, she altered her writing instruction to give the children greater responsibility and the necessary skills for editing their own writing.

Margaret initially perceived word processing as a tool to eliminate the need for children to recopy entire texts after errors were found. She hoped that this would "make writing and editing a less tedious chore for the children." But she found that the task of entering text into the word processor was a "tedious" task itself in that, for some, it simply "took too long." In response to this problem, she devised a series of alternative procedures for editing texts with word processing, all of which included an adult typing in the child's text. In some cases, the text was typed from the child's paper and pencil draft with initial errors included. The child and teacher and a peer then corrected the errors on the screen and printed a corrected final copy. In other cases, the child and teacher marked corrections on the paper and pencil draft, and then an adult typed in the corrected text and printed a final copy while the child and a peer observed. (See Figures 3.3a and 3.3b for the evolution of these and other editing procedures.)

The vignette that follows describes an event in the fall of the second year of Margaret's work with word processing. Each of the children in the reading group had composed a story about a pet. Two of the children had composed their stories using word processors and the other five children composed theirs using paper and pencils. When the stories were complete, Margaret Price took the group to the word processors for a lesson on editing. The focus of the lesson was both the literacy skills and the word processing skills needed to complete this task.

> Miss Price sits down in front of the keyboard and retrieves the first of the two stories written at the computer. Together, the group reads through the story, locating and correcting each error in punctuation, capitalization and spelling. She allows the children to identify errors first; she then points out those they have missed. For each correction made, she talks through and demonstrates the word processing procedure needed. For example, she places a great deal of emphasis on how to move the cursor to the proper location; although most of them have learned that the delete key will remove errors in the midst of text, few have become adept enough at moving the cursor to make this an efficient procedure for them.
>
> When the first story is corrected and printed out, the other is retrieved. The same procedure is followed: children look for and tell how to correct errors; Miss Price identifies and corrects errors they have missed; and Miss Price types in the corrections and prints out the final copy. For each of the five children who have composed their stories with pencil and paper, she types in their text as it appears on the paper and then the class edits their story on screen.

Initially, Margaret had corrected children's texts written at the word processor or asked an adult assistant to help the children edit their writing. But when the children edited with adult assistance at the word processors, they not only demonstrated that they could find many of their own errors, but, in some cases, became very interested in making certain that final copies were perfect. With this new information about the children's willingness and ability to find their own errors, Margaret altered her expectations of how much responsibility her children could take for editing their own texts. Subsequently, when children wrote at the word processor and saved their texts on a disk, they took the corrected paper printout to the computer with a partner. The author of the text sat at the computer and made the corrections indicated on the paper copy. The other child's task was to hold the printout, show the typist where the next correction was to be made, and to assist in locating necessary keys or solving word processing problems. Not only did Margaret give children greater responsibility for editing their own texts, she altered the social context in which editing was done. Rather than editing directed by an adult, adults coached children in the task, and children assisted other children.

Margaret shaped her implementation of word processing in ways that did not disrupt her ''organized routine'' and ''harmonious classroom atmosphere.'' She shaped the tool to fit her practices of instructing, providing assistance, allotting time, and assigning tasks. Over the two years, however, the tool helped to shape her practice. She took on primary responsibility for providing word processing instruction, altered her assessments of her children's ability to find and correct errors in their own writing, and altered the social context in which editing was accomplished.

Bev Winston

If Margaret Price's evolving uses of word processing could be called a process of winnowing, then Bev Winston's might be thought of as a process of exploring. Together Bev and her children explored the capabilities of the word processors and the children's capabilities as writers. Her tongue-in-cheek remark early in the first year of the project, "I guess when they get bored with playing with it I'll teach them to do something with it," betrayed her uncertainty about appropriate uses of word processing in a kindergarten writing program. There were no preestablished routines for teaching writing and no clear expectations about how much writing skill her children could achieve to build word-processing practices. The writing instruction that word processing would eventually support was in the process of evolving.

Over the course of two years, Bev created approaches to teaching writing as she created approaches to teaching word processing. The development of her use of word processing paralleled the development of her understanding of and confidence in her instruction of beginning writers. Her perceptions of children's early literacy, and her role in their development, shifted in response to her experiences with both word processing and writing. So too did the goals and practices that characterized the classroom culture in which her children learned to write.

Figures 3.4a and 3.4b provide an overview of the writing tasks and arrangements for providing time, assistance and instruction that Bev established as she introduced the children to both word processing and recording ideas in print.

For Bev, the question of practice that was immediately foregrounded was that of task. What should kindergarteners do with a word processor? What could they do? Following questions of task were questions of instruction. Bev explored freely—tasks and routines were devised, abandoned, or used sporadically as she gathered information from her observations of her children's capabilities as writers and users of word processing. These tasks were of four types: dictation to an adult, unsupervised exploration of the word processors, supervised exploration, and writing with an adult. Implicit in the terms that described each category were her arrangements for providing or not providing assistance to the children as they worked. Less obvious, yet clearly related to the tasks themselves, was the need for and provision of instruction in word processing skills. Consequently, Bev's answers to questions of task, assistance, and teaching evolved together.

Tasks, Assistance, and Teaching Skills. Bev's decisions about word processing were based, not only on her evolving practices and the culture of her classroom, but also on her perceptions of children's abilities as writers and users of technology. Prior to the introduction of word processing and the required writing curriculum, Bev had observed children copy words and sentences from the chalkboard, using pencil and paper. Looking back on her writing instruction in the previous year, Bev commented:

Figure 3.4a
Bev Winston (1st Year)

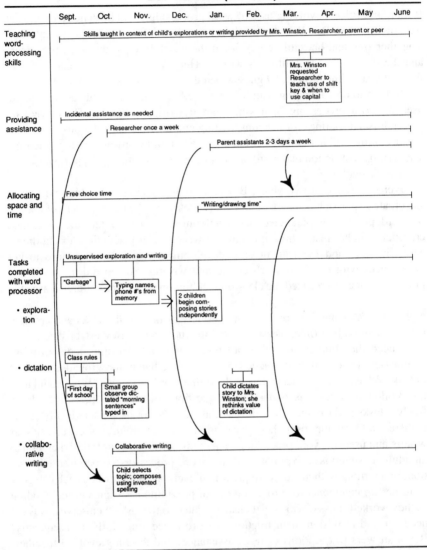

What I did before, considering what I do now, I guess was just very minimal. . . .
We started out just drawing pictures and then probably not until after Christmas did
we attempt any kind of writing. It was after they had a few, shall we say, letters
under their belts . . . beginning sounds so they could work with something.

Based on these observations and her "wait and see" approach to the new writing
curriculum and word processing, she planned to begin formal instruction on

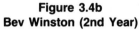

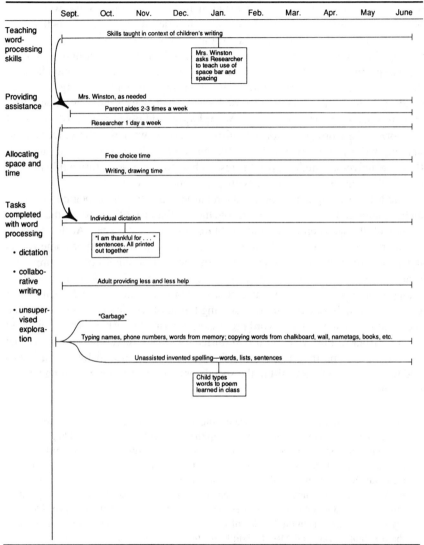

Figure 3.4b
Bev Winston (2nd Year)

letters, letter sounds, and writing in the middle of the year, as she always had. In keeping with this plan, she arranged for her children to "play" at the word processor, which involved primarily exploring the keys and watching to see the effects they could produce on the screen. At times an adult was present to oversee their explorations, but no efforts were made to instruct them in word processing or writing skills.

However, early in the school year, the children working at the word processor displayed interest and considerable skill in representing words that they could spell from memory or copy from material in the classroom. Some were even composing sentences and attempting to write brief stories using known words and invented spelling. Encouraged by their show of skill and enthusiasm for writing, Bev began instruction in handwriting and phonics earlier in the fall than she had planned. In addition to full group instruction in handwriting and phonics, Bev scheduled a 15- or 20-minute drawing/writing time daily. During this time, children drew pictures and composed single words or sentences about their drawings using invented spellings. Accordingly, additional time was scheduled for work at the word processor that mirrored the new writing activity. During the drawing/writing time, two to four children went to the computer with an adult (teacher, university student, parent, researcher) to compose a story while the rest of the children drew and wrote with paper and pencils.

The following vignette captures the relationship between the beginning writer and an adult coach as they worked together at the task of recording the child's ideas with the word processor during March of the second year. At this point in the year, some children were still dictating stories; most could type some words independently from memory and, with the help of an adult coach, compose a sentence using invented spelling (see Figure 3.4b). This event represents a midpoint in the range of Bev's use of word processing that falls between that of the child sitting beside the adult, observing the adult type in his or her words, and the child sitting alone at the word processor, entering his or her own text without adult assistance. Furthermore, it is significant in that it represents an activity that eventually became the major form of word-processing use in Bev's classroom and marked a significant shift in the social context surrounding beginning writing experiences.

[Mrs. S, the mother who assists each Thursday, arrives and Bev sends Sara and Kelly to the computers while she winds up the writing/drawing time and begins the morning exercises with the rest of the class. Mrs. S. sits between the girls and reminds each to type their names first. Kelly begins and Mrs. S. reminds her to use a capital 'K' and how to make a capital letter. Kelly is giggly today and is having more difficulty than usual deciding what she will write about. After a half-hearted effort to write about her new barrettes, and to compose the formula sentence 'I love my teacher,' she hits upon the idea of writing about her boyfriends. "I have four of them I think!" She and Mrs. S. laugh together over this and then set to work. "I liv" has been painstakingly spelled out by Kelly with Mrs. S. simply confirming her choices of letters as good ones. When Sara looks over from her work at the adjacent computer and announces that she will probably copy Kelly's idea (and presumably her text), Mrs. S. gently reminds the girls where each was in her sentence. Kelly makes a space and then types 'mi.']
     'mi'

Kelly: [She adds another space without being prompted and announces] I made a capital space! [She has by simultaneously pressing the shift key and the space bar.]

Coach: Do you know how to spell 'boyfriend'? [Kelly answers with gales of giggles, and still giggling, she continues to type.]
           bo

Coach: [elongating the end of the word] Boy-yuh.

Kelly: Yuh—yuh—yucky! [All three giggle together]

Coach: The next letter is 'y'. [Kelly finishes typing her sentence.]
           liv   mi   boyfnds

[Kelly types the names of each boyfriend from memory. Mrs. S tells Kelly that in addition to leaving a space between each name, she should follow each with a comma because she is "making a list". Kelly wants to follow the list with the words "are my boyfriends". She types 'rmi' as Mrs. S says the words aloud. Mrs. S. points out that she has already written the word "boyfriends" and asks if she can find it on the screen and copy it. Kelly can and does.]
           rmi   boyfnds

Coach: End that with a period. [She points at the correct key and Kelly presses it. Mrs. S asks Kelly to read what she has written and Kelly does so flawlessly. Together, Kelly and Mrs. S. follow the commands on the cue card attached to the printer. Mrs. S. reads off the keys and the number of times each should be pressed, and Kelly finds the keys and counts the keypresses. The printer begins to clatter away and Kelly runs to the back of the table to see her printout.]

Mrs. S and Kelly collaborated on the production of her written text. In addition, Mrs. S provided flexible, responsive literacy instruction in the context of the production of this text.

In Bev's first year, word processing was primarily used by the children as another material to experiment with. Children explored all the keys, discovering the effects each had on the screen display. Their final products were random strings of letters and numbers that Bev Winston and Barbara Gold called "garbage" (see Figure 3.4a). For a brief period at the beginning of the first year, children were invited to dictate stories to adults, who typed in their stories as they observed. When some children became impatient watching an adult at the keyboard and became capable of inventing their own spellings, children and coaches began collaboratively to compose stories. They shared responsibility for deciding what letters to use to represent their spoken words, but full responsibility for typing remained with the child. Dictation was then abandoned, and free exploration and collaborative writing were the dominant uses of word processing.

Late in the spring of the first year, one of the more proficient writers asked Bev to type his dictated story. As she typed in the story, which was both longer and more complex than any he had previously composed alone or in collaboration with a coach, she found many opportunities to extend his writing skills. At this point, Bev reassessed her decision about word processing tasks and the methods of providing instruction and assistance with word processing. Looking back, it was clear to her that, in the first year, with no clear idea of kindergarten children's capabilities as writers or users of word processing, adults had followed children's leads supporting them in their explorations or collaborative composition of texts. During this time Bev was carefully collecting information about what she could reasonably expect of the children and what roles adults could play in the children's growth as writers. Based on her observations, in the second year Bev shifted the use of word processing toward purposeful tasks clearly designated as "writing," with more direct intervention and instruction from the coaches (see Figure 3.4b). At the beginning of the second year, Bev arranged for parents to be present for the first 20 minutes of the class day to take two to three children's dictation or coach them as they wrote with the word processors while the rest drew and wrote with pencils and paper. In addition, the researcher or Bev acted as coaches at the word processors during free choice activity times, and children continued to work alone or with friends at the machines when no adults were present to assist.

By January of the second year, while watching over the shoulder of one of her children composing enthusiastically with a friend, Bev commented to the researcher:

> We did it right this year. Lots of dictation. Some are still just doing dictation. We held off writing [independently and with an adult coach] until they were ready.

Dictation not only provided opportunities for coaching in word processing and literacy skills, it also shaped the children's perceptions of the tool. The presence of an adult other than their teacher in the classroom, the fact that Bev made certain that every child had regular opportunities to work at the word processor with an adult ("Did you go to the computer with Mrs. S yet?"), and the very language used to invite the children to the word processor at these times ("It's your turn to write a story") set their work at the word processors apart from the children's independent activities during other parts of the day. These signals marked this as a purposeful activity and an important activity in which an adult invested her undivided attention, setting it apart from many other activities that did not require invitation and were not so carefully attended by an adult. Not only were almost all of the children's efforts at these times purposeful attempts to record meanings, the expectation that word processing was always to be used for this purpose seemed to be building. In the early fall, children began composing their own words, sentences, and stories using invented spelling.

Although children's greater success in the second year may be attributed to the fact that they had experienced word processing first as a tool used by adults to record their words rather than as a machine to explore on their own, as they had in the previous year, it is likely that they were influenced as well by Bev's stronger emphasis in her curriculum on words and how they are recorded. Embedded in her routine of recording daily sentences on the chalkboard, for example, were impromptu lessons on phonics, capitalization, punctuation, spacing, and the process by which one might decide what letters to use to represent a particular word. Bev's increased emphasis on writing skills earlier in the kindergarten year was certainly attributable to the district-wide mandate to teach writing and to the writing workshops she had been required to attend during the previous year. But some of this change in the learning opportunities that she provided was the result of her own observations of her children's writing with word processing. Early in her first year of work with word processing she saw that children who struggled to draw individual strokes in order to form letters, composed full sentences and short stories using invented spelling when writing with the word processor. Composing skills that had been masked by children's difficulties in recording letters with pencils on paper were revealed to Bev when they wrote with the word processor. As the children's use of the tool revealed their capacities to represent words in print, Bev's choice of tasks with word processing and her provision of assistance and instruction shifted to accommodate her growing understanding of her children's writing development.

Allocation of Time. Time for word processing was dependent, among other things, upon the vagaries of a public kindergarten schedule. Early dismissals, conference days, field trips, and programs disrupt half-day kindergarten schedules even more seriously than they do regular full day schedules. Unsupervised exploration, which took place during free play periods when children explored and set their own tasks with traditional kindergarten materials, occurred whenever free play was not preempted because of schedule changes. Coached writing and supervised exploration took place whenever an extra adult was available or when Bev could free herself from other responsibilities.

Bev kept a mental tally of who had not worked with an adult at the computer recently, and was certain every child was invited, but not forced, to participate regularly in one of the supervised uses of word processing. Once a child started work at a word processor, no other child was permitted to interrupt. Children worked through opening exercises and group meetings if necessary. Only when the class had a formal lesson, or left the room for music or gym, did children have to end their turns.

Like the children in Margaret Price's class, Bev's children demonstrated writing skill at the word processor that was frequently masked by the difficulties they experienced when writing with handdrawn pencil strokes. The introduction of word processing provided both teachers with new evidence about their children's capabilities. Both responded to this new information by altering their writing instruction. In addition, Bev's observations led her to create a setting for learning to write that included regular sessions in which a novice writer was paired with an adult writer to jointly compose texts. The effect was the creation of a social context for learning to write that differed significantly from that of traditional full class writing instruction. A similar context evolved out of a different set of circumstances in Barbara Gold's classroom.

Barbara Gold

As we have seen, one of Barbara Gold's fundamental goals for her children was that they experience success as learners in general and as writers in particular. For Barbara, the importance of success and the perceived complexity of the word processor as a writing tool brought issues of assistance and appropriate writing tasks to the foreground. Her initial decision to bring children to the word processor to dictate stories to an adult coach not only allowed children to experience success in their first encounters with written language, but also created opportunities to instruct children in word-processing and writing skills. Like Bev Winston, Barbara's answers to questions of task, assistance, and instruction were interdependent, as Figure 3.5 indicates. Particular tasks required particular kinds of assistance and instruction.

Assistance, Tasks, and Teaching Skills. Through the first half of the school year, Barbara or the researcher assigned to her room sat with each child at the word processor as he or she dictated a story. The purpose was for children to see their words represented in print and begin to "make the connection" between speech and print as the adult typed their sentences. Children were prepared for these sessions in full class discussion that served as both stimulus and rehearsal for the stories they would eventually dictate. Frequently, children had a drawing or art project that they used at the computer to serve as a prompt for their dictation or reminder of the prewriting discussions. The stack of children's art work next to the computer served as a waiting list of children who had not yet had a turn to complete the writing project. When every child in the class had dictated a story on the assigned topic, all of the stories were bound in a book or displayed in the classroom or hallway. A new topic was then introduced, and a similar procedure followed. In this way, each child successfully created a text that was produced in perfectly printed form. However, Barbara soon found that far more than "seeing their words in print" was being accomplished during dictation sessions. Important literacy and word processing skills were also being learned.

In the following excerpt, Barbara worked with Sung, who was just learning English, as he dictated his first story at the word processor. As they worked together at the word processor, their interactions provided opportunities for Sung

Figure 3.5
Barbara Gold

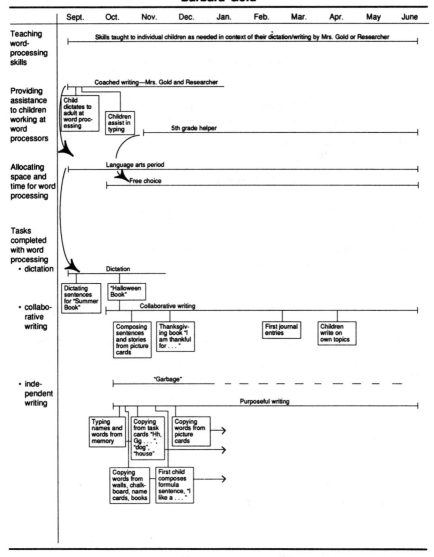

	Sept.	Oct.	Nov.	Dec.	Jan.	Feb.	Mar.	Apr.	May	June
Teaching word-processing skills	|—	Skills taught to individual children as needed in context of their dictation/writing by Mrs. Gold or Researcher								—|
Providing assistance to children working at word processors		Coached writing—Mrs. Gold and Researcher								
		Child dictates to adult at word processing	Children assist in typing	5th grade helper						
Allocating space and time for word processing		Language arts period								
		Free choice								
Tasks completed with word processing										
• dictation		Dictation								
		Dictating sentences for "Summer Book"	"Halloween Book"							
• collaborative writing			Collaborative writing							
			Composing sentences and stories from picture cards	Thanksgiving book "I am thankful for . . ."			First journal entries	Children write on own topics		
• independent writing			"Garbage"							
			Purposeful writing							
		Typing names and words from memory	Copying from task cards "Hh, Gg . . .", "dog", "house"	Copying words from picture cards						
			Copying words from walls, chalkboard, name cards, books	First child composes formula sentence, "I like a . . ."						

to learn, not only word-processing skills, but literacy skills in the context of his own piece of writing. Barbara began by asking Sung to tell something about himself. Getting no response, she asked a series of questions about his home and family. His one-word response, ''Dog,'' was then the basis for a jointly composed ''story.''

Sung: Dog

Coach: Your dog? Do you have a dog? Or would you like to have a dog? [pause]
You'd like to have one? Give me a sentence to put down.

Sung: Dog.

Coach: OK, that's a word. Can you tell me in a whole sentence?

Sung: It is a dog.

Coach: It is a dog? OK. Can you help me make a capital letter? [Sung nods] OK,
you push this [shift key] down and I'll push the 'i'.

[Coach types the 'i' then the 't'.]
         It

Coach: OK, that spells 'It'. Can you give me another word?

[Sung presses the space bar, Coach types 'is', then points to the word on the
screen.]

Coach: This says 'is'. Can you give me another space?
         It is

[Sung presses space bar.]

Coach: Can you make a little letter 'a'? Can you find an 'a' on the keyboard?

[Sung searches and finds it, then reaches for the shift key with his free hand.]

Coach: No, not with a capital.

[Sung types 'a'.]
         It is a

Coach: [pointing to each word on the screen as she reads] "It is a . . . ." Now I
need another space.

[Sung presses space bar.]

Coach: OK, "It is a . . . ." what?

Sung: It is a . . .

Coach: You said, "Dog." Do you know how to spell dog?

[Sung does not respond, so Coach says each letter name as she types the word
'dog'.]

Coach: D . . . . O . . . . G. Now when we come to the end of a sentence, we put
a dot or a period. Would you like to put the dot?
         It is a dog

[Coach points to the correct key and Sung types it. She goes on to explain how to space between sentences.]

Coach: Now, first off, you put two spaces.

[Sung presses the space bar twice, using two hands at once.]

Coach: Super!

In a short time period, Barbara questioned, supported, and responded as Sung composed. She typed his words as he spoke them and enlisted his help in holding down the shift key and making spaces. Although this event took place during the first month of first grade, she addressed the difference between a word and a sentence, introduced the conventions of spacing between words and using periods to mark the ends of sentences, modeled using spaces and using capital letters to mark the beginning of a sentence, and read and reread his piece to help him recall his place in his thought. They talked about his idea, clarified whether he was talking about a dog he owned or one that he wished he owned. Only her instruction in the use of the space bar and shift key were specific to writing with word processing. All her other interactions with Sung could have occurred if they had been working with pencil and paper. However, when writing with word processing, Sung had access to prolonged and personalized interactions at every writing session. (Sung's experience is further considered in Chapter 5.)

The perceived mechanical complexity of the word processor as a writing tool led Barbara to create a context in which experienced writers were paired with beginning writers. This learning context was available at no other time in the class day. The presence of an experienced writer significantly altered the context in which the children first composed stories in the kindergarten and first grade classrooms, and composed and edited in the second grade and to a lesser extent the third grade. The mature writer enriched these experiences by modeling, providing instruction in skills as they became necessary in the context of the child's writing, and helping the child maintain focus on ideas to be represented without getting lost in procedures for recording those ideas. Furthermore, the mechanical procedures and special keys used to record certain print conventions such as capitalization and spacing became occasions for discussion and on-the-spot instruction in literacy skills.

Allocation of Time. Barbara's decisions about when word processing would be used were not only dependent upon the tasks she wanted the children to complete, the necessity of providing adult assistance in order to complete successfully a particular task, and the availability of adult coaches. For example, implicit in the decision to arrange for the children to dictate stories is the need for a mature writer. Consequently, time for dictating stories was arranged when Barbara was free of other classroom responsibilities or the researcher was scheduled to be in the classroom. Similarly, when time was available in the children's schedule but no adult coaches were available, the computer was available as a free choice activity when other work was completed. At this time children either worked independently, copying words and letters from task cards, the chalkboard, or posters, or composed stories with the help of a fifth-grade coach. Turns for word-processing use during the language arts period were regulated. Each child had an equal number of opportunities to participate in the assigned writing tasks. Word-processing use at other times of the day was determined by the children's choice.

Like the children in Margaret's and Bev's classes, children in Barbara's class encountered some of their earliest writing experiences in a social context in which a child and a mature writer wrote collaboratively. Although adult coaches were provided because teachers and researchers initially believed that young children would need help with the technical aspects of word processing, most children mastered the necessary features of the system relatively quickly, as we demonstrate in Chapter 4. But the adult coach stayed on to contribute to the process of composing, encoding, revising, and editing, thus significantly altering the social context surrounding early literacy experiences and the opportunities available to children to learn to write.

In this altered context for learning to write, Barbara's perceptions of her children's abilities to manage the word processor, and her interpretations of word processing as a tool for beginning writers, shifted. She began to expect more and different kinds of participation from her children as they completed writing tasks. Soon after the writing event described above, coaches moved their chairs away from the keyboards and the children moved their chairs in and took over much more of the typing. As the tool changed hands, so too did the sense of ownership and responsibility for the text. Soon writing tasks changed as well. Dictation gave way to collaborative composition and then to children writing with occasional prompting from the coach. The change that took place in the ways Barbara deployed word processing over the course of a school year is best described as a careful, measured evolution mediated by ongoing reflection on practice. Later in this chapter, we return to look more closely at the process by which Barbara's uses of word processing and thinking about learning to write evolved.

Debby Perrone

If the changes in Barbara Gold's practice could be described as evolutionary, then changes in Debby Perrone's uses of word processing might be characterized as cumulative. Debby's methods of providing group instruction were slowly replaced by more individual instruction. But in every other way—assistance to the children, allocation of time, and assignment of writing tasks—Debby accumulated practices. That is, she built upon rather than replaced the word-processing practices that had come before. In this manner, word processing began to pervade her class day, not only in actual time when in use, but also in impact on more and more of her curriculum.

Figure 3.6
Debby Perrone

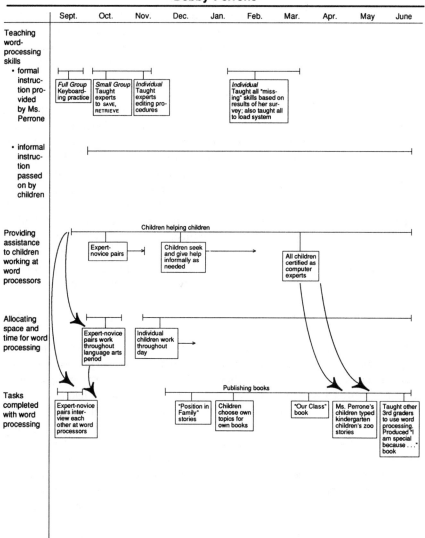

Teaching Word-Processing Skills. For Debby, decisions about instruction and assistance with word processing required immediate attention, as Figure 3.6 indicates.

Debby was an avid writer and enthusiastic teacher of writing, and she planned to have her children do a great deal of writing. It was important, therefore, that they learn to enter text with relative ease and speed. For this reason, Debby chose to teach basic keyboarding techniques (Kahn, 1988; Kahn, Avicolli, & Lodise, 1988) as well as procedures for entering, printing, and saving text. Instruction in additional procedures, such as forcing pages, numbering pages, and indenting, was provided as needed in the context of her writing curriculum. For example, when she taught the children to compose and format a ''friendly letter'' to a teacher who had just had a baby, she and the children learned to indent on the word processor in the context of a meaningful writing task.

Debby's methods of providing instruction became increasingly more individualized through the year. As we have seen, initial keyboarding instruction and practice were provided to the class as a full group. Shortly thereafter, she taught the group of 12 computer experts to save and retrieve files. Later in the fall, she provided individual instruction in editing procedures to each of the computer experts. As the ''experts'' passed their knowledge along to their classmates, word-processing skills spread informally through the class. In January, Debby took an informal survey of her children's abilities to perform basic word-processing skills. On the basis of this information, she met with several children each morning before opening exercises until she had tutored each child in skills that he or she had missed or forgotten. Over the course of the year, Debby's initial methods of providing instruction shifted from full group to instruction tailored to needs of small groups and finally, to individual children.

Providing Assistance. The ability to instruct and help a peer was an important goal in itself in Debby's classroom. Peer assistance also ensured that all of Debby's children could productively use word processing as soon as possible. Debby's practice of selecting and training computer experts to provide assistance to their classmates was patterned after Tina Santori's procedure developed in the previous year. By spring, however, each of Debby's children had been ''certified'' as a computer expert, so that every child was capable of helping and expected to help classmates. Peer tutoring was extended to include teaching other third grade classes to use word processing. Debby planned a writing project in which every child in the three-space classroom contributed a page to a book that recorded what was special about third grade and what was special about each of the authors. Finally, at the end of the year, Debby and a kindergarten teacher paired third grade typists/coaches with kindergarten authors to produce a book that documented the kindergarteners' trip to the zoo.

In this steady cumulative fashion, teaching and helping others to use word processing spread beyond the walls of her classroom and beyond her grade level. No longer a means but now an end in itself, providing assistance to others had built steadily on the foundation of her expert–novice pairs in which children learned to give and receive help in a productive and supportive manner.

Allocation of Time. Just as the practice of peer helping expanded in a cumulative fashion, so too did the allocation of time for word processing.

Initially the children in Debby's language arts class used word processing to complete their assigned tasks during the morning language arts period. Early in the school year, Debby's children demanded more time to use the word processors than their language arts periods permitted, and children in her homeroom who were assigned to other teachers for language arts were eager to learn to use word processing like their classmates. In a research meeting in early October, Debby opened her remarks by declaring that:

> I wish that all I had to be teaching right now was word processing because I love it and I'm excited about it and . . . the enthusiasm among the kids is something you can't put a lid on! . . . It's like breaking my heart every day when I have to say, 'No, you can't go to the computer because [we have to do something else].'

Debby responded by permitting children from both her language arts classes and homeroom to work at the word processors before school, during class meetings, movies, recess, social studies, and science, in addition to the language arts period.

The net effect was that the activity of writing began to pervade the school day. With writing liberated from its language arts time, Debby and her children devised uses for word processing at almost all times of day and for a wide range of purposes. Eric even found a way to make his request to write during an art class seem appropriate. This example illustrates the child's perception of appropriate times to write at the word processor and the lengths to which he would go to have the opportunity to do so. A researcher wrote in fieldnotes:

> Sharon Cohen, a university student, was conducting a lesson on American Indian art. Eric had just completed his project and asked Ms. Cohen if he could go to the computer. When she hesitated, he added, "Because I want to write a story . . . about Indians." When Ms. Cohen said that he'd have to ask Ms. Perrone, Eric went to her and said, "Ms. Cohen wants to know if I can use the computer."

Permission, of course, was granted, and writing was introduced into yet another part of the class day.

Word-Processing Tasks. As writing with word processing came to pervade Debby's class day, the number and diversity of writing tasks grew as well. To the writing tasks already assigned in language arts class, Debby added larger and larger projects such as book-length stories by individual children, books co-authored by the entire class, and, as described above, a book co-authored by all children in the shared classroom space. Children generated their own ideas for writing with word processing as well, just as Eric had done. By the second month of school, children had opportunities to write daily journal entries with word processing and even to take spelling tests there. New word-processing tasks were added to old, just as additional times to use word-processing were accumulated, and additional ways of sharing word processing expertise were devised.

In late October, Debby recounted what she regarded as a highly significant event in the growth and spread of word-processing skills and use in her classroom. The researcher recorded the following notes on their conversation:

Ms. Perrone greeted me with a big smile and told me that the neatest thing happened yesterday. She was absent and when she returned to school this morning there were printouts in her basket, which meant that someone had been able to get the computers working in her absence. She asked the children how this had happened and they told her that Paul had taken care of it. Apparently they had asked the substitute teacher whether they would be able to use the computers and she said that she did not know what to do with them. At that point Paul volunteered to get them started. Ms. Perrone told me with great pride that he turned the computers on, booted the Bank Street Writer, loaded in the printer codes, and during the morning helped four different children print their work.

Debby elaborated on this in her journal.

This is a kid who is NOT a computer expert. He, however, loves the computer and any free minute he has he wants to write a story. I taught him how to boot the machines and a few other things that I've only showed him and he remembers everything! . . . I was really excited to know that the kids didn't have to miss the computer while I was out sick. At this point, my computers are on every single minute of every single day. . . . I am trying to expose as many kids to it as I possibly can. Kids in my homeroom are being coached by kids in my Language Arts groups. Also kids in my spelling [group] are taking pretests and posttests on it and they love it too! Again, anyone in my spelling [group] who also has me for Language Arts is coaching the kids with no experience. . . . I feel that [word processing] should NOT be wasted for one minute during the day, especially since all the kids want to learn to use [it].

Over the course of the year, word-processing use continued to grow in this steady cumulative fashion.

The decisions Debby made about who would use word processing, how time for word processing would be allocated, and the tasks to be completed with word processing led to cumulative changes in the kinds and amount of writing done in her classroom. These changes were clearly related to the introduction of word processing, but not the direct result of its introduction. The impact of word processing on the classroom culture was mediated by Debby's—and her children's—ever-expanding interpretations of writing and word processing and the ways in which instructional time could be allocated.

Tina Santori

The word-processing tasks Tina Santori assigned and the ways she allotted time and space for word processing varied considerably over time. As Figures 3.7a and 3.7b also indicate, however, her methods of providing word-processing instruction and assistance remained relatively stable.

Speaking from her considerable experience using word processing and other software in her classroom, Tina summed up the impact of using word processing on her teaching.

> [The] . . . way that it has changed for me is the numbers . . . the amount of computers, the amount of time I can get the children on.

Tina's insights are supported by the observations we made in her classroom over two years. They indicate that the culture of Tina's classroom remained relatively constant, and the decisions she made about initial deployment of word processing remained in use.

Teaching Word-Processing Skills. Over time, Tina's decisions about teaching word-processing skills and grouping children for instruction were consistent. Changes were of quantity, pacing, and sequencing of instruction rather than of content of instruction. Looking back at the end of the first year, Tina had been pleased with the outcomes of her full group skill lessons and found that the use of the video equipment and individual keyboards had been particularly effective. She used the same instructional methods the following year and taught the same skills, which were selected to help the children master the technology of word processing. Tina also continued occasionally to teach procedures such as "COPY" and "SEARCH and REPLACE," which demonstrated special capabilities of the software and "really hooked" the children on word processing.

On the other hand, Tina expressed dissatisfaction during the first year of the project with the quality and amount of writing that the children produced with word processing. She reported in group meetings and interviews that, at some points during the year, the children's progress in writing was impeded by using word processing. During the fall of the first year of the project, for example, Tina had commented in a group meeting:

> To tell you the truth, right now the computers are really a burden. [They're] not helping the children with their writing.

Our observations of fourth graders during this same time period provide supporting evidence for Tina's perceptions—before they learned keyboard familiarity, using word processing significantly interfered with fourth graders' fluency and clearly did not "help them" with their writing. (This finding is discussed in much greater detail in Chapters 4 and 5.) In an interview at the end of the first

Figure 3.7a
Tina Santori (1st Year)

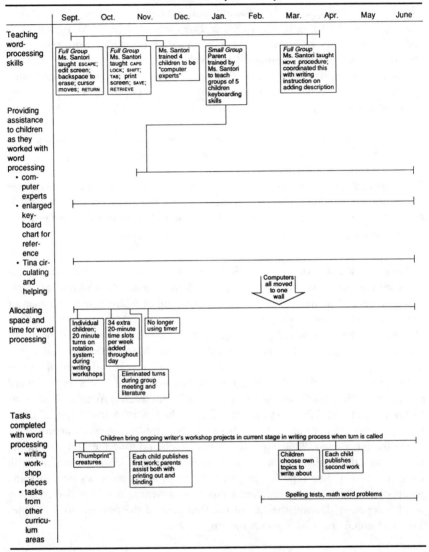

year, Tina elaborated on her assessment of the impact of word processing on the children's writing.

There was SOME improvement, but I can't say it was what I had hoped for from them.

Figure 3.7b
Tina Santori (2nd Year)

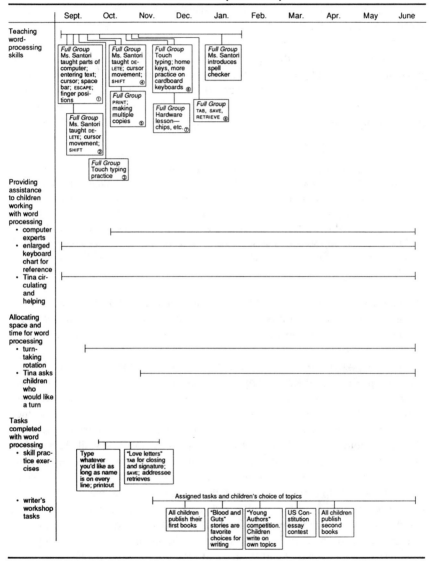

Tina had rightly observed that, early in the year, too much of her fourth graders' attention was focused on the mechanical procedures of using hardware and software rather than on their writing. The following year she decided to increase the number of word-processing skill lessons and to present these to the children earlier in the year (see Figure 3.7b). Keyboarding skills were interspersed among the skill lessons rather than taught following skills lessons by a parent, as they had been the first year. Word-processing instruction that had been spread over four to five months during the first year of the study was compressed into the first two months during the second year.

Another change in Tina's word-processing instruction was the way she related it to instruction in the writing process. During the first year she taught word-processing skills and the writing process simultaneously. Following word-processing skills lessons, children were given opportunities to practice the new skills in the context of a writing assignment. In an interview at the end of the first year, she shared her thoughts about more effective ways to teach word processing:

> In the beginning I was really trying to get them into the writing process. I think I would let them do more play. I would let them do their names—I didn't know they were doing this but I found it on their disks. They put their names all the way down the screen. That seems to be one thing all of them wanted to do. . . . [But] what I was trying to do was to put the two—the writing process and the computer—together, and they weren't ready for that. So I think I would just continue the writing process, but as a separate entity from the computer and then combine [them].

During the second year, Tina followed through on her reflections about the need to teach writing and word processing separately, although she continued to use the methods of instruction that she had found successful the previous year.

Providing Assistance. Tina's instruction was designed to equip her children to use word processing independently, although she circulated among the children whenever she was not conducting writing conferences or small group lessons. Throughout her lessons, children were reminded that they would be "on their own" and that they needed to attend carefully. Tina provided assistance to her children in both years of the study by recording on a keyboard wall chart each of the word-processing procedures as she taught them. Within the first few months of each school year, Tina also trained and certified computer experts who would be available to help their classmates with problems and load the machines daily throughout the school year. Training and certification were formal procedures in which Tina met individually with the trainees and arranged for them to practice in preparation for the certification test she would administer. Those who passed were awarded a badge and certificate, and their names were displayed for all to see.

Over the course of each year, children continued to refer to the enlarged keyboard chart when necessary and were helped by Tina when she was available. Computer experts were called upon less often as the class as a whole became more skilled and as many children became capable of providing help to one another. Children often sought assistance from classmates working at neighboring computers. It was not uncommon, for example, for a child to ask, "Where's the SHIFT?'' or ''How do you get this thing to move up there?'' and for a peer to reach over and press the necessary key. Informal help from peers continued through both years .

Allocation of Space and Time. In Tina's busy three-space classroom and tightly scheduled class day, both space and time were precious commodities. Although her classroom was the same size as all of the others, she had four or five computer systems with printers operating in her classroom during most of the 2-year period. Allocation of computer equipment was jointly decided by project members. Researchers and teachers had agreed that fourth graders would need more equipment, because they would write longer pieces and need more computer time. Over the course of two years, Tina tried a number of different methods of allotting time and arranging classroom space. She initially clustered computers together so that she could attend to several children at once. Later she moved the computers to reduce distractions or to meet children's needs for either assistance or privacy.

In response to children's interests and enthusiasm about word processing, Tina increased the number of time slots posted on the turn-taking chart by making word processing available for writing before school, during recess and lunch, and during group meeting and literature times. She thus provided 34 20-minute turns each week in addition to the regularly scheduled turns during language arts period. The newly scheduled times worked out well with the instructional schedule except for those scheduled during group meetings and literature. When children used the computers at those times, it was difficult for both the children at the word processors and the children sitting near them in the large group activities to concentrate on their tasks. Furthermore, when she conducted full group lessons, Tina preferred to know where all the children were and to have all of them work directly with her.

By November of the first year, Tina no longer had children time their 20-minute turns, since they had found it too difficult to remember to set the timer. The rotation system for turn taking remained, but children were permitted to work for longer than 20 minutes if they wished. This procedure was satisfactory, because most children tired in about 20 to 25 minutes anyway. During the second year, regulated turn taking was used when the children were completing the assigned word-processing exercises described below. Otherwise, Tina often simply asked which children were interested in using the word processors each day, and then selected children to take turns at the machines.

Tasks to be Completed with Word Processing. The nature of the writing tasks children completed with word processing reflected the relationship Tina constructed between teaching word-processing skills and teaching the writing process. In the first year, she embedded children's first word-processing experiences in the context of a writing task. Children practiced word-processing skills as they composed or transcribed text from a paper-and-pencil draft of a "writers' workshop'' assignment. Having found this unsatisfactory because it was too difficult for children to learn word-processing skills and writing skills simultaneously, Tina devised specific practice exercises for the second year to develop the word-processing skills she taught in a series of full group lessons. Many of these exercises incorporated some of the "unofficial" play activities she had discovered her children doing during the previous year, such as repeating their names and writing messages to one another, but also gave the children opportunities to learn the basic skills of word processing.

During the second year, word-processing practice exercises such as those described above were separated from the writing assignments that children also completed with word processing. When it was a child's turn to use a word processor for writing (rather than for learning word processing itself), for example, the child could bring a partially completed paper-and-pencil draft of an ongoing writing project and transcribe it onto the word processor and then continue to compose. Or the child could choose to begin a new piece of writing by composing directly at the computer. Some children chose to skip their turns if they occurred when the writers were involved in paper-and-pencil compositions. This avoided having to drop one piece and begin a new topic at the word processor, or having to use computer-turn time to transcribe an already-composed text. Some children chose to use their turns to transcribe completed paper and pencil drafts in order to produce clean final copies.

As the following vignette reveals, Sean chose the common option of beginning a new topic when he took his turn at the word processor rather than continuing with his ongoing writing workshop piece. Sean's experience was similar to those of many of the children in his class: he chose a popular topic—horror movie sequels—which attracted the attention of several classmates. A very good typist and a relatively fluent writer, Sean was also skilled in managing the word processing system, and on the occasion below, he was asked by classmates to demonstrate the use of the spelling checker that Ms. Santori had taught the class to use the previous week.

[Sean sits down at the computer and gets right to work. He enters the title of today's horror tale and moves immediately to the action.]

Carie II Wars   by Sean

One day Carie blew up Kansas. She had a lot of fun . . .

[A small crowd begins to form. Two boys, Jake and Sammy, watch as Sean adds to the piece.]

Now she is a demon. Right now she is arguing with the devil. She is saying the devil is to nice.

[Sean uses the spelling checker, a device new to all of them, at the request of his audience. The word search identifies 'Carie' as a possible incorrect spelling. The group decides that it is spelled with two r's. Sean makes the necessary changes.]

[Sean continues writing with many crowd-pleasing sentences about fireballs and screaming. His completed story is indeed, in his words, 'gross, terrifying and evil.' Sean ends his tale by converting all the characters to 'the good side.']

[Sammy returns to help and watch Sean operate the spelling checker once more. When they find no errors, they print the document together.]

The writing task Sean elected allowed him to begin and complete a composition at one sitting. Assistance, in this case, was not necessary. In fact, he was asked by several others to demonstrate a word processing skill that the class was just learning. Sean's peers contributed to his writing indirectly as an audience that appreciated as much violence and gore as possible.

Other writing tasks that children in Tina's class completed with word processing were assignments in other curriculum areas. Children took spelling tests, completed vocabulary exercises, and wrote word problems for math class using the word processors. Some children even requested to do their homework assignments on the word processors when they had free time during the day.

Overall, Tina's practice remained the most stable of all of the teachers in the study. Changes in her work with word processing occurred when she responded to observed needs in her children, such as the difficulty of composing and learning word-processing skills simultaneously, or the need for more frequent turns to use the word processors. At these points the ongoing culture of her classroom and her work with word processing were in dynamic interrelationship, and changes in practice occurred. But in many ways, initial practices and the ongoing culture of the classroom remained stable.

INTERRELATIONSHIPS OF CULTURE
AND WORD PROCESSING: A CLOSER LOOK

In each of the five classrooms where we observed, classroom culture and teachers' ongoing practices influenced the ways they designed opportunities for children to learn and use word processing. In short, teachers shaped the tool. But, as we have seen, using word processing also shaped classroom cultures in ways that ultimately altered many of the learning opportunities made available to children. Over time, children had opportunities to learn to write differently, as we will see in detail in the following chapters. Furthermore as the preceding vignettes and discussions indicate, the effects of classroom culture and word processing were dynamically interactive over time—initial uses of word processing were shaped by the existing classroom culture, but, over time, working with word processing also altered classroom culture. Altered culture then shaped new ways of teaching and using word processing. The process was continuous and compounded on an ongoing basis. As we have seen, however, the extent of the interaction between classroom culture and word-processing use differed from classroom to classroom.

The evolution of the coaching relationship and the altered learning oppor-

Figure 3.8
Barbara Gold
Interrelationships of Classroom Culture
and Word-Processing Use Over Time

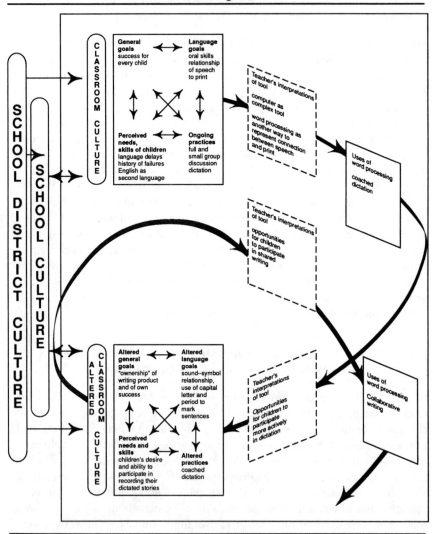

tunities in Barbara Gold's first-grade classroom provide a clear example of the interactive effects of classroom culture and word processing. Figure 3.8 illustrates the dynamic interrelationships of culture, teachers' perceptions and interpretations, and word processing use over time.

Critical features of Barbara's classroom culture were her goals—that children understand that their spoken words can be represented in print, and that every child be successful and gain confidence as a writer; the perceived needs of her children—extensive oral and written language experiences and successes to counteract a history of school failure; and her ongoing practices—using a language experience approach that emphasized speech-print connections, and the Peabody Language Development program, which focused on oral language and concept development. The critical characteristics of word processing were, ironically, its perceived mechanical difficulty as well as the ease with which it produced and placed perfectly formed letters and its potential as a new tool for recording children's speech in print. But these were not separate influences. They interacted, each shaping and being shaped by the other.

Barbara had determined that the capability of word processing to produce perfectly formed and correctly positioned letters could be used to support her goal that all of her children, even those for whom printing was laborious and fraught with mistakes, feel successful as writers. However, the perceived difficulty for 6-year-olds of using a technically complex word-processing system made it appear likely to Barbara Gold and to researchers that children would meet failures more often than successes at the word processor. For the teacher, this perception called into question the capability of word processing to boost a child's self-concept as a writer and precluded the option of sending children to work alone at the word processor to take advantage of its capability of producing perfect print that they could not produce with paper and pencil.

Initially, an alternative use of word processing was found within the teacher's repertoire of ongoing practices—the child-dictated story. In reading groups as well as in full class meetings, children dictated sentences and full "stories" to the teacher, who recorded their words on chart paper or the chalkboard. By choosing dictation as the child's first experience with word processing, the teacher both solved the problem of ensuring success and met several important goals. The adult could handle any mechanical difficulties, while pointing out the connection between the child's spoken ideas and the text on the screen. Every child was successful every time he or she dictated at the word processor. It is possible that either the characteristics of word processing alone, or the ongoing teaching practices in this classroom, might have led to the selection of dictation as a use of word processing. In this particular classroom, both Barbara's classroom culture and her interpretation of the capabilities and limitations of word processing interacted to contribute to her decision to use word processing for dictated stories.

Word-processing use was both determined by ongoing practices and the teacher's goals, and it altered ongoing practice in significant ways. The very practice of having children dictate stories at the word processor was further mediated by the teacher's perceptions of children's work at the word processor and her evolving goals for the children. Whereas dictated stories were consistent with the first-grade teacher's ongoing teaching practices, this use of word processing seemed to hold less promise for helping children achieve positive self-concepts about themselves as writers. Not even the production of a flawlessly printed record of his or her dictated words could lead a child to feel truly successful as a writer if he or she did not participate in some way in the production of that printed story. It was important to the teacher that the child feel a sense of ownership of the stories dictated at the word processor so that he or she might feel legitimate pride in them.

Based on her observations of her children dictating stories at the word processor, Barbara's perception of the word processor shifted somewhat. She began to see it as a writing tool uniquely suited for sharing between teacher and child. The child could successfully participate in recording ideas by typing letters or words he or she knew, as well as holding down the shift key, pressing the space bar, or adding the period at the end of each sentence while the adult performed the rest of the task. The keyboard could be reached and the screen remain easily visible to both participants without shifting the position of the writers or the writing surface, as must be done with paper and pencil. The uniformity of print left no record of who had actually "written" the most. But perhaps more importantly, the lure of the keyboard that invites a child to touch, the appeal of using a tool associated with adults, as well as the ease of producing letters on the screen, made it almost impossible for a child to be excluded from actively participating in recording his or her story. Dictation gave way to a new writing event, collaborative writing, in which the child was encouraged to type familiar letters or words, as well as hold down the shift key, press the space bar, or add the period at the end of each sentence while the adult coached and performed all the rest of the word processing. Every child could legitimately feel successful each time he or she wrote with the word processor. (Coached word-processing events are described in Chapter 5.)

Over time, however, definitions of "success" in collaborative writing shift-ed. Early in the year, remembering that one's name began with an 'M' and finding and typing that letter at the keyboard was an accomplishment worthy of pride. As children gained experience as writers and their skill grew, however, so too did the teacher's and children's perception of what constituted success. Soon, inventing spellings for whole words or even sentences was a reasonable goal. As the shared definition of success shifted, so too did the the social context surrounding writing. Almost imperceptibly, the adult's role shifted from collab-orator to coach. Scaffolding once necessary for the child to achieve success was no longer necessary, and the scaffolding "self-destructed" (Cazden, 1972) as children took over word processing and composing tasks once managed by the adult. (In Chapter 6, the continuum of adult participation in children's writing is discussed further.)

Both classroom culture and the use of word processing interacted over time. The result of this interaction was the evolution of new contexts in which children learned to write. Figure 3.8 summarizes the interactive effects of word-processing use and the culture of the first-grade classroom described above as they evolved in just the first weeks of the school year.

Alterations in the culture of the classroom are recorded down the left side of the figure; alterations in word processing use are recorded down the right side of the figure. Arrows indicating influence of one variable on the other demonstrate that classroom culture and word processing use both influenced and were influenced by the other. As the figure indicates, the effects of classroom culture on word-processing use, and the effects of word processing use on classroom culture, were not direct but were mediated by the teacher's interpretations and perceptions. Furthermore, the interactive effects of classroom culture and word-processing use were compounded, their effects accruing over time.

Although the use of word processing selected and the effects on the classroom culture illustrated in Figure 3.8 were specific to this classroom, the interactive effects of word-processing use and classroom culture were characteristic of each of the five classes in our study. In each case, the teacher's goals and ongoing practices, and her uses of word processing, evolved in a mutually dependent relationship. The figure provides a way of understanding this relationship. It explains the ongoing culture, practice, and goals in a classroom as the foundation from which change in practice evolves. It calls attention to the role of the teacher's interpretation of word processing as a pedagogical tool and her interpretation of the uses that the children make of this tool. Finally, it demonstrates that the classroom culture in which children learn to write is continually changing, and offers different learning opportunities as the culture evolves and the children and the teacher grow in their understanding of writing and word processing.

SUMMARY AND CONCLUSIONS

In this chapter we have provided description and analysis of the initial and evolving uses of word processing in each of the five classrooms. We have argued that teachers' decisions about the deployment of word processing must be understood within the context of the school district, school, and individual classroom cultures. Further, we have made the case that the relationship between classroom culture and word-processing use is neither linear nor direct. We demonstrated that classroom culture and word-processing use are interdependent—each affects the other, and these effects are compounded over time.

We demonstrated as well that the relationship between classroom culture and word-processing use is mediated by the individual teacher's perceptions of her children and of word processing as a writing tool. Classroom culture, word-processing use, and teachers' perceptions are in dynamic interrelationship, shaping and being shaped by each other over time.

Because these uses each teacher made of word processing evolved in response to her unique classroom culture and to perceptions of her children and of word processing as tool, children in each of the five classrooms received different kinds of instruction, learned different word processing skills, were assisted in their uses of word processing in different ways, and used word processing in different writing tasks for different amounts of time. In the following chapter, we examine the ways children in each of the five classrooms learned to use word processing.

chapter 4
Hunting, Pecking, and Checking: Learning to Write with Word Processing

Chapter 3 has given us a sense of the range of opportunities that were created for beginning writers to learn about writing and word processing. As we have shown, the nature of the learning contexts in each classroom depended on teachers' goals and values, their existing reading/language curricula (including the writing tasks they assigned or invited), their perceptions of the benefits of word processing, and the ways they allocated space, time, and assistance to beginning writers who were using word processing. Over time, as tools and tasks interacted with the social processes of classrooms, these learning contexts changed. They were shaped by teachers' evolving conceptions of word processing as a writing tool and of children as developing writers. In most cases, a dynamic relationship developed between classroom cultures and teachers' interpretations of word processing. In short, the teachers shaped the tool at the same time that the tool shaped the teachers. As a pedagogical tool, word processing also shaped the writing theories and practices of the children who used it. These gradual shaping processes, and the ways beginning writers developed writing/ word processing skills, are the foci of the next three chapters.

In this chapter, we provide a close look at how beginning writers worked within the learning contexts that evolved in their classrooms—that is, how 5- to 10-year-old children learned to write with a tool that was radically different from the paper-and-pencil tools to which they were accustomed and which contained the raw capacity to alter radically their composing strategies. Staying close to observations of individual children, we identify the features of word processing that were learned, the difficulties that were encountered, and the ways children incorporated word processing into their prior and emerging writing strategies. We demonstrate that, although they experienced some difficulties due to misconceptions about word processing as a tool or unfamiliarity with the computer keyboard, all of the children whom we observed eventually learned to enter text and to manage some elements of the word-processing system. On the other hand, with few exceptions, beginning writers did not learn to use the features of word processing for which it is universally heralded. That is, they did not use the "MOVE" command, the "COPY" and "MERGE" features, or the "SEARCH AND REPLACE" function, all of which allow powerful conceptual and organizational revisions of text. Nor did they use word processing to produce speedy experimental first drafts which helped them move into new understandings of their ideas, a composing strategy which is also widely touted as a benefit of word processing. On the contrary, our data reveal that most beginners composed and edited serially and sequentially, using word processing to facilitate easy production and modest alteration of essentially single-iteration texts.

We make the case, nonetheless, that word processing was a powerful writing tool for beginners, but powerful for reasons different from those that explain the experiences of older, more competent writers. Because word processing managed many aspects of the production of print, beginners were able to use it to participate in higher-level writing tasks such as encoding and topic forming. Because it foregrounded certain features of written language, beginning writers had unusual opportunities to learn both procedural and propositional knowledge. And because beginners often worked at word processing with the assistance of adult coaches, they were able to produce more linguistically and substantively advanced texts than they could have produced independently. In short, working with word processing interacted with the language and social contexts of classrooms to allow beginning writers to think about and practice writing in new ways. In this chapter we emphasize the specific features of word processing which children learned, and in the next two chapters we argue that using these features shaped the opportunities children had to learn to write differently.

WRITING WITH PAPER AND PENCIL
AND WRITING WITH WORD PROCESSING

Writing with word processing and writing with pencil and paper are different for all writers, whether adults or children. But because many of the concerns of beginning writers have to do with the physical production of text, word processing has the potential to shape children's writing practices in ways that are dramatically different from their paper-and-pencil practices. When young children write with pencils on paper, for example, they must be concerned with left-to-right as well as top-to-bottom progression, the correct and legible formation of individual letters, the accurate placement of letters on lines, spacing between words, appropriate pressure on the pencil point, and erasure of errors without ripping or smudging the paper. When a child pushes a button at the word processing keyboard, however, the machine forms each character perfectly and locates it appropriately on the page/screen. Like a typewriter, word processing takes care of left-to-right/top-to-bottom progression, proper letter formation, and the positioning of letters in a straight, continuous line. Pushing a key is clearly less physically demanding for the beginning writer than drawing a letter on paper, and thus has the potential to free the writer to concentrate on other issues. These features of word processing have prompted writers and researchers to recommend the tool for young children (Daiute, 1985a; Graves, 1984; Smith, 1986).

Although typewriting shares some features with word processing, the former involves physically affixing letters to paper, which, as Kane (1983) points out, "might as well be carved in stone" because they are so difficult to erase and impossible to move around. The capacities of word processing to delete and insert with ease and to move words from one place to another make it a powerful writing tool, significantly different from other tools. The young child who composes serially and chooses to erase what he or she has just typed, for example, can do so without making the writing space messy. In addition, the word-processing screen is flexible in a way that paper is not. If a child chooses to add a word to a paper and pencil draft, he or she must either squeeze the additional word into the tiny space between two other words, write within the space above the word but below the previous line, or write the word in an unused marginal space and draw arrows to the desired location. When even a few insertions of this kind are made to a text, rereading is difficult if not impossible. With word processing, on the other hand, a different concept of "space" operates. Because it shifts all the words that follow to create space for the insertion, word processing enables the entirely legible insertion of words, sentences, and paragraphs of any length at any point in the text. By the same token, when a child chooses to remove material from a pencil-and-paper draft, he or she must erase or cross words out. With word processing, however, the program closes up the space as characters are deleted, and again leaves an entirely legible screen. The "paperlessness" of word processing is abstract—there is considerable physical distance between the keyboard where text is entered, the screen where it appears, and the printer where hard copy finally emerges. And a writer need never touch the paper until a final copy is made. In another sense, however, the continuous capacity of word processing to create and close up space creates a writing experience in which there is always available a clear, properly ordered, visible text. For the beginning writer the latter may be more concrete than trying to imagine how a text will eventually look when squeezed-in letters and words are elongated, cross-outs are repaired, and arrow-marked sentences are inserted into their proper places.

Editing, correcting, or revising with pencil always means marking up and messing up the paper and usually rewriting the entire piece if clean copy is required. Although some of the current pedagogical literature on writing emphasizes that children will learn that writing involves multiple drafts when they are freed to mess up their papers (Calkins, 1986; Graves, 1983), teachers often complain that children view recopying as anticlimatic at best and punishing at worst. Publishing "the good copy" occurs in many classrooms at the end of the writing process. When a child drafts with pencil and paper, producing good copy is done after the drafting is completed, after revisions are composed, after corrections are made. At this point the thinking is complete, and producing a flawless final copy becomes a laborious physical task at which young children frequently make new spelling mistakes or omit words and even whole lines. Word processing has the potential to treat the production of "good" copy as the mechanical activity that it is. When children write with word processing, they automatically have an un-marked-up screen when they are finished, and a neat and legible hard copy instantly available. The perfection of clean white space and neat even lines (albeit a superficial and potentially misleading brand of perfection) is possible and painless with word processing. Using word processing significantly changes the meaning of "a written draft," making it more fluid and slippery as a "step" in the writing process and often completely merging the notions of final draft and published copy.

Word processing handles for writers many of the tasks involved in the physical production of print, tasks which are almost always taken for granted by experienced writers but which are often major stumbling blocks for young children. But writing with word processing also introduces its own additional set of concerns, including finding the appropriate keys for letters, numerals, and marks of punctuation, using the space bar and shift keys correctly, and applying the appropriate amount of keyboard pressure. In some cases getting used to these features involves trading in a pencil stroke (e.g., the tiny arc of the comma) for the comparable keyboard button (e.g., locating the "[,]" key in the bottom, right-hand row between the "M" and the "[.]"). In other cases the word processing activity is qualitatively different from the paper-and-pencil activity. For example, with paper and pencil, the writer signals the separations between words by leaving empty space between them. This is accomplished by *not* writing in a particular spot. With word processing, the writer also separates words by leaving empty space between them, but this is accomplished by *putting space in* rather than leaving it out. The writer actually creates space on the screen by pushing the keyboard's space bar.

Many of the tasks of word processing are also characteristic of typewriting. But word processing has additional tasks that are uniquely its own, including correctly positioning the cursor by manipulating arrow keys or moving a "mouse" across a pad, deleting by using the appropriate keys, and understanding the differences that may exist between what appears on the screen and what will appear on a hard copy. In addition the size of the word-processing screen determines the amount of text the writer may view at one time and, depending on the overall length of a piece, sometimes leaves the writer without concrete signals about text length and paginal relationships. Users of word processing must also learn to manage, or have set up and managed for them, some features of the system itself—booting the program, saving and retrieving files, printing hard copies, and so on.

BEGINNING WRITERS' PRECONCEPTIONS
AND MISCONCEPTIONS ABOUT WRITING
WITH WORD PROCESSING

We make the case throughout this volume that we cannot adequately understand the ways teachers and children used word processing for writing without understanding the learning contexts they jointly constructed. An important but generally unexamined part of that context for beginning writers is the difference, detailed above, between writing with the tool of word processing and writing with the tools of paper and pencil. In other words, children begin their experiences with word processing based on their preconceptions about how paper and pencil work as tools for writing. In many cases these *pre*conceptions about paper and pencil writing are *mis*conceptions about writing with word processing. All of the 5- to 10-year-old children whom we observed had had previous experiences using paper and pencil as well as other hard surface writing and drawing tools. Even kindergarteners knew how these tools worked, and the second, third, and fourth graders whom we came to know had been doing school-sponsored paper-and-pencil writing for several years before our study began. The children's behaviors at the keyboard often illuminated their a priori expectations for the tool of word processing and made it clear that paper-and-pencil preconceptions were a critical part of the learning context.

The older children we came to know had had a great deal of experience with written language, and they certainly had a firm grasp of the alphabetic sequence. They were annoyed with the arrangement of letters on the typewriter keyboard, which begins at the second from the top row and proceeds left to right with the letters, "Q," "W," "E," "R," "T," and "Y." Computer professionals, who refer to this arrangment as the "QWERTY keyboard," have pointed out that, although it originated in order to avoid jam-ups of frequently used keys on the manual typewriter, the QWERTY arrangement is now completely obsolete but apparently here to stay. Third and fourth graders knew only that QWERTY had no logic that they could discern, and, until they developed basic keyboard familiarity, it greatly delayed their attempts at finding the keys they needed. During his first attempt at word processing, for example, fourth-grader Brad paused in his search for letters and, somewhat frustrated, demanded, "How come they just can't put these things in alphabetical order?" The arrangement of the keyboard, which was not in any order to which the children were accustomed, was not what they expected it to be, and the alphabet, the only letter arrangement to which they were accustomed, was no help in finding keys.

More important than the alphabetic sequence, however, were the children's expectations about how writing with the tool of word processing would happen based on their preconceptions about how it happened with the tools of paper and pencil. Children at all grade levels came to the computer knowing that they pushed keys rather than manipulated a pencil, and some even did fancy fingering impressions of speedy typists who ended each line with a flourish. Nevertheless, almost all of the children implicitly expected writing at the computer to be like writing with pencil and paper. They assumed that computer "space" would be as finite and inelastic as paper space is. They assumed that erasing or making other changes would be difficult. And they assumed that trying to insert a word into an existing text would type over the words already there. Interestingly, these misconceptions are precisely those elements of word processing that make it more desirable than paper and pencil and lead most adult writers to celebrate its capacities. In order for children to begin to write with word processing and understand the capacities of the new tool, however, their misconceptions about it had to be dispelled. In some cases the children made their own discoveries about how their new writing tool worked, in some peers shared their knowledge with one another, and in many cases adults showed children how to take advantage of the capacities of word processing and directly pointed out its special features.

Many children, for example, did not assume that they would be able to insert words and spaces into a text that they had already keyed in with the computer. One way to think about this response is that children were operating from a kind of spatial conservation. In their experience, space was limited and finite—a zero-sum rule applied. When they began their work with a new tool, children expected computer screen space to operate like the space on paper. They assumed that the space they saw on the screen at any given moment was all that there was. Eventually most second, third, and fourth graders adjusted to the limitless space of word processing. When they made this adjustment, they started to write somewhat differently.

Similarly, many children assumed that erasing letters and words, or making corrections, would be difficult and taxing with word processing, as it was with paper and pencil. They were dismayed the first time they pressed the wrong key by mistake, but delighted when they saw that an unwanted character could disappear so easily. In interviews at the end of the year, children described in detail the painful process of erasing pencil marks from paper in contrast with the easy process of erasing from the computer screen without the trace of a mistake. Polly, a second grader, commented, "I like writing on the computer . . . it's hard on paper because you have to keep sharpening your pencil and when you erase stuff, it makes a smear. *I write differently with computer . . .* I make changes with the computer, [but I only] sometimes [make changes] with paper because I don't like making erasing on my paper."

Polly's conclusion was true for many children. In important ways, they learned to write differently with the computer. For example, the fact that corrections could be made easily and cleanly on the computer screen had important and immediate consequences for second, third, and fourth grade writers. Children were often reluctant to make changes to their paper-and-pencil pieces, and early in the year, when adults asked children whether they wanted to make additions or corrections to their word-processed texts, their responses were the same. After children learned how easily corrections could be done with word processing, however, they edited with enthusiasm and diligence, often asking what else needed to be fixed. In a certain sense, word processing changed the standard of excellence for many of the children. With the tool of paper and pencil, they corrected their texts within the limits of their own frustrations and their own physical abilities—the standard was something like "It's good enough" or "That's all I can do, my hand's too tired." With a new tool, many children were eager to correct their texts to the standard of what they perceived as perfection—they would "fix" until all the "fixing" was done. One child even corrected an error on a piece of writing already posted on the bulletin board when it was pointed out to him by his older brother at back-to-school night.

Of course "perfection" in this sense often meant "free of all the surface errors which the writer noticed or someone pointed out." As we suggested in our discussion in Chapter 2, error-free production is not the equivalent of overall quality of writing. But for the young writers in our study, readily producing a text with fewer surface errors was important. As Bartlett (1982) points out, "For elementary students, at least, choice is likely to depend less on the constraints of a particular context than on the ease with which a strategy can be executed, particularly on the amount of physical text rearrangement and content integration required" (p. 359). Editing, a writing activity that was valued in second, third, and fourth grades, could be executed with the tool of word processing without requiring physical text rearrangement and often without much content integration.

LEARNING TO USE WORD PROCESSING

Over the course of one school year all of the beginning writers who worked with word processing learned the skills needed to enter and change text and to manage some features of the system. In fact, children at every grade level, even kindergarten and first, became proficient enough with word processing to teach some of their skills to other children. This was true despite the fact that children experienced initial difficulty learning the computer keyboard and unlearning their inappropriate expectations for word processing as a writing tool. The following sections illustrate the ways in which beginning writers learned how to press keys to produce letters and words on the screen, how to use the space bar and the return key, how to make capital letters, and how to erase characters. Additionally, children in grades two through four learned how to insert and delete text in order to edit their writing, and in some cases, they learned both *to revise* their writing and *how to use* word processing to facilitate their revisions.

Figure 4.1 summarizes the word processing operations which were learned. The horizontal axis of the figure divides word processing into four bundles of features for entering text, editing text, formatting text, and managing files.

Within each bundle, the specific word processing features used to accomplish the given process are listed. Hence, for example, the bundle "entering text" includes pressing keys, using the space bar, using the shift key for capitalization and other punctuation, using the "caps lock" key for capitalization, and using the "back-arrow" key to erase. (We distinguish "erase" from "delete" because of their conceptual differences, which are discussed later in this chapter.) The vertical axis of the figure separates grade levels, kindergarten through four. The blocks created at the junctures of the two axes are solid black, cross-hatched, or solid white, indicating, respectively, widespread, scattered, or no instances of usage at each grade level.

The younger children we observed in kindergarten, first, and second grade generally worked with adult coaches when they wrote with word processing. Therefore, their uses of the word-processing features on Figure 4.1 were commonly accomplished with the assistance of a coach. On the other hand, third graders sometimes worked with coaches and sometimes worked independently, and fourth graders usually did not work with adult coaches. Generally we found that what beginning writers learned was a function of both their developmental capacities and skills and the focus of the writing programs in their classrooms. To a great extent, children learned to control those features of word processing that enabled them to meet their teachers' expectations for writing and complete the tasks assigned to them. In keeping with the literature we reviewed in Chapter 2, we found that word processing itself did not initiate new strategies for writing or teach children new ways to write and revise their work. Figure 4.2 provides some global information about the amount of instruction/exposure that was required for beginning writers to get started with word processing. The figure is constructed around the same horizontal and vertical axes used in Figure 4.1 (i.e., bundles of word processing features and individual grade levels), but Figure 4.2 also conveys approximate information about the number of times adults taught particular word-processing features to groups or individual children. It is important to note that Figure 4.2 represents the number of initial teaching episodes adults provided to accomplish beginning-level skill only. It does not imply that beginning writers "mastered" each feature of word processing within two or three sessions, or that teachers thought they had. Rather, after initial exposure, word-processing instruction was ongoing and largely informal. Children often helped one another, coaches were available to help younger children, and teachers offered continued instruction to individual writers on an as-needed basis.

Locating Letters/Entering Text

There was a great deal of variation in the strategies 5- to 10-year old children used for locating and pressing letter keys on the word processing keyboard. To a certain extent, variation was the result of knowledge of language, the individual child's fluency, and digital dexterity, as well as the prior assumptions about

Figure 4.1
Features of Word Processing Learned by Beginning Writers

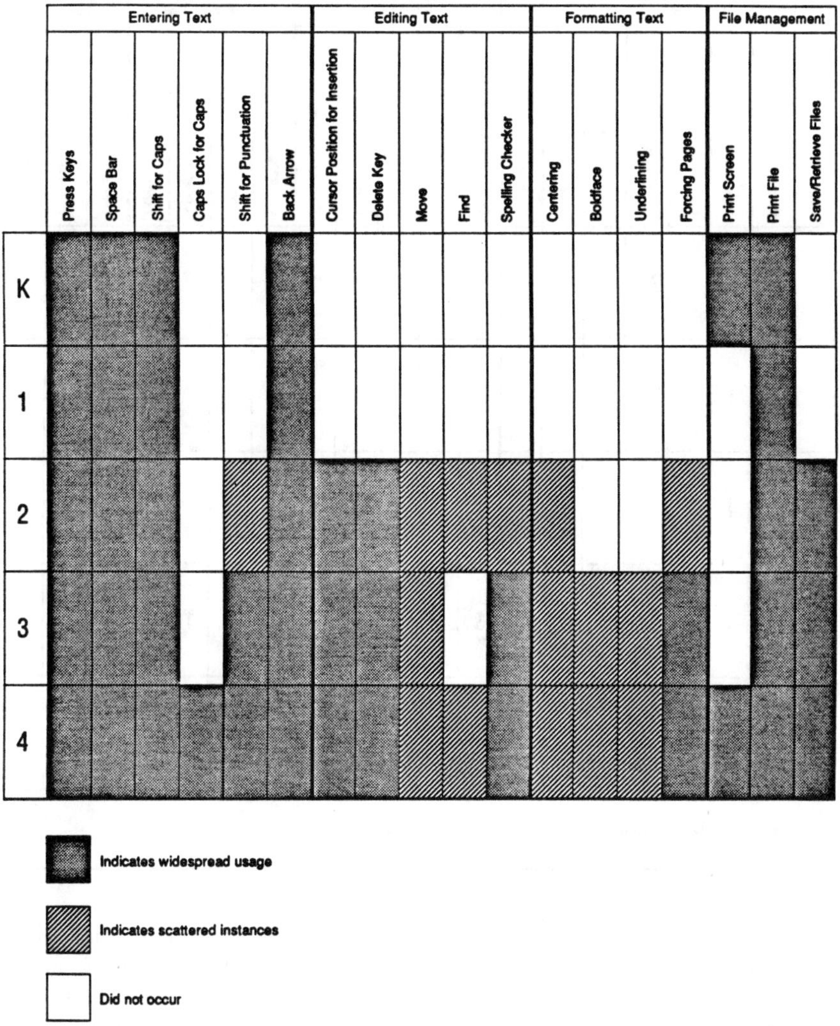

	Entering Text						Editing Text					Formatting Text				File Management		
	Press Keys	Space Bar	Shift for Caps	Caps Lock for Caps	Shift for Punctuation	Back Arrow	Cursor Position for Insertion	Delete Key	Move	Find	Spelling Checker	Centering	Boldface	Underlining	Forcing Pages	Print Screen	Print File	Save/Retrieve Files
K																		
1																		
2																		
3																		
4																		

Indicates widespread usage

Indicates scattered instances

Did not occur

writing that he or she brought to the task. In the sections that follow we look first at second, third, and fourth graders, whose keyboarding experiences are closer to adults' initial experiences with word processing, and then turn to kindergarteners and first graders, whose experiences were quite different.

Second-, Third-, and Fourth-Grade Children. When second, third, and fourth graders began to use word processing, locating letters on the keyboard was

Figure 4.2
Instruction Required to Get Started with Word Processing

Grade	Kind of Instruction	Entering Text						Editing Text					Formatting Text				File Management		
		Press Keys	Space Bar	Shift for Caps	Caps Lock for Caps	Shift for Punctuation	Back Arrow	Cursor Position for Insertion	Delete Key	Move	Find	Spelling Checker	Centering	Boldface	Underlining	Forcing Pages	Print Screen	Print File	Save/Retrieve Files
K	One to one	1	1	2-3			1												
1	One to one	1	1	2-3			1												
2	One to one, some group	1	1	2		1	1	2	3			1				1		3	2
3	Whole group and some one to one	1	1	2		1	2	3	3	1		2	1	1	1	1		3	3-4
4	Whole group Already knew	1	1	1	1	1	1	1	1			1	1	1	1	1	1	1	1

Numbers indicate how many times teachers taught a skill to whole group.

time-consuming and sometimes frustrating. (We are making an artificial distinction here to try to clarify the aspects of writing which were problematic during beginning word processing. We use the word *compose* to mean, roughly, thinking of the words one wants to write, *encode* to mean selecting the letters needed to form the words, *inscribe* to mean physically printing or typing the letters, and *transcribe* to mean transferring the spelling of a word from one medium to another—usually paper-and-pencil draft to computer keyboard.) For the older children we observed, searching for keys significantly interfered with writing because it slowed down their inscribing rates and threw off their composing/inscribing rhythms. These children were fluent enough at encoding and inscribing that they could represent their ideas with paper and pencil more or less as they composed them. Although their spelling and punctuation were far from flawless, they were able to encode and inscribe automatically—at least in reasonably approximate (and readable) form. For these children the need to hunt for the letter keys at the computer keyboard severely disrupted the composing process.

Severe disruptions meant that the texts some children actually produced during their first word-processing turns were striking for their errors and their brevity. Clarence, for example, was a fourth grader who seemed generally puzzled by the word-processing enterprise and was markedly unproductive during his first turn at the computer. His writing was slow and laborious, and, unlike many other children, he was unwilling to experiment much on his own. At the end of a 20-minute period, he had transcribed only one line from his prewritten paper-and-pencil draft, and these three lines contained a number of errors not made on the initial draft. His experience, excerpted in the sequence below, clearly illustrates the disruption that keyboarding initially caused for children who could already encode and inscribe automatically with paper and pencil.

[Clarence has been assigned to describe an imaginary creature. He studies the screen where his teacher has typed in the title from his paper and pencil draft, "GOOFYO EXNAME," to get him started.]

GOOFYO EXNAME

[The name, pronounced Goofy-O, is modeled after his teacher's sample description which uses "Getty-o" as the name for the imaginary creature. "Ex-name" is linked in Clarence's view to the notion, "brand X."]

Clarence: Hmmmm. . . [His intention is to follow the title with the first line of his paper and pencil draft of the description, 'My name is Goofyo Exname . . . ' and then continue transcribing at the keyboard from the draft. He searches for and types "m", not realizing the cursor is at the beginning of the same line that already contains the title.]
m   GOOFYO EXNAME

[He shakes his head, drawing back in recognition that he has not done what he intended to do. Clarence looks over the keys, points to the screen to find his place, searches over the keys again, looks over his paper again and the keys again. Leaving the cursor where it had been, he continues to type. His intention is still to type, "My name is" followed by the name of his creature.]
m   im   iiiiiiii   GOOFYO EXNAME

Clarence: Oh! [Looks up at screen.] Where's erase? [Scans the keyboard.]

Karen: (a classmate who is using the computer next to Clarence's) This is erase. [Points to and then presses DELETE key, she deletes for him the title of the creature.]
m   im   iiiiiiiii

Clarence: Oh. [Looks at the screen, points at each letter with his finger, searches for the cursor keys, tries three times to use the DELETE key as Karen did. However, the key will not now delete the letters because there is no text to the right of the cursor. What he actually needs to do is to use the BACKARROW key which erases text to the left of the cursor.] (See Appendix for a description of how the DELETE and BACKARROW functions operate on the IBM keyboard.) [Continues to press the delete key for thirty more seconds while nothing happens, then tries the "D" key, still trying to erase his text.]

m   im   iiiiiiiii   d   d   d   d   d

Clarence: Erase! This ain't erase! [He is somewhat frustrated, but also puzzled, continues to struggle with the DELETE function, but finally turns to Karen and taps her shoulder.]

Karen: What do you want? (annoyed)

Clarence: Erase! (nervously emphatic)

Karen: You . . . ! [Looks at his screen] What? You're still over there? (shocked) We only have ten minutes lef . . . [Looks again at Clarence's nearly empty screen]. Just . . . wait . . . [Reaches over and pushes delete, but nothing happens]. Wait. . . you want to erase all that? [Moves cursor over, then uses delete key, which now works because the cursor is to the right of the text]. Wait . . . just wait. . . the whole sentence? [Deletes everything with delete key so the screen is now blank]. Now start all over again! And (starts to yell) don't make. . .

Clarence: Shush. Shush. [Tries to quiet her, then tries to retype in the name of his creature, but gets too many "O's" when he presses the key too hard and it automatically repeats.]

gooooooooo

[Clarence tries to delete as before without success. He searches the keyboard, then looks over at Karen, but doesn't disturb her again. Finally he locates the cursor arrow, moves it to the "g" and deletes all with the delete key. The screen is now blank again. Then he types in "goo".]

goo

Clarence: All right! There's goofy, come on goofy . . . [Talks to the screen.]

Karen: 'Cause you're goofy [barely looking over].

Clarence: 'Cause you are too. [Not really paying much attention to her, continues to type, calling out each letter as he locates it]. F-F-F . . . [Searches for and then types "f"] . . . Y-Y-Y-Y-Y [Searches for, types "y", looks down, points with finger to find his place in the draft.] . . . X-X [Searches for "x", types "ex"] . . . N-A-M-E [Searches for each key, types in "name"] . . .J-J-J-Juice [Searches for each key, types in "juice".] . . . Y-O [types in "yo"].

goofyo exname juiceyo

Clarence: Foolish clown [reading from draft] . . . [Searches for, types in "foo"]
. . . L-L-L-I-S . . . [Types in "lis"]. Where's H? [Types in "h"',
then "clown"].
goofyo exname juiceyo foolishclown

Karen: You press these two for printing? [Poised to print her story, seems to
be addressing no one in particular.]

Clarence: [Pauses, watches her print out her completed story, then continues. He
types "he" but does not leave a space after it]. I-S- [searches, types
"is"].
goofyo exname juiceyo foolishclown heis

Clarence: Silly . . . L-L-L [types "si"]. Where's L-L-L? [Searches, types "l"',
then "y"] Silly . . . silly. . . He is silly. Too-too [Searches for "t,"
can't find it.]. . . You're messing me up [Talks to the keyboard]. Too!
Too! Where's T? [Finds and types "t" but has not left a space.]
goofyo exname juiceyo foolishclown heis sillyt

Clarence: [Looks at "sillyt"] What is this? How do you erase? [Deletes "t".]
T-O . . . [Types "to" but does not leave a space after it]. M-E
[Searches, types in "ne" by mistake for "me."'.]
goofyo exname juiceyo foolishclown heis silly tone

Clarence: [Looks up at screen] Tone! (astounded) Tone! [Looks at screen in
confusion.] What?

[Timer sounds to signal the end of his turn.]

Karen: Time's up! (Announces with a flourish.) You didn't even finish your
first sentence??? [Stares at Clarence's screen in exaggerated amaze-
ment].

Clarence: Will you just shut up? [Backs up with cursor, positions it correctly,
and uses the "DELETE" key to delete "tone"]
goofyo exname juiceyo foolishclown heis silly

Clarence: [He pushes back his chair with some relief). Who's next?

Clarence's first turn at the computer lasted a little less than 20 minutes. To many
adults who have read this excerpt, his experience with word processing seems
almost tortuous—painfully slow and counterproductive in many ways.
Clarence's confusion, coupled with Karen's taunts, make for an experience that
is difficult to interpret as educational. It is interesting, however, that, by the
conclusion of his first sitting at the computer, Clarence had indeed mastered the
delete function and had begun to develop a talk–hunt–peck rhythm, albeit an
extremely slow one, that allowed him to enter text. It is also interesting that even
children like Clarence, among the poorest keyboarders in the room, chose to
work at the computer whenever they could, reported in end-of-year interviews
that they preferred writing with word processing to writing with paper and

pencil, and in subsequent turns at the computer, improved enough to enter and change text without undue confusion or hesitation. Clarence's laborious hunt-and-peck contrasts sharply with David's more fluid actions, reported below.

David, also a fourth grader in Clarence's class, had an initial experience at the computer which is strikingly different from Clarence's. Although the Clarence excerpt represents his first turn at the computer and David's represents his second, their juxtaposition provides some sense of the enormous range and variation that occurred in what children of about the same age were able to do early on when they began to write with word processing.

[David is using word processing to compose a new story which he seems to have a clear idea about in his head. His method goes something like this: think up two or three words, hunt and peck these out as quickly as possible on the keyboard, take a cursory glance at the screen just to get your place, stop and think of the next few words, repeat.]

[David types slowly but steadily with almost no verbalization. He uses one finger of his left hand to peck out the words, although he occasionally reaches around with his right index finger to type a letter on the opposite half of the keyboard.]

[He stares at the screen for a second, then looks down at the keys and begins to type.]

There was a cat that lived in a hat.

[Presses "return" key.]

And the cat loved the hat and onw

[Looks up, realizes that "onw" is incorrect. Erases using "DEL" key and types in "one," then continues in the same style as above. Does little rereading of the actual text on the screen. Looks at it only to find his place and to check when he thinks he has made a typing error.]

one day a

[Presses "return" key.]

mos

[Looks up, erases "s" and types "-use." He slides his fingers over the keyboard row-by-row to find the letters he wants, using one finger of his left hand.]

mouse came to the hat and the cat said

[Presses "return" key.]

ho are you. I,

[Looks up at the screen, erases the comma.]

David: How do you make a, uh . . . ? (to Maxie, a classmate who is using the computer next to his).

Maxie: How do you make a what?

David: How do you make, you know those like commas (motions with his hand to indicate a short arc), only they go at the top?

Maxie: Yeah . . .

[Johnny, the "computer expert," comes by to help.]

David: How do you make those commas, you know like "I'm"?

Johnny: Yeah, I know it's here . . . [Scans all the keys on the keyboard, doesn't locate the apostrophe.] Should be here somewhere . . . [Still has trouble finding it, finally tries the quotation marks key, checks it out on the screen, then erases it, keeps looking.] Here. [Finds the apostrophe, types it in.]

> **I'**

David: [Nods, continues to type as before.]

> **I'm FRED**

[Erases "RED," types in "-red."]

> **Fred the**

[Erases "the" continues to type.]

> **the cat said**

David: How do you spell, "why"?

Maxie: W-H-Y.

David: Oh yeah.

> **whu**

[Erases "u," continues to type.]

> **why are you here the mousesaid**

[Erases "sesaid," retypes "-se," adds a space, then types "said" and continues.]

> **mouse said I ned**

[Erases "d."]

> **need a home then why did you come here**

Compared with many children we observed, David moved quickly and intently at the computer. He had no trouble spelling and did not lose the train of his words as he worked. His row-by-row hunting strategy was effective, and his sense of when to look up at the screen to check for typographical errors was quite accurate. David was unusual in his intense and quiet labor at the word processor. He worked about

20 minutes and managed to get three full lines of newly composed text into the machine. This was considerably faster than many other fourth graders during their initial attempts at word processing. Further, David was relatively independent, talking little to the person sitting next to him and asking for little assistance. Following David's computer turn when his class met to talk about their writing for the day, David described the story he was working on. He seemed pleased by what he was doing and quite satisfied with his progress.

As Clarence's contrast makes painfully clear, there were fourth graders as well as second and third graders who were not as facile as David and whose hunt-and-peck systems were not as efficient as his after their second turns at the computer. But David was fairly typical of third and fourth graders in that he worked steadily and productively; he developed a hunt–and–peck system which was comfortable for him and which did not seem to interfere with his thinking; and, by end of two or three turns at the computer, his composing fluency was consistent with and supported by the rhythm of his word processing. Hunt-peck-talk-check patterns varied considerably from child to child, but after they became familiar with the keyboard, most children developed a rhythm that did not interfere with composing.

David's experience is also typical of the relatively systematic search strategies that second, third, and fourth graders devised to locate letters on the keyboard. Many ran their fingers over the rows of keys in a continuous "S" or backwards "S" pattern, repeating to themselves the names of each letter they were seeking. Some children hunted first on the right side of the keyboard and then on the left, while others circled the keyboard with their fingers as they searched with their eyes. Children who developed methodical hunting strategies were acting from some understanding of typewriters or computers as well as from knowledge of the systematicity of written language itself: they knew that all English words were composed of the same 26 characters, that all of these were located on every keyboard, and that the positions of particular characters on the keyboard did not change. Within about three turns at the computer, these children developed enough familiarity with the keyboard to overcome any initial frustrations they might have had and begin their letter searches in the appropriate sectors of the keyboard. As would be expected, the locations of the most frequently used letters were learned before less frequently used letters.

Second graders were also slow to locate letters when they began using word processing. Hunting for letters, however, did not seem as frustrating for them as it was for their older peers. This was the case because they usually worked with a coach at the word processor and because their composing/inscribing rhythms were slower in the first place. In other words, their spelling was not so automatic as it seemed to be for third and fourth graders. It took second graders some time to think of the individual letters they needed in order to encode particular words. Fortuitously, the length of time needed for hunting and pecking the letter seemed to be about the same as the length of time for thinking up the letter itself. Hence the hunt-and-peck rhythm was balanced and not disturbed by the introduction of word processing.

Learning Period for Word Processing. It was clear across grade levels that there was a relationship between what children could already do with paper and pencil and the extent of their adjustment to word processing. Third and fourth graders, usually adequate spellers and fairly fluent composers, were impatient at first because they knew what they wanted to write and they knew how to spell, at least approximately, most of the words they wished to use. Because they did not know key locations, however, they were slowed down enormously in their attempts to enter text. For these beginners, there was indeed what we called, in a preliminary report, a *learning period* during which they could not both learn the features of word processing and use the tool effectively for their writing (Cochran-Smith et al., 1986). As we pointed out, during the learning period, which seems to exist for adults as well as children, attention is focused on the task of learning to use word processing more or less at the expense of writing. During this learning period, which lasted until children had had two to three turns at the computer, word processing was not very productive for third and fourth graders. Like Clarence, many laboriously hunted, pecked, and checked their typing against paper-and-pencil drafts, and produced little written text. On the other hand, what was also going on during this learning period was that children were learning the word-processing system and gaining enough familiarity with the keyboard to use it productively in later writing sessions.

Fourth-grade teacher Ms. Santori, who was experienced with computing as well as word processing, anticipated that her children would need a learning period when they first began working with word processing. In order to separate composing from inscribing, she assigned the children to transcribe at the keyboard what they had already composed with paper and pencil. Although the teacher wisely separated composing from learning word processing with this procedure, she also unintentionally introduced a third new task. In order to transfer words from paper to computer screen, the children had to follow along on the paper-and-pencil draft at the same time that they checked it against what appeared on the monitor and also struggled to locate letters on the keyboard. This proved to be very difficult for some beginners, resulting in a fitful sequence of actions that proceeded something like this: read a bit of paper-and-pencil text, search for the first letter of the first word, type in the letter looking down at the keyboard, look up, check the screen to see whether what actually appears is what you intended to type, if not fix the mistake by deleting and searching again for the letter, if so look down and find the place where you left off on the paper, look up again at the screen to verify what you already typed, look down to check the paper again, search for the next letter in the word, and on and on. It is easy to see that this process was not very effective.

During the second year of our project, Ms. Santori changed the procedure.

She introduced her fourth graders to basic features of word processing in a whole-group lesson and then had children enter the date and playful variations on their names as the "text" for their first word-processing turn. She had realized early on that for fourth-grade children, who had some degree of composing fluency, the task of composing needed to be separated from the tasks of learning word-processing operations and keyboard locations, but without introducing new visual or manual tasks. Her second-year process worked much more effectively than her first-year process.

The learning period shortened somewhat during the second year of our study, partly because teachers like Ms. Santori had a good sense of which features of word processing children could quickly master and which they would need in order to get started with word processing. Also an influence, however, was the fact that some of the children who worked with word processing during the second year of the study had already learned it the year before. When Linda and Abdul came to use the word processor early in their third-grade year, for example, it was clear that Abdul recalled from his second-grade experiences how to use the shift key, the backarrow delete key, the general locations of specific letter keys, the period button, the space bar, the return key, and the entire procedures for "SAVE" and "RETRIEVE." It is possible that, eventually, elementary schools will have compatible computer and word-processing materials across the grades in their classrooms. If this is the case, we believe it is likely that the learning period for word processing will decrease in length each year, until, by the time they reach the upper grades, children will be quite comfortable with word processing as a writing tool and will require almost no initial learning period at the start of each school year. Instead, over the course of each year, they will acquire increasingly sophisticated word-processing skills as they work at increasingly complex writing tasks.

A contradiction in our findings is that, although it took second-, third-, and fourth-grade children relatively few turns at the computer to master enough word processing and keyboarding skills to enter texts, it took a very long time, in absolute terms, for the children to get their turns. This problem had to do with the ratio of children to computers, the ways computer time was scheduled, and the number of children within individual classes who had access to the computer. In the fourth grade, for example, Ms. Santori wanted to provide equal word processing access to all the children in her own class and also provide initial exposure to the children in the adjoining fourth grades. In order for all the children to have two or three 20-minute turns at the computer during writing workshop time, it took almost three months. Since word processing instruction began the first of October, this meant that the first semester was nearly over by the time all the children had had their initial experiences. This suggests that there are critical dilemmas about the minimum amount of computer equipment necessary for effective classroom use and about equity of computer access. Over time our data reveal that, in some cases, there were ways around these dilemmas, while in other cases there were not. These issues are discussed further in the following chapter.

Kindergarten and First-Grade Children. For kindergarten children, "playing" at the computer served a purpose that was similar to that served when the older children used their own names as the "text" to enter at the keyboard during their initial word-processing turns. That is, kindergartners' "playing" at the keyboard separated the task of composing from the task of learning how the tool of word processing worked. During the first few weeks of the year, for example, Mrs. Winston allowed her kindergarten children to choose the word processor from among many games, toys, and other educational activities during "choice time" in her classroom. When they chose word processing, kindergarteners literally "played around" with keys, and arm and finger positions, and also experimented with the sounds that could be produced by the keyboard and the printer. Although it was not Mrs. Winston's intention, free play at the keyboard provided the children with practice and with orienting opportunities that prepared them for later work inventing spellings, copying word labels, and otherwise entering text.

Unlike their older peers who eventually developed relatively efficient hunt-and-peck systems in order to enter text at the keyboard, the younger children we observed had a different kind of experience. They "entered text," but for them this meant everything from selecting specific or random keys to produce a string of letters, to copying words from signs or labels posted around the room, to creating meaningful messages by inventing their own spellings. Younger children approached the task of locating letter keys in a different fashion from their older schoolmates. Some kindergarteners, for example, did not assume the systematicity of language or the constancy of computer equipment. They did not assume that letters would necessarily be in the same positions on the keyboard each time they had a turn at the computer, nor did they think that the keyboard on one machine in their classroom would necessarily contain the same set of characters as the keyboard on a second machine. One child who was working at the keyboard to copy a word from a picture dictionary was unable to find the appropriate key after considerable hunting. Thinking that he had finally discovered the reason he was having so much trouble, he turned to an adult nearby and asked, "Does this thing *have* an R?"

Similarly, kindergarten, and some first-grade children were unsure about the significance of the order of letters in written words. They were not like second through fourth graders, to whom it was obvious that one could not type a letter for a particular word out of its particular sequence. When older children were hunting for the next letter of a given word and found instead a letter they would need later in that word, they kept a finger on the letter found serendipitously while continuing their original search for the next letter in the word, but of course they did not type the letter out of sequence. When the same thing happened to kindergarteners, however, the situation presented an interesting dilemma. They were uncertain about the effects of typing a needed letter out of sequence and somewhat unwilling to forego the advantage of a letter found without a hunt, as the following excerpt indicates.

[Gordon and Katie are working to type Gordon's last name, "McEntire," which is printed on a paper they have beside them. Lew, a silent observer, is anxious to participate in the activity either to help or interfere with the writing event. Although he has some knowledge of the keyboard, he never talks.]

[Gordon has already typed M.]

M

Gordon: Now I gotta get me a . . . C . . .a . . . C . . . [Searches for keys, runs his fingers over the keyboard, stops at a letter, shakes head.] That ain't it. . .

Katie: [Also searches for keys.] A. . . A . . . [Lew reaches toward the keyboard.]

Gordon: Lew!

Katie: A . . . . . . W! [Finds "w", points to it].

Gordon: W? . . . . .No . . . . I need that letter. [Points to C in "McEntire" on the paper.]

Katie: N! N! [Points to the letter on the paper.] Where's the N?

Gordon: I need the C! I need the C! The C! That's hard to find. [Lew reaches over from the side and types in the C.]

MC

Gordon: You hit it, Lew? Thanks! Thank you! OK, now I need THAT letter. [Points to E on paper] . . . That letter there . . . [Lew reaches toward keyboard again, but Gordon pulls Lew's finger away, then sits with left elbow raised toward Lew as if to fend him off.]

Gordon: What? [Still trying to find the "C," Lew reaches forward.] Where is it, Lew? . . . Where?

Katie: [Spots the "N" on the keyboard, points to it.] Do you want to do the N first? 'Cause the N is right there [pointing]. [Lew has slipped his hand in to type something.]

Gordon: No (to Katie), I know where the N is (very patiently).

Katie: [Still pointing to the "N."] Wanna do the N first ?

Gordon: Mmm, OK. Let me do the N. Let me do the fast N and then we'll do that number. [Motions toward the "E" in his name which is written with curved lines rather than in straight block form] . . . Do that one.

MCN

Gordon: Now we gotta do . . . we gotta push this back.

Katie: We gotta do the T . . . the T!

Gordon: No, we gotta do THAT . . . find THAT . [Points to "E" on paper.]

Katie: Oh, here it is. [Finds "T."]. . . . [Lew has removed cover from the function keys portion of the keyboard and is about to press them.]

Coach: Please don't press the . . . these keys while Gordon's working. That will mess up his work. You did very well helping him find the other letters though.

Gordon: He helped me find one.

Coach: Yes, he did. He found the C for you, didn't he?

Katie: [Reminds them of her idea.] Gonna do the T first? . . . You better do the T first, it's right here! [Points to key.]

Working together with word processing prompted kindergarten children to talk about written language in ways that they did not do when they wrote with paper and pencil. In this excerpt, Gordon and Katie talked with each other about some of the constraints of written language as they wrestled, albeit unknowingly, with the question of whether order counts in the formation of words. Katie operated on the principle that a bird in hand is worth two in the bush—she insisted that they ought to type the "N" and then the "T" whenever they happened to find them on the keyboard. After all, she seemed to reason, they needed the letters eventually, so why not take advantage of the fact that they had found them easily on the keyboard? Gordon was less certain. He seemed to want to follow the sequence of the letters on the paper, but Katie's persistence and his own desire to preserve his turn at the computer convinced him to just type in a "fast N" when they found it, before he tried to continue with the proper sequence of the word. Lew had fewer doubts about what letters were needed. Silently he located and tried to type each letter. Essentially the children were struggling with what Clay (1975) has called the "directional principle," or the constraint in written language that requires that letters are drawn and ordered in a particular sequence. Clay cautions that it is unwise to assume that the relationships of letters put together in left-to-right fashion in order to make words are obvious to children. Kindergarteners' collaborative work using word processing called their attention to and made more obvious the issues of direction, sequence, and order in the making of words. As we show in many of the examples that follow, working with word processing foregrounded many features of written language for beginning writers. Furthermore, their experiences with word processing often occurred in altered social learning contexts, especially in situations where two or more children worked together to compose a message or copy a label. These situations bolstered children's attention to the details of composing and encoding. Consequently, working with word processing provided kindergarteners with unusual opportunities to learn about the workings of written language.

Many of the kindergarten and first-grade children in our study were just learning to form letters. For them writing by hand was a laborious process that involved many subtasks. It required them to remember or recognize needed letter forms and then draw them by applying the right amount of pencil pressure, positioning letter forms frontwards, right-side up, and left to right; locating them evenly on lines in a continuous left-to-right, top-to-bottom fashion; and leaving spaces where appropriate to indicate word and sentence separations. Because there were only two computers in their classrooms, kindergarteners and first graders composed by hand to practice letter forms most of the time. When they worked with word processing, however, many of the physical difficulties of handwriting were subtracted out. Even for children who could form letters easily, pushing a button was easier than forming a letter by hand. But when they composed with word processing (as often as three times a week for some children, as rarely as once every two weeks for others), they could concentrate on producing text rather than drawing letters.

Kindergartener Anna provides a good example. Anna knew the names of many of the letters and understood quite well that a string of letters "said" something. She could create stories that were quite elaborate when she had the chance to compose orally. But Anna was not an advanced printer compared with others in her class, and she was just beginning to control a pencil well enough to draw recognizable letters. In her paper-and-pencil journal, Anna wrote random letters and occasionally copied words from signs and labels on the walls around the classroom. On rare occasions she tried to invent spellings with paper and pencil, but these episodes were brief, with a few isolated words produced. Managing the pencil seemed to exhaust most of Anna's energy.

Working with a coach at the word processor, however, Anna had a different experience. Her work was purposeful and deliberate, and her attention to the task never strayed. In many instances she scanned the keyboard efficiently and located letter keys easily, but she also asked for help when she needed it. As she worked with word processing, it became clear that Anna was able to isolate many of the individual sounds in words and then select letters to represent them. With word processing, she composed and entered a meaningful text, using her knowledge of letter names to invent the spellings for her message. In an important sense, entering text with word processing uncovered Anna's considerable skill at encoding. The experience gave her the chance to demonstrate her language skill and practice ways to encode words, and it also gave adults the opportunity to see more of what Anna could do.

Although the example that follows provides a good sense of how Anna located keys and entered text at the word processor, it cannot begin to convey the delight in her voice as she figured out what letters were needed or how to make the computer do what she wanted it to do. This was an activity that Anna thoroughly enjoyed. Ms. Paris, a member of the research team, had been asked by the teacher, Mrs. Winston, to coordinate activities at the word processor and help individual children as they worked.

[Anna is sitting at the computer waiting for Ms. Paris who is checking the printer.]

Anna: [Knows exactly what she wants to do and is anxious to start.] I wanna make a . . . a story . . . How do you spell, "once"?

Coach: [Finishes checking to see that the printer is set up correctly for large type.] OK, what is it you wanted to type?

Anna: Once . . .

Coach: OK. Once . . . once. . . w-w-w-once (exaggerating the first sound of the word) . . .

Anna: Y! (Readers who are not familiar with the logic of invented spelling are invited to note that the *name* of the letter "y" does indeed begin with the sound usually represented in English by (the letter "w.")

Coach: OK, put a Y there.

Anna: I know where the Y is. [Looks for key.]

Coach: Where is that Y ?

Anna: Right here! [Finds "y."]

Coach: OK.

Anna: Y. [Types "y"].

    y

Coach: OK, once . . . once-s-s-s-s . . . (exaggerating the ending sound of the word). Do you hear anything else in there? Once-s-s-s . . .

Anna: S?

Coach: OK.

Anna: Y- S . . . Y - S . . . is it really S after Y?

Coach: It's got an S sound in it.

Anna: Um hmmm . . . [Searches for the key.]

Coach: Once . . . there it is. [Points to "s."]

Anna: Ah ha! . . . Thank you! [Types "s."]

    ys

Coach: What's the next word? Once . . . once . . . how about the next word you need . . . once *upon* . . . Is that the word?

Anna: P!

Coach: OK. First, before we put the P, do you remember what this bar is for? [Points to space bar.]

Anna: P!

Coach: Press the space bar. [Anna presses it.] Now you can start "upon" right there. [Points to cursor on screen.] Once upon . . .

Anna: P!

Coach: Ah, yes.

Anna: Where's the P?

Coach: It's on the top row of the letters. Do you see it anywhere?

Anna: That ? [Touches "p."]

Coach: That is it. Do you hear any other sounds in that word . . . "upon-n-n-n-n" . . .

Anna: Upon-n-n-n-n . . . P! [Types in "p."]
        ys p

Coach: Upon-n-n-n-n-n . . .

Anna: Uhhh . . . N!

Coach: OK, N, good for you! [Anna finds "n" quickly, types it.]
        ys pn

Coach: OK, once upon . . . now make a space again . . . [Anna moves
        to space bar without hesitation, presses it]. What's the next word? Once
        upon . . .

Anna: Uh.

Coach: Uh. Oh, boy . . .

Anna: O.

Coach: OK. [Anna finds "o" in about four seconds, types it.]
        ys pn o

Coach: OK, space bar . . . [Anna presses it] . . . once upon a . . .

Anna: Time!

Coach: OK!

Anna: T! I need T. Is that T? [Points to "x" key.]

Coach: Nope, that is the X.

Anna: Is that? [Points to "return" key.]

Coach: No.

Anna: Is that it? [Points to "t."]

Coach: Sure is! [Anna touches it, but holds it down for too long.]
        ys pn o ttt

Anna: Oooooh! I made too many T's!

Coach: Uh oh, what are you going to do about that?

Anna: Gonna eraase it!

Coach: Do you know how?

Anna: Um hmm . . . no.

Coach: Do you remember when Lew was erasing things?

Anna: Yes.

Coach: What did he press?

Anna: Hmmmm [scanning keyboard] . . . That ? [Points to "return."]

Coach: Ummmm.

Anna: That ? [Points to "DELETE."]

Coach: That's the one! [Anna uses single keystroke to erase "ttt" and the space].

Anna: There's the O. [Points to screen.] Now I need to make the T.

Coach: How about the space first? [Anna presses space bar]. There you go! OK, now your T. [Anna reaches for "t" immediately and types it.]
    ys pn o t

Coach: Time . . . Once upon a time . . .

Anna: Tuh tuh tuh taahh taahh . . . tuh tuh . . . taahh taahh . . . o . . . tuh taah o . . . uhh . . . H!

Coach: OK. [Anna finds "h" in two seconds, types it.]
    ys pn o th

Coach: Time . . . ti-i-me-m-m-m-m-m-m-m-me.

Anna: We need a space! [Presses space bar.]

Coach: Mmm, we're not done [with] "time" yet. We need to put the "time" letters all close together . . . all the letters that say "time" stand next to each other, then there's a space. Are you done [with] the word, "time"? Once upon a tiiime-m-m-m-m-m . . . Anything else you hear?

Anna: M!

Coach: M! You're right! [Anna finds "m" in two seconds, types it in.]
    ys pn o th m

Coach: Do you want that M to be next to the rest of the letters in "time"?

Anna: Yeah, but it doesn't look like the M.

Coach: Here, let me sharpen that up. [Adjusts the brightness of the computer screen.] Does that look more like an M to you now?

Anna: Yeah.

Coach: The screen was too bright. Do you want to move that M so it's next to the rest of the letters in "time"? [Anna nods] How could you do that?

Anna: I don't know.

Coach: Hmmm . . . Could you erase it and move it?

Anna: Yeah!

Coach: OK, show me how you would do that. [Anna backs up one space then looks at coach with puzzled expression]. Ah ha . . . now the M is going to be typed right where that flashing light (referring to cursor) is. How can you move that flashing light back? [Anna holds finger over BACK-SPACE and looks at coach]. Hmm . . . give it a try [Anna does] . . . It works! Wait — is it right next to it yet? [Anna peers at screen and shakes her head.] Not quite . . . [Anna BACKSPACES one more time.] There you go! Now do your M.

[Anna's story continues in this manner until she has this message on the screen: "ys pn o thm r ys o hs." Translation: Once upon a time there was a house.]
[At this point Anna notices that "once" and "was" are both spelled the same way on the screen—"ys."]

ys pn o thm r ys o hs

Anna: Wait! That one [pointing to "ys" at the beginning of the line] and that one [pointing to "ys" at the end of the line] are the same.

Coach: Uh oh. Wait a minute. Let me read it to you . . . and see if they're the same words. Once upon a time there was . . . [Points to each word on the screen.] . . . once [Points.] . . . was [Points.] . . .

Anna: Wuh . . .

Coach: Are they the same word?

Anna: No!

Coach: No! Wait . . . there must be a sound missing in one of them. On-n-n-n-n-n-n-ce . . . on-n-n-n-n-n-n-n-n-n-ce. . . Do you hear a sound in the middle of that one?

Anna: Yeah!

Coach: What do you hear in the middle there?

Anna: On-n-n-n-n-n-n-n-n . . .ce . . . . S!

Coach: Ah, you hear that S and that's why you typed the S. Are there any other sounds in there? Once . . . on-n-n-n-n-n-n-n-n-ce . . .

Anna: Wuh . . . wuh . . . Y!

Coach: That's right, and you have the Y up there. [Points.] There might be another letter in the middle though. On-n-n-n-n- n-n-n-n-n-n . . .

Anna: N-n-n-n-n-n-n-n-n-n-n-n . . .

Coach: Listen to this. I'm going to say your name, and listen to the sound in the middle. An-n-n-n-n-n-n-n-n-n-nah . . .

Anna: H!

Coach: An-n-n-n-n-n-n-n-n-n-n-n-n-n . . . What's that sound?

Anna: N?

Coach: Yeah, it is. The trouble is that we've got to get the N right in the middle there. Hm. . .

The capacity of word processing to handle the correct formation, spatial orientation, and linearity of written text supported Anna's efforts to invent her own spellings and convey a meaningful message. Remembering the shape of the needed letter (or finding it on the alphabet chart that was on the wall of the classroom) and then hunting for it at the keyboard was a much easier task for Anna than was the task with paper and pencil, wherein she herself had to draw each needed letter. Graves (1983) has pointed out that young writers are preoccupied with production, concerned with "imbalances" between the way they would like their writing to look and the way it actually looks. Graves suggests that the issues of production, including spelling, aesthetics, and handwriting, are often handled by the end of second grade, depending on the emphasis of the teacher. Using word processing intervened in this process for many beginning writers. The technology of word processing handled many of the issues of aesthetics and handwriting before Anna and her kindergarten and first grade friends could have handled them for themselves, probably regardless of teacher emphasis. One way to think about invented spelling is that it allows children to write before they can spell. By the same token, using word processing allows beginning writers to compose before they can handwrite.

It is interesting that Anna, who certainly did not have any more typing speed than Clarence or other older children, was not frustrated by the process of locating letters. As we have pointed out above, the critical factor in determining whether word processing can be used effectively by young children is probably not some absolute minimum typing speed, but rather the relationship between the rate at which a child figures out what letter is needed and the rate at which he or she is able to locate that letter on the keyboard. For Anna, the relationship was balanced—with the help of the coach, she listened to a given word, figured out which discrete sounds she could hear (usually an initial sound and then a final sound), picked a letter whose name sounded like the sound she had heard, and then hunted for the appropriate letter on the keyboard. The figuring-out process took at least as long as the hunting–pecking process, and often took longer, so there was no frustrating interruption to the composing process. Third and fourth graders' experiences were dramatically different: they knew which letters they wanted as soon as they had decided on the language to use, so there was little, if any, figuring-out of the kind kindergarteners did. Until they developed basic keyboard familiarity, then, there was an annoying imbalance between composing and inscribing rates that was simply not an issue for the younger children.

There is some evidence that in order for children to use word processing successfully, they need to be able to type at least as quickly as they write by hand (Fidanque, Smith, & Sullivan, 1986). Wetzel (1985) suggests that the ability to type 10 words per minute allows children to make adequate use of word-processing programs. Our research was not intended to measure typing speed, but the experiences of the children we observed offer some general support for the finding that handwriting and keyboarding speed need to be roughly equivalent. Although there was a great deal of variation both across and within grade levels, most children used word processing in ways that seemed effective for them when their keyboarding speed was relatively consistent with their composing/inscribing rhythm.

Coaches for kindergarten and first graders played a critical role in establishing and maintaining the composing/inscribing balance, often by serving as a kind of mental place holder for the children (Paris, Barton, & Shelow, 1988). In Anna's example, the coach repeatedly reminded Anna of where she was in the composing/figuring-out/hunting-and-pecking process. She prompted, "What's the next word . . . once . . . once . . . how about the next word you need . . . once upon? . . . is that the word?" after Anna had finished writing "once", and "Do you hear any other sounds in that word . . . upon-n-n-n. . .?" after Anna had found the key for "p" in "upon." The coach's prompts sustained the balance by reminding Anna whether she was in the middle of a word, ready for the next word, ready for the next idea, or ready to review the text she had produced thus far. In doing so, the coach not only modeled many aspects of composing, but also helped Anna retain the thread of meaning of her story even as she worked on individual bits of letters and sounds.

The role played by the coach in word processing events like this one is related to Flower and Hayes's (1981) argument that writers move between a variety of plans when they write, especially from high-level plans for an entire piece to lower-level plans for specific words and sentences, and then back up to high-level intentions. The ability to switch from one kind of plan to the other, which is often difficult for writers, is controlled by what Scardamalia and Bereiter (1983) have called the writer's "executive routine" and what Calkins (1986) referred to as a child writer's developing "executive function," or internalized ability to shift back and forth from writing to reading. When beginning writers worked with word processing, adult coaches often bolstered the executive routines by keeping youngsters on the track and helping them figure out where they were. Repeatedly shifting between the big idea to be represented and the multiple little tasks necessary in order to translate the idea into written language is a process often difficult for young children. Together, the word processor and the presence of a coach scaffolded this shifting process for young writers like Anna. Without a coach Anna would not have been able to do this activity.

As beginning writers worked to locate keys and enter text at the keyboard, coaches and word processing together provided many opportunities for children to learn the practice of encoding. In their interaction regarding the "once upon a time" message, for example, the coach repeatedly helped Anna hear the discrete sounds in the words she wanted to write by exaggerating particular word parts, especially initial and final consonant sounds. Interestingly, the coach seldom offered evaluation or comment about Anna's choices of letters, which were almost always logical and often correct. Rather, she modeled the process of elongating various parts of words and picking out the letter forms that could be used to represent them. In interactions of this sort Anna and other beginners had many opportunities to explore grapheme–phoneme relationships. The critical role of the coach is developed in further detail in Chapter 5.

Hunting, Pecking, and Talking. As many of the above examples have indicated, the hum of children "talking out" their keyboarding actions was present in every grade at the beginning of both years when we observed. Our audiotapes reveal a steady stream of talk for most children, supporting the tricky balancing act of coordinating thought processes with actions at the computer and working out a manageable rhythm. Some children like kindergartener Tommy said each of the letter names aloud as he searched for them. Tommy hummed, "T . . . . O . . . . MM . . . . Where is Y?" while others like second graders Ernie and Melina talked to support or check their actions. Ernie repeated, "Up . . . . up . . . . up," as he moved the cursor up one line, and Melina chanted in syncopated style, "Delete M, (pause) space (pause)," as she changed "andm" to "and milk". April narrated her own actions one by one by chanting the moves she should make:

[April sits at the keyboard, working farily independently on a story.]

April: What do I need to do? . . . I need a space bar.

[Hits the space bar, then continues to write and make corrections to her story.]

April: Now if only I could find the K . . .

[Process continues as April continues singing and humming as she talks herself through cursor movements, which are tricky for many children because the numeric keypad must be used to move the cursor to the left: 4, right: 6, up: 8, and down: 2.]

I need to move the cursor down so I need the 2 [moves to the numeric keypad, presses the 2] and across so I need the 4 [moves to the keypad, presses the 4].

As the school year progressed, word-processing events grew more and more silent, particularly in grades two through four. Eventually, many children seemed not to need the support of talk in order to manage the operations of word processing. This finding is in keeping with Vygotsky's (1978) general notion that external speech is often used as a support for difficult or unfamiliar tasks. And several researchers have pointed out that early writing is often accompanied by verbalization (Calkins, 1986; Cioffi, 1984; Graves, 1983) or what Cioffi has called young children's "oral writing," or articulating words as they write them on the page. Early on as they learned to use word processing, beginning writers seemed especially to need the support of talk to carry out the challenging juggling of figuring out messages, finding the correct letters, and managing the required word-processing operations.

Spacing, Erasing, Capitalizing, and Punctuating

In addition to learning how to locate letter keys and enter text, beginners at all grade levels learned how to use the space, erase, capitalize, and punctuate features of word processing. As we have pointed out, however, they developed these skills within quite different classroom situations. Just as there were differences in children's experiences finding letters on the keyboard that were related to their knowledge of alphabetical order, handwriting speed, and writing fluency, we found that there were differences between younger and older children in their uses of word processing to represent print conventions.

Second-, Third-, and Fourth-Grade Children. Ryle's (1949) distinction between *propositional knowledge* (i.e., knowing that) and *procedural knowledge* (i.e., knowing how) provides a useful way to understand some of the differences that older and younger writers experienced in learning spacing, erasing, capitalizing, and punctuating on the computer. For older children, as for most adult writers, learning how to allow for spaces between words, how to make capital letters, and how to insert other marks of punctuation with word processing is for the most part procedural knowledge. That is, writers know *that* spacing and basic marks of punctuation are needed, and learning to do so at the computer is merely a matter of learning the appropriate keystrokes that are equivalent to their paper-and-pencil strategies.

For fourth graders, learning to capitalize the title of a piece, for instance, meant simply learning how to use the shift key. In fact they were dissatisfied when, in one instance, they did not receive the keyboard information they needed in order to insert the punctuation they knew was required. Intending to simplify the initial keyboard experience during their first turns at the computer, Ms. Santori had told the fourth graders simply to leave the "CAPS LOCK" key pressed down at all times, so that lower/upper-case changes would not be at issue. She intended to teach them how to use the shift key at a later session. Nearly every fourth grader we observed, however, assumed immediately that the computer had the capacity to produce both upper-case and lower-case letters and, slightly misunderstanding the teacher's directions, used the "CAPS LOCK" key as one would a shift key, pressing it and releasing it for each individual letter they wanted to produce in upper case form. (Ms. Santori quickly modified her teaching plans and presented information about how to use the shift key, as soon as she observed what was happening.)

For children who were not so certain about written language conventions, however, the mechanical procedures of word processing underscored certain propositions about language and hence reinforced propositional knowledge at the same time that children acquired procedural knowledge. For example, in Miss Price's class, mastering capitalization was an important skill that was emphasized in the district-wide writing curriculum for second grade. When children edited pieces they had composed with paper and pencil or with word processing, they were often expected to concentrate on correcting capitalization errors. For some children, word processing maneuvers seemed to call their attention to capitalization. To change a letter in a text created with word processing from lower case to upper case required that the child writer execute an intricate series of moves. The writer had to position the cursor to the left of the appropriate letter, delete the lower case letter, depress the shift key, press the appropriate letter key while keeping the shift key in depressed position, release the shift key, and then move the cursor to the next appropriate point in the text. This procedure, which is considerably more complicated than simply drawing an upper case letter form above the lower case form crossed out by the teacher, seemed to play a role in children's learning.

For example, second grader April had typed an entire story with no capital letters at all. An adult worked with her at the word processor, coaching her through the procedures for changing a single lower case letter to its upper case form. Immediately afterwards, April worked on the rest of the piece independently. Without difficulty she appropriately corrected the first letter of the first word in the remaining sentence in her piece. In subsequent word processing events, April generally remembered to capitalize, often talking herself through the procedures she needed to use the shift key appropriately. The intricacy of the moves themselves seemed to require her to pay attention to the activity more closely than she had when she recopied her writing and inserted Miss Price's red-marked corrections. The multiple actions required to capitalize letters with word processing (procedural knowledge) underscored the fact that initial words did indeed need to be capitalized to indicate the beginnings of sentences (propositional knowledge).

Initially, the intricacy of the physical moves needed for capitalization was a source of minor frustration for some children. Some youngsters behaved as though capitalization were a test of reflexes, trying to press the shift key and the letter key at precisely the same moment rather than first holding down the shift key and, while doing so, pressing the letter key. It was necessary to show children that, unlike their experiences with other keys, the shift key could be held down indefinitely without reproducing a character, and that the shift key only worked in combination with a letter key. One kindergartener, who selected the shift key randomly, tried holding it down by itself and, when he saw that nothing happened, reported to us that the key was broken. Despite some minor initial snags, however, all second through fourth-grade children learned to type capital letters with little difficulty.

In addition to proper spacing and capitalization, second, third, and fourth graders also learned to erase text. We are making a distinction here between erasing and deleting text: we use *erase* to mean removing words or characters more or less as they are entered onto the screen. We use *delete* to mean removing text after it has been produced. The distinction is a relative rather than an absolute one. It differentiates between erasing, that is, making changes linearly at the point of initial text production, and deleting, or making changes after the point of initial production by entering into an existing text. The erase/delete distinction which we are suggesting separates points in time when changes are made rather than the kinds of changes made. It is not equivalent to the distinction, often made in the composing literature between editing and revising, which discriminates minor word- and sentence-level changes from more significant conceptual-level changes. In fact, the older youngsters in our study deleted text (that is, they removed text well after it had been entered) in order to do both surface-level corrections (often referred to as *editing*) as well as to remove letters or words that created somewhat more substantive changes in the text (usually referred to as *revising*). Our data reveal that erasing was a way for beginning writers to change texts while still remaining in a linear mode of production. Deleting, in contrast, required that writers step back and make changes by entering into an already existing stream of words and sentences. Deleting moved beginning writers into a recursive mode, and, with very rare exceptions, it was simply not done by kindergarteners or first graders.

Like the younger writers we observed, who are discussed in the next section, second, third, and fourth graders frequently erased text as they composed primarily to correct typing or spelling errors. When the error was noticed shortly after it had occurred, older children often erased to the point of error, just as younger children did, and continued to enter text linearly. Many of these errors were typographical, probably a result of lack of touch-typing skill rather than of actual misspelling or word choice alterations. The composing patterns of Angela, the fourth grader in the example that follows, are fairly representative of the older children in our study who had developed some, but not extensive, keyboard familiarity. Angela was composing a new story directly at the keyboard. She worked steadily for about 20 minutes.

[Angela sits at the keyboard, composing the story she will eventually use as her entry for the 'Young Authors Contest.' She uses her right and left index fingers and her left thumb for space bar. She is able to locate letters quite quickly. She looks primarily at the keyboard, typing in three words or so and then checking them on the screen. With more difficult words, she looks up at the screen.]

THIS PERSON

**This person's name is Helen. Helen
likes to listen to Europan**

[Deletes 'Europan,' replaces it with 'European.']

likes to listen to European

Angela: [Reads screen, shakes her head.] Oh, I forgot. [Deletes 'European,' types in,' DEPECHE MODE.']

likes to listen to DEPECHE MODE

Ms. Cochran-Smith (the researcher who is observing): What is that (puzzled, looking at screen)?

Angela: A rock group . . . [Continues typing.]

> **likes to listen to DEPECHE MODE while
> she does her homework. Helen f**

[Erases 'f' and space, moves cursor back to 'Helen.']

> **Helen's favorite 3 people in this world
> are her parents and her cousin Georges**

[Erases 's' and continues.]

> **cousin George. She likes her cousin
> George because they both like the samd**

[Erases 'd' and continues.]

> **same things and because they get ak**

[Erases 'k' and continues.]

> **along with eachother. She likes her
> parents now more than ever because
> she understands them.**

[Erases period, continues.]

> **most of the time.**

When Angela completed the typing, she reread the whole text, then immediately saved and printed the piece. When questioned by Cochran-Smith about whether or not she planned to revise the piece, she indicated that she had no plans to do so. Using a linear erase mode while composing with word processing is a strategy common to adult writers as well as to the older children in this study. Often it is simply easier to back up and erase three or four letters or even a few words, and then continue to type linearly, than it is to move one's fingers off the keyboard and then manipulate the cursor with arrow keys or mouse pad. But the composing patterns of the third and fourth graders we observed represented more than simple adult-like typing convenience. They reflected the fact that the children's composing was for the most part linear and sequential. They used the capacities of the word processor to make easy erasures, but not to alter texts as they composed. The linear nature of second, third, and fourth graders' composing with word processing is in keeping with what Bereiter and Scardamalia (1982) call the "what next" strategy common to young writers. They point out that youngsters' composing strategies are unlike those of experienced adult writers who engage in many kinds of conceptual, organizational, and specific planning as they compose (Flower & Hayes, 1981). In contrast, children are more likely to write one word, phrase or sentence, and then link it to the next without an overarching "controlling purpose" (Hillocks, 1986).

The linear pattern of composing was supported by the ease with which beginning writers could erase text with word processing by backtracking briefly and then continuing forward, attaching one piece of information to the next. Obviously word processing does not offer only the capacity for easy alteration of typographical errors or word-level features. It also has the raw capacity to support powerful recursive alterations to texts as, and after, they are being produced. As we discuss in the section that follows, however, nonlinear alterations were not common in the writing of the beginners we observed, particularly when they worked without a coach at the word processor. To a certain extent, a basically linear procedure was in line with classroom writing instruction. It was emphasized in second, third, and fourth grades, and indeed it was a central part of West Brook School's "process writing" curriculum, that first drafts should be completed quickly without undue attention to form and without stopping to make spelling or punctuation corrections. Revision and editing were encouraged for later drafts, following conferences with teachers or with peers. In truth, however, later revisions and editions generally cleaned up first attempts, correcting surface errors and sometimes adding details to the initial text. They were seldom on the order of significant meaning-level changes, and linear composing with erasing to the point of error was commonplace.

Kindergarten and First-Grade Children. Unlike their older schoolmates in second, third, and fourth grades, the younger children in our study were not aware of many of the conventions of printed language. For them working at the word processor with an adult coach often provided opportunities to learn propositional knowledge about the conventions of print almost simultaneously with procedural knowledge about the word-processing system. In other words, as adult coaches showed young children *how* to hit the space bar, *how* to depress the shift key and then strike a letter key, and *how* to locate the "period" keypress on the bottom row of the keyboard, they were at the same time teaching them *that* written words are separated from one another by empty spaces, *that* certain words are started with upper case letters, and *that* groups of words that belong together are marked off with capitalized letters and end-point punctuation.

The presence of an adult provided opportunities for coaching children in word-processing procedures. It also created unusual opportunities for coaches to present and point out extensive information about written language. Although the latter was not the initial intention of teachers who set up coaching situations for children, our data reveal that most of coaches' efforts were aimed at teaching about the conventions of printed language or the activities of composing rather than teaching the logistics of word processing. Anna's word-processing experience, presented earlier, serves as a good example by demonstrating the way coaches focused on spacing as they worked with young writers to produce texts.

Several brief pieces of that excerpt are repeated below, with italics marking those exchanges that emphasize spacing.

Coach: OK. First, *before we put the P, do you remember what this bar is for?* *[Points to space bar.]*

Anna: P!

Coach: *Press the space bar. [Anna presses it.] Now you can start "upon" right there. [Points to cursor on screen.] Once upon . . .*

[Procedure continues as presented earlier with Anna typing in "pn" for "upon."]
>   **ys pn**

Coach: OK, once upon . . . *now make a space again . . . [Anna moves to space bar without hesitation, presses it]. What's the next word?* Once upon
. . .

[Session continues until Anna has typed, "ys pn o th," for "once upon a time.]
>   **ys pn o th**

Coach: Time . . . tiiimmmmmmmmmmmme.

Anna: *We need a space! [Presses space bar.]*

Coach: *Mmm, we're not done [with] "time" yet. We need to put the "time" letters all close together . . . all the letters that say "time" stand next to each other, then there's a space. Are you done [with] the word, "time"?* Once upon a tiiimmmmmmmme . . . Anything else you hear?

In the parts of the exchange that are in italics, it is clear that the coach was teaching Anna, albeit not necessarily intentionally, both *that* words are set off by white space (propositional knowledge) and *how to* create space with word processing (procedural knowledge). The emphasis, however, is propositional knowledge, especially the notion of *word-ness*—that is, the idea that little groups of sounds that are said together also stand together when they are represented with letters, and that they are then marked off on either side with white spaces. Repeatedly, the coach pointed out that using the space bar was associated with finishing the letters that represented one group of sounds and beginning another. On the other hand, the coach devoted little time to the procedural knowledge that space was created by pressing a special bar. Finding and pressing the bar was something Anna picked up immediately. Early in the session, it is not clear that Anna understood the concept, and her own insertion of space after "th" may indeed suggest that she had inferred a spacing rule that had something to do with the number of letters that were strung together rather than with any internalized sense of word-ness. It is more probable, however, that Anna had simply not heard any more sounds in the word *time* and was indeed finished with it (thus adding space appropriately) until the coach emphasized the "m" sound at the end of the word. Support for this interpretation is suggested by the fact that, as the session continued, Anna more readily inserted space after each word. Additionally, over the next few months when she worked more independently with word processing, Anna automatically inserted space around each word for which she invented the spellings. As Phenix and Hannan (1984) have suggested, the positive act of creating space by pressing the space bar of the word-processing keyboard may emphasize word-ness for young children. It seemed to do so for Anna and for many of the beginning writers in our study. More important to emphasize, however, is that, in our data, it is clear that it was the active exercise of pushing the space bar coupled with the coach's words that drew children's attention to this and other print conventions.

Mrs. Winston and Mrs. Gold had been concerned that the capital letters that appeared on the computer key presses for each letter would present a problem for their kindergarten and first grade children, partly because the key press labels, which were upper-case letters, would not match the characters that would appear on the screen—lower-case letters (unless the shift key were used). The teachers were especially concerned because they stressed the recognition and use of both upper- and lower-case letters in their curricula. They wanted children to break away from the practice of thinking and writing with all upper-case letters, and, especially for the children's own names, to use upper case for the initial letter but then continue with lower-case letters. To encourage children to recognize both upper and lower case, the teachers remodeled the keyboards by putting stickers with paired letters (that is, Aa, Bb, Cc) on the keys.

Teachers also used the word processor as a way to reinforce their specific instruction about the circumstances for using lower- and upper-case letters, as the example below demonstrates and as Figure 3.4b pointed out. In this event, Mrs. Winston had asked Ms. Paris to coach the children at the computer, emphasizing lower- and upper-case letters, just as Mrs. Winston was doing in class. It was clear to her that working with word processing provided a potent opportunity for children to talk directly about written language.

[Barbie and Michael are working side by side at two computers. Each has typed in his or her name using all lower case letters.]

Barbie: I made "Barbie." [Motions to her screen where "barbie" appears.]

Michael: I wrote "Michael" right there. [Points to screen where "michael" appears.]

Coach: How would you two like to learn a trick today? You know when Mrs. Winston is teaching you to print your name, she tells you to make a capital letter—a capital "B" first [nods to Barbie] and she tells you to make a capital "M" first [nods to Michael]? Do you think you can teach the computer to make capitals like Mrs. Winston is teaching you to make capitals? Have you ever found that anywhere on the computer?

Both: No . . .

Coach: OK, I'll show you the trick. Do you see that arrow key right there? [Indicates the "SHIFT" key.]

Michael: Yeah.

Coach: OK, hold it down with one finger . . . [Demonstrates.] OK? Why don't you use this (left) hand? . . . Hold it all the way down . . . [Michael and Barbie each hold down the "SHIFT" key, look up at the screen to see what they have typed.] Just keep it down. Did anything happen up on the screen?

Michael: No . . .

Coach: No, nothing happened. It's sending a message into the computer there (pointing) saying, 'The next letter Michael types, make it capital. The next letter Barbie types, make it capital.' Now hold that key down and type the first letter of your name . . . while you're still holding that key down . . . OK? Now, look! [Barbie uses the shift key correctly to make a capital B and then releases the key.]
   B

Now . . . [Nods toward Michael.] You can lift up your finger just like Barbie did, and type the rest of your name. [Michael does the same.]
   M

Barbie: Yeah . . . that was neat!

Coach: That's pretty neat, isn't it? You taught the computer how to make a capital letter . . . just like Mrs. Winston is teaching you.

[Michael erases capital "M" and then proceeds. Types in "ca."]
   ca

[Michael remembers to hold down the "SHIFT" key. Types in "AC."]
   caAC

[Michael erases "aAC" then types in "AT."]
   cAT

Michael: What? Why did that happen?

Coach: What do you mean, what happened?

Michael: [Points to "c."] Why did that come to a lower case letter?

Coach: Because you're not holding that down. [Points to the "SHIFT" key.] When you hold that down, it will be a capital. Hold that down, and then press that (the "C").

Barbie: I want to try it again.

Coach: OK . . . (to Michael) That's called the shift key. There's how you do it.

Barbie: I want to do it . . . I wanna do a big Y!

Michael: I'm gonna erase it . . . [Deletes "cAT."] Hold, uhhh . . . [Presses shift key.] C . . . A . . . T! There!

CAT

It is interesting that, just one month after this lesson on capital letters, Michael and his friend, Micky, had a long discussion as they worked together at the word processor. The two boys experimented and argued about how to get "higher letters" (their memory of their teacher's phrase "upper case") and in what writing situations they might need them. They also discussed the appropriate times to push the "return" key. The collaborative context in which the two boys worked together, and the fact that word processing foregrounded capitalization, provided an opportunity for them to talk about some of the conventions of print as well as the word-processing procedures for representing those conventions.

Like second through fourth-grade children, the kindergarteners and first graders in our study frequently erased individual characters, words, and sometimes even whole texts. Unlike the older children, however, the younger ones never deleted text. We have shown that working at the word processor, for the kindergarteners and first graders, was sometimes an opportunity to play with bits and pieces of printed language, sometimes an opportunity to invent their own texts or copy existing texts, and sometimes even a video-game-like activity. The youngsters erased bits of print in all of these situations. The example below, for instance, reveals the way kindergarteners and first graders regularly erased in order to "eat up letters, "PAC-MAN style. The child in this example does not have the intention of making a particular change in the text but rather is toying with the speed and visual appeal of the screen image.

[Joel comes to computer to begin his turn. Unintentionally the child who has used the computer before him has left his story on the screen. With great enjoyment, Joel presses the DELETE key and makes loud engine noises as the cursor races across the screen, eating up letters as it goes.]
[Joel continues to press the DELETE key until all the letters disappear, laughing with obvious delight. The coach, looking over to find out the source of Joel's amusement, joins in his laughter.]

Joel: Speed Racer Erasing! (clearly delighted)

[The speed racer show ends too quickly for Joel. He wants to try the whole procedure again, so he quickly fills half the screen with random typing, and again races the around the screen to erase all of the marks. As he does so, he continues to making loud engine noises and other racing sound effects. As the cursor "eats up" the last marks, he announces with a flourish to anyone who can hear him that he has completed his task.]

Joel: I win!

Kindergarteners did not erase simply to create exciting visual displays or to provide the action for their own sound shows. They also erased bits of text with specific intentions in mind, often in order to correct mistakes they had made as they typed, or because they had changed their minds about what they wanted to say. The example below illustrates that first-grader Melinda could easily manage this function at the keyboard in order to change her text.

[Melinda is working at the computer with a coach to compose a story inspired by a picture card for, "tie." She has already typed, "My dad wears a tie. i like to play with a top. I like to play with . . .]

> **My dad wears a tie. i like to play with
> a top. I like to play with**

Melinda: [Types "m."] Y. Y, Y, Y, Y . . . [Types "y."].
>   **my**

Melinda: My . . . 'I like to play with . . . the . . .'

Coach: But you already said, 'my.' [Points to text on screen.]

Melinda: Tree.

Coach: OK, make a space. [Melinda presses space bar.] OK.

Melinda: No. 'I like to . . . play with . . . my . . .' uh, uh . . .

[Melinda has changed her mind about the text, but now seems to feel stuck with the sentence frame, "I like to play with my . . . "]

Coach: You can change the "my" if you don't like it.

Melinda: OK.

Coach: OK, do you know how to get rid of it? [Unassisted, Melinda uses the "DELETE" key to erase "my."] Right. What do you want to say instead?

Melinda: I. . .

Coach: 'I like to play with . . .'

Melinda: My . . . 'I like to play with . . . the . . . tree.'

Coach: "The!" OK. Do you know what the word, "the," looks like? Have you seen it?

In kindergarten and first grade, although children removed text, they always did so in a linear manner. If they noticed an error three characters back or even one or two words back, they "ate up" all of the text to the point of the error in order to continue to enter text linearly. They did not delete text, that is, enter into an existing text after it had already been composed in order to remove particular letters or words and leave the remainder. Nor did they ever enter into existing text to insert new text. Hence, for kindergarten and first-grade children, erasing was a way to change text with ease but, more importantly, to continue to move forward, from left to right and top to bottom. The emphasis on linearity was clear in instances when children altered significantly the content on their pieces partway into them by erasing to the point of a new idea and then starting again. In other words, children of this age did add new information to their stories, and sometimes they changed to a completely different idea, but their composing remained linear. For example, kindergarteners Michael and Nicky began to write a piece about a "G.I. Joe" show they imagined they might attend. They had typed in several lines of text about the number of tickets that would be needed. Their conversation and their topic shifted, however, and they decided to copy the spelling for a word and picture they selected from the picture dictionary. To do so, they erased most of what they had produced, but continued with the same sentence beginning. This process allowed them to change their idea but maintain the linear production of their piece.

Inserting, Deleting, and Revising Text

In addition to entering and erasing text, the second, third, and fourth graders we observed also broke into existing texts in order to edit text (that is, insert and delete characters in order to correct surface errors) and revise text (that is, insert and delete information or reorganize pieces of text). These composing strategies are qualitatively different from those used by kindergarten and first graders, who never edited or revised, although they did, as we have shown, erase bits of text as they composed. These differences are not surprising given the fact that entering into an already-produced text requires a more abstract sort of thinking than does adding onto or taking away from the end of a text. This pattern is in keeping with close observations of young children's paper-and-pencil writing (e.g., Calkins, 1983, 1986; Graves, 1983) that indicate that there is a developmental progression within which children first revise their texts by adding onto the end and only later begin to make changes within them. Entering into an existing text which has been produced with word processing is in a certain sense doubly abstract—it adds to a process which is already somewhat abstract (i.e., the abstraction of imagining the new text which will exist when certain words are inserted into or removed from an existing text) the additional abstraction of the "paper-less" creation of space for an insertion and closing up of space left by a deletion.

Editing with Word Processing: Inserting and Deleting. The second, third, and fourth graders we observed were expected to edit some of their writing in order to obtain final copies that were more or less error-free. Essentially this meant that they were to enter into the stream of writing that had already been produced and correct errors by inserting and deleting bits and pieces of text. Word processing supported and made much easier this established practice of the writing program, especially when children had composed their initial drafts with word processing, or, in some cases, when someone else had keyed in a text which a child had produced with paper and pencil. Children usually edited their texts independently in third and fourth grades and often with the help of a coach or a peer in the second grade.

The procedures for editing with word processing were sufficiently simple for children to master. In some cases, as we pointed out above, children learned both propositional and procedural knowledge about language as they edited, but in other cases, they simply learned how to do with word processing what they already knew to be part of the activity of writing with paper and pencil. The latter instances were those in which beginning writers already knew that some words were spelled incorrectly, that their sentences had missing or unwanted words, and that they needed to attend to standard punctuation. The example below illustrates common editing procedures.

[Second grader Julie is working on her story with Miss Carlisle, a third year elementary education student from the university who helps in Miss Price's class twice a week. She is also assisted by her classmate, Abdul. Her paper and pencil story has been typed into the computer ahead of time by Miss Price. Her unedited text reads as follows.]

Me and my brother at camp

Part one
Me and my brother Danny were siting on
a stone at are camp. I said to Danny do
you like to walk down the hill I will
he said We haved fun going down the
hill.

Back at camp
Prat two
Back at camp me and my brotehr played
ball we haved lots of fun playing ball

[Julie corrects "my" in the title so it reads "My," by moving the cursor, deleting the "m" and inserting the "M."]

Julie: Now where is my paper, where is my next . . . [Looks to her paper and pencil copy to find the next problem which has been marked by the teacher.] There! [Points to error on paper.] "Brother" . . . [Moves cursor just to the left of "b."] All right now, I push the B.

Coach: Help her out Abdul, if you see what she should be doing. Maybe you can hold the copy over here so you can both look at it.

Julie: [Types in "B" in the title.]
        Me and My Bbrother at camp

Coach: How do you get rid of it? [Points to "b." in the title. Julie deletes "b" easily.]
        Me and My Brother at camp

[This process continues with Julie moving the cursor to each error spot and the coach filling in any word processing procedural information which is needed. Abdul plays little part in the activity, apparently more interested in trying to carry on a conversation with the university student.]

Julie: [Refers to paper copy.] Now I have to go all the way to "sitting."

[Abdul and the coach have a brief conversation about his grandmother's computers. Meanwhile Julie has been using the cursor movement keys to move to the word, "sitting," written in her text as "siting."]

Julie: I know. I need a t. But I don't need a capital.

Coach: Find a t.

Julie: I can fix this one because I'm already there. [Inserts "t."]
        Me and my brother were sitting on a
        stone at are camp.

[The coach points out that Julie has another mistake in the same line which she has overlooked. While Julie fumbles with cursor movement keys to get to "are," Abdul tries another discussion-starter with the coach. This time the topic is video games.]

[Julie: types an "o" in front of "are."]

        oare

Julie: Come on (to Abdul), you're not helping me! I have to find a "u." I have to find a "u."

[Julie looks for the key, and Abdul draws his attention back to the keyboard.]

Abdul: A "u?" . . . Here . . . [Matter-of-factly points to the correct key, then turns his attention back to his attempted conversation with the coach.]

Julie: Now I go . . . [Types in a "u."]. . . There we go. [Deletes the "a," moves the cursor to the "e" and deletes it.
        Me and my brother were sitting on a
        stone at our camp

[This process continues with Abdul eventually helping Julie find errors and manage the word processing procedures. The completed piece, error-free, is printed out at Abdul's directions.]

Like Julie, many children in second, third, and fourth grades developed systematic ways of editing their work. They generally started by locating the cursor at the beginning of a line and moving along it until a mistake was located. Some children then erased an entire misspelled or mispunctuated word and started again, typing in the correct form of the whole, while others deleted the individual incorrect parts, preserving any characters which were correct and inserting around them the additional characters needed. Still other children chose to insert all of the correct bits and pieces that were needed in a word and only then to delete the incorrect pieces. To transform "are" to "our," for instance, Julie transformed the word in five steps: *are, oare, ouare, oure, our.* Strategies like Julie's, which create successive approximations of the correct spelling of a word, are quite complex. They require the writer to formulate and hold a mental image of the correct configuration of a word, interject additional characters around those that are already inscribed, and then preserve and/or discard the original characters. This means that the writer must attend to, and make a decision about, every single character in a given word. For some writers, this proved to be a highly valuable opportunity to examine closely the ways in which words are spelled. (This is discussed in more detail in Chapter 6, where we analyze the experiences of one child over time.)

Like most other second graders, Julie, who was by no means the most skilled manager of word processing or the best keyboarder in Miss Price's class, had no difficulty following the errors that the teacher had marked on her papers. Word processing allowed beginning writers to much more easily complete a task which was required in Miss Price's classroom: correcting the errors identified by the teacher in order to produce a "good copy" of the piece. As Miss Price had hoped, word processing took the tediousness out of the process and greatly relieved the physical hardship it imposed on some children.

Julie's experience was similar to those of many second graders and some third graders who used word processing to edit their stories. In the first year of our study, second graders initially worked from a draft on which their teacher had identified their errors. Eventually, they shifted to working with a coach who helped them find errors themselves or, if they could not locate errors, pointed them out to the children directly on the screen. Often, once children knew that an error existed, they knew how to fix it, and they learned to manage the word processing procedures for doing so after a few turns at the computer. April's experience was typical. The coach had helped her identify and change the sentence "I get alot of toys" to "I got alot of toys," so that the verb tense would be consistent with the first line of her story, "I went to Circus Town." Immediately afterwards, April was able to find the usage errors in the sentences "We get balloons and pizza at the party" and "We has fun" without assistance. She changed each of these sentences to past tense, using the correct word-processing procedures as well as the correct spellings for the words.

With the help of coaches who prompted them to reread their texts, children as young as second grade were able to enter into the stream of existing texts to make editing changes as well as the content integration that these changes required. The coach supported the task as much as was necessary for the individual child, although this varied considerably. For instance, a coach provided more assistance to April than to Julie in the two instances reported above. The coach supported the children's realization that changes needed to be made, and the word processor supported the ease with which they could make them. Children rarely complained about making editing changes when they wrote with word processing, although they frequently did so when they wrote with paper and pencil, since it required them to start over again with good paper and recopy their texts.

The kind of editing we have been describing here—entering into the stream of existing text to delete and insert words or letters— was never done by the younger children in our study. As we mentioned above, kindergarteners and first graders composed and erased in a completely linear way. Indeed, there is only one instance in our data where a coach suggested to Anna, the kindergartener we met earlier, that she could intervene in a text to add a word which she herself had noticed was missing. In this instance, both the word-processing procedure and the idea itself were extraordinarily difficult for Anna to handle, even with the full support of a coach. Anna grew tired during the long word-processing event, an unanticipated occurrence, since she generally worked at the word processor for as long a turn as she could wangle and often had to leave the computer before she felt ready. Like many of the other kindergarteners and first graders whom we observed, Anna was apparently not ready to conceive of the composition of connected text as anything but a linear process.

In contrast, second graders were easily coached about how to edit their texts, insert missing words, correct spellings, and change capitalization and punctuation. The insertion of tiny changes, such as those made by April and Julie and many of the second graders we came to know, are sometimes brushed off by researchers and practitioners as mere tinkering with texts in ways that are not meaningful. Instead the literature on teaching writing urges teachers to help children rethink and revise their writing organizationally and substantively. In contrast, however, our data indicate that it may be that surface-level tinkering is an important first step toward eventual revision for beginning writers. It may be that minor changes help beginning writers prepare to make more significant changes later on. For the children we observed, working with word processing with the assistance of a coach seemed to support the notion that it was possible to break into, and edit, text at a point in time after the text had been initially produced.

Over time, using word processing allowed children themselves to control many parts of the editing process. For example, especially after a new "Bank Street Writer" package with an online spelling checker arrived midway through the first year of our study, children had a tool for correcting the majority of spelling mistakes on their own, before teachers saw their drafts. In the third and fourth grade, this meant that children had a new learning opportunity—they speculated about the spelling of a word and then immediately used the spelling checker to evaluate that attempt. This allowed them both to test their spelling approximations with few risks and to receive precise and immediate feedback about their attempts. Third and fourth graders learned to use the spelling checker easily. Even one group of second graders which was introduced to its use seemed able to understand that the spelling checker located instances of incorrect spelling rather than incorrect usage. (Analysis of the ways children used the spelling checker is provided in Kahn and Fields, unpublished manuscript.)

Revising with Word Processing. Second, third, and fourth graders used word processing to revise as well as edit their texts. In almost all cases in second grade, and in some instances in third grade, children revised with the assistance of an adult who coached them through the strategies they needed. Working with a coach proved to be an important learning opportunity wherein children were not simply using word processing to make revisions which they already knew how to make with paper and pencil. Instead they were learning *that* writing could be altered in substantive ways, and *that* it often needed to be altered to accommodate the reader. When adult coaches worked with children to use word processing, they asked questions and provided information that urged children to think about their writing from the perspectives of eventual readers. Reading from the perspective of a reader removed in time and space from the context in which writing has been produced is an abstract and sometimes difficult activity. Presumably experienced writers engage in this process internally, alternating between the roles of readers and writers, anticipating the ways audiences will make sense of their words, and asking various questions of themselves. Coaches' direct questions made some of this process concrete. As they asked of young writers some of the questions experienced writers may ask themselves, they essentially filled in for the absent reader. These interactions made the usually internalized and implicit process of composing more externalized and explicit.

In the example that follows, third grader Scott produced a first draft of a leprechaun story, a topic which had been assigned to all the children in his class. He informed us that his teacher, Mrs. Perrone, had suggested that the children answer three questions as they wrote: how they would catch a leprechaun, how they would get the leprechaun to show them to his pot of gold, and what they would buy with the pot of gold. Scott worked independently at the word processor to produce the following draft.

[Scott works without difficulty locating letter keys or entering text, including proper use of space bar, shift key and "period" key.]

> **I would go to ireland and on A dark
> night I wuld try to here tapping. I
> wuld get I wuld get A cage and put
> it in A cage. I wuld buy a stereo
> and a tape for it.**

[Scott reports that he is finished. The coach asks him to read his text aloud. When he does, he notices the repeated "I wuld get" in line two. He deletes the extra words without difficulty and again indicates that he is finished with the piece.]

> **I would go to ireland and on A dark**
> **night I wuld try to here tapping. I wuld**
> **get A cage and put it in A cage. I wuld**
> **buy a stereo and a tape for it.**

Coach: Now I don't know what Mrs. Perrone said to you. [The coach is reminding Scott that she wasn't there when the teacher asked the questions or framed the whole assignment, even though she does now know the three question. She is trying to get Scott to think about how a reader would understand the text if she had no knowledge of the way the assignment was framed.] Right? *What* is it that you would put in a cage?

Scott: [Rereads piece, looks puzzled.] A leprechaun.

Coach: Did you tell us that anywhere? How about if we start . . . This is fine . . . but I think maybe you should start with something that says, 'If I were trying to catch a leprechaun I would go to Ireland . . .' Huh?

Scott: What do you mean (upset)? You mean erase all this? [Motions to what now appears on the screen.]

Coach: Oh no you don't have to do that. Now if you were writing this story on paper [and you wanted to add something], would you have to erase all this and start again?

Scott: Yes (worried).

Coach: We don't have to do it that way [shakes head]. . . If you type in [something new] right here. . . [Points to the top of the screen.] What's going to happen to the rest of the words?

Scott: Probably going to go forward.

Coach: That's right. They're going to move over and make room for anything else you want to add up there. [Points.] So . . . what do I need to know if I'm the reader?

Scott: I guess . . . uh . . . I don't know . . . [Puzzled, doesn't seem to get what the coach is trying to convey about a reader who hasn't heard the teacher's three questions.]

Coach: Well, you tell me that you would go to Ireland and on a dark night you would try to hear tapping and you would get a cage and put it in the cage and you would buy a stereo and a tape for it. Now there are some other things that I need to know in this story.

Scott: Like for what would I buy it for?

Coach: What is this a response to, Scott? What question are you answering with, 'I would buy a stereo and a tape for it.'

Scott: 'What would I buy?'

Coach: If the leprechaun . . .

Scott: . . . took me to the gold.

Coach: Yes. But you didn't say that. So I don't know that if I'm the reader, right?

Scott: Oh, now I get it.

Coach: You understand what I'm saying? I don't know why you're going to Ireland, because you didn't say anything . . .

[Scott starts to move the cursor down through the text.]

Coach: You could stay at the beginning because you have a problem right at the beginning. I don't know why you want to go to Ireland and hear tapping.

Scott: I should erase this. [Anxious to begin editing.]

Coach: You don't have to erase this.

Scott: Leprechauns would go to . . . No, I would go to Ireland . . .

Coach: OK why would you go to Ireland and on a dark night you would try to hear tapping?

Scott: To catch a leprechaun.

Coach: Oh. You want to put that at the beginning of the sentence . . . 'To catch a leprechaun I would go to Ireland?' But you don't have to erase.

[Scott begins to type, inserting additional text right at the beginning of the existing text.]

To cath A

[Coach supplies the spelling of "leprechaun," Scott continues typing.]

leprechaun I would go to Ireland . .

Coach: Ok. Now I know why you're going to Ireland. 'To catch a leprechaun I would go to Ireland.' [Reads the text from the screen.] Now I know what you're doing here.

[Session continues with coach asking questions and rereading bits of text, supplying spellings and pointing out misspellings, and helping with punctuation. At the end of the session, Scott's story reads as follows:]

**To catch a leprechaun I would go to
ireland and on a dark night I would
try to here tapping that would be a
leprechaun. I would get a cage and
put the leprechaun in a cage. I wuld get
the money from the leprechaun's pot of
gold. I would buy a stereo and a tape
for the stereo.**

In this writing episode, Scott and his coach were wrestling with a basic requirement of written language. Unlike oral language, the meaning of which often
depends on a context of immediate verbal give and take, written language must
carry much of the interpretive context in the text itself. Scott had omitted from
his text a considerable amount of the information that would be needed by a
reader who was removed in time and space from the context in which the text
was produced. Mrs. Perrone had inadvertently contributed to the situation with
the structure of her assignment. When she told the class to respond to three
questions, she unintentionally signalled a dialogic language mode. Although it is
extremely unlikely that he could have articulated his assumption, Scott implicitly
assumed that the teacher's three questions to which he was responding were
somehow embedded in the text he had created. The coach explained, questioned,
and coaxed to try to get Scott to see his writing from the viewpoint of someone
who had not heard the teacher's questions.

This is a difficult concept for 7- and 8-year-olds who are often not yet aware
of the needs of a future audience, or, as Graves (1983) suggests, have not
"decentered" enough to shape their writing according to the needs of its
eventual audience. Even more difficult for beginning writers is the realization
that school assignments generally operate according to the conventions of standard formal writing. Regardless of the fact that the actual eventual reader of the
piece (often the teacher) knows the context in which it was created, and that
the reader could easily ask for additional information when reading the piece, the
writer must write as if this is not the case. Essentially, the writer must learn to
produce text that provides orienting information and explicit comment on the
purpose and use of the piece. In this particular instance Scott and his fellow third
graders were required to anticipate the lack of knowledge of eventual readers,
even though in reality there were to be none.

Despite the struggle and some early confusion, Scott's second draft was
clearly better than his first. With the help of the coach who prodded him along,
Scott filled in some of the information that was missing from the story. Word
processing made it easy to add the needed information and eliminated the
necessity of erasing and recopying. It is evident in the excerpt that Scott was
willing to be coaxed into thinking more about his potential reader only after he
had been assured, and then convinced, that it would not necessitate erasing and
copying over. Scott's episode points out the valuable role played by the tool of
word processing, but also the critical role which the coach played in word-
processing events. Using word processing to revise with the assistance of a coach
was much more than a process of learning operations for already-existing
revising strategies. Often it was also a matter of learning revision strategies in the
first place.

Working with a coach, Scott had the opportunity to learn a little bit about
attending to audience when he wrote. Supported by the capabilities of word
processing, coaches also helped children learn about reorganization and about
the ways in which a text might unfold from a prewriting activity into a draft . In

one instance in our data a child even learned to use the ''MOVE'' command, a particularly powerful revision tool for adult writers. This instance was atypical: beginning writers almost never used the ''MOVE'' function, but sometimes a single instance serves as a powerful demonstration of what is possible with the support of word processing and of the ways children may learn to revise through their experiences working with a coach.

[Dicky has written a ''prewriting list'' for a book about his favorite ice hockey team. Prewriting, or brainstorming, are common activities for the children in Dicky's second grade class and in most of the other classes in our study. Dicky's list has not been composed in logical order, but, as per the instructions for brainstorming, in the order ideas occurred to him. He seems uncertain as to the purpose of this prewriting activity or what role his list is to play in the book he was expected to make eventually. His initial prewriting list is reproduced below.]

> **they are good**
> **i like them**
> **they are my favort team**
> **i like the fights**
> **get mad**
> **they check a lot**
> **they skate**
> **i like the guys the most**
> **they are the best**
> **i like to watch the games**
> **they have 2 shirt home and away**
> **home shirts are white, orange**
> **away scirts are red, orange black**

[The coach invites Dicky to ''rearrange stuff'' if he wants to, before he saves his work on the computer. With some prompting from the coach, Dicky eventually reorders his text so that it is arranged by topics. At first the coach reads aloud to him the ''prompts'' that appear on the screen during the ''MOVE'' function, but after several operations, Dicky completes these independently. His rearranged text reads as follows:]

> **i like to watch the games**
> **they are good**
> **i like them**
> **i like the guys the most**
> **they are the best**
> **they are my favort team**
> **they have 2 shirts home and away**
> **home shirts are white, orange**
> **away scirts are red, orange black**
> **i like the fights**
> **get mad**
> **they check a lot**
> **they skate**

Dicky's experience with a coach demonstrates a way of working with a prewriting list that seemed to help make the connection between prewriting and drafting. When the session began, Dicky was unclear about how his list might be used as the basis for the piece he was writing. With word processing as a support, and with an adult coaching him through the process, his prewriting list *became* his book in a quite literal way—he expanded his list, ordering it more logically. He broke into his text to add information and to rearrange ideas. The example also indicates that Dicky, only a second grader, seemed to understand both the purposes and the procedures of the "MOVE" function. It was clear as he reconstructed his keystrokes that he remembered the mechanical process he had used for the "MOVE" command and that he knew why he had used it. Interestingly, this child saw almost immediately the value of the "MOVE" function, since he turned to the child next to him and volunteered to show her how to do the same thing with her prewriting list. Word processing supported his understandings in a variety of ways—as Dicky rearranged phrases on the screen, he was always able to reread the story. He did not have to follow arrows or staple extra pieces of paper to his list the way he might have done with paper and pencil. Using word processing demonstrated dramatically that lists of ideas and tentative topics could indeed have a direct and valuable role to play in the creation of drafts.

A few second graders, and many third and fourth graders, eventually revised with little or no coaching from adults. As they worked, they were able to insert missed words or phrases as well as add new ideas to their writing. Often, as Matthew did in the example below, they shaped their writing gradually to elaborate and clarify their ideas. Matthew was quite a fluent writer who composed and revised his work relatively easily; he had come to the computer to compose an assigned story about his "favorite skill," which was bowling. In this example the coach primarily provided information about how to manage word-processing operations, and how to spell the words which Matthew requested.

[Matthew sits down at the computer and begins to type his story. He locates letters relatively easily and uses the shift key with no difficulty.]

Favoriteskill

[Matthew immediately notices the missing space between the two words, so the coach demonstrates how to move the cursor to insert space. The coach is observing and providing needed information whenever needed by Matthew or the child using the computer next to his. Matthew resumes typing.]

Favorite skill

My favoriteskill

[Uses cursor control keys to insert space and continues typing.]

is bowling

Matthew: How do you spell 'because'?

Coach: B-E-C-A-U-S-E

Matthew: [Continues to type.]
    becauseyou

Coach: Your favorite skill is bowling 'because you' . . . you need a space.

Matthew: [Inserts a space, deletes "you," and continues to type.]
    I can roll the ball

Matthew: [Reads the piece to himself.] 'My favorite skill is bowling because I can roll the ball . . . down the alley . . . [Looks to coach.] How do you spell 'alley'?

Coach: A-L-L-E-Y.

Matthew: [Types.]
    down the alley

Matthew: [Talks to coach.] I go up my grandmother's house and she has a bowling alley across the street from her house. It's across the street, a big street near my old school.

Coach: Does somebody cross you?

Matthew: Yea. My cousin. He's ten. [Continues typing, talking softly to himself.]
    andtry to all 12 pins

Matthew: [Talks to coach.] I try to knock a lot of pins down. Like the first time I tried I knocked about eight pins down, then nine.

Coach: That's good.

Matthew: I only got twelve when I started to bowl.

Coach: [Reads the screen.] 'Try to . . .' Wait . . . you're missing a word. [Points to screen.] Do you want 'knock' in here? [Points to screen.] You can just type it in now.

Matthew: [Moves cursor to insert 'knock'.] How do you spell knock?

Coach: K-N-O-C-K.

[Matthew types.]
    andtry to knock all 12 pins down.

Matthew: Ok now I have to put in a space.

[Session continues with coach providing spellings when asked. Matthew inserts space whenever he needs to and seems comfortable at the keyboard. Text now reads:]
    My 10 year oldcousin taught mehow to
    bowl

Matthew: [Talks to coach.] Should I put a period and then, 'My cousin comes with me?'

Coach: [Studies screen.] You could do that. Then what you would have is, 'My ten year old cousin taught me how to bowl. My cousin comes with me.' Or you could say, 'My ten year old cousin taught me how to bowl and he comes with me.' Then you don't need a period.

[Matthew nods and continues typing.]

and he comes with me

[Session continues as above. Matthew's completed piece reads:]

Favorite skill

**My favorite skill is bowling because I
can roll the ball down the alley and try
to knock all 12 pins down. My 10 year
old cousin Arty taught me how to bowl
and he comes with me. Me and my
cousins Arty and Nikki go with their
dad Arthur DeLeon we go when I sleep
over my Nan's house**

Throughout this session Matthew asked the coach for spellings and for minor word-processing information. In turn she pointed out surface problems in the text—a missed space, an omitted word—and supplied spellings. But Matthew also developed new information in conversation with the coach, and her responses invited him to elaborate. In two instances over the course of the event, Matthew tried out alternate versions of sentences as he talked with the coach, exploring the possibilities of embedding some phrases within others. The coach's responses supported Matthew's tentative approach to his writing by helping him try aloud two versions of the same sentence and leaving the decision up to Matthew. Both the use of word processing and the opportunity to work with a coach gave Matthew the chance to experiment with his writing as he figured out what he wanted to say about bowling, his favorite skill. When his piece was complete, Matthew was pleased with the outcome. He immediately requested four copies—one for himself, one for Cousin Nikki, one for Cousin Arty, and one for his mother.

In each of the events described above, word processing facilitated revising for beginning writers. It is important to note, however, that most of these revisions were relatively minor. Although they moved beyond the editing of surface features and the linear deletion or insertion of bits of text, they generally did not significantly alter substance or conceptual framework. The one instance when revision substantially altered organization—Dicky's hockey team story—was the exception rather than the rule for beginning writers. On the one hand, then, it is clear that using word processing did not prompt beginning writers to revise. On the other hand, it is also clear that using word processing did prompt teachers to set up coaching situations for beginning writers. Within the context of these learning situations, coaches prompted beginning writers to revise, and word processing facilitated the revisions they learned to make. In other words, within an altered social context where beginners worked with adults to negotiate texts on a joint basis, the raw technological capacity of word processing facilitated new ways of thinking about writing and revising.

In Chapter 2, we analyzed the literature on the effects of word processing coupled with various computer prompting programs. We suggested that the importance of this research was insight into the nature of the instruction that seems to scaffold uses of word processing rather than information about the specific form such instruction might take. Woodruff et al. (1981–1982) use the term *procedural facilitation* to argue that writing assistance which reduces the cognitive demands of writing while allowing writers to control lower as well as higher-level aspects of writing is most effective. One way to understand the revising exchanges of coaches and beginning writers is to interpret the coach's role as offering procedural assistance. This assistance highlighted language issues, such as spelling, punctuation, and sentence structure, as well as content issues such as the amount of information to provide for the audience and the way to organize a piece. Emphasis on word-processing procedures was secondary, even with a somewhat complicated operation like the "MOVE" command.

What we want most to emphasize here is that beginning writers were willing to respond to coaches' suggestions because word processing made it possible to do so without extreme effort. Our analysis makes a subtle, but critical, connection about the ways beginning writers used the tool of word processing to edit and revise their work: (a) Word processing, in and of itself, did not teach or prompt beginning writers to edit and revise their writing in new ways. (b) Adult coaches, in and of themselves, did not teach and prompt beginning writers to edit and revise their writing in new ways. (c) Adult coaches, working with beginning writers who were using the tool of word processing, offered procedural assistance by suggesting cognitive strategies for writing, while the tool of word processing offered procedural assistance by reducing the burden of lower-level aspects of text production. (d) This combination of human and technological assistance helped second-, third-, and fourth-grade beginning writers learn to revise and think differently about revising.

SUMMARY AND CONCLUSIONS

In this chapter we have provided many cameos of beginning writers learning to use the capacities of word processing to enter, edit, and revise text as well as manage some of the basic operations of word processing. Our data reveal that beginning writers initially approached word processing with expectations based on their prior experiences with language and with paper-and-pencil writing. In certain ways, this was problematic—some beginners were disconcerted by the nonalphabetic keyboard and found cursor movement and deletion procedures puzzling. In other ways, this was liberating—many beginners commented explicitly that they added more detail when they wrote and were willing to find and correct more errors. In all cases, beginners started to write differently when they began to work with a new tool, a tool that demonstrated by its very features that the most important thing about writing was not aesthetic production or avoidance of alterations. We have analyzed the manner and speed with which beginners adjusted to word processing partly as a function of what they could already do with paper and pencil. This resulted in an oddly inverted outcome— kindergarteners and first graders, who had less experience and less skill with written language, could often more readily establish an effective balance between encoding and typing speed than third and fourth graders, who were adequate spellers and composers, and hence were seriously troubled by their inability to locate letters on the keyboard.

The capacity of word processing to handle the formation, spatial orientation, and linearity of written text supported the efforts of many beginning writers to encode their own messages through invented spellings. This meant that very young writers could deal with more advanced aspects of written language— encoding as opposed to copying or tracing over letter forms. It also meant that older beginning writers could sometimes attend to issues of topic and information instead of neat copying of final drafts and insertion of minor corrections. As we argue here and in the following chapter, this ratcheting-up process for all beginning writers was not the function of word processing alone, but was instead the result of the ways the tool interacted with the evolving learning contexts of various classrooms.

Further, we have argued that, although beginning writers generally did not use its most powerful features, their work with word processing created robust opportunities to learn propositional and procedural knowledge about language. Beginning writers learned, for example, the procedures for *how* to create white space using the computer keyboard's space bar and *how* to break into a continuous text to insert additional information. But they also learned the propositional information *that* words are marked off by white spaces, and *that* written texts must account for the discontinuity between the knowledge base of the writer and the knowledge base of the eventual reader.

In the next chapter we move beyond global description of what beginning writers learned to do with word processing. We look closely at individual word-processing events and at the factors that account for variation across and within events.

chapter 5
WORD PROCESSING: IS IT A FELICITOUS TOOL FOR BEGINNING WRITERS?

In preceding chapters we have looked at teachers, beginning writers, and word processing from two perspectives, beginning with the teaching cultures of the classrooms in which word processing was introduced and moving to the experiences of particular children as they learned about writing and word processing. In the course of these chapters, we have offered glimpses of beginning writers for whom working with word processing seemed highly effective, as well as beginning writers for whom it was frustrating or simply unremarkable. In this chapter we consider more specifically the usefulness of word processing as a beginning writer's tool. Readers will find little, however, which directly addresses the bottom-line question, "When they use word processing, do beginning writers write better?" We have intentionally avoided this question because, as we demonstrate in this volume, it is unlikely to have a single answer or prove to be a particularly productive question. How word processing can be used most effectively in elementary classrooms is not likely to be understood apart from the ways individual teachers and children work within particular instructional contexts. How word processing affects the quality, quantity, or processes of writing by beginners is not likely to be understood apart from the ways these are embedded within, and mediated by, individual social situations.

Questions about the quality and quantity of writing produced with word processing are not the right questions to ask about the experiences of 5- to 10-year-old children who are in the process of emerging as writers and for whom issues of fluency and print production are still central. To consider the usefulness of word processing as a writing tool for beginners, we need to look beyond the correlations usually explored with older writers: the production of lengthier texts, the commission of fewer errors, the occurrence of more revisions, the creation of a greater number of drafts, the improvement of attitudes, and so on. When considering beginning writers, we need instead to look closely, not only at the ways word processing is used within the instructional contexts of primary school education, but also at the value of the writing tool within these contexts. Two alternative questions are ultimately more valuable to the educational community: "In what ways and under what conditions does word processing function as a felicitous writing tool for beginners?" and "What do those conditions look like in various classroom settings?" Two analytic constructs provide a framework for answering these questions—the notion of word processor as a *felicitous writing tool* and the notion of individual writing episodes in which word processing is used as *word-processing events*. Using these two constructs to examine word-processing episodes across grade levels, we conclude that word processing can indeed function as a felicitous writing tool for beginning writers when task and learning context are constructed in ways that enable the individual child to take advantage of the facilitative features of word processing. We also point out, however, that this kind of structuring is not always possible and not always desirable.

FELICITOUS TOOLS AND WORD-PROCESSING EVENTS

Felicitous Tools

We use the phrase *felicitous tool* to capture the sense in which our questions about word processing and writing depart from the common view, which sets up word processing as an independent variable and writing performance as a dependent variable. Our questions, which require interpretation of events rather than correlations between input and outcome variables, argue for an alternative sense of what is significant. *Felicitous* is a term that is usually paired with such English synonyms as *appropriate, apt, befitting, applicable, desirable*, and *convenient*. Its Latin root, however, is *felix*, translated into English as *happy*, and the other English derivatives that share the root—*felicitate, felicific*, and *felicity*—all connote some sense of causing, expressing, or intending happiness. In the phrase *felicitous tool* we have tried to retain, in the term *felicitous*, the suggestion of happiness originally embedded in the root to signify a tool "happily paired with," or "particularly well suited for," certain kinds of writing tasks, writers, or writing contexts. Accordingly, the phrase *felicitous tool* is used in this volume to describe word processing when it is used in circumstances that make it unusually well suited for beginning writers and the tasks they are trying to complete within particular situations. On the other hand, the term is not used to characterize the tool of word processing when it is used in circumstances that make it either not well suited for beginning writers or merely as well suited for them as other common writing tools.

Snyder and Palmer (1986) make a related point in an interesting discussion of the potential of computer technology in our society. They point out that computers can be used for many tasks in the world, but ultimately their worth depends on their capacities as tools to help us perform our tasks in ways that are *significantly better* than the ways we could perform them with other tools.

Tongue in cheek, Snyder and Palmer comment that we could, after all, use a helicopter for transportation to the corner grocery store, but this would not necessarily be an effective or cost efficient use of the tool. They raise a number of important questions about the uses of computers for writing and other school tasks:

> Does it make sense to use the computer in the service of education? Obviously it can do a lot of swell things, although like any tool it can do some things better than others. . . . A computer can integrate graphics, text, and sound, but in many cases a book might do a better job of getting the point across. Poor resolution, screen glare, unimaginative graphics, and eye-boggling typefaces combine to make readability something less than one of the computer's strong points. A computer can be used as a writing instrument, along the lines of Papert's computer-as-pencil vision, but a real pencil or a piece of chalk might be just as good. . . . Should we use it to teach? Not unless it can be made to help teachers do their job, and unless the software content is in keeping with subjects they already teach. . . . These decisions shouldn't be made arbitrarily, on the basis of availability or convincing advertisements, but in relation to a host of other factors. . . . And if [using computers] makes sense in relation to other educational priorities. (pp. 59-60)

Snyder and Palmer's critique of the uses of computer technology in education reminds us that tools are revolutionary only when they help us perform our tasks better and/or allow us to perform new tasks that are considered to be significant. Ultimately, decisions about what is significant educationally must be made by educators and not by computer technologists. Given the expense, the large space demands, and the limited accessibility of word-processing equipment relative to the low cost, the compactness, and the virtually universal availability of papers and pencils, "felicitousness" seems a reasonable criterion for word processing as a writing tool. We need to know in what ways and under what circumstances, if any, word processing can help teachers and students do important writing tasks *better*, and not just *as well as*, paper and pencil. A criterion of this sort is one that could have far-reaching implications for elementary school policy and curriculum.

Weizenbaum's (1976) argument, introduced in Chapter 1, emphasizes that the tools we use shape the ways we understand the tasks we do and even shape who we are as users of tools. Through our tools we act on the world, but our tools, in turn, act on us as we work to understand the world. Throughout this book we have analyzed the ways in which word processing *can* be a particularly powerful tool for writing. Accordingly, it has the potential to have a powerful impact on the ways young children understand and carry out the task of writing. In order to determine whether or not word processing *is* a felicitous tool for beginners, however, it is important to consider how it shapes their theories and practices of writing and how it functions in the writing demonstrations that are available to them. To consider the felicitousness of word processing, we examine uses of word processing within individual writing events.

Word Processing Events

In Chapter 1 we defined a *word-processing event* as a specific kind of literacy event in which one or more persons use computer word processing to create or modify a piece of writing and/or to read, respond to, or otherwise use a piece of writing created with word processing, and in which word processing is central to participants' interactions.

Our data reveal that word-processing events, which functioned as part of writing instruction and practice in all five classrooms where we observed, were structured along four dimensions: (a) *specific writing task*; (b) *developmental constraints, abilities,* and *concerns* of individual child writers; (c) *learning/ teaching processes* involved; and (d) relevant *capabilities of the word-processing* software and hardware. Each of these four dimensions, summarized in Figure 5.1, is discussed in the following section.

The Writing/Word-Processing Task. By *writing/word-processing task* we mean the precise writing activity a beginning writer is assigned to do or chooses to do with word processing, including the multiple smaller tasks that comprise the larger task and the skills and knowledge necessary to complete and coordinate each of these. There are both broad-brushed differences between very unlike writing/word-processing tasks and more nuanced differences between different versions of the same task. For example, using word processing to invent the spellings for single words or phrases is obviously quite different from using word processing to edit a final draft in order to correct spelling errors. The former requires that the writer select a word that he or she knows orally, identify one or more phonemes within the word (usually by repeating the word aloud and elongating one of its sounds), select a letter to represent that sound, locate the appropriate letter on the keyboard, press the key appropriately, and begin the process again either by finding the place within the same word and continuing or selecting a new word. In this task, encoding is the central endeavor. There is little or no attention to "meaning" in its usual sense in composition, and organization and style are simply not at issue. The task of editing an existing text for spelling, on the other hand, requires that the writer read systematically through the text, identify each instance of nonstandard spelling, locate the cursor at the point of the error within the word, use the appropriate key to delete the error, use the appropriate key(s) to insert the correction, and begin the process again either within the same word or with a new word. Issues of form as they affect the meaning of the entire piece are central to this task. Like the task of invented spelling, encoding is still the major issue in editing, but it occurs by comparing existing spellings with some sort of mental template for standard form or with the correct spelling supplied by an expert resource. (Use of a computerized spell-check system obviously changes the task.) It is clear that the differences in skills and knowledge necessary to complete these two different

Figure 5.1
Word Processing Events: Four Dimensions

1. THE WRITING/WORD PROCESSING TASK

Question: What is the exact nature of the task?
What smaller tasks are contained within the larger one?
What word-processing skills are needed to complete and coordinate all parts of the task?
What reading/writing skills are needed to complete and coordinate all parts of the task?

2. THE INDIVIDUAL BEGINNING WRITER

Question: Independently or with a coach does the child have the skills needed in order to do the task?
Is the child functioning at the appropriate developmental level in order to perform the needed skills?
Does the child have the fine motor, visual and coordination skills needed?
Does the child have the word-processing skills and experiences needed?
Does the child have the reading/writing skills and experiences needed?

3. THE LEARNING/TEACHING CONTEXT

Question: Does the learning/teaching context support the child's completion of the task?
Does the learning/teaching context include references, resources, and consultants that are helpful to the child?
Does the learning/teaching context include adequate instructions concerning the task?
Is the amount of time allotted sufficient for completion?
Is allocation of turns at the computer sufficient for completion of of the task?
Does the instructional program include opportunities for the child to learn the the word-processing skills needed to complete the task?
Does the instructional program include opportunities for the child to learn the writing/reading skills needed to complete the task?

4. THE WORD PROCESSING HARDWARE/SOFTWARE

Question: Are the features of the word-processing software/hardware particularly well-suited to the child's completion of the task?
Do features of word processing foreground writing/composing issues that are relevant to the child?
Do features of word processing manage production issues that are of concern to the child?
Do the features of word processing contribute to the development of the child's theories and practices of writing?
Do the features of word processing make easier or quicker drafting, revising, editing, or publishing strategies that the child is expected to use?
Do the features of word processing make drafting, editing, revising, or editing strategies and skills easier for the child to learn?
Are the word-processing procedures sufficiently simple for the child to handle?

encoding tasks—inventing spellings for individual words and editing continuous text—are enormous.

On the other hand, typing a sentence using standard spelling and punctuation seems a fairly undifferentiated writing/word-processing activity, but there are subtle differences inherent in variations on this task as well. For example, composing an original sentence at the word processor requires that the writer have an idea, decide how to render it, either remember or approximate standard spellings and letter forms, and manage the keyboard sequences necessary to enter the words and marks of punctuation. This process of composing a sentence is significantly different from transcribing a sentence that has already been composed on paper with pencil. When transcribing, the burdens of composing the sentence are removed, but the burdens of orchestrating visual and manual actions is heightened, and the need to juggle visual attention to paper-and-pencil text along with attention to screen and keyboard is added. Producing a sentence that one knows by rote (e.g., "Now is the time for all good men . . ." or "Today is Friday, June 9, 1989. . .") is a third variation on the entering-a-standard-sentence task. Since it does not require composition or reading and rereading from a prepared draft, the rote sentence task is primarily a process of managing the mechanics of word processing by balancing attention to keyboard and screen. None of these three versions of the specific writing task of entering a complete sentence of text is, in and of itself, easier or more difficult than another. Rather, relative ease or difficulty in completing any of them is a function of the interaction of the task with the skills and abilities of the writer, the structure of the learning environment, and the word-processing technology itself. All of these together comprise the context in which word processing is used, and the task itself is a central determinant of that context.

The Abilities and Skills of the Beginning Writer. By *abilities and skills of the beginning writer*, we refer to both the developmental constraints and abilities of the child and the composing and word-processing skills he or she possesses. Again there are enormous differences between the abilities and skills of 5- to 10-year-old beginning writers, both across and within age and grade level groups. For example the broad-brushed developmental differences between a kindergarten child and a fourth-grade child are quite substantial. Many kindergarten children have undeveloped perceptual and fine motor skills as well as limited, but emerging, knowledge of the relationships between sounds and printed symbols. Kindergarteners are seldom experienced writers who can fluently produce in standard print the messages they can produce orally. Similarly, the youngest children within this age group generally have little experience with the computer keyboard and often little knowledge of the alphabetic sequence. Fourth graders, on the other hand, usually have mature fine motor skills and firm mastery of fundamental sound-symbol correspondences. With a repertoire of thousands of words they can automatically produce in written form, the basic production of print is ordinarily not an issue. Although fourth graders still make many spelling and punctuation errors, they can generally represent most oral messages in intelligible written form. Further they often have quite well-developed knowledge of the structure of story as well as some notion of the importance of attending to the "other" who will serve as the eventual reader for a piece. For fourth graders in writing classrooms where issues of style and organization are stressed, students often learn to make revisions in their writing that affect significantly its meaning.

Of course, as the many qualifying phrases in the above descriptions emphasize, there are tremendous differences within same age groups as well as across age groups. Some fourth graders, for example, have well-developed keyboarding and computer skills based on outside-of-school experiences; others have never used a keyboard. Some second graders are basically fluent writers who compose coherent and reasonably well-organized stories, while others of the same age struggle with the basic production issues of spelling and handwriting. Some first graders can read an existing text and check for errors in capitalization, while others are just beginning to invent spellings for single words and phrases. Some third graders can independently manage the "SAVE," "RETRIEVE," and "PRINT" functions of word processing, while others have difficulty inserting a disk into the drive. There is not an ideal implied in any of these cameos of word-processing/writing skills, nor is any particular grouping of skills more likely to lead to felicitous use of word processing for writing. The question of felicity is entangled in the interplay of all four factors, and additional nuances are embedded within each.

There are aspects of children's development about which educators can do very little at any single point in time. For example a child who is developmentally unready to make the association between abstract marks on a page and the oral sounds of spoken language is unlikely to be aided by spelling lessons at the computer keyboard. Similarly, a child who cannot conceive of the idea of entering into an existing text is unlikely to be aided by instruction in how to delete unwanted characters from the computer screen. We include in the category of "individual beginning writers" the constraints of developmental levels as well as the development of current and emerging skills. On the other hand, there are a number of skills which children can manage with the help of a more experienced writer/word-processing user even though they cannot manage them on their own. As we saw in word-processing events in Chapters 3 and 4, for example, an adult can sit with a child as he or she works at the keyboard and fill in the word-processing/writing skills needed in order both to hear the sounds in individual words and find the letter keys needed to represent those sounds. By the same token an adult can walk a child through the procedures needed to insert additional information into a keyboarded text at the same time he or she teaches the child about the need to insert information for greater clarity of meaning. When we refer in this chapter to the skills and abilities that the individual writer brings to a word-processing event, we mean both those writing/word-processing skills that the writer can manage and control independently and those skills that the child can manage with the assistance of a coach.

The Learning/Teaching Context. We have emphasized throughout this volume that the *learning and teaching cultures* that exist in classrooms are different from one another. We have also emphasized that learning/teaching culture in a single classroom shapes the ways in which the individual teacher chooses to deploy word processing in that setting, just as, in turn, evolving uses of word processing shape the learning/teaching environment. As we have pointed out, all five classes where we observed were "process writing" classes, in that West Brook School District had adopted a language arts curriculum that emphasized writing as a five-step process of prewriting, drafting, revising, editing, and publishing. All five teachers attended school-wide and district-wide in-service training sessions about writing instruction and were conversant with the process writing literature and language. Further, all five teachers were attentive to writing as part of the language arts curriculum: they adhered to requirements set by the district for individual age and grade levels (e.g., covering the prescribed writing assignments and skills emphases for each grade level), and they implemented required classroom routines (e.g., encouraging invented spelling, brainstorming sessions for prewriting, or editing conferences with teacher or peers).

As Chapter 3 makes clear, however, these activities were carried out in quite different ways across classrooms. Teachers instituted most fully those new procedures that supported their ongoing programs and goals. They completed what they considered to be unsuitable district-wide writing assignments quickly and then devoted instruction to assignments more geared to their overall programs. They paid least attention to recommendations they believed were not developmentally appropriate for their children. As we argue in Chapter 3, we can no more consider "the writing process classroom" as *the* learning/teaching culture for the use of word processing than we can consider "using word processing" as an independent treatment introduced into that context.

In this chapter we make the case that learning/teaching processes are a central influence on the felicitousness of word processing as a tool for writing. But we mean more than the general learning cultures of individual classrooms. We also mean the many contexts constructed by adults and children within the larger milieu of the individual classroom—the details of the many individual settings in which writing tasks are assigned and completed. We include here especially the nature of the social interactions that occur between children and adults, or children and their peers if they work together with word processing. We also include the extent and kinds of composing instruction provided, the extent and kinds of word-processing instruction provided, the composing processes a child is encouraged or expected to utilize in writing, time and access limitations and opportunities (e.g., length of time allotted for the completion of assignments, length of time allotted for individual "turns" at the word processor, how "turns" are allotted), the extent and explicitness of directions given for particular writing tasks, resources and reference materials available, past emphasis or instruction concerning the kind of task assigned, and availability of word processing cue cards, computer experts, or other consulting resources. It should be evident that "learning/teaching processes," conceived of in this way, change continuously, altered at times even from one minute to the next or from one child's work space to the next.

For example, when a first grader goes to the computer to enter text by inventing the spellings for various words, having the lower- and upper-case forms posted with pictures representing initial sounds and displayed on charts around the front of the room is a significant part of the learning/teaching context. Similarly, the third or fourth grader who has a 15-minute "turn" at the computer every three weeks works within a different kind of learning context from that of the second grader who works for more than 65-minutes during one sitting at the computer and then has a similar opportunity a few weeks later. A second grader who writes a piece based on a story from the reading book used in class has a different learning context when he or she uses the book itself as a resource for spellings and ideas from the experience he or she has without the book. A fourth grader whose class always brainstorms prewriting lists together approaches this same task at the word processor in a way that is different from the approach of a child who has not participated in brainstorming. A kindergartener who uses the word processor to "practice words" has one experience when the words come out of his or her head and another when the words come from label cards on the walls around the room or from a picture dictionary made available as a reference. Most importantly, perhaps, a first grader who sits with an adult and jointly negotiates a written text at the word processor works within a very different learning/teaching context from the context he or she might experience when working with word processing independently. Human collaboration is situated in a particular context and is responsive to the needs of that situation. Clearly, these detailed features of the learning/teaching context overlap intimately with the skills of the child and the requirements of the writing task.

Capabilities of Word-Processing Software/Hardware. The fourth factor that structures word-processing events includes *word-processing software*, and to a certain extent, hardware itself. Obviously the capacities of word processing do not change from one word-processing event to the next, but the relative importance of these capacities to the individual writer and to the specific writing task do vary considerably. It is interesting, for example, that, when adult professional writers describe the advantages of word processing, they never mention the fact that word processing is beneficial because it manages for them the correct and even production of individual letter forms as well as the appropriate and continuous progression of text from left-to-right across, and top-to-bottom down, the page. They do, however, almost always emphasize the enormous benefits of the "MOVE," "INSERT," and "DELETE" functions. Word processing always offers the capacity for both the former and the latter, and, in fact, one cannot do much of anything at a word processor (even random punching of keys) without taking advantage, albeit unknowingly, of the capacities of the former. What is emphasized as the ''miracle'' of word processing, however, tends to depend more on the user and on the conditions under which he or she works than on actual technology.

As we have pointed out in Chapter 4, for example, third and fourth graders were often confused by the QWERTY keyboard. Before they had developed basic keyboard familiarity, the arrangement of the keyboard was a relevant and disadvantageous feature of the word-processing hardware that structured word-processing events for them. For kindergarteners and some first graders, on the other hand, the capacity of word processing to position letters correctly in space, free of reversals and inversions and automatically allowing enough space to the right and below for the next letter, was an extremely relevant capacity of word processing software. The examples that follow make clear which of the features available with word processing was relevant during any given word-processing event.

A FELICITOUS TOOL FOR BEGINNERS?

Our data clearly reveal that one word-processing event varied from another whenever there were differences in one or more of the four dimensions described above. Further, we found that we could not make inferences about the usefulness of word processing for one writing event based simply on its usefulness for another event. Rather the contour and shape of each event depended on the dynamic interplay of these four factors. Figure 5.2 builds on Figure 5.1 and emphasizes that word-processing events were the outcome of these four factors as they were interactively related. To determine the felicitousness of word processing for the writing events of a particular classroom, we must consider the ways in which these four factors converged or diverged in particular instances. Figure 5.3 provides a way to think about the relationships of word-processing/ writing tasks, individual beginning writers, learning/teaching processes, and the capacities of word processing.

Figure 5.3 provides a way to address the question, ''What are the conditions under which word processing is a felicitous tool for beginning writers?'' It is constructed along the lines of a truth-table to emphasize the interconnectedness and interdependence among the factors that play a part in the answer to the question. The table begins with the writing/word-processing task to be completed (across the top of the figure). Analysis of conditions includes consideration of whether or not the beginning writer has the skills needed to complete the task, what the learning/teaching context is and whether or not it supports completion of the task, and whether or not the features of word processing itself are well suited to completion of the task (down the left side).

Figure 5.2
Dynamic Interplay of Four Factors in Word-Processing Events

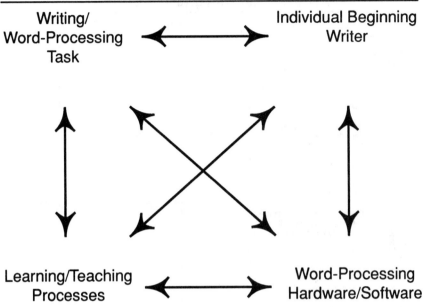

Writing/
Word-Processing
Task

Individual Beginning
Writer

Learning/Teaching
Processes

Word-Processing
Hardware/Software

As the figure makes clear, a "no" answer to any one of the three major questions in columns B through H leads to a "no" answer to the final question, "Is word processing a felicitous writing tool?" On the other hand, a "yes" answer to the final question requires a "yes" to each one of the three major questions, as indicated in column A. Hence, there are seven different pathways to the conclusion, "No, word processing is *not* a felicitous tool for beginning writers," while there is only one pathway to the conclusion, "Yes, word processing *is* a felicitous tool." Constructed in this way, the truth table provides a systematic procedure for analyzing writing events accomplished with word processing and an appropriately conservative way for judging its value as a writing tool which is in keeping with our definition of felicitous.

The seven pathways leading to a "no" answer to the final question suggest that it would be unlikely that word processing would function very often as a felicitous tool for beginners. However, our data belie this suggestion, displaying instead a wide array of examples in which word processing was indeed used as a felicitous tool at all grade levels, kindergarten through fourth. Our discussion in the next section reveals that there is an additional factor that has a powerful influence on each of the others and is, in a certain sense, embedded within each of the questions of the truth table. This factor is the teacher. As we reveal in the

Figure 5.3
Conditions Under Which Word Processing
was a Felicitous Writing Tool for Beginners

Dimensions of Word-Processing Events	Questions	Word-Processing Tasks							
		a	b	c	d	e	f	g	h
The Skills of the Child	Does the child have the skills needed in order to do the task? OR With the help of a coach, does the child have the skills needed to do the task? OR Is the task altered so that the child has the skills?	YES	YES	YES	NO	YES	NO	NO	NO
The Learning/Teaching Context	Does the learning/teaching context support the child's completion of the task? OR Is the learning/teaching context altered in order to support the child's completion of the task?	YES	YES	NO	YES	NO	YES	NO	NO
The Word-Processing Software/Hardware	Are the features of word processing well suited to the child's completion of the task? OR Is the word processing software/hardware altered so that it is well suited to the child's completion of the task?	YES	NO	YES	YES	NO	NO	YES	NO
	IS WORD PROCESSING A FELICITOUS WRITING TOOL?	YES	NO	NO	NO	NO	NO	NO	NO

examples that follow, the teacher is central in almost every event, often intervening to redefine the task, bolster the skills of the writer, modify learning/teaching processes, and even temporarily redesign the computer hardware or software in order to make it possible for word processing to function as a felicitous tool. Figure 5.3 also emphasizes that, within any given classroom situation, word processing may be used as both a felicitous and an unfelicitous tool for writing instruction, depending on variations over time or from child to child along any of the four dimensions.

HUNTING, PECKING, AND CHECKING:
REVISITING BEGINNING WRITERS

Analyzing word-processing events according to the interplay of factors in Figure 5.3 provides a perspective that cuts across the events presented in the two previous chapters. The discussion that follows both illustrates how the notion *felicitous writing tool* functions as a way to examine beginning writers' uses of word processing and provides a sense of the specific circumstances under which word processing does and does not function felicitously for 5-to 10-year-olds. The examples make clear that, for different word-processing events, different factors are the critical determinants.

Clarence Revisited

As we pointed out in Chapter 4, Clarence's first turn at the word processor was a tortuously slow event that produced very little text. Clarence's experience is a clear example of a writing event in which word processing was a decidedly unfelicitous tool.

(1) *The Writing/Word-Processing Task.* Clarence's task was to enter text at the keyboard by transcribing from a paper-and-pencil draft on which he had composed a few paragraphs of description about an imaginary creature, the "Goofyo Exname." In order to transcribe, Clarence had to look intermittently at three different places—the paper (to see what text was supposed to come next), the keyboard (to find the proper letter keys), and the computer screen (to check to see whether what he thought he had entered was indeed what he had entered). With the paper-and-pencil text, Clarence found his place by rereading, then pointing with his finger to "save" the place each time he looked away to the screen or the keyboard. With the keyboard, he had to locate individual letter keys as well as manage the procedures for spacing, erasing, and moving the cursor. On the screen, Clarence had to keep track of the text he had typed in so far and the point of new entry as indicated by the flashing cursor. On the other hand, because he was transcribing from a pencil draft rather than composing, Clarence did not have to come up with an idea for his creature, decide on the wording to render his idea, or construct properly punctuated sentences. The task was strictly a matter of transcribing and managing word-processing features from which the requirements of composing had been removed. In and of itself, there is nothing about this task that is unfelicitous or inappropriate— secretaries routinely transcribe from printed text with ease and speed. It was the interrelationship of the task to the skills of the writer, the context of the event, and the computer hardware/software, however, that was problematic.

QUESTION #1:   What is the nature of the writing/word-processing task?

ANSWER #1:   The task requires use of the computer keyboard to transcribe several sentences of text from paper-and-pencil draft to word-processing screen.

(2) *The Individual Beginning Writer.* Clarence had all of the visual, motor, and coordination skills required by the transcribing task, and he had the reading/writing skills needed as well. The lack of word-processing skills was what tripped up Clarence, although his difficulty in this area was clearly not his own failing. He simply had too little knowledge of the keyboard and was forced to hunt for every letter, often losing his place on the screen and on the paper while he searched. As handicapping as his lack of keyboarding skill was his lack of knowledge about how to erase and position the cursor, which caused him considerable confusion. The only help Clarence had was Karen's somewhat grudging and quite annoyed pointing out of the "DELETE" key. Interestingly, as we mentioned in Chapter 4, for the class that entered fourth grade the year after Clarence's did, the beginning word-processing task was different. Because of her experiences the previous year, Ms. Santori realized how difficult it was for some children to juggle reading and rereading a paper-and-pencil draft with checking the screen and finding their way around the keyboard. Consequently, she altered the task so that it did not require transcribing as well as keyboarding. The new assignment for the first turn was to use their name and the date as the "text" to be entered at the keyboard. In this way, although the task was still to inscribe and not compose text, the selected text was one the children knew by rote and hence did not require mental maneuvering of an original idea nor physical manipulation of a piece of paper. Interestingly, the task of entering name and date is not unlike the traditional "Now is the time for all good men . . ." sentence often used by adults when they are unfamiliar with a typewriter or computer keyboard.

QUESTION #2:   Can the child manage the skills needed to complete the task, or, with the help of a coach does the child have the skills needed to do the task, or, is the task altered so that the child has the skills?

ANSWER #2:   No.

(3) *Learning/Teaching Processes.* Ms. Santori had provided basic word-processing instruction to all of the children prior to their initial turns at the computer. In a whole class lesson, she demonstrated how to enter text using the keyboard, how to move from the text entry screen to the editing screen, how to use the "DELETE" and "BACKSPACE" keys to remove text, how to use the numeric keypad for cursor movements, and how to use the return key. She had also talked with the children about writing a description of an imaginary creature,

instructing them to include the name, habitat, eating habits and behavior of the creature. Her sample piece was about a creature named "Getty-o" who lived in a bowl of spaghetti—Clarence's creature was presumably patterned after the teacher's. Although the amount of instruction the teacher provided in word processing was not sufficient to overcome Clarence's lack of skills, it was sufficient for some fourth graders in his class.

Further, due to the luck of the draw for computer neighbors, he was paired with a partner who was quick to criticize and unwilling to help. Although Ms. Santori valued independent learning and wanted the children to figure out procedures for themselves at the computer, she encouraged some informal collaboration. Other children in Clarence's class were often much more helpful to their peers than Karen was, coaching them on word-processing procedures they had mastered or experimenting together to find a given key or try out a new operation. Random selection had also placed Clarence as one of the last in the class to receive his 20-minute initial turn at the computer. That meant that his turn occurred weeks after he had written his paper-and-pencil draft and weeks after he had received initial word-processing instruction with the whole class. The amount of time that elapsed was undoubtedly a factor in Clarence's difficult first encounter with the word processor.

QUESTION #3:   Do the learning/teaching processes support the child's completion of the task, or, are learning/teaching processes altered to support the child's completion of the task?

ANSWER #3:   No, not enough.

(4) *The Word-Processing Hardware/Software.* For Clarence the QWERTY keyboard was clearly a detriment of the word-processing hardware, and the procedures required for erasing and moving the cursor were somewhat confusing, especially given the two different procedures possible for deletion on the IBM keyboard (see the Appendix for a description). Further, with the IBM hardware and the Bank Street software available when this study began, "what-you-saw" on the screen was not "what-you-got" when you printed out a hard copy. This also caused some confusion for Clarence and others. Of course word processing did produce correctly formed, rightly positioned characters, and it did automatically manage the linearity of text production for Clarence as well as for any other user of word processing. It also offered the raw capacity for large scale reorganization of information, easy deletion and insertion, and so on. But production was not a writing issue for Clarence, and he was not trying to compose and/or revise his story as he worked. These features of word processing, although available, did not match his needs for the task. What Clarence needed was more support for locating letters on the unfamiliar nonalphabetic keyboard and more review of deletion procedures, or possibly temporary alteration of the hardware until he gained more keyboard familiarity.

QUESTION #4:   Are the features of word processing well suited to the child's completion of the task, or, is the word-processing software/ hardware altered so that it is well suited to the child's completion of the task?

ANSWER #4:   No.

It is clear that, during Clarence's first-time at the computer, word processing was not a felicitous tool for writing or writing instruction. If anything, it was a particularly unfelicitous tool, and the writing episode was particularly unproductive. Clarence's experience, then, is an extreme case—a paradigm of word processing as unfelicitous tool for the beginning writer.

QUESTION #5:   Is word processing a felicitous writing tool?

ANSWER #5:   No.

But we must also consider Clarence's experience in light of the time frame in which it occurred. The event occurred within the "learning period" for Clarence during which he was developing keyboard familiarity and basic operations management. It is difficult to imagine ways to alter the word-processing event significantly enough so that it would function as a genuinely felicitous tool during most third or fourth graders' first few times entering text at the computer. As we pointed out in Chapter 4, the discrepancy between handwriting fluency and keyboard unfamiliarity is simply too great for many beginning writers to overcome at this point of development. It may be the case that beginning writers like Clarence, for whom production is not a major concern but keyboarding is, will simply have to endure a learning period which is unproductive for writing but, we repeat, *not* unproductive for learning word processing. As we know, Clarence did conclude his 20-minute stint at the word processor having more or less mastered the delete function and the locations of some letter keys.

Finally, it is important to remember that there are some possibilities for altering the initial word-processing event even for third and fourth graders. Several of these were designed and tried out by Ms. Santori and Mrs. Perrone during the second year we observed in their classrooms: providing more keyboarding instruction before children take their first turns; providing a "coach" or computer expert to work with the child to fill in those parts of the task which he or she cannot do; altering the task so that composing and/or transcribing issues are not in question; and making learning/teaching processes more supportive of the child's completion of the task by providing cue cards, longer time periods in which to work, more turns more often, or word-processing partners who collaborate to figure out new procedures together.

Anna, Sung, Scott, and Matthew Revisited

Earlier in this volume we saw how a number of beginners wrote with word processing—kindergartener Anna invented spellings for a story about a house, first-grader Sung composed a sentence and used appropriate capitalization, punctuation and spacing, second-grader Matthew composed and revised a story about his bowling skills, and third-grader Scott added missing information to his description of how to catch a leprechaun. These four episodes represent quite different word-processing tasks, learning/teaching processes, and writers' skill levels. However, all of them have two features in common. First, as we show below, in each of the four events word processing functioned as a felicitous writing tool for the beginning writer. And second in each event, there was active participation by an adult coach—that is, a more experienced language user who worked with the child and filled in for him or her those parts of the writing and word-processing task that the child could not do alone. Working with a coach and using word processing as a tool frequently shifted writing events into a zone of proximal development (Vygotsky, 1978) for beginning writers and enabled them to complete more advanced writing tasks and solve more complex writing problems than they could accomplish independently. The discussion below revisits the word-processing events of Anna, Sung, Scott, and Matthew according to the four dimensions of task, skills, learning/teaching processes, and hardware/software. It reveals that the specific capabilities of word processing coupled with the collaboration of coach and child were the critical determinants of felicitousness in each of these events.

(1) *The Writing/Word-Processing Task.* Anna came to the computer to compose a story by inventing spellings. As we have pointed out in Chapter 4, this is a complex task to complete independently: following the formation of a phrase or sentence, it requires the identification of discrete sounds within words, decisions about how to represent them, location of letters on the keyboard, and keeping track of how much of the overall message has been produced. Like Anna, Sung came to the computer to compose a "story," but his real task was to come up with a topic, describe it in one sentence, and then begin to isolate specific words within the sentence. To do this task independently, a writer figures out how to spell a word (possibly sound-by-sound through invented spelling, possibly by using other resources), then locates and presses the appropriate letter keys one at a time until he or she determines that the word is complete, and then inserts a space after the word. To continue, the writer reviews the sentence, remember his or her place in it, selects the next word, and begins the process again. When a word ends a sentence, the writer finds and uses the appropriate key to insert a period, leaves a space bigger than the spaces inserted between words by pressing the space bar twice, and then uses the shift key to capitalize the first letter of the next sentence (see also Paris et al., 1988). A beginning writer who completes this task independently needs a sense of the relationship of written and oral language, some sense of letter-sound relationships or standard spellings, and a concept of "word-ness" and "sentence-ness," as well as the punctuation and spacing conventions of printed language used to signal them, the ability to reread/review a sentence to find the current place, and the word-processing skills of locating and pressing letter keys, using space bar and shift keys appropriately, and reading from the monitor. Anna and Sung, as beginning users of written language, faced complex writing/word-processing tasks. These tasks were different from one another, but they were also quite different from the tasks confronted by second-grader Matthew and third-grader Scott.

Matthew came to the computer to begin a new piece. He had been assigned to write about a special skill he had and then illustrate his piece with a stick-figure drawing. To complete this task, Matthew had to choose an initial topic (i.e., his skill at bowling) and then elaborate by including additional information (i.e., his cousins, his uncle, and the bowling alley). To craft an interesting story, Matthew needed to try out different versions of sentences and phrases, select those he preferred, and erase those not needed. As he worked, it was important that he reread his text frequently, identifying important information he might have omitted, and then deciding how to say it and where to insert it. In addition, Matthew needed to encode and punctuate appropriately as well as manage the word-processing procedures for text entry, cursor movement, insertion, erasure, capitalization, and spacing. The major emphasis in Matthew's task was developing a particular idea within a larger topic.

Third-grader Scott, on the other hand, had already independently composed the first draft of a story about a leprechaun, following three guiding questions his teacher had suggested. During his word-processing event, he was expected to revise and edit the piece. To do so independently, a writer rereads the piece on the screen, notices that there are missing referents, incomplete pieces of information, and few connections between sentences. He or she then decides on additional information to clarify the topic, composes new sentences and phrases that carry the needed information, figures out where to insert that information in the existing text, and deletes other phrases that are by then redundant or nonsensical. Throughout this process the writer must keep his or her place and reread the piece repeatedly, taking account of an audience removed in time and space, and figuring out the connections between this audience and the three prompting questions the teacher provided. Finally, the writer finds and corrects spelling errors by correctly manipulating cursor and delete keys and inserting corrections into the running text. This task requires attention to composing and revising as well as managing the operations of word processing. To rewrite the text, the writer alternates between the role of a removed reader who has not heard the teacher's three guiding questions and a present writer who experiments with alternative sentence structures but is also mindful that, when one sentence or word changes, it frequently requires a number of other changes as well. The major emphasis in this task is clarification of meaning.

Anna's, Sung's, Scott's, and Matthew's tasks were quite different. We make the case below that despite differences in tasks, in all four of these cases the presence of a coach coupled with the use of word processing as a tool transformed the tasks entirely and made for particularly felicitous uses of word processing as a writing tool for beginners.

QUESTION #1: What is the nature of the writing/word-processing task?

ANSWER #1: To compose a story by inventing spellings and locating letters on the keyboard (Anna).
To produce a complete sentence and inscribe it in print at the keyboard (Sung).
To compose an interesting, elaborated essay, using word processing to insert and delete text (Matthew).
To transform a set of answers into a a story by revising and editing a draft, using word processing to insert and delete (Scott).

(2) *The Skills of the Individual Beginning Writer.* Neither Anna nor Sung, Scott, or Matthew, had the writing and word-processing skills needed to complete independently the tasks outlined above. Anna was advanced in her ability to compose stories orally and, it turned out, quite advanced in her ability to hear the sounds in words and choose appropriate letters to represent those sounds, but she had poor fine motor skills and her early printed work was far less controlled than that of others in her class. Sung, on the other hand, had difficulty orally composing a sentence of just a few words, and his teacher was working to help him develop the ability to elaborate on an idea. In addition, he lacked basic concepts of word and sentence, and had little if any idea of sound-symbol relationships, punctuation, or capitalization. In contrast, as we saw in Chapter 4, Matthew was a quite capable second-grade writer who could compose and revise as he worked, even occasionally trying out on his own some alternate versions of text and using some complex sentence structures. Matthew had limited word-processing skills, however, because he had had only one introductory lesson at the computer early in the school year prior to the experience in the event described here. Matthew also needed frequent spelling assistance. Scott, in third grade, was able to represent his sentences in print both with paper and pencil and with word processing, but he lacked knowledge of revising strategies as well as awareness of the need for revision. Specifically he lacked the ability to see spots where a gap in the information made it virtually impossible for the reader to infer the meaning of the text, a phenomenon Ms. Santori liked to call a "pot-hole" in a child's writing. Scott was also unfamiliar with the word-processing operations needed for revisions of this kind.

QUESTION #2:   Does the beginning writer have the skills needed in order to complete the task?

ANSWER #2:   No, neither Anna nor Sung, Scott, or Matthew, had the skills needed in order to complete the tasks independently.

Despite the fact that none of the four children discussed above had the skills to complete their writing/word-processing tasks independently, each was able to do so with help. The role of the adult coach was central, since; in a very dramatic sense, it altered both the task and the child's ability to complete the task. In each case the coach was able to take advantage of certain features of word processing in order to collaborate with the child to function at a higher level of written-text production than the child could achieve alone. The role of the coach is similar to the teacher's role described in Cochran-Smith's (1984) study of storyreading in a nursery school. Building on Vygotsky's (1978) notion of mediation and Bruner's (1978) concept of scaffolding, Cochran-Smith (1988) suggests:

> Simply put, mediation means that a more experienced language user (teacher, parent, or someone else) fills in some of the gaps that exist between children and the print they are attempting to read, write or use in some way. . . Through mediation, children extend the ways they can use and understand print beyond those ways that they can already perform by themselves. With the help of a teacher, who is more experienced with print than they are, children are able to participate in a wider range of literacy events. As time goes on, the teacher provides less and less help until children are able to make sense of and use print by themselves. (p. 110)

In word-processing events, the coach was central, but, as we have seen, it was the introduction of computer word processing into the classroom in the first place that had prompted the creation of the coached writing situation. Thus we assert that the effects of coaching and the effects of word processing were completely entangled. For this reason, we discuss the special role of the coach in conjunction with the relevant features of word processing in Section 4 below, following our discussion in Section 3 of the learning/teaching contexts for each of these word-processing events.

QUESTION #2:   With the help of a coach, does the child have the skills needed to do the task?

ANSWER #2:   Yes.

(3) *Learning/Teaching Processes.* In Anna's class children dictated stories to Mrs. Winston and also wrote words or short sentences to illustrate their drawings. Further they had a daily writing/drawing period during which they independently drew pictures and wrote accompanying words or phrases using invented spelling or copying from classroom labels. In Sung's class, Mrs. Gold worked to support oral language development as well as familiarity with the basic conventions of printed language. She encouraged story dictation, read aloud to the children, conducted group discussions, and worked extensively with the Peabody Language Program, emphasizing the use of complete sentences. At the computer and elsewhere in her classroom, children were assigned tasks with ample enough resources that their success was assured. Matthew's and Scott's classes were entirely different from Anna's and Sung's. In each there was emphasis on the stages of writing, especially prewriting and editing. Children were comfortable with brainstorming and listmaking, and they received instruction in either how to make the corrections marked by their teachers on their final drafts or how to edit their own work. Neither Matthew nor Scott had had much instruction, however, in the kinds of revisions a coach helped them do—moving chunks of information around within an existing text, inserting missing information, or experimenting with language and form.

One of the most important characteristics of the learning/teaching context for all four of these word-processing events was the amount of time during which youngsters had access to the computer. Real time varied across events, of course—Matthew worked with a coach for 45 minutes and Scott for 50, while Sung and his coach collaborated for only 20 minutes and Anna and coach worked for just over 30. In each case, however, beginning writer and coach had enough time to complete the writing task in one sitting. They were not interrupted or delayed, and they did not have to switch back and forth between word processing and pencil-and-paper production. Teachers' awareness of timing, and the actual amounts of time which they provided children to work at the word processor, were major determinants of the supportive learning/teaching context in these writing events.

Adequate time and accessibility, and the frequent conflicts between these two, were central determinants of the felicitousness of word processing as a writing tool. In most of the classrooms we observed, in order to structure the learning/teaching context so that children had enough time to complete writing tasks (or discrete portions of writing tasks), not all children could have equal computer access. The five teachers we observed had differing beliefs about issues of equity and access. Miss Price, for example, provided computer access for children whom she believed would most benefit from working with a coach at the computer. Children were selected for a variety of reasons, from their need for extra help with writing and reading, to their already-established competence as writers. Others, whom she believed would not benefit from word processing as much because they were likely to be easily distracted by the machinery, were given few opportunities to work with word processing beyond the initial introductory experiences available to all children. Consequently in Miss Price's room, when children worked with word processing, they almost always had ample time to work with a coach to complete a writing task. On the other hand, some children in her room had almost no computer experience beyond the whole group's introductory word-processing lesson.

Ms. Santori, on the other hand, was committed to equity of access for the children in her fourth-grade classroom and even for children in the other fourth-grade classes who shared the three-space open classroom area with hers. Consequently, every child in Ms. Santori's class had access to writing with word processing during the course of the year, although children often had to alternate between the tools of word processing and paper and pencil even within the course of a single writing task. This meant that a child might begin a writing assignment with paper and pencil and then, when his or her turn was called for the computer, bring along the partially completed draft to transcribe at the keyboard. By the time the text was transcribed, the computer turn was over, which often reduced the capacities of the word processor to those of a typewriter. The dilemma many older grade teachers confronted was equity for all beginning writers, on the one hand, versus adequate time to use the word-processing tool productively, on the other. This was a difficult tradeoff, discussed in more detail in the final section below. For Anna, Sung, Scott, and Matthew, however, there was adequate time to work and there were more than adequate resources, especially the presence of a coach, but this was not the case for all children.

QUESTION #3: Do the learning/teaching processes support the child's completion of the task, or, is the learning/teaching context altered to support the child's completion of the task?

ANSWER #3: Yes, especially with the help of a coach (see below).

(4) *Coaching Interactions and Word-Processing Software/Hardware.* Anna's, Sung's, Scott's, and Matthew's experiences are typical of the word-processing events of many children in the kindergarten, first-, and second-grade classrooms, and to a lesser extent the third-grade classroom, where we observed. These events demonstrate that working with an adult who coached them in word-processing procedures, writing strategies, and, in most instances, both of these, provided children with opportunities to engage in more advanced writing events than they did when they worked independently with paper and pencil. Hence, when adults and children worked together in one-to-one coaching situations, word processing functioned as a particularly felicitous tool for beginning writers.

Obviously there is an immediate question to be asked about the nature of coached word-processing events—was it the difference between writing with word processing and writing with paper and pencil that was important, or was it the difference between writing with a coach and writing independently that was important? We are arguing here that it was *not* word processing alone that altered the learning opportunities for the beginning writers in our study. But we are just as clearly arguing that it was also *not* coaching alone that made the difference in these classrooms, although we believe that coaching often does alter the participation structures in classrooms with or without the use of word processing. Rather we are claiming here that coaching and word processing were related synergistically during writing events. In other words, both had effects that were *greater than*, and *different from*, the effects that either one would have generated independently. Furthermore, because word processing automatically managed or made easier many of the production and revision issues that were of concern to beginning writers, there was more time in coached writing events for coaches to help children concentrate on issues of language. Hence these two factors *together*—word processing and coaching—had a significant impact on opportunities for beginners to learn to write differently.

This point is somewhat similar to one made by Clark and Salomon (1986) in a recent review of the literature on media and teaching. They suggest that, even in cases where the introduction of media produces dramatic results in student achievement, it is not the medium per se that produces the change but rather the curricular reform that accompanies its introduction. We are arguing a subtly but significantly different case here. We are not claiming that it was the introduction of a particular kind of technology that produced a change in the learning opportunities beginning writers had, but we are also not crediting the curricular change alone with these changes. Rather, we found that it was the concurrent introduction of a new tool (computer word processing) *coupled with* the introduction of a curricular change (the coached writing event) that made for significant alterations in the learning opportunities available to beginning writers.

(a) *Coaching, Word Processing, and Print Production.* In many instances collaborating with a coach at the word processor temporarily removed issues of production from the writing task. Anna, for example, had considerable skill at orally composing stories and at identifying the sounds within words—indeed, she was one of the best "invented spellers" in her class. That is, she was able to figure out nonrandom and developmentally appropriate approximations of the standard spellings of words (see seminal work on early spellings "invented" by young children in Chomsky, 1971; Harste et al., 1984; Read, 1971). But Anna's motor coordination was not strong, and her paper-and-pencil efforts were often single words or simple phrases. A pair of examples of Anna's writing displays the contrast between writing with word processing and writing with paper and pencil. Interestingly, these examples, which were produced in the spring of her kindergarten year, were written on the same topic and indeed composed on the same day. Their contrast points out the way in which the automatic production of word processing supported the coach's efforts to help Anna develop a story (see also Paris et al., 1988).

[When she comes to the word processor to work with a coach, Anna refers to the story she has written earlier in the day.]

Anna: I was writing a story on a piece of paper. Well . . .

Coach: Was it about Fuzzy too (a stuffed rabbit the teacher had used earlier in the day as a discussion starter)?

Anna: Yeah. It was about him coloring the Easter eggs and he has a Easter basket and Easter eggs in it.

Coach: Wonderful! Tell me, do you want to write a different story about Fuzzy, or do you want to continue your old story and make it longer?

Anna: I want ta . . . ummmmm . . . talk about what I do . . .what I do at Easter.

Coach: Oh wonderful! It will be an "Anna story" instead of a "Fuzzy story."

Anna: [types in her name]
                anna

[Anna continues to type the names of her two brothers without difficulty. She backspaces in order to correct omitted capital letters. The adult coach discusses with her the difference between using the "shift" and "caps lock" keys, then Anna continues to type.]

          Anna   Isaac   Ben

Coach: OK [reading her piece so far], 'Anna, Isaac, Ben . . .'

Anna: Can you tell me how to write Nate?

Coach: Yes, I can.

Anna: [Presses space bar 5 times, very deliberately.] There. 'Nate,' now . . . [Presses "caps lock," types "N", then looks up at screen, releases it.]
         N

Coach: Good job, you saw that sign come on, didn't you and you knew you wanted it to go away. [Refers to signal on screen that indicates that the "caps lock" key is depressed.] What do you think is next? Naaaaaaaaaaaaaate . . .

Anna: A?

Coach: Yes, ma'am. Good for you. [Anna types in 'a.']
         Na

Anna: I know . . . T?

Coach: Yes! [Anna types in 't.']
         Nat

Anna: Is that all?

Coach: This seems silly, but there's an E at the end. It doesn't make any sound . . . all it does is make 'A' say 'ay.' Sometimes 'A's' say 'ah,' but if you put an 'e' at the end, it will 'ay' like in 'Nate.' [Anna types "e."]
         Nate

[Barbie, the child at the next computer, is sounding out a word. She asks the coach whether she should use a 'C' or a 'K.' Anna offers an answer.]

Anna: I always put 'C' because 'C' is usually right . . . a 'K' isn't [right] that much [thinks a moment] . . . and 'C,' 'K' and 'S' go together . . . 'K' and 'C' go together and 'C' and 'S' go together . . . 'C' sometimes makes 'S's' sound, and 'S' sometimes makes 'C's' sound, and 'K' sometimes makes 'C's' sound, and 'C's' sound sometimes makes 'K's sound.

Coach: Isn't that confusing! But you understand that very well.

[Barbie asks for help again, and Anna turns back to her own keyboard, continues to work to produce "Easter egg." Types in 'E,' then 's,' 't.']

Est

Anna: Now R . . . I can't find R . . .

Coach: There it is. [Points.]

Anna: Easterrrrrrrr . . . [Types in 'r.']
Estr

Anna: Now 'Easter eggs' . . . [Presses space bar 4 times.] AAAEEeeggggs . . . [Types 'a.']
Estr a

Anna: Oh dear . . .[Backspaces to erase and replace 'a' with 'A.'] Aaaay.. [Types 'y.'] . . . eggs . . . [Types 's.'] Oh dear . . . [Types 'r'.]
Estr Aysr

Anna: [Reads.] 'Eggs.' Oh dear . . . [Backspaces to erase 'r' then types 'g.']
Estr aysg

Anna: [Reads from the screen.] 'Easter eggs.' [Announces to coach, points to screen.] I made 'Easter eggs!'

Coach: Yes you did. Good for you! What comes after 'Easter eggs'?

During this word-processing session, which lasted about 25 minutes, Anna collaborated with the coach to create her second Easter story of the day. Anna's efforts demonstrate considerable encoding skill as she actively experimented with letter-sound relationships. Her description to Barbie of her own strategy for deciding whether to use 'C' or 'K' is particularly telling; it indicates her awareness of rules of frequency in spelling, and suggests that her encoding strategies are systematic and reasoned.

Despite the occurrence of several side conversations, Anna managed to produce the following story during her word processing turn, "Anna Isaac Ben Nate has a Estr aysg hnt thhn we go To Chrch." (Translation: Anna, Isaac, Ben, Nate has a Easter eggs hunt Then we go to church.) Her paper and pencil Easter story, written the same day, appears in Anna's own hand in Figure 5.4. This text reads, "hSEY CLrsh ESdrs Ahyegs." (Translation: Fuzzy colors Easter eggs.)

The paper and pencil text produced independently is different in several ways from the story produced collaboratively with a coach and with the tool of word processing. The paper-and-pencil story is just four words and rather difficult to decipher even for experienced invented-spelling readers. Anna's sentence con-

Figure 5.4
Anna's Easter Story

veys one idea, and much of the meaning in the story is carried in the picture, which, as Anna herself pointed out in an earlier comment, indicates that Fuzzy is a rabbit and that he has an Easter basket full of eggs. Anna's story with word processing is more than three times the length of her paper-and-pencil story. It has two main ideas in two complete sentences connected by the word "then" to indicate a temporal relationship between the two. This comparison is one of many available in the collection of Anna's work. In most instances she produced longer, more coherent, and more connected texts with word processing and was able to explore in print some of the forms and devices she used in her verbal compositions. In contrast, Anna often produced only strings of words with paper and pencil. For example, one paper-and-pencil text read, "orange SHHR HRT Blue." (Translation: "Orange, star, heart, blue.") On the other hand, she almost always produced connected text with word processing—stories, sentences, and even riddles.

As Anna worked to enter text at the keyboard, the presence of a coach, and the tool of word processing, together provided many opportunities for her to learn about written language. In the excerpt above, the coach helped Anna hear the medial vowel sound in "Nate," just as earlier in the year Anna had often needed help to hear initial and final consonant sounds. The coach sometimes offered evaluation or comment about Anna's choices of letters, which were almost always logical and often correct. But more often she modelled the process of elongating various parts of words and picking out the letter forms that could be used to represent them. In interactions of this sort Anna and other beginners had many opportunities to explore grapheme-phoneme relationships and to practice the process of encoding. Coaches also taught minilessons about language in response to children's questions and the strategies they demonstrated, such as the quick lesson on "silent E" offered by the coach when Anna wondered whether she had finished a word. Interestingly, Anna's comment to Barbie about when to use "C" or "K" reflects the style and form of the coach's earlier comment about when to use a "silent E."

The capacity of word processing to handle the correct formation, spatial orientation, and linearity of written text supported Anna's efforts to invent her own spellings and convey a meaningful message. Remembering the shape of the needed letter (or finding it on the alphabet chart that was on the wall of the classroom), and then hunting for it at the keyboard, was a much easier task for Anna than was the paper-and-pencil task wherein she herself had to draw each letter. Graves (1983) has pointed out that young writers are preoccupied with production, concerned with "imbalances" between the way they would like their writing to look and the way it actually looks. Graves suggests that the issues of production, including spelling, aesthetics, and handwriting, are often handled by the end of second grade, depending on the emphasis of the teacher. Using word processing intervened in this process early on for beginning writers like Anna. The technology of word processing handled many of the issues of aesthetics and handwriting before Anna and her kindergarten and first-grade friends could have handled them for themselves, probably regardless of teacher emphasis. Using word processing often allowed beginners like Anna to compose and wrestle with written-language conventions before they could handwrite. When they worked with coaches using word processing, beginning writers were not bound by the limitations of their own fine-motor coordination and penmanship skills and therefore had the opportunity to compose without all the attendant problems of print production.

That word processing took care of certain aspects of print production was recognized explicitly by some of the younger children for whom it was a central concern. In an interview at the end of his second grade year, for example, Mark commented that he preferred writing with word processing because it was fun and because it was easier than writing with paper and pencil.

> You don't have to write what you want. All's you have to do is put down the letter you want and then you just press the letter and it does it and it don't write fast or anything unless you push it fast. It always writes neat letters, and it's never sloppy because you don't have to erase the letter. You don't have to write the letter down . . . like make the lines and stuff. You just push the button.

Mark's comments are precise and reflect the gratitude often expressed by second, third, and fourth graders that word processing negated the necessity for "hurting your hand." Coupled with coaching, word processing became, not just a felicitous, but a powerful tool for writing instruction. It allowed coaches to concentrate with children on issues of written language—from which sounds represent which letters at the youngest levels, to which information is needed to construct a complete story at the intermediate levels—rather than issues of physical production of letter and word forms. The temporary liberation from production chores freed some beginning writers to concentrate on meaning and also, eventually, to formulate new theories of writing itself—what writing was about, what counted most in writing tasks, and where one's attention should focus.

There were many instances in our data where word processing gave beginning writers opportunities to demonstrate some of the written language skills they already had but were not able to make visible when they wrote with paper and pencil. In the absence of children's ability to perform, that is, to make their competence visible to teachers and others, it is unfortunately easy to assume that writing problems reflect deficits in basic competence rather than particularities of production. Using word processing as a writing tool often clarified the distinction between the beginning writer's language competence and his or her performance, and also unmasked that competence. This distinction is related to Hymes's (1974) argument for a view of language competence that includes knowledge of how to perform within specific social situations. Eschewing Chomsky's emphasis on competence as the native speaker's tacit knowledge of grammaticality, Hymes argues that competence is a much broader aspect of language that cannot be understood independent of the social situation in which it is demonstrated, and including notions of grammaticality as well as appropriateness, occurrence, and feasibility. Although not entirely like the distinction we are making here, Hymes's notion helps to emphasize that what we can know about a child's competence with written language is limited if we look only at his or her performance with certain kinds of writing tools. Examining what beginning writers can do with the tool of word processing allows a broader view of the beginner's competence. Word processing unmasks more of the child's competence and removes assessment of competence from the narrow view of performance in a particular paper-and-pencil writing situation where the physical demands are especially heavy.

(b) *Coaching, Word Processing, and 'Windows on the Mind'*. Many recent studies of children's writing have been framed in relation to Vygotsky's (1978) theories of learning and development. His ideas are particularly useful here, because they emphasize both that children use signs and tools from the social context in order to construct their own knowledge, and that these tools are used in social situations. Vygotsky theorizes that children eventually internalize what they first learn from their manipulation of tools within social interactions with others. Vygotsky directly links the development of "practical intelligence" (tool use) and the development of the use of signs (language use):

> Although practical intelligence and sign use can operate independently of each other in young children, the dialectical unity of these systems in the human adult is the very essence of complex human behavior. Our analysis accords symbolic activity a specific *organizing* function that penetrates the process of tool use and produces fundamentally new forms of behavior. (p. 24)

Vygotsky's theories provide a way of understanding coached word-processing events wherein adults demonstrated interpersonally (i.e., within social interactions where they jointly negotiated texts with beginners) the use of the computer as a writing tool and, in doing so, often provided children with new models for the activity of writing, which over time began to be internalized and used intrapersonally (i.e., by the individual writer himself or herself). Writing at the computer made it possible for adult coaches to support children's writing in two ways that are unique to the tool.

First, using word processing with a coach often allowed children to participate in writing events in ways that were not possible with paper and pencil. This was especially apparent in the cases of the least able language users we observed. Sung's computer episode, where the teacher, Mrs. Gold, carried the burden for almost everything in the writing event, is a clear example. She elicited Sung's initial sentence, isolated specific words within it, supplied the spellings, reread the text as they went, and decided on the punctuation that was needed. Sung was able to compose the initial declarative sentence using a sentence frame which he had learned in class, but could certainly not have selected words within it, let alone spelled them or produced appropriate punctuation. In the coached event at the word processor, however, Sung actively participated by jointly producing the piece—he pushed the space bar between words and at the end of the sentence, held down the shift key when a capital letter was needed, and later typed in the period as well as his name and one word in the sentence. These are minor contributions, and Mrs. Gold undoubtedly controlled the episode and did most of the work, but Sung participated in a way that is different from the earliest efforts at composition in many classrooms where children dictate sentences and then watch as adults inscribe them. Sung's role was more active—he did much more than simply look on as an adult composed and inscribed. He literally had a finger in the physical and active production of the text. Further, he had the opportunity for close individual contact with an experienced written language user who modelled out loud for him some of the strategies that competent writers use.

That Sung's teacher discussed issues of punctuation and capitalization with a child who could barely speak English is remarkable, but this phenomenon was not at all uncommon when adults coached children using word processing. Coaches routinely discussed issues of punctuation and capitalization (e.g., "OK, now you just need a period there. Right there cause that's the end of a sentence."), and children consequently incorporated this language (e.g., "period," "capital," "higher case letters") into their own discussions of texts produced at the computer.

Like Sung, kindergartener Lewis was not an able language user. In fact, during the whole year of kindergarten prior to our study, Lew had never spoken. Primarily because of his language difficulties, he had been retained. Despite the fact that Lew demonstrated no willingness to speak during the first part of his second year of kindergarten, Mrs. Winston coached him at the computer. She encouraged him to type his name, and, undaunted by his minimal response, she behaved as if Lew could understand, respond, and function as a user of written language.

[Mrs. Winston has helped Lew type in his name by guiding his index finger and saying the names of the letters as she pressed the keys with his finger.]

Coach: Now eat the letters up. Let me see you eat the letters up . . . Here, this one right here. [Points to the DELETE key. Lew presses this key alone and erases his name.] Great! Now do it again! Let me see you write your name again . . . Go ahead! Hit the L . . . Here you go! . . . Come on! . . . Have it come up on the screen . . . [Throughout her urging, Lew just sits, looking at Mrs. Winston.]

Coach: Look . . . Hit it! . . . Watch it come up on the screen. Go ahead. [Lewis hits the "L" and then the "E" keys.]
    LE

Coach: Mmmhmm . . . then what? [Lew looks at keyboard, looks at coach, coach touches "W" key, then Lew reaches for it.] That one . . . [Lewis types in "W."
    LEW

Coach: What's the next letter in your name . . . Look up here. [Points to his name written on a piece of paper.] What else do you need? [Lew touches "S" key, then looks at Coach.] Before that . . . [Lewis touches "I".] Uh huh! [Lewis types "I," then "S."]

LEWIS

Coach: Look what you did, 'Lew! I'm proud of you! Now what do you do? [Wants him to type his name again.] What a smart little boy you are! Can you do it again? Can you do that again? I'm not even going to look . . . You go ahead and do it for me . . . Type your name! I'm going to look over this way. [Turns toward center of the room and puts her hand over her eyes.] Go on, Lew . . . Get it on the screen . . . [Gordon stands behind Lew to watch.]

Gordon: Can I try my name too?

Coach: After Lew types his name, Gordon can have a turn . . . I'm not even going to look. . . . Go ahead. [Slowly, deliberately, Lew types each letter without looking at the monitor, but looking frequently at Mrs. Winston.]

LEIWS

Coach: [Ooh! Lew! Is that how you spell it? Is that how you spell it? Hmmm? Lew just looks at coach.] Let's go back a couple of letters. [She erases 'IWS.']

LE

Coach: After L-E then what? What letter's next? [Lew types in W]

LEW

Coach: Uh huh . . .Then what? [Lew types in I.]

LEWI

Coach: And then . . .? [Lewis types in S.]

LEWIS

Coach: Bravo! (clapping). Know what I think we oughta do? We're gonna print that out . . . for you. Watch this, Lew! [Coach carries out print procedures. Lew looks at keyboard occasionally and out at the room.] Let's go over [to the printer] and look . . . Come on! . . . [They walk around to the printer.] Look, Lew look! It's your name ! Congratulations! Here! [Hands him printout.] You can take that home!

Despite his extreme reticence, Mrs. Winston managed to encourage, cajole, and prompt Lew into typing most of his name. Like Sung, Lewis had the opportunity to participate more actively in a written-language event because of the use of the tool of word processing. The tool gave Lewis a chance to participate, even though he would not speak and was not able to write his name with paper and pencil. Unfortunately, Lewis made little progress with word processing or in other areas during his second year of kindergarten, and at the end of the year he transferred to another school. Nevertheless, the chance to write with word processing was something of a success, albeit a very small one, for him.

The second unique feature of coached word-processing events is closely related to the first. Not only was even the most beginning-level child able to participate more actively in the joint negotiation of a text, but the coach was also able to participate more actively in the child's writing. The visual publicness of the computer screen gave the coach access to the child's ongoing composing processes that was deeper and perhaps closer to what the child was thinking and learning about writing as he or she worked than was the access the teacher had when the child wrote with paper and pencil. Following Papert's (1980) seminal work , Weir (1989) and others have proposed that the computer's capacity to act as a "window into the mind" that enables teachers to concentrate more on children's learning and less on their ability to produce expected answers or standard products may well be the computer's most important contribution. Weir points out that, in mathematics or science, the publicness of computer problem solving is critical: "There is something about the public nature of the activity. There it all is, up on the screen for all to see, each problem-solving step available for scrutiny in a way that pencil work scribbled in a corner of the page never is" (p. 63). In a different sense this was true of coached writing events completed with the tool of word processing—they made external some of the internal moves of beginning writers and hence allowed teachers to intervene during, rather than after, the point at which a particular piece of writing was taking shape. Further, because of the ease with which text could be erased, deleted, and inserted, children seemed willing to try out more of their ideas on the screen than they might have with paper and pencil.

Matthew's word-processing event about his skill as a bowler is an especially good example of the way writing with word processing can make it possible for the knowledgeable teacher to see more visibly the beginning writer's operational theories of writing. Matthew had had few previous turns with word processing when he began to compose his bowling story, but he was a remarkably fast learner and a good paper-and-pencil writer. He was able to move easily between his general images of bowling and the more specific tasks of choosing language, spelling words correctly, and managing word-processing procedures. Because he sat at the word processor with a coach, the coach was able to see what Matthew was producing in relation to what he was saying as he worked and both support the possibilities Matthew entertained and make additional suggestions about the formation of sentences. For example, the coach wondered aloud whether Arty's name ought to be specified, and she suggested that "Cousin Nikki" could easily be added to the story after Matthew talked about him. Both these suggestions were incorporated into Matthew's story. The coach also had access to the options Matthew himself perceived for different versions of sentences, and she both supported his consideration of alternatives and, in some instances, taught him new strategies for embedding one sentence within another. The coach's role in Matthew's word-processing event was not as active as the role of the coaches in Sung's and Lew's word-processing episodes, but it was an extremely important role nonetheless.

The extent to which the coach participated in Scott's composition of the leprechaun story fell somewhere between the participation of Sung's and Lew's coaches, on the one hand, and Matthew's coach on the other. Through their conversation at the word processor it was clear to the coach that Scott was simply answering three questions he had been given about catching a leprechaun. The coach worked hard to get inside Scott's thinking, listening to his responses, and studying his writing on the screen. The differences between Scott's initial and final pieces of writing clearly demonstrate that the coach was able to help Scott create a more linguistically sophisticated piece than he would have been able to produce alone. But observation of Scott's word-processing event also leads us to two other important points. The first is reiteration of the fact that it was the conjunction of word processing and coaching, and not simply coaching, that enabled Scott to make revisions in his writing. He repeatedly questioned the coach about how much erasing he was going to have to do to respond to her suggestions, and it was not until the coach assured him that he could revise without erasing everything that he settled down to work with her to negotiate a story with more information in it.

The second point that Scott's story reveals is that coaching with word processing makes a child's writing and his internal moves so public that it may be easy for a coach to intrude too much—to intervene fully and take over the writing so that it no longer belongs to the child. We believe that there is a fine line between taking advantage of the felicitousness of word processing as a writing tool to respond to children's writing, on the one hand, and using it to control the event on the other. The line between the two is uncertain, and although it appears that the coach provided just enough help for Matthew, it is unclear in Scott's event whether the coach seized an appropriate pedagogical moment to help him begin to read and understand his writing as a distanced reader would, or whether she led him through a series of steps he might not have understood.

In many "process writing" classrooms, it is a recommended practice that beginning writers meet with their teachers in one-to-one writing conferences about their work. Generally, conferences occur after the child has composed an initial draft (or some part of it) to which the teacher responds and then encourages the child to revise and produce a subsequent draft. This method of instruction is sometimes thought of as reactive teaching. It involves what Graves (1983) argues is one of the most critically significant aspects of writing instruction—a waiting, responsive kind of teaching: "Follow the child, let the child talk, let the child understand that what the child knows is primary" (p. 101). On the other hand, in his well-known review of research in writing, Hillocks (1986) criticizes the notion that writing instruction ought to be merely reactive, suggesting instead that it ought to "seek to develop or promote experiences which will allow children to move from one level of competency to higher ones" (p. 18). Both reactive teaching and direct instruction are global terms for broad-stroke patterns of behavior that occur over time and across observations of multiple classrooms. However, both of these terms fail to capture the nature of individual events or situations and what we observed when we looked closely at beginning writers over time—that coached word-processing events created a learning opportunity in which teachers could both react and respond to children's writing as it unfolded *and* instruct directly about writing strategies and word-processing procedures.

As Weade and Evertson (1988) have suggested, close observations over time raise serious questions about whether global descriptions hold up or capture the whole story about classroom interactions. Our observations over two years indicate that the word processor, as a potentially felicitous tool for writing instruction, eliminated part of the dichotomy that may or may not exist between reactive teaching and direct instruction. Because it functioned as a window into some of beginning writers' internal strategies while their writing was in the process of unfolding, word processing allowed coaches to both react to, and direct, the process. The "window" let the knowledgeable teacher see the writer's operational theories of writing more clearly and provide more continual responsiveness.

QUESTION #4:   Are the features of word processing particularly well-suited to the child's completion of the task, or, is the word process-ing software/hardware altered so that it is well-suited to the child's completion of the task?

ANSWER #4:   Yes, the features of word processing coupled with the sup-port of a coach who worked with the child were particularly well suited to Anna's, Sung's, Scott's, and Matthew's com-pletion of their writing tasks.

The word-processing experiences of Anna and Sung, Scott, and Matthew (and even Lew, who struggled so to get his name on paper) were generally positive ones. The dynamic interplay of the tasks they were assigned, their own writing and language skills, the learning/teaching processes that supported them (espe-cially coaching), and the capabilities of word processing itself made it possible for word processing to function as a felicitous writing tool. As we will see in the next section, however, word processing was not always a felicitous tool for beginning writers. But, as the above experiences demonstrate, there was a wide array of situations in which this was clearly the case.

QUESTION #5:   Is word processing a felicitous writing tool?

ANSWER #5:   Yes.

Independent Writers Revisited

Many of the word-processing events we have labeled so far in this chapter as "felicitous for writing instruction" have included an adult coach who worked with a beginning writer to compose and jointly negotiate a written text. As Chapter 3 makes clear, however, the fourth graders whom we observed did not work with coaches in the ways kindergarteners, first, and second graders did. Instead, in most instances fourth graders worked independently at the computer, although there was an informal and generally supportive network of peer helpers, computer experts, teachers who worked as editors, and researchers who answered questions. The third graders we observed worked with coaches on many occasions but also had many opportunities to work independently with word processing. Further, the third and fourth grade writing programs included both peer conferencing about story drafts and informal coaching about word-processing operations. Nevertheless, in both grades, except when third graders worked with adult coaches, they generally wrote their own individual pieces with word processing and did not collaborate with one another to compose joint texts. In this final section we revisit the word-processing events that were common for fourth graders and frequent for third graders—events where children used the tool to compose, edit or revise individual writing with some informal peer assistance but without the help of a coach.

As we reported in Chapter 4, during the initial learning period, word processing was generally not a felicitous writing tool for third and fourth graders who struggled to familiarize themselves with the keyboard and manage the operations of word processing. (It is worth noting that word processing is generally not a felicitous writing tool for adult writers during the learning period either, although, as we have pointed out, adults' learning periods are often much briefer than children's.) After the learning period, however, there were many instances in which word processing functioned as a felicitous writing tool when third and fourth graders used it independently, as well as many instances in which it did not. The section that follows provides an explanation for the discrepancy among these basically similar word-processing events. This explanation emerges from analysis of their four structural features and the ways these were interactively related. Our analysis indicates that learning/teaching processes were the determinant factor. (Learning/teaching processes are represented in Figure 5.3 as Question #3. This question is considered fourth in the discussion that follows, since it was the critical determinant.)

(1) *The Writing/Word-Processing Task.* When they used word processing, third and fourth graders were expected to compose, revise, edit, or produce final copy of texts of a variety of types from interviews and personal experiences to descriptions and brief explanatory essays. In some instances children worked from partially completed paper-and-pencil texts, while in others they composed with word processing itself. Whether or not paper and pencil were used as tools in production of a piece for which the writer also used word processing depended on the ways writing programs were structured and the ways time and access to word processing were allocated. (These are discussed with learning/teaching processes below.)

QUESTION #1:   What is the nature of the writing/word-processing task for independent writers?

ANSWER #1:   These tasks require the use of word processing to compose, encode and inscribe text (i.e., develop ideas and represent them in standard spelling by locating the proper letter, punctuation, and erasure keys); revise (i.e. , enter into running text to insert or delete particular parts); edit (i.e., enter into continuous text to correct spelling, punctuation, and usage errors); or produce final copies of original texts (i.e. , print out clean text appropriately arranged in page or booklet format).

(2) *Individual Beginning Writers.* Discrepancies between felicitous and un-felicitous uses of the word-processing tool in independent writing were initially puzzling to us. We reasoned that, if differences in writing/word-processing skill were the factors that explained the discrepancy, then word processing would function more felicitously for fourth graders, who generally had more advanced skills, than it did for their third graders. But this was not the case, and observed variations in writers' skills proved to have little explanatory power for the variations among events. After the initial learning period, most children in both the third and fourth grades had enough writing and word-processing skills to compose texts and to do some revising and editing on their own or with the informal assistance of classmates or adults. In other words, for most of the independent writing tasks assigned or selected in both third and fourth grades, writers had sufficient skills.

QUESTION #2:   Can the writer manage the skills needed to complete the task, or, with help can the writer manage the skills needed to do the task, or, is the task altered so that the child has the skills?

ANSWER #2:   Yes, either independently or with informal help, third and fourth graders had the skills needed to complete the tasks.

(4) *Word-Processing Software/Hardware.* It was not the difference in children's skills, then, that determined whether or not word processing functioned as a felicitous writing tool. Nor was it a discrepancy between task and the tool itself. Word processing had capacities that were generally well suited to completion of the composition, revision, and editing tasks that children undertook. As a writing tool, word processing made for ease of revision and production of texts for the very reasons we have discussed throughout this volume—easy and traceless erasures, deletions, and insertions; continual provision of clean, legible copy; removal of the necessity for rewriting drafts and recopying final products; and effortless production of professional-looking booklet, page, and column-type formats.

QUESTION #3:   Are the features of word processing well-suited to the child's completion of the task?

ANSWER #3:   Yes

(3) *Learning/Teaching Processes.* Despite many similarities across events, the word processor sometimes functioned as a felicitous tool for independent writing events and sometimes did not. Our data suggest that all other features being more or less equal, the discrepancy had to do with learning/teaching processes and contexts. When it was possible to structure the learning/teaching context to support the *completion* of writing tasks with word processing, then word processing was a felicitous writing tool. Often, however, because of complex schedules, numbers of children, cross-class grouping, and limited amounts of equipment, it was not possible to create situations in which children could complete writing tasks with word processing, and instead they had to switch back and forth between the tools of paper and pencil and computer. When this was the case, word processing generally did not function as a felicitous writing tool.

In Mrs. Perrone's classroom it was often possible to integrate word processing into many time slots and hence to use computers throughout the school day. It was common in her classroom, for example, for a child to work busily at each computer station during math, science, and reading periods, as well as during the time officially designated for writing. This meant that, even though there were only two computers in the classroom, children had regular and frequent turns, and, when they wanted to, they could continue their work by writing at lunchtime, before and after school, or during other classes. This gave children the opportunity to carry their work through to completion (or at least through to completion of some discrete portion) while using word processing. Continuity of work with the tool was possible.

For example, Mrs. Perrone followed Ms. Santori's lead and planned to have every child in her class compose an original book during the spring semester. For most of these books, Mrs. Perrone had children compose, conference, revise, and publish using word processing. To accomplish this task, word processors were in use steadily during the entire school day. At all times, a child worked at each computer to compose, revise, or publish a book. In this way writers had the opportunity to use the computers for a long enough time period to benefit from its facilitating features for editing, revising, and publishing professional-looking final copies. In an odd way, this outcome was analogous to felicitous uses of word processing at the lower grade levels. As we have pointed out, in kindergarten, first, and second grades, children usually completed their writing in one sitting. Especially in kindergarten and first grades, a piece of writing was to a great extent defined by the sitting itself—whatever a child finished within his or her time allotment at the word processor *was* the final draft, "published" in the sense that it was printed out for the child to take home at the end of the day.

Revision and editing were not issues in the lower grades, and consequently opportunities to return to the computer to finish one's work were not necessary. In contrast, however, in third and fourth grades, revision and editing were expected, and children did not complete their pieces in one sitting. They wrote longer pieces that often extended over a several-day, and sometimes a several-week period. When older children worked continuously enough at the computer to complete a piece of writing, word processing functioned as a felicitous tool.

In Ms. Santori's class, however, it was not possible for children to have access to the computer throughout the day. As we pointed out in Chapter 3, the class was taught as part of a "three-space" arrangement wherein teachers team-taught many subject areas; exchanged children for reading, math, and language arts groups; and held many cross-class, grade-level, and whole group activities. The time limits on subject area periods were not flexible, and the needs of 90-some children and three teachers had to be taken into account when scheduling decisions were made. The children whom Ms. Santori taught for language arts, and the primary group with whom she worked with word processing, were not necessarily part of her homeroom group and therefore many of them were not even in her room space during most of the day.

Further Ms. Santori's goals for word processing included equity of access to computers and basic familiarity and confidence about the tool for all her students. Moreso than many other teachers did, Ms. Santori and her teammates thought of all of the fourth graders as their students and hence considered each of them as their joint responsibility. Ms. Santori wanted all of her own students, as well as every fourth-grade child, to have an opportunity to work with word processing and begin to be comfortable with the technology. After they had developed basic keyboard familiarity, for example, the children in her language arts group taught all the children in the other two fourth grades how to enter their names and dates at the keyboard, use a few basic word-processing commands, and write a brief newspaper article. Essentially, Ms. Santori had three goals for word processing—providing general exposure and familiarity with the tool, making access to technology equitable for all children, and helping children use word processing as a felicitous tool for their writing. Each of these is an educationally sound and ambitious goal, but, when coupled with limited amounts of equipment and complicated daily schedules, they are also goals that are in conflict with one another. This created a genuine dilemma for Ms. Santori—a teaching situation for which there is no clear solution, but instead only various strategies for managing and coping (Lampert, 1985).

Ms. Santori recognized the dilemma early in the project, noting that there simply was not enough instructional time or enough word-processing equipment to meet all of her goals. Equity, and the development of positive attitudes about technology, took precedence for Ms. Santori, so she chose to structure her classroom for maximum exposure for the largest number of children. The end result was that fourth graders had access and exposure to word processing on a much broader scale than the children at any other grade level in the school. On the other hand, the individual child also had less total time at the computer. Individual turns, lasting about 20 minutes each, occurred about once a month, depending to a great extent on what special programs, snow days, in-service meetings, swimming schedules, assemblies, and holidays had occurred during a given month to interfere with the well-organized schedule. This meant that a given child might be at any point in a writing project when his or her turn came up. If the child had already composed a paper-and-pencil draft or part of one, he or she would end up spending the time transcribing the draft at the keyboard. Although children frequently made some revisions as they transcribed and therefore seemed prompted by the use of word processing to think about their writing, there was often little time remaining to make revisions by the time they had keyed in their initial drafts. This created a situation where the writer had a draft preserved with word processing but could not use the facilitative features of the tool to revise or edit it until the next turn occurred (a turn which might occur weeks later). By the same token, although a child who composed a draft directly at the computer was free of the difficulties of transcribing from a paper-and-pencil draft, he or she rarely had the opportunity to also revise and edit that same piece at the computer.

Despite the difficulties and the insufficient time and equipment, fourth graders still preferred word processing to paper and pencil, and many of them especially liked to use it for the creation of final copies of their work, since it eliminated the need for erasures, white-outs, and crumpling-up-and-starting-again with pen and "good paper." Unfortunately, as Ms. Santori pointed out, irregular and short turns at word processing, coupled with long periods of time in between, often reduced the powerful features of word processing to the status of a very expensive and very fancy typewriter. This was not what Ms. Santori wanted for her students, but there was not enough equipment and scheduling flexibility to allow for both extended use and broad equity.

Ms. Santori's dilemma touches on what may be one of the most critical aspects of the deployment of computer technology in the public schools— inequity of computer access, expertise, and instruction, often based on the class, race, ethnicity, and gender differences of school children and school populations broadly. On the basis of a recent national survey of over a thousand schools, for example, Cole and Griffin (Cole, Griffin, & the Laboratory of Comparative Human Cognition, 1987) drew several conclusions: middle- and upper-class children have more access to computers than do poor children; poor children are more likely than upper- and middle-class children to be instructed with drill-and-practice rather than "cognitive enrichment" software; and, regardless of class or ethnic origin, girls have less involvement with computers than boys do in school (Laboratory of Comparative Human Cognition, 1989). Ms. Santori taught in a working-class school where many children did not have access to computer expertise and equipment in their own homes. She believed that these children would be better prepared for middle and high school, as well as for later employment, if they had early positive experiences with computer technology. Faced with the dilemma of equity versus felicity for writing, Ms. Santori chose equity for all of the children in her charge.

Other Examples

There were many other individual occasions when word processing functioned as a felicitous tool as well as occasions when it did not. In each of these it is possible to see which of the four features of word-processing events was the critical determinant. For example, a few kindergarten children did not have a real sense of cause and effect. These children were not able developmentally to make the conceptual connection between what was typed at the keyboard and what appeared on the screen, let alone the connections between these and what was later produced by the printer. For these children, word processing was not a felicitous tool, and it is unlikely that any amount of coaching or reference material would have made it so. For children who are just beginning to connect oral language with its graphic representations, we believe that paper and pencil and other hard-surface marking tools are probably more useful tools for writing instruction.

In a similar vein, some children, even as late as second grade, approached the word processor completely unsystematically. They pressed keys randomly, seemed unaware of the consistency with which a given key produced a given image, and impulsively erased everything on the screen. For these children the permanent and more limited features of paper and pencil were more felicitous for writing. Second-grader Dennis, for example, came to the computer uncertain about what he wanted to write. As he tried out ideas, he consistently erased each one, although at one point he had managed to compose a long, disorganized run-on sentence. Despite its problems, the sentence had four ideas in it and could have been developed into a writing piece with the help of a coach. Before this could occur, however, Dennis abruptly erased everything away in several bursts of the delete key. For him, it was simply too easy to erase with word processing and too hard to keep his fingers off the keys. Word processing was not a felicitous writing tool for him.

Several teachers experimented with whole class or large-group activities using the word processor. For Miss Price's introductory computer lesson, she intended to sit at the keyboard and type in one sentence contributed by each child (the computer version of the group experience story commonly used in early childhood classrooms). This word-processing event proved, in Miss Price's words, "a disaster," simply because the children could not see the words as they appeared on the monitor, had to wait too long in between their turns with nothing to do, and became impatient. Chart paper and magic markers would have been more felicitous tools. In a similar activity, Mrs. Winston commonly wrote the "morning sentences" on the chalkboard as various children in her kindergarten class dictated them aloud. At one point she instructed her aide to type the sentences simultaneously at the computer keyboard so that all the children could have a copy to take home each day. Word processing was wonderful for the production of multiple copies of the daily sentences, but it was not felicitous on the occasions when Mrs. Winston assigned small groups of children to sit with the aide and watch her type in the sentences. The idea, of course, was for the children to observe as an experienced writer selected the appropriate letters to represent the words and sentences that were dictated. Like Miss Price's experience, however, this word-processing event proved unsuccessful. The kindergarteners had too little to see, found the screen and keyboard too distant, and wanted to type not watch—the chalkboard worked much better. There were many uses of word processing which, like those just described, were tried out and, when they proved unfelicitous, abandoned.

On the other hand, we observed many unplanned word-processing events where it functioned as a felicitous tool as well as some special circumstances which combined to make for unexpectedly felicitous uses of word processing. Matthew, for example, was immediately able to take home copies of his bowling story for his cousins and uncle, each of whom had functioned as characters in the piece. This helped him develop more of a sense of audience and purpose for his writing. In another instance, Susan and Gwendolyn used word processing to compose a joint story about planting sweet potatoes. They constructed the story by alternating turns typing and helping; the visible monitor and the computer keyboard made the activity possible. This sort of collaboration was rare with word processing, but joint writing was nonexistent in their classroom when children used paper and pencil. First-grader Ho Sook was one of the first in her class to begin writing on her own. She used formula sentences (e.g., "I like . . .," "Today is . . . "), learned in class, as a scaffolding for her own compositions. Although it was not necessary due to the automatic "wrap-around" feature of the software, Ho Sook used the "RETURN" key after each line she produced. The physical action of tapping the key seemed to reinforce the sentence frame idea for her, and because the repeated words were exactly aligned in each successive line, they helped her to spell them correctly and to remember what to type next. Min Cha, literate in Korean but not in English, used word processing to practice composing sentences made from the sentence frames he had learned in his ESL class. In Min Cha's circumstances word processing was quite felicitous—he could practice encoding English words and constructing English sentences while the computer modelled the actual shaping of English letter characters, which were quite different from those he was used to. And finally, as we will see in the following chapter, for second grader Nicky transcription from paper-and-pencil copy provided spelling and reading practice and prompted him to focus on the patterns of written language. In several instances, by the time he had transcribed a given word several times, Nicky found that he had indeed learned how to spell it and could correctly reproduce it without referring to the paper-and-pencil draft. These examples make clear that word processing was not always a felicitous writing tool, nor was it always the desirable tool to use. In some instances it was not desirable or possible to structure the learning environment to support word processing. Rather, the appropriate action was to use other writing tools.

SUMMARY AND CONCLUSIONS

Our data reveal two major findings about the use of word processing as a writing tool for beginners. First, in the majority of word-processing events across grade levels, word processing functioned as a felicitous tool. That is, there were many ways in which it was particularly well suited for work with beginning writers, especially because of its facilitating role in the production of print and hence its capacity to provide opportunities for beginning writers to participate more actively in writing events. Further, as we have seen, word processing was very frequently used in coached writing events wherein more experienced language users worked with beginners to negotiate joint texts. This arrangement allowed beginning writers to produce more sophisticated writing than they could produce independently, provided coaches with unusual insights into the strategies and skills of the writers, and provided opportunities for children to learn both propositional and procedural knowledge about written language.

The data reveal a second major finding. As Figure 5.2 indicates, there are many obstacles to the effective use of word processing as a tool for beginning writers and many pathways that lead to the conclusion that word processing is not a felicitous tool. However, as the many examples in this chapter reveal, word processing was often a particularly felicitous tool for beginners. Close analysis indicates that teachers themselves were the most critical factors in determining felicitousness. Teachers intervened in every aspect of word-processing events—providing coaches for children who did not have the writing and word-processing skills to manage tasks independently, providing book, poster, and human resources, structuring writing tasks at which children could succeed, and even altering computer hardware (by adding stickers to the keyboard) and software (by drawing rebus-like cue cards for "PRINT" and "SAVE" operations) so that children could manage it. In this way teachers made word processing a felicitous writing tool for the beginning writers in their classrooms by discerning the relevant capacities of the software itself and then making it work to support their instructional programs.

Finally this chapter also emphasizes that questions about beginning writers' uses of word processing for writing are quite complex. They generally cannot be asked or answered for the short term or in global ways that cut across grade levels, school and classroom contexts, and individual children. Rather analyses like the one provided here can offer richer ways of understanding the dimensions of writing events and the nuances of word-processing use.

chapter 6
NICKY'S STORY:
ONE CHILD LEARNS
TO WRITE DIFFERENTLY

Chapter 3 of this volume discloses how five elementary teachers introduced, understood, and used word processing in their classrooms. As the chapter reveals, there was considerable variation in teachers' understandings and deployment of the tool. Taken together, variation and change across five teachers and over two years reveal the remarkable interpretability of word processing as a tool for the writing curriculum. They verify Papert's (1980) early assertion that the computer is the "Proteus" of machines, and also serve as evidence that tool software, such as word processing, may be particularly Protean among program possibilities. But the variation and change documented in Chapter 3 not only reveal the power of teachers to shape the tool of word processing to fit their individual curriculum goals. They also reveal the power of the tool to shape and shift teachers' perceptions. Over time, using word processing prompted teachers to think differently about writing, and, concurrently, word processing made it possible for them to structure children's opportunities to learn to write in ways that were qualitatively different from their opportunities to write with paper and pencil. Thus, as we have shown, there was a long-term interactive relationship between the opportunities teachers offered children to learn to write and the capacities and requirements inherent in the word processing tool.

In Chapters 4 and 5, this volume also provides a series of images of beginning writers learning to use word processing in five elementary classrooms. Together these images demonstrate both the range of 5- to 10-year-olds' skills with word processing and considerable variation in the ways they used it to support their writing practices. As we have shown, some uses of word processing were immediately helpful and supportive of children's writing strategies, while others, like transcribing paper-and-pencil texts at the computer keyboard, were cumbersome, often interfering with what children could have done more efficiently with the tools of paper and pencil. Most importantly, the images of beginning writers in Chapters 4 and 5 reveal how word processing interacted with the social processes of classrooms to shape the ways participants learned to write differently.

Chapters 3, 4, and 5 tell us little, however, about how individual children progressed over time or how their particular uses of word processing shaped, and were shaped by, their interactions with teachers and coaches. By following the experiences of one particular child, the present chapter combines the lenses of the previous chapters, each bringing into focus a different aspect of work with word processing. In this chapter, we look closely at 7-year-old Nicky and trace his development in writing, word processing, and literacy over a 2-year period. We make the case that Nicky wrote according to his theory of writing, and that he constructed and reconstructed his theory of writing according to the ways he was coached and instructed to practice writing within the social contexts of his classrooms. We show that the most important learning context for Nicky was constructed through the language interactions of coach and child wherein they jointly negotiated texts and demonstrated the activity of writing.

Writing with a new tool was a powerful experience for Nicky, allowing him to break certain connections that had hampered his writing and enabling him to forge new connections that eventually facilitated it. In this chapter we combine excerpts from word-processing episodes, examples of written work, and quotations from Nicky and his teachers to demonstrate that, while production problems occupied Nicky's attention, he believed that writing was about production, a theory that significantly interfered with his ability to use writing to communicate. When coaches helped him develop strategies for handling some of the issues of production, and when he had the opportunity to use a tool that minimized production difficulties, however, Nicky began to use writing to make meaning. We argue in this chapter that the shift in Nicky's attention was made possible by his opportunities to work closely with his teachers and to use word processing as a writing tool.

LOOKING AT ONE CHILD

In the literature of oral and written language development, there are a number of portraits of single children over relatively long periods of time, from Halliday's (1973) study of a 9- to 18-month-old child "learning how to mean" with oral language, to Calkins's (1983) description of one youngster learning how to write and revise during her third- and fourth-grade years. Case studies like these focus on the particularities of single children. They seek to develop enlightened views of the language learning processes of individuals rather than to abstract generalizations that are globally applicable to other cases. Most of the case studies in early oral and written language development explore language learning in home and community settings (see, for example, Baghban, 1984; Bissex, 1980; Butler, 1975; Crago & Crago, 1983; Scollon & Scollon, 1981; White, 1981). Few examine the ways these interact with classroom processes, although this perspective is especially needed to increase our understanding of school-sponsored literacy development. Nicky's portrait, presented in this chapter, provides an image of a beginning writer and his classroom tools and tasks. At the same time, it suggests a number of language-learning issues that often come into play when children learn to write with word processing.

One of the most important things we know from language and literacy studies is that children constantly build and test theories about how language works and how it is used in various settings (Bissex, 1980; Genishi & Dyson, 1984; Lindfors, 1987). Within their social interactions with others, children construct and test theories of language in use, but also constantly rethink and reconstruct them. As Nicky's story unfolds in the following pages, it is possible to glimpse the dynamic relationship between theory and experience. Nicky writes according to his theories of writing, and, as his theories change, so do his practices—but equally important, as his practices change, so do his theories. Nicky's powerful language and literacy development over two years was closely related to the word-processing events he and his coaches constructed. Nicky's story emphasizes how important it is to attend to the writing tools children use as they interact with others to learn to write.

We focus on Nicky in this chapter for two reasons. First, in comparison with the other children we came to know, Nicky was "average" in several ways. At age seven, he was in the middle of the 5- to 10-year-old age span of beginning writers whom we observed. As a child in the middle, he was well beyond the point of learning individual letter forms and names, but he was clearly unable to write with speed or fluency. Further, despite the fact that he was in the lowest reading group and was clearly not the best writer in the second grade, Nicky was not among the worst. Nicky's access to the computer was comparable to that of many of the other second graders in his class. Like his classmates, Nicky initially worked at the word processor with the help of an adult coach, and later worked independently, and he used word processing about as frequently as many other children. Although he eventually developed keyboard familiarity and basic skill at managing the word-processing system, Nicky was never labeled a *computer expert*, the title used in some classes for the most adept computer users who were often designated as trouble-shooters and helpers for others. In fact, Nicky thought of himself as a slow typist but still preferred typing to handwriting. Nicky's ordinariness illuminates some of the difficulties and successes that were typical of many of the beginning writers we observed as they learned to write with word processing. In one sense, then, Nicky's story is a story like all of the others in this book—it demonstrates that word processing and the ways teachers used it in their work with children were interactively related. What Nicky could do with writing at any given moment can be understood as the outgrowth of his instructional interactions with his teachers about what writing was, what it was for, and what was important about it, as well as the ways writing was practiced in Nicky's classrooms.

On the other hand, Nicky was a child who made extraordinary progress in language and literacy development during the two years that we knew him. His status as a reader changed from membership in the lowest second-grade group to competent membership in an average group. His status as a writer changed from painstaking draw-er of virtually meaningless text to winner of the second grade "gold pencil award" in the school-wide "Young Authors' Contest." Despite the fact that, mid-year, Miss Price considered retaining Nicky in second grade, by the end of the year she had moved him up in reading group status so that he was functioning well in a low average group. Likewise, Mrs. Perrone switched Nicky's reading group position during his third grade year from a lower to a higher reading level, skipping several of the small steps in between groups. Without prompting from us during the course of the study, both teachers remarked about Nicky's unusual progress and were surprised by how well he was doing. In short, Nicky was a beginning writer who broke through to fluency with written language during the period we observed. And as this chapter makes clear, participating in word-processing events seemed to play an important role in the breakthrough.

We focus on Nicky, then, because he was both ordinary and extraordinary. He was typical of other children in word-processing expertise and opportunity. In the conventional ways that schools measure talent and ability, however, Nicky was below average. But Nicky's progress as a user of language was not so ordinary, nor were the ways his writing changed during the years when he was seven and eight years old. It was the interplay of ordinary and extraordinary that prompted us to look more carefully at Nicky, and over time it was Nicky who showed us most clearly the forces that shaped his literacy development.

NICKY—FROM RAINY DAYS TO MAKING CARS

Seven-year-old Nicky was a Greek-American child of a bilingual, working-class family. He spoke Greek at home and in the classroom to Greek friends when they communicated privately. Nicky had a shy manner, often speaking in almost a whisper, and his frequently slumping posture at the beginning of his second grade year seemed to indicate a defeated air. When he worked at reading "seatwork," he often had difficulty concentrating, as the following field note reveals.

> Nicky is doing his workbook page sprawled over a chair, sagging, brow furrowed. He has a hard time attending to the task, yawns, looks around the room, rearranges the books on the desk, yawns again, listens to Miss Price's conversation with Dean. All this has taken five minutes at least. Finally he begins to draw a picture, tuning out the conversations around him.

Although his spelling and decoding skills were very poor, Nicky was also somewhat of a perfectionist, and he displayed beautiful handwriting. He eagerly contributed to discussions about stories in a way that suggested he had understood, but he approached written activities with less enthusiasm.

When we first met him, Nicky was in the lowest of nine reading groups constituted across three second-grade classes. His teacher, Miss Price, had been informed by Summit Grove's reading specialist that Nicky's instructional reading level was *preprimer*. This designation, commonly used in reading programs structured around basal reading materials, was intended to indicate that Nicky was ready for only the most beginning tasks of formal reading instruction and was significantly below the level considered "average" for a second grader in the West Brook School District. Children in other second grade reading groups at Summit Grove were instructed with materials classified at the levels of primer (P1, P2, P3), the second half of the first-grade year (1^2), the first and second halves of the second-grade year (2^1, 2^2), and the first half of the third-grade year (3^1). In addition, a number of children in Nicky's class, designated as *gifted*, were instructed with materials well above second-grade reading levels in special pull-out enrichment programs.

When the second-grade year began, Miss Price described Nicky as "the best of the worst." She meant that, compared to the other children in the lowest reading group, Nicky seemed to her to have the most ability despite an obvious lack of skills. She noted that Nicky had a great deal of difficulty with the discrete parts of printed language. He could not decode or spell adequately, and he had trouble remembering sight words. On the other hand, Miss Price commented that he seemed to have the ability to understand—he could say what stories were about, predict what would probably happen, and correctly identify the sequence of story events.

The extent of Nicky's progress as a writer over the 2-year period we knew him is illustrated through the comparison of two pieces of writing—one produced with paper and pencil in November of Nicky's second-grade year, and the second produced with word processing 15 months later in February of his third-grade year. Side by side in Figure 6.1, the two pieces underscore the dramatic changes in Nicky's writing from the rainy day story to his essay on how to build a car.

The contrasts in these two pieces are startling. "A Rainy Day" is a beautiful product. It boasts carefully drawn, uniform letter forms and reflects a great deal of attention to size, spacing, and layout. The punctuation marks are accurate and perfectly aligned. Nicky's penmanship indicates well-developed small motor coordination, attentiveness, and steadiness of hand. Despite its meticulous letter forms, however, the piece is also striking for its dull language and repetitive sentence structure. Three of the four sentences, which Nicky wrote to describe a picture of a boy decked out in raingear, begin with identical words, "the boy is," and the one sentence that avoids the same opening phrase repeats its basic structure and verb. Even for practiced readers of invented spelling, the first sentence is difficult to read, since the graphophonic similarity of "uglppe" and "umbrella" or "kraye" and "carrying" is limited. Further, there is almost no sense of voice in the piece—it is hard to discern any relationship between "the

Figure 6.1
The Rainy Day/How to Make a Car

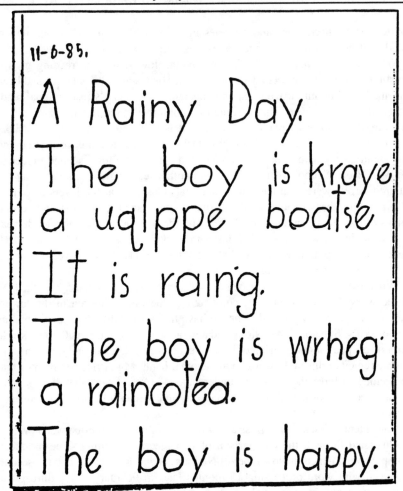

11-6-85.

A Rainy Day.
The boy is kraye
a uqlppe boatse
It is raing.
The boy is wrheg
a raincotea.
The boy is happy.

How to Make a Car

You will need wood, wires, gears, tools, metal, nails, motors, generators, tires, 1 belt. First get a 5-foot piece of wood. Put the motor in the back of the wood. The motor has to be powerful and fast to have a nice ride. If you put the wheels in freewheel, it will be harder, so I suggest you don't do freewheel. Put the wheels about 1 foot from the motor. Then connect the belt, the motor, and the wheels together. Then get the generator and put it next to the wheels. Connect the gear to the generator. Adjust the gear so it is tight against the wheel. Then get one wire and connect it from the generator to the motor. Get two small pieces of metal. Nail one piece to the 5-foot piece of wood and the other to about a 5-inch piece of wood. Put a spring between the pieces of wood. Connect 1 from the piece of metal to the motor and the other to the generator. Then get a 1-foot piece of wood. Nail it to the middle of the wood. Then put the front wheels on. Make sure they turn. Connect two pieces of string to the wheels and the steering wheel. Make the body and you're done. You would have to pull it to get the generator started.

boy'' and Nicky, or for that matter, any interest Nicky might have had in such a boy or his rain equipment. Despite its attractiveness, the piece makes little sense and does not seem intended to communicate with an audience, whether immediate or distant.

To produce the rainy day piece, Nicky functioned as scribe. He was a careful calligrapher of letter forms whose task had everything to do with appearances and little or nothing to do with meaning. The piece was written to fulfill a writing assignment and to display Nicky's considerable penmanship skills. A few weeks before he wrote "A Rainy Day," Nicky had shyly confided to us that he had been "the best writer in first grade." This meant that Mrs. Jeffries, Nicky's first-grade teacher, had found that he had the neatest penmanship and the best-crafted letters of anyone in her class. Every day in first grade, Mrs. Jeffries encouraged Nicky to copy the morning sentences from the blackboard in his meticulous and deliberate way, transcribing them one letter at a time from board to paper. Every day, Nicky reported, it had taken him until well into the afternoon to complete the job of carefully drawing each letter. But Nicky had persevered at the task and had been rewarded with the teacher's praise and the flattering label "best writer." The rainy day piece reflects the careful attention that Nicky had learned to give to neatness and penmanship.

"How To Make a Car," produced with word processing some 15 months later, is as attractive and as legible as the handwritten piece. In fact, because of the mechanical uniformity of lettering size, alignment, and shape, the car piece is even more perfect-looking in form. But "How To Make A Car" is most remarkable for its contrast to "A Rainy Day." Unlike the rainy day sentences, the sentence structure of the car essay is complex and varied, even including embedded clauses and a variety of compound objects and descriptors. There is a clear sense of chronology and order to the list of car-making directions, which are extraordinarily rich and detailed. The vocabulary is precise and appropriately technical. And it is clear in the piece that Nicky knows what he is talking about. He speaks in the strong voice of an expert on car-making as he addresses a less knowledgeable reader, even couching his direct instructions in the more polite guise of friendly advice, "So *I suggest* you don't do freewheel." In addition, Nicky includes reasons for his directives, incorporated to convince the reader that "the motor has to be powerful and fast to have a nice ride" and cautioning that, if the wheels "are in freewheel, it will be harder." Nicky takes into account the probable lesser experience of his reader, pointing out some aspects of car-making that are no doubt obvious to an expert like him: "Then put the wheels on. Be sure they turn."

There is no question that the piece is intended to communicate accurate information about something Nicky cares about. It stands as both a way for him to review the many steps required in car making and a practical list of instructions for a reader who wants to learn about the process. The piece reflects Nicky's attention to recording information precisely, completely, and in sufficient detail to help the novice. To produce the piece, Nicky functions as holder and sharer of knowledge, a role which stands in sharp contrast to his role in the rainy day piece as calligrapher of proper word and letter forms. Although it is professional looking (even though it is only a draft), the car making piece discloses little visible attention to appearances, because appearances are simply not at issue in its production.

There is no question that there are dramatic contrasts between "The Rainy Day" and "How To Make A Car." But the argument we are making in this chapter goes beyond the surface and structural differences in Nicky's early and later writing. We also argue that there were largely invisible but equally dramatic shifts in the underlying ways Nicky understood the activity of writing, and further, that these shifts were shaped by the interplay of the tools and tasks Nicky used for writing during word-processing events. Weizenbaum's (1976) volume on the relationships of computers and human reason is helpful in this regard. He begins a chapter on tools with the assertion that "the stories of man and of his machines are inseparably woven together" (p. 17). Our argument here is a parallel one—that Nicky's story as a writer is inseparably woven together with the story of his writing tools. In other words, "Nicky's Story" of change and development in writing during his second and third grade years is also a story about word processing and about paper and pencil. Weizenbaum suggests that tools are not just instruments, not just devices that accomplish particular practical ends. Rather he claims that, regardless of their primary practical purposes, tools are also "pedagogical instruments" that shape the ways we see the world and imagine its reconstruction. Weizenbaum emphasizes that pedagogical instruments are vehicles for shaping the ways we understand and carry out various activities.

> Tools and machines do not merely signify man's imaginativeness and its creative reach, and they are certainly not important merely as instruments for the transformation of a malleable earth. . . . A tool is also a model for its own reproduction and a script for the reenactment of the skill it symbolizes. That is the sense in which it is a pedagogic instrument, a vehicle for instructing men in other times and places in culturally acquired modes of thought and action. The tool as symbol in all these respects thus transcends its role as a practical means toward certain ends. . . The tool is much more than a mere device: it is an agent for change. (p. 18)

One way to understand the transformation in Nicky's writing from November of one school year to February of the next is in relation to the tools he used to complete particular writing tasks. When Nicky worked with paper and pencil, the tools modeled their own reproduction and served as a script for the reenactment of the activity of writing. In short, the tools themselves supported Nicky's past experiences as "the best writer in first grade" to emphasize that writing was about penmanship and neatness. The tools themselves helped teach Nicky that his internal theory of writing was accurate: the lines of the paper stressed alignment, the relative immutability of the hard-marking pencil stressed first-round precision, and the dexterity required to manipulate properly the slender writing utensil stressed that writing was laborious physical work. The task conveyed a related script for the enactment of writing: description of a nameless picture stressed distance between the writer and his subject, expectation that the task would be completed during seatwork time stressed the status of the activity as a fleeting skills exercise, and absence of an audience stressed that communication was neither intention or issue. The task itself—describing a picture—invited Nicky to produce caption or label-like sentences about the picture rather than to create a story or essay related to the picture.

In contrast, when Nicky worked with word processing to create the building-cars piece, the tool provided a script for the reenactment of the activity of writing that was quite different from the paper-and-pencil script. Word processing emphasized that neatness and calligraphy were minor aspects of writing, essentially managed by the tool itself. Instead, word processing, as pedagogical instrument, supported the idea that writing was about ideas. It emphasized that handwriting and paginal or linear arrangements were mechanical concerns that were less important than what one had to say and how one could say it with written language. Because word processing made it so easy to do, it emphasized that part of figuring out what one had to say was trying out and changing actual words and sentences. The task also conveyed a different script for writing. Nicky chose his own topic for the piece, created especially for the "Young Authors" contest, an annual school-wide writing event at Summit Grove Elementary. He knew contest pieces would have multiple readers who were interested in how much writers knew about their topics. Nicky chose a topic on which he could write as expert, and a tool that would encourage him to include as much detail as he needed.

As juxtaposition of the two texts makes clear, Nicky made a remarkable shift from rainy day to making cars. Over time the powerful tool of word processing prompted Nicky to forge new connections between theory and practice, and eventually to revise his theories of writing. "Nicky's Story," presented in this chapter, provides a sense of how one child learned to write differently—how the tool of word processing interacted with the social processes of word-processing events to shape the ways he practiced and thought about writing.

READING NICKY'S STORY:
A CONCEPTUAL FRAMEWORK

As Nicky's pieces attest, word processing, as pedagogical instrument, provides a script for writing that precludes a narrow focus on penmanship. Hubbard (1985) has suggested that writers who regularly use word processing adapt over time to the capacities of the machine, carrying out most frequently those activities that the machine does best. In short, the "ontology of their writing processes" comes eventually to "recapitulate the technology" of word processing (p. 26). With beginning writers, however, the technology is only partly responsible for the ontology of writing processes, and the tool provides only a partial script for reenactment of the skill. For beginning writers who do not have clear internal scripts for the activity of writing, the teacher, the writing task, the social processes of the classroom, and the unique ways these come together with the writing tool in individual writing events provide the rest of the evolving script.

Writing with Word Processing as a Sociocognitive Activity

As we have mentioned in earlier chapters, Bloome (1987) points out that teachers and students negotiate definitions of literacy when they participate in literacy instruction and when they interact with one another and with the texts stipulated or permitted by the curriculum. Similarly, Green and Weade (1987) define reading as the outcome of both the social and instructional events of classrooms (i.e., interpersonal processes) and the strategies and skills of individual students (i.e., intrapersonal processes). These views, which emphasize that literacy is a sociocognitive activity embedded in the social and linguistic contexts of classrooms (Bloome & Green, 1984), provide a conceptual framework for interpreting what was going on with one individual child as he learned to write with word processing. Nicky's development as a writer over the course of a 2-year period can be understood as the outcome of the dynamic interrelationship of his evolving theories of writing, on the one hand, and the ways he practiced writing with word processing and paper and pencil on the other. But both of these can be understood only in terms of the ways they were embedded within, and interacted with, the learning/teaching cultures of his classrooms, especially the notions of writing demonstrated and negotiated.

A conceptual framework that captures the dynamic relationship of the individual's theories and practices and the social processes constructed in the classroom is represented in Figure 6.2. The figure emphasizes that a beginning writer's ways of practicing writing are reciprocally related to the writer's evolving ideas or theories about writing. Simultaneously, both practices and theories are embedded within, and shaped by, the notions of writing demonstrated generally in the classroom and specifically within given writing events. All of these—practices, theories, and demonstrations—are embedded within the larger social and language processes and teaching culture of the classroom. An interpretive framework of this kind highlights the fact that beginning writers' experiences with word processing are both nested within, and built out of, the language and social interactions constructed in the classroom.

As Figure 6.2 indicates, the "beginning writer's practices" for any given piece of writing (represented on the left-hand side of the diagram) are essentially the writing events in which he or she engages. These are characterized by the

Figure 6.2
A Sociocognitive Framework for Understanding Word Processing and the Beginning Writer

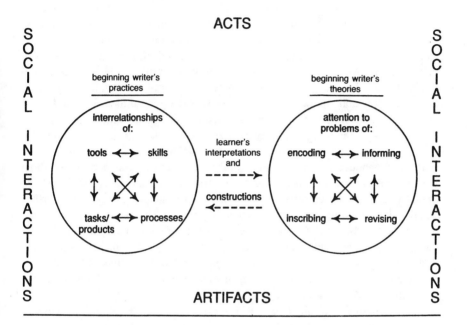

interrelationships of writing tools used, tasks/products assigned or selected, reading/composing/encoding/inscribing skills of the writer, and the processes in which the writer engages. The "beginning writer's theory" underlying a specific piece of writing (represented on the right-hand side of the figure) is evidenced directly through ongoing comments and/or indirectly through the "problems" to which the writer attends in the writing—production problems (encoding and inscribing) as well as communication problems (informing and revising). "Writing demonstrations" are made up of the dynamic interrelations of writing acts, artifacts, and social interactions in classrooms. Acts include teachers', coaches' and students' instructions, responses, assignments, and other classroom actions that convey messages about how the activity of writing is done. The artifacts used by actors include writing tools, writing materials, and models offered when writing is demonstrated. Social interactions refer to the ways in which actors and artifacts come together, often through the medium of language, to respond to, refer to, use or create written texts of any kind.

Notions of Writing: Demonstrations, Theory, and Practice

Mrs. Jeffries, the first-grade teacher who had dubbed Nicky "best writer," wrote sentences on the board and instructed her students to copy them neatly and carefully onto lined newsprint pages. Miss Price assigned second graders to write stories about classroom experiences, such as a trip to the local supermarket or their project sprouting sweet potato plants. Miss Carlisle, a university education student who assisted in Miss Price's classroom, introduced word processing by announcing to each child that it could help them add ideas or make changes to their writing. And Mrs. Perrone presented writing in a series of stages and directed third-grade children to write in various forms, including poetry, dialogue, letters, and opinions. She also provided opportunities for children to publish books from their favorite pieces. As they assigned children writing tasks or worked with them on individual written texts, each of these adults provided information about the nature of the activity of writing. Miss Price signalled that writing was about meaning and not penmanship when she assigned a story about the children's own experience rather than instructing them to copy a standard text or describe a preselected picture as they had often done previously. Miss Carlisle conveyed a similar message by immediately pointing out to each child who came to work at the computer that he or she was working with a tool particularly well equipped for appending ideas, inserting words and spaces, and producing early drafts during which they need not be concerned with spelling. Mrs. Perrone indicated that writing was an ongoing process within which different concerns were appropriate at different times.

Each of these actions are *demonstrations of writing* that instantiate and convey notions about what writing is, how its tools are used, how it functions in school and elsewhere, who participates in it, and how it is learned and developed. Smith (1981) suggests that demonstrations, or opportunities "to see how something is done," are essential aspects of learning, as are learners' active engagements with demonstrations and their expectation that learning will take place. Smith asserts that multiple demonstrations are continually available to learners through people's actions and the products or artifacts they use, although, he notes, many demonstrations may be inadvertent or out of keeping with the intentions of the actor. A book, he explains, demonstrates how books are designed and organized, how pictures and text relate to one another, and how sentences are punctuated and words spelled. By the same token, a teacher demonstrates not only how teachers talk, dress, and ask questions, but also how teachers feel about both their subject matter and their students.

Following Smith's general discussion of the role of demonstrations in learning, Harste et al. (1984) develop more extensively the notion *literacy demonstrations* as part of a conceptual framework for understanding language and literacy learning. Like Smith, they emphasize that there are many demonstrations available in any language event. What a learner does or does not respond to is partly a function of the social interactions of the participants in the demonstration and partly a function of the experiences of the individual learner who seeks unity and coherence across demonstrations.

> Any literacy event provides a variety of demonstrations which are available to language learners through the actions of the participants and the artifacts of the process. The learning of these demonstrations involves the active mediation of the language user. . . . There is no inherent sequence to the order in which the demonstrations involved in literacy are learned; rather, which demonstrations are learned are a function of which demonstrations are highlighted by a literacy event as they transact with the interests, purposes and personal history of the language user. . . . Unity and the search for unity across past and current texts, becomes the propelling force in literacy learning. (pp. 180-181, 185)

Both Smith and Harste et al. assert that language demonstrations are available to learners through people's acts and the artifacts they use or produce. These two features—acts and artifacts—are helpful in understanding the nature of the writing demonstrations made available when Nicky and other beginning writers used word processing. Demonstrations were the result of the interrelationships of artifacts (that is, writing tools, writing tasks assigned or selected, and final products required) and acts (that is, participants' instructions, responses, and other classroom actions) as they came together in language and social interactions. In one sense Nicky's story is a story of the writing demonstrations which he helped to create and out of which he actively constructed his evolving theories and practices of writing. Examining these demonstrations in relation to Nicky's written products and the word-processing events constructed out of the talk of child and coach over a 2-year period provides a glimpse of the ways Nicky made sense of demonstrations as well as which aspects of demonstrations he seemed to be learning.

Nicky's story is also a story of theory and practice—that is, of the ways in which his changing practices of writing and his emerging theories of writing were reciprocally and dynamically related. By "writing practices" we mean the way the individual child writer constructed writing events—what he or she made of the various writing opportunities available in the classroom in terms of tools, tasks, products, and processes. As we have seen, for many beginning writers the opportunity to interact with a coach during writing events was the most critical aspect of the beginners' writing processes. For Nicky, writing practices included the ways he carried out the writing tasks assigned to him, the composing processes with which he was invited or assigned to engage, the ways he chose to utilize the writing tools available to him, and the written products he created. In short, writing practice was the way in which Nicky himself practiced the activity of writing and helped to construct writing events.

The most important aspect of Nicky's writing practice, especially as he initially learned to write with word processing, was his social and language interaction with adult coaches around and during word-processing events. As they worked with word processing, Nicky and his coaches (and later on, Nicky independently) constructed a learning context where he was able to practice writing in ways that were qualitatively different from his writing practices with paper and pencil. Theories of writing, in the sense used here, were the ideas about what writing was and how it functioned that were implicit in Nicky's practice of writing and/or explicit in the language of writing interactions and direct commentary and the ways he constructed the meanings of writing events. As we will see in the many vignettes that are woven throughout this chapter, the most consequential development in Nicky's theory of writing was a shift away from concentration on production and toward concentration on content.

Word processing played a compelling role in this shift. Not only was it a powerful composing tool that offered the writer the capacity to insert, delete, and reorganize text without effort and without physical traces, it was also a powerful pedagogical instrument with the capacity to break through old notions of writing and begin to forge new ones. For Nicky, as this chapter makes clear, the power was in the capacity of word processing to manage enough of the issues involved in the mechanical production of text so that he could concentrate as well on content and communication. When production problems occupied all of Nicky' attention, he had apparently believed that writing was about production, especially beautiful handwriting and neat papers. This theory of writing as well as the considerable physical effort required for Nicky to be "the best writer" made it nearly impossible for him to write for meaning or use written language to act on the world. In contrast, when coaches helped him learn strategies for handling some of the issues of spelling, and when he worked with a tool that, by itself, handled many of the issues of aesthetics, he learned to turn his attention to communication problems and began to develop strategies to address some of these.

NICKY LEARNS WORD PROCESSING

Like most of the beginning writers we came to know at Summit Grove, Nicky had had little prior experience with computers and virtually none with word processing. Like most second graders in Miss Price's class, Nicky learned only two of the basic features of word processing during his first lesson—how to enter text and how to insert and erase within the text. Despite the fact that neither of these features is among the powerful options tauted in the word-processing literature, together they allowed most second graders to get started, and, as soon as basic familiarity with the keyboard developed, prompted teachers and children to report that word processing was a helpful and preferred writing tool. But much more intriguing to us than the discovery that youngsters needed minimal word-processing exposure to begin to use the equipment was the discovery that, for many children, using word processing began to reshape their ideas about writing almost immediately. As the following excerpts reveal, Nicky began to write differently as soon as he started working with a coach at the keyboard.

In his first lesson, Nicky worked with Miss Carlisle, a third-year elementary education student from the university who observed and assisted in Miss Price's classroom a day and a half a week as part of pre-student-teaching fieldwork requirements. Miss Price had instructed Miss Carlisle to work with individual children to complete the writing assignments the rest of the class was completing with paper and pencil in order to expose each one to the basics of word processing. When it was Nicky's turn to work at the computer, the assignment the class was working on was a story about their recent trip to the supermarket. Pedagogically, the point of the trip had been both to visit a neighborhood establishment and to learn that food items are categorized into four basic groups. The culminating activity was the preparation and eating of a fruit salad made with items purchased at the grocery store.

The three lengthy excerpts that follow represent Nicky's introduction to use of the word processor as a writer's tool. They provide a great deal of detail about how a coach helped one child get started with the tool. During the initial session, Miss Carlisle pointed out the relationship between keyboard and monitor and emphasized that it was easy to make changes with word processing. She also taught the basics of text entry—how to press keys, how to erase unwanted characters, and how to insert spaces and type capital letters. But these excerpts also provide considerable information about how Miss Carlisle demonstrated to Nicky what writing was about, and how it could be practiced differently from the ways he had been doing it. The excerpts below demonstrate that, in just one session, Nicky began to learn that writing with word processing was an activity that was significantly different from writing with paper and pencil.

[Nicky settles in at the computer, ready to begin his first lesson with the coach.]

Coach: Have you ever typed on anything before?

Nicky: No

Coach: Well, welcome to the new experience! When you type any of these letters [points to keyboard], they're going to appear on the screen [points to monitor]. Want to try typing just any letter? [Nicky types in an "f."]
   f

Coach: See? Now to erase that letter, use this button up here . . . [Points to the backarrow key.] Try it. [Nicky pushes backarrow, "f" disappears.]

Coach: And it's gone! You want to make a capital letter? Use this button. [Indicates the shift key.] Say I want to make a capital. . . [Types in "A," demonstrating correct use of the shift key.]
   A

Coach: You have a capital letter. Do you want it there? What do you do to get rid of it? [Nicky uses the backarrow correctly to erase "A".]

Coach: If you ever want to make spaces between words, this is the space bar and you make spaces between the words. [Types "d," then "o," and "g."]
dog

[Presses the space bar emphatically.]
Now I'll type "cat." [Types in "c," then "a," then "t."]
dog   cat

See that. Easy? All right. [Deletes "dog" and "cat."] What I thought you could do . . . I want to take your Acme story that you wrote yesterday and type it into the computer and then we could make some changes on it, and you're gonna see how easy it is to make changes on it because you don't have to use your eraser.

Nicky: Do I have to use the stuff on top? [Points to his name and date at the top of the draft paper.]

Coach: Sure. Put your name on it. Do you want to copy it?

Nicky: (nods) Where is the capital?

Coach: That's this one [points]. That little arrow. [Nicky types "N," correctly using the shift key.]
N

Coach: Good.

Nicky: Is this "I" (uncertain)? [Points to the "I" key.]

Coach: Um-hum. They're all capital letters (referring to the letters as printed on the keyboard), but they'll come out small on the screen unless you use the capital.

Nicky: How do you do the numbers?

Coach: You don't have to unless you want to. Do you want to type in your date?

Nicky: No.

Coach: Then just start typing your story. You can even change it if you don't like it. I just thought that this would give you something to start off with and then we can add to it.

Within minutes Miss Carlisle had introduced Nicky to almost everything he needed to know in order to enter text. Nicky immediately understood the connection between what he typed at the keyboard and what appeared on the screen. Although he needed reminders about key location and basic operations during his subsequent word-processing episodes, Nicky got the main idea of these during the first session. With help, he entered text, inserted space, erased text, and made capital letters. His only initial confusion, caused by the appearance of the key for the letter, "I," which did not show the horizontal bars at top and bottom and to him looked more like a lower case "L," was momentary.

Overall, Nicky adjusted easily to the keyboard and, like most of the children whom we observed, was remarkably unintimidated by the equipment. By the end of the session, Nicky was able to locate the keys he needed without apparent frustration, even though he needed to search for some keys for as long as a minute.

During the first part of the initial lesson, Miss Carlisle's demonstration emphasized the linear production of text. Essentially she showed Nicky how to do with word processing what he could already do with paper and pencil—put letters together to form words, leave spaces to indicate divisions between them, make capital letters, and erase the last one or two characters to correct an error. In most cases, she showed Nicky how to trade in a series of pencil strokes for a single keystroke: the stick and ball combinations required for letters like "b," "d," "B," and "g" were replaced by solitary keystrokes, as were the three- and four-stroke diagonal and hump formations of letters like "w," "m," "M," and "K." The tradeoff was an economical one for Nicky—writing with word processing required less physical dexterity, less manual pressure, and less cognitive work (Daiute, 1986), since Nicky did not have to remember how to draw the letters but instead had only to recognize them on the keyboard. Locating letter keys, a burden which was added when one wrote with word processing, did not seem to create an imbalance in the rhythm and ratio of Nicky's composing and encoding. In one sense, then, Nicky was writing differently with word processing within a few minutes—he simply did not have to work as hard as he did with paper and pencil in order to inscribe the letters he wanted.

The introductory session continued as Nicky typed in the story he had pencilled onto a rough draft and brought with him to the machine. When he asked for spellings, Miss Carlisle encouraged him to type the sounds he heard and pointed out that spelling perfectly was not important except at final-draft time, assuring him, "That's good enough. I can read it." The excerpt below is a continuation of the one above.

[Nicky has typed in his name and "I."]

Nicky: How do you spell 'ate'?

Coach: Do the best you can. This is so close (tapping 'eyat' on his rough draft). Just sound it out the best you can. If we ever make a real final perfect copy of it, we'll fix all the spelling and stuff but for now just get down the words. Spelling's not that important right now. . . [While she talks, Nicky has been scanning the keyboard.] What are you looking for?

Nicky: The E.

Coach: It's up there (points to top row). Just keep looking. [Nicky finds the "e."] Good!

[Nicky continues to type in what he has on his paper-and-pencil draft. He searches for letters systematically, running his fingers across the rows of keys. Eventually he transfers what he has written on his rough draft to the computer screen.]

> **Ieyatfrstand vegetables andzaywr good.**
> [Translation: I ate fruits and vegetables and they were good.]

Coach: Well, you typed what you had in. Can you think of anything else about the trip that you liked or that you remember? [Nicky shakes his head.]

Coach: Nothing? Did you have a favorite fruit or vegetable?

Nicky: My favorite fruit is . . . Is pear a vegetable or a fruit?

Coach: A pear? A pear is a fruit. Did you have that yesterday, two days ago?

Nicky: Yeah.

Coach: Would you like to add that in?

Nicky: Yeah.

Coach: Go ahead.

[Nicky turns to keyboard and continues the text, stopping twice to insert missed spaces between words.]

> **Ieyatfrst and vegetablesandzay wr good**
> **my frt**

Nicky: That's 'favorite.' [Points to 'frt.']

Coach: Um-hm.

Nicky: Is there 'fruit' on that? [Refers to the rough draft paper where he thinks he might find the correct spelling.]

Coach: There it is. [Points to 'frst' on draft.]

[Nicky types 'frst' from draft, inserts spaces where appropriate, then sits for a long time.]

> **my frt frst is**

Coach: What are you thinking of?

Nicky: 'Pear.'

Coach: How to spell it?

Nicky: Yeah.

Coach: What sounds do you hear in it?

[Nicky turns to keyboard and types in, 'p,' then 'r.']

> **my frt frst is pr**

Coach: Do you remember anything about the walk that was fun, or not fun? You
             guys walked all the way down there. What did you do for the fruit salad?

Nicky: I cutted up apples.

Coach: Do you want to add that?

Nicky: Yeah.

As the work of coach and child continued, Nicky was writing more and more
differently from the ways that were usual for him. The focus of his writing at the
computer was *not* penmanship, which, until this session, had been the main
concern of Nicky's efforts. On the contrary, penmanship and neatness were
automatically managed by the equipment itself. But Miss Carlisle, who insisted
throughout the session that spelling was not the focus either, demonstrated that,
when writing with word processing, the focus could be the "truth" of an
experience that Nicky had had with his class. She urged Nicky to include in his
story information about anything that had actually occurred on the trip as well as
his feelings and responses to it. Miss Carlisle prompted Nicky to continue each
time he stopped. She asked him what had happened on the trip, how he reacted to
it, and what role he had played in creating the fruit salad. She invited Nicky to
add detail to his story based on the validity of his own experience, and Nicky did
so until he announced suddenly that he was finished. In her demonstration, Miss
Carlisle not only pointed out that writing was about content rather than production alone, but also demonstrated that a way to develop the content of writing
was to add on additional information about the event to a text that had already
been produced.

When Miss Carlisle and Nicky talked at the word processor, Miss Carlisle
urged Nicky to spell words as best he could. Encouragement to spell words
incorrectly was a new experience for Nicky and one that was not in keeping with
the notions of writing generally conveyed in his classroom. Miss Price required
that children spell words correctly and did not view invented spellings as part of a
developmental process. She provided correct spellings when children asked for
them, posted spelling models in the room, and edited children's work by writing
correct spellings above the children's words in red pen. Nicky was not very
comfortable inventing his own spellings, and, as we show in the section on
spelling that follows, he was acutely aware of correct and incorrect forms of
words. Nevertheless, Miss Carlisle's demonstration introduced the idea that
spelling was not the only focus of writing.

The excerpt below is a continuation of the initial word-processing event
between Nicky and Miss Carlisle. The text that Nicky had constructed so far was
as follows.

> **Ieyatfrstand vegetables andzaywr good.**
> **My frt frst is pr i ct apl**
> [Translation: I ate fruits and vegetables and they were good.
> My favorite fruit is pear. I cut apples.]

Nicky: That's all.

Coach: That's all? Do you want to type in 'that's all'? [Nicky shakes his head.] No? You all done? [Nicky nods.] Do you see any . . . Uh, go back and read what you wrote. Read it out loud.

Nicky: [Looks at the screen and tries to read his story aloud.] Did I forget to put spaces?

Coach: Um-hum. Do you want to fix that? [Nicky looks doubtful.] It's real easy. No eraser! Instead of pushing this all the way . . . Uh . . . [Points to the backarrow.] What does this do when you push it?

Nicky: It takes the letter away.

Coach: It takes the letter away (nodding). Well if you wanted to get all the way back to there [points to first place where space is omitted], you wouldn't want to erase the whole line would you?

Nicky: No.

Coach: No, that was a lot of work. You use these arrows . . . You see these arrows over here? [Points to cursor key.] . . . Watch what it does. [Presses the key which moves the cursor to the left.] Makes it go that way (nodding left). Now look at this arrow, the #6 arrow [Points to cursor key.] There's a 6 on top of it.

Nicky: Makes it go back.

Coach: Makes it go the other way. And it doesn't erase anything. So you want to go all the way back, push this one until you're back where you want to be. You put it on the first letter of the next word and it will put a space in the right place. [Nicky tries it, successfully]. There you go.

[Nicky uses the #6 cursor movement key to move through the text, checking for omitted spaces and inserting them where needed.]

I eyat frst and vegetables and zay wr good My frt frst is pr i ct apl

Coach: See what happened. You inserted all those spaces and it got to be a line longer. Can you read the whole thing out loud now?

Nicky: [Rereads the story aloud.] 'I ate fruits and vegetables and they were good. My favorite fruit is . . .' [Stops right before 'pear' when he realizes it is missing the word 'a' in front of it.] Can you go back to here (pointing to space before 'pear') and write the 'a'?

Coach: You want to write the letter, right? Of course you can.

[Nicky uses the cursor movement key without further prompting to move through the text to locate his place.]

Coach: You want it behind ''pear,'' right? Read it out loud to yourself and then you'll figure out where you want it. [Nicky finds the place, shows it to Miss Carlisle with his finger, hesitates.]

Coach: It won't erase it, so you just type over it right there.

As the session with Nicky continued, Miss Carlisle taught him how to insert spaces within the text that he had already produced. Because they break up the linearity of text production, insertion and deletion within existing text are two of the most critical features of word processing. For any writer, these two features make writing with word processing qualitatively different from writing with pencil and paper. As we demonstrated in Chapter 4, breaking into existing text to insert more text or space and/or to delete text from an already existing text was conceptually out of reach for most of the kindergarteners and first graders whom we observed. The inability of young children to break into existing text is not surprising when we consider that to do so requires both the conceptual ability to deal with the paperless abstraction of adding space to a computer screen and the ability to reread and rethink an idea. Nonetheless, it is the power of word processing to break neatly and effortlessly into a stream of text that makes it possible for meaning to emerge as one works with the tool. Interestingly, this notion was not at all difficult for Nicky, a child whose standard school tests indicated that he was at an early first-grade or even kindergarten level, barely ready to profit from formal reading instruction.

In his first word-processing session, Nicky worked with a coach to construct a story about his class trip to the supermarket. One way to think about his introductory lesson is in terms of the word processing skills he learned— how to use the shift key, space bar, backarrow key, and the cursor movement keys. He also learned that he could insert letters and words anywhere within his text, and, when he unintentionally inserted extra spaces, he learned how to remove those as well. At the end of the session he learned how to save and print his work and then clear the screen for the next child. But another more important way to think about Nicky's first lesson is in terms of what he began to learn about writing. Nicky began to learn that writing was not simply a process of laborious calligraphy— forming perfect letters, staying on the lines, leaving even spaces. Rather, it was a process that required attention to words, not just letters; to meanings, not just lines; and to the ordered coherence that emerged between spaces, not just the even placement of spaces themselves.

NICKY LEARNS TO WRITE DIFFERENTLY

Over time Nicky began to understand writing as a process of discovering, clarifying, and relaying information. His evolving theory of writing can be seen as both *a result of* changes in the ways he practiced writing with word processing and also as *a reason for* the changes in the ways he practiced writing. Likewise his evolving practices of writing can be seen as both *a result of* the new ways he thought about writing and also as *a reason for* his reconstruction of his theories of writing. The conversations constructed by coaches and child formed the teaching/learning context within which Nicky learned to use word processing and shaped the ways he thought about writing. Further, the ways Nicky thought about writing shaped the ways conversations were configured and the ways Nicky wrote with (and without) word processing. The images of Nicky working with coaches, and later working more independently, to write with word processing are best understood within the sociocognitive framework we have posited, a framework which places in the foreground the interrelationships of writing demonstrations and beginning writers' theories and practices of writing as they are embedded within, and constructed out of, the social and language interactions of classrooms.

Problems of Writing: Production and Communication

Flower and Hayes (1981) have suggested that writing is a series of problem-solving activities involving skills that are organized more or less hierarchically and procedures that are summoned recursively. Experienced writers tend to plan and attend more to problems of content and organization in their writing, while inexperienced or weak writers are often preoccupied with problems of mechanics. (See Hillocks, 1986, for a comprehensive review of the composing-processes literature.) Usually as writers gain experience, skills such as spelling and handwriting become so automatic that they demand little conscious attention, thus freeing writers to concentrate on topic, revision, and information (Scardamalia & Bereiter, 1983). Along somewhat similar lines, Graves (1984) posits a sequence of problems to which writers attend: spelling, motor-aesthetics, conventions, topic and information issues, and revision of texts. He suggests that children attend to spelling concerns first, and address issues of topic and revision only after they have solved their spelling and motor-aesthetic problems. Indeed Graves's (1984) conclusions about young children, as well as empirical studies of basic adult writers (Hillocks, 1986), suggest that writers who cannot solve their spelling and motor-aesthetic problems may be seriously impeded in writing for a lifetime. Following these lines of research, we turn to the writing problems Nicky and his coaches tackled. This provides one way to gain insights into his changing cognitive strategies and his evolving theories of writing as they were embedded in the conversations that surrounded and supported word-processing events.

Over two years, Nicky and his coaches tackled two types of problems in his writing: (a) problems of print production, where handwriting and spelling were critical; and (b) problems of meaning, where content, selection/organization of information, and presentation to an audience were important. In one sense, these two kinds of problems were related hierarchically: the first type had to be managed before the second could be tackled. For instance, while Nicky was completely preoccupied with problems of paper-and-pencil inscribing, he seemed unable to attend to problems of meaning. Within the context of conversation with an adult, and with word processing as a regular writing tool, however, the situation changed. Word processing itself took care of some production problems, and he and his teachers collaboratively devised ways to manage some others. Consequently, Nicky and his teachers were able to tackle both the first and the second type of problems more or less simultaneously—as they worked together, they began to address communication problems because they could satisfactorily manage production problems.

Tackling Production Problems: Handwriting. Production problems are of two basic kinds: handwriting, or issues involved in inscribing letter forms on paper; and spelling, or issues involved in encoding sounds into letter symbols. As we pointed out in Chapter 4, the task of inscribing requires young children to attend to left-to-right and top-to-bottom progression, even alignment with appropriate adjustment for upper- and lower-case letters, marking off word and sentence units with standard spacing conventions, drawing letters in recognizable and attractive form, and maintaining sufficient speed. For beginning writers, these can be formidable tasks that engage all available attention and exhaust all available energy, leaving little for content and communication issues. Indeed there is some evidence that there is a correlation between production speed and ease, on the one hand, and the quality of written work on the other.

Although Graves (1984) argues that spelling is the first concern for beginning writers, followed by a concern for the appearance of the writing on the page, we found that Nicky was concerned foremost about what the paper looked like. As we saw earlier in this chapter, Nicky's rainy day story provides a clear example of writing of the sort he had been encouraged to produce in first grade. The piece reflects preoccupation with beautifully drawn handwriting, less attention to encoding, and almost no attention to meaning. When Nicky began second grade, he brought with him the ''best writer'' experience, and he essentially equated writing with handwriting. He wrote as if neat and correct production of letter and word forms were the central tasks of the writer.

The strong connection Nicky made between handwriting and writing hampered his ability to create interesting, extended prose. Opportunities to work with a coach with word processing began to interrupt that connection for Nicky and suggest other connections. The piece produced in the excerpt that follows provides a sense of how Nicky worked with a coach to use word processing in his first word-processing session following the initial introduction with Miss Carlisle. Although he had developed only minimal word-processing skills and had to be reminded about some of the basic operations, Nicky's finished piece, ''Making Friends Happy,'' was longer than anything he had written in his paper-and-pencil journal at that point in the year. Miss Price was especially impressed with the length of the story, since the other second graders in her class, who had composed with paper and pencil, had produced just one sentence on the topic. Nicky not only wrote at length but, as the excerpt indicates, also combined sentences and revised as he wrote. He was coached during this event by Mrs. Kahn, one of the researchers who had been asked by Miss Price to help the children with word processing instead of simply observing. As the excerpt below indicates, Mrs. Kahn took advantage of the capacity of word processing to manage some production problems in order to demonstrate to Nicky that the process of writing could include sentence combination and revision. The combination—tool and interaction with a coach—made it possible for Nicky to attend to the content of his piece rather than just to its appearance.

Nicky: I'm supposed to write about making friends happy.

[Coach and Nicky have a brief conversation about what the topic means.]

Coach: What do you think she means by making friends happy? We'd better start with that because you're in trouble (laughing) if you don't know what she means.

Nicky: How to make them happy . . . You could give them something like candy or stickers.

Coach: Is that a way you would make them happy, by giving them candy or stickers?

Nicky: Yeah.

Coach: Do you have a friend that you do that with, that you share things with? Does that friend give you things back?

Nicky: Not all the time.

Coach: Not all the time. It's not like going to the store where you give them one and they give you one, is it? But sometimes you get stuff back and it makes you happy? So it works both ways, huh?

[Session continues. Coach helps Nicky type in a list of words he might want for the story across the top of the computer screen. He dictates, 'friends, happy, stickers, candy, buy, them, toys, play, soccer, basketball.' Then Nicky is ready to type in the title he has selected, 'Making Friends Happy.']

Coach: Remember how to make a capital letter? [Points to shift key.] You hold down this arrow and the 'M' . . .

Nicky: This? [Points to shift key.]

Coach: Press that one down and just hold it. [Nicky does so.] Now find the 'M' and press it just once. [Nicky does so correctly.] Okay, now you let go of this button. [Nicky releases shift key.]
              M

              'Making friends happy . . . Making . . .' [Repeats the title.]

Nicky: Is 'making' up there? [Nods toward list of words.]

Coach: No it's not. Want to take a shot at it? It's pretty close to the way it sounds . . . 'Making . . .'

Nicky: E?

Coach: No, it's an 'A'. [Nicky hunts for and finds the key.]
       Ma

Nicky: K?

Coach: Yes. [Nicky types it in.]
       Mak

Nicky: E?

Coach: No, you drop the 'E' it's just an 'I' . . . 'I,' 'N,' 'G.'

Nicky: Is this the 'I'? [Points to 'I' keypress.]

Coach: Yeah, that's the 'I'. It looks like an 'L', doesn't it?

Nicky: 'I' . . . 'N'. . . 'G.' [Says each letter aloud as he types it in.]
       Making

Coach: OK, now what do you need?

Nicky: 'Making friends . . .'

[Session continues. Nicky has no trouble announcing the sentences he wants to write. The coach assists with spelling, verifies as Nicky picks out words from the word list, and helps him insert a space when he requests help. After a few minutes, the text reads as follows.]

> **Making friends happy**
> **I make my friends happy.**

Coach: Good. Okay. [Reads.] 'I make my friends happy.' It's about time, I guess, to say how you do that, hum? What would you like to say?

Nicky: 'I make my friends happy when I buy them stickers and candy.'

Coach: Ok, do you want to make that all one sentence?

Nicky: Yeah.

Coach: Do you want to add that on to this sentence? [Points.] Or do you want . . . [Nicky interrupts.]

Nicky: Add on to this sentence. [Nicky is definite about what he wants to do.]

Coach: OK, back up and take out the period. It's not the end of the sentence [now].

[Session continues with Nicky adding information about his friends, asking the coach for spelling and word processing information where needed, and revising his sentences. He frequently refers to the word list at the top of the screen.]

> **Making friends happy**
> **I make my friends happy when I buy**
> **them stickers and candy. they buy my**
> **stuff back. I like to play soccer with**
> **them.**

Nicky: I want to write 'I like to play soccer with my friends.' (Indicates that he has changed his mind about how he wants the final sentence to read.]

Coach: What do you have to do?

Nicky: Take out this. [Points, deletes the word, 'them,' and the period, types in 'my friends.']
I like to play soccer with my friends.

[Announces the next sentence.] 'And they like to play soccer with me . . .'

Coach: How does it go together?

Nicky: I'll take out this period. [Deletes the period and adds the phrase. The finished text reads as follows.]

Making friends happy
I make my friends happy when I buy
them stickers and candy. they buy me
stuff back. I like to play soccer with
my friends and they like to play soccer
with me.

The length and a good bit of the content of this piece can be attributed to Nicky's conversation with Mrs. Kahn, who sat with him at the computer, coaching and encouraging. There is no question that the prompting of an adult helped Nicky to extend and expand his writing, even though the purpose of having the adult there in the first place was to coach him in word-processing strategies and make sure he could handle the equipment without mishap. But, as we pointed out in Chapter 5, it was impossible for coaches to teach about word processing without teaching about writing. As a novice at the computer, Nicky needed help from the coach to know that he could erase a period and add on to a sentence. While at first glance this piece of information seems to be about word processing, it is also about writing. Suggesting that it is possible with word processing to combine two sentences also conveys the idea that it might be desirable.

But the coach did not make all the difference in Nicky's writing. The word-processing tool itself modelled the way in which Nicky was to understand the activity of writing. The tool, as pedagogical instrument, managed handwriting for Nicky, so that beautiful letters were simply not an issue. Instead Nicky and Mrs. Kahn focused on spelling, either using the word list or encoding words together, and they focused on content—what Nicky bought to make his friends happy, what games he liked to play with them, and their mutual enjoyment of one another. The writing demonstration that they jointly constructed carried the message that writing was not equivalent to drawing, copying, or inscribing, but was instead an activity that centered on information and ideas.

As the year progressed and sessions like this one continued, two intriguing things happened to Nicky's writing. On the one hand, his paper-and-pencil handwriting regressed. It no longer appeared so labored and crafted, letters were not perfectly formed, and some of his writing could even be called sloppy. On the other hand, the content of his stories, whether created initially with word processing or with paper and pencil, grew longer and more involved. Nicky's draft of a story about baby elephants (see Figure 6.3) was written with paper and pencil during Nicky's second grade year after he had participated in just three

Figure 6.3
Baby Elephants

word-processing sessions. The example reveals a noticeable and curious deterioration in Nicky's penmanship.

Clearly the elephant story is different from the rainy day story (Figure 6.1) in quality of penmanship, with its unevenly spaced letters, its lack of uniform size, and its irregular sticks, balls, and humps. However, while the elephant story is poorer aesthetically than the rainy day piece, it is at the same time extraordinarily more rich than the latter in content. For example, although both stories have four sentences, the sentence structure of "Elephants" is much more complex than that of "A Rainy Day." "Elephants" has two sentences with embedded adverbial clauses, which spell out the conditions under which the major sentence propositions are true—'when it's hot' specifies the conditions for elephants going near the water, and 'when baby elephants can't find their mother' conveys the condition under which other elephants take on the job of parenting. Even the two simple declarative sentences ('baby elephants run fast' and 'elephants are fat') contain colorful information and add substantively to the piece. Overall the piece is coherent and interesting—it makes it clear that Nicky is something of an expert on baby elephants, a topic he had been reading about in class.

Near the end of his second-grade year, we asked Nicky to explain why the stories in his paper-and-pencil journal were no longer painstakingly drawn and beautiful.

Mrs. Kahn: Do you remember what your handwriting looked like at the beginning of second grade?

Nicky: Yes.

Mrs. Kahn: What happened that made you willing to write sloppily?

Nicky: I got sick and tired of being so slow and never getting my work done. Besides on the computer it doesn't matter . . .

By handwriting more quickly, and therefore less laboriously, Nicky had found that he could get his work done, knowing that his final copy could still be produced beautifully on the computer. The baby elephants piece, composed with paper and pencil, makes it clear that Nicky's theories of writing were changing, not just the way he practiced writing with word processing. He was realizing that writing was a process of organizing and presenting information, not just producing pleasing print.

Tackling Production Problems: Spelling. Over time, then, Nicky came to think and talk about writing as an activity about meaning, not just aesthetics. Working with word processing played an important role in the evolution of Nicky's ideas, since it handled for him the attractive production of print and allowed him to focus his attention elsewhere. But it is misleading to think that writing with word processing helped young writers like Nicky because it allowed them to ignore the production issues that are unavoidably part of the activity of writing. Far from avoiding the production issue of spelling, for example, working with word processing gave Nicky opportunities to concentrate on spelling that were not available to him when he wrote with paper and pencil. In the making-friends excerpt, for example, Nicky and Mrs. Kahn spent some of their time talking about spelling and working out ways to encode words like "making."

When Nicky wrote with a coach at the computer, he had opportunities to work on spelling in three ways: (a) transferring correct spellings from a model created during initial composition of a draft or by the coach during the word-processing event, (b) manipulating letters through successive approximations of standard spellings during an editing period, and (c) after the midpoint of his second-grade year, using an online spelling checker to verify his best-guess attempts. When Nicky composed his making-friends piece, for example, the coach suggested a method that she had seen William, another second grader in Nicky's class, initiate independently. When William came to the computer to write a poem, he had, without prompting or suggestion, typed in a list of words that he thought he might use, then used the list as a reference while he composed. When the piece was complete, he had erased the list from the screen. When Nicky wrote his piece, the coach offered at the beginning of the session to type a list of words that Nicky thought he might need for the story. Nicky immediately responded by asking whether the words would "stay up there" on the screen and was assured that they could be erased when the story was complete. Knowing that the list would not be part of the printed product was critical to Nicky. His first concern was the aesthetics of the piece, and the capacity of word processing to produce text on the monitor that could be hidden or easily expunged when hard copy was produced honored Nicky's commitment to appearances.

As we saw in the preceding example, when he wrote the making-friends piece, Nicky referred to the word list constantly. Although he had serious deficiencies in reading, he was usually able to find the word he was seeking if it appeared on the list and he usually knew when the word was not on the list. To transfer a word from the list into the text of his story, he chanted the first few letters to himself, slowly found each of those on the keyboard and typed them in, looked up again at the word list to locate the next few letters, and then repeated the process. This spelling procedure provided auditory, visual, and kinesthetic support for spelling. As the year progressed, Nicky transferred larger strings of letters with each glance at the model. In February, when he transferred the word *elephants* from paper-and-pencil copy to computer screen, he was able to produce the entire spelling of the word with one glance at the model by the time he completed the piece. The capacity of word processing to reduce the physical strain of handwriting and to provide temporary supporting text in the form of a word list gave Nicky a chance to study standard spellings, rehearse the spellings orally, and then reproduce them on the computer screen.

Obviously a version of this transferring activity can be accomplished with the tools of pencil and paper and often is in classrooms where children use word banks, personal dictionaries, or prewriting lists to aid them in initial text production. Word processing does not really change the nature of that activity. But transferring from a model at the word processor was an activity that was especially efficient for Nicky, since none of his energy was siphoned off by the need to concentrate on remembering, producing, and correcting letter forms. Further, when he wrote with word processing, the transferring activity was embedded within the larger context of conversation with a supportive coach who provided the initial spelling list and helped Nicky keep track of where he was in the process. And then of course, the need to produce a "good copy" by writing everything over again on special paper simply disappeared with word processing.

Using word processing also enabled Nicky to practice spelling in a second way, a way that was unique to the tool. Although Miss Price regularly edited children's work for spelling and punctuation errors, she frequently chose not to have her second graders handwrite good copies, because the process was tedious and often resulted in new mistakes and omissions. As often as possible, however, she did choose to have children use the the word processor as a tool to produce good copies, reporting that she particularly valued the machine because it took the sting out of recopying. Working with a coach to edit their texts with word processing prompted Nicky and other beginning writers to concentrate on spelling at the appropriate point in the process, that is, at the point of final rather than first draft. In the following example, Nicky worked on the correct spelling for the word *mammal* which he had spelled *mamle*. As per Miss Price's instructions, he had circled all the words in the piece which he thought might be misspelled, then brought his circled draft to the computer. (Miss Price had typed children's first drafts intact the night before, so that they could edit them at the machine.) Mrs. Kahn, who was observing and coaching, helped Nicky as he worked through the piece and showed him how to use the cursor movement keys and both delete keys that the keyboard offered. Nicky paid close attention as she pointed out that, if he typed in a letter, the letters that appeared after it would move over, and that, if he deleted a letter, the space where the letter had been would automatically close up. Out of his talk with the coach, Nicky eventually developed a strategy for correcting his spelling. (Underlined words are those that Nicky had circled on his own before coming to the computer.)

> **A bear is a <u>mamle</u>. The mother bear <u>sets</u>**
> **with the baby bear. <u>Ontill</u> it is big. A bear**
> **<u>hebrnte</u> all <u>wnlter</u> long. <u>Ontill</u> it is spring.**
> **A bear is big**

[Coach reviews Nicky's paper-and-pencil draft.]

Coach: So you figured out which words are not spelled right, and you got them all. . . Let's find the first one, which is this one. [Points to 'mamle'.]

Nicky: Mammal.

Coach: Mammal. Can you get the cursor over to the word mammal?
This is the arrow that moves this way (points to cursor movement key.)
So you want to move this light (points to blinking cursor on the screen) to
where you want to make a change.

Nicky: There. [Points to 'mamle' on screen.]

Coach: Right. There—exactly.

Nicky: I have to get it on the "l"?

Coach: Yes because let me show you what the right spelling of "mammal" is.
Do you want to take a guess at it or do you absolutely have no other idea?
[Nicky indicates he has no idea; Mrs. Kahn prints 'mammal' at the top of
his draft.] Move the cursor to the "l" . . .

Nicky: On top of the "l"?

Coach: Right on top of the "l". That means that the next letter you type will be
next to the "m" and the "l" will move over, ok? Because the correct
spelling of "mammal" is M-A-M-M-A-L. [Taps paper.] Though this
[indicating Nicky's spelling, "mamle," on the screen] was perfectly
sensible. Unfortunately it's not right, but it was perfectly sensible. So
what you want to add is . . .

Nicky: [Interrupts.]. . . is M . . . A . . . [Nicky immediately types in "m" and
"a" in between the second "m" and the "l" of his original spelling to
form, 'mam(ma)le.']
       mammale

Coach: Exactly. Now what else do you have to do to "mammale" to make it
right? We still have an 'e' there. [Points.]

Nicky: Erase the E. [He makes the changes with some consultation about
whether to use the back-arrow erase key or the delete key.]
       mammal

Coach: Got it! OK. What next? [Points to circled word on paper and pencil
draft.] 'Sets'? Should that be 'sits?'

Nicky: [Shakes his head no.] 'Stays.'

Coach: Let's find the word on the screen.

Nicky: It's right over there. [Points to 'sets' on the screen, correctly moves the
cursor to it.]
       sets

Coach: Now what do you want to change? We're going from that word [points to
the word "sets" on the screen] to this word [prints 'stays' at the top of
the paper]. Wouldn't it be easier to erase the whole word and put the new
word in . . . Or would you like to . . .

Nicky: [Breaks in.] Erase the E. [Deletes 'e' on screen.]
           sts

Coach: Now what?

Nicky: Erase the S. [Indicates the second 's', deletes it.]
           st

[Nicky then correctly types in "ays," and the word is completed.]
           stays

Consistently, Nicky chose not to erase a whole word and rewrite a word, as he did with pencil and paper and as the coach suggested might be easier. Instead Nicky figured out a system for correcting spellings that generally worked like this: check the spelling on the screen letter by letter against the correct spelling on paper (usually supplied by the teacher who had edited his work or supplied by the coach within the word-processing event), move the cursor to the first wrong letter, delete it, insert the correct letter, and repeat the process until the word on the screen was perfect. Nicky consistently began his corrections at or near the beginning of the word and then proceeded to the end of the word, even when, in positioning the cursor, it might have been more efficient to work "backwards" on a word. This process meant that Nicky attended sequentially to every letter in a word and stopped to consider its appropriateness.

When Nicky transformed *hebrnte* into *hibernate*, for example, he paid close attention to every correct and incorrect letter. He also repeated letters and syllables aloud to himself as he worked. This kind of letter-by-letter building of the correct spellings of a word within an already-existing approximation of that word was only possible with word processing, where deleting and inserting letters takes place on a mutable screen, rather than a much less flexible piece of paper. Nicky corrected *hibernate* without prompting from the coach, using the strategy he had worked out earlier with the coach's help through the following moves.

Word on the screen	*Nicky's changes*
hebrnte	delete "e", insert "i"
hibrnte	delete "r", insert "e"
hibente	delete "n," insert "r"
hiberte	delete "t," insert "n"
hiberne	

In this process Nicky made four changes in the word, each one a delete–insert combination move that altered one letter in the spelling of the word. After the fourth move when the cursor was on the final "e" of *hiberne*, the coach interrupted. As the conversation below indicates, she saw that if Nicky typed in "a" and "t" together, he would need only one more delete-insert move, and he would have the complete correct spelling of *hibern(at)e*.

Coach: What would happen if you typed in "A-T" right now?

Nicky: It won't fit.

Coach: Because you'll need space for it? [Nicky nods.] No . . . the computer
will make it move over (reassuring). Try it. Try typing in just the "A-T"
and see what happens to the "e" [Uncertain, Nicky types in 'a,' then
't.']

hibernate

Coach: What happened to the "e"?

Nicky: It moved over.

Coach: It just moved over (confirming).

Nicky's response that the letters would not fit is surprising in one sense. The
example above indicates that Nicky inserted four letters in four separate word-
processing moves where there seemed to be no spaces, but because he did them
one at a time—a kind of one-for-one exchange—this was apparently a different
process for him than inserting more than one letter. He had to be assured that,
when he typed in several letters at once, there would indeed be space for them.
We found that this kind of information had to be supplied again and again to the
beginning writers we observed. They assumed that writing with word processing
was like writing with a typewriter on paper until they eventually saw for
themselves that the computer screen was not like paper, that letters, words, and
even whole sentences could be inserted anywhere on the screen. The questions
and suggestions coaches offered played a pivotal role in the children's eventual
realization, even though children certainly did not always learn what coaches
demonstrated about writing with word processing. When beginning writers did
develop the notion that computer space was limitless, many of them, like Nicky,
began to use word processing to write differently.

As he made corrections, Nicky recited letters and syllables, watching the
screen intently and seeing the conventional spellings of words like *hibernate*
emerge in his text. The practice of using word processing to edit his work by
producing closer and closer approximations of standard spellings seemed valuable for Nicky. It gave him an opportunity to look closely at the individual letters
within words and to produce final copies in which all the words were spelled
correctly, an accomplishment that was important to Nicky. He wanted his pieces
to be spelled right, and he was willing to make all the necessary corrections
himself with word processing. In one instance Nicky overheard Mrs. Kahn
supply the correct spelling for *pumpertrucks* to Andrew, who sat and worked at
the computer next to Nicky's. Nicky, who was also writing about firefighters,
immediately looked up to check the writing on his own screen, found his spelling
of the word (*pmprtrucks*) and, referring to the other child's screen, corrected as
he was composing.

We have made the case that both the inherent capacities of word processing as a writer's tool, and the ways in which teachers and coaches demonstrated that the tool could be used, helped Nicky learn to write. The ability to create progressively more perfect text on the screen as each mistake was corrected was in sharp contrast to Nicky's experiences correcting text with pencil and paper. When his teacher pointed out his spelling and usage errors on paper, she marked up his paper with red pencil, crossing out misspellings and writing correct spellings wherever there was space on the paper. When she was finished, the paper was less legible than it had been before, and if Nicky wanted a "good copy," he had to start from the beginning and copy the whole piece over. We wonder whether it was difficult for Nicky, whose first concern was aesthetics, to believe that his corrected piece had been "fixed" or made "better" by the teacher's corrections when, in fact, it looked worse than his own initial draft had looked and required still more laborious effort from him. Nicky's experience with word processing enabled him, not only to produce a legible draft just by pressing buttons, but also to amend that draft, again by pressing buttons, in such a way that his draft remained consistently neat as it became progressively more accurate instead of messier and more illegible.

Over time Nicky had many opportunities to work at word processing with a coach as well as independently. He had opportunities to "sound out" spellings, to use word lists and books as resources for conventional spellings, to correct his own words at the computer letter by letter, and to use a spelling checker to confirm or disprove his hypotheses about spelling. These opportunities changed his practice of spelling and eventually led to dramatic changes in what seemed to be Nicky's theory of spelling. When he began writing in second grade, he seemed to regard spelling as an irrational act that was beyond him. He asked for help frequently and dared only to guess single letters. In his "The Rainy Day" story, he spelled the word umbrella *uqlppe*, a guess which has little graphic or sound–symbol correlation to the standard form. However, when we look at Nicky's "best guess" spelling four months later, it is clear that he was developing a different theory about written words, a theory that included both the notion of sound–symbol correlation and of visual cues. In his rough draft of "The Firefighters," for example, he wrote extinguish as *extingwersh*, a reasonable approximation of the sounds he heard in the word. There is also evidence that he was using visual cues to reproduce spelling: he wrote *poeple* for *people* and *srchlitgh* for *searchlight*, using spelling patterns that are not phonetically based. Nicky's changing practices of correct spelling, and his evolving theories about the ways words were put together, enabled him to solve some of his spelling problems. We are not suggesting that Nicky became a perfect speller because he used word processing, but by the end of third grade, Nicky had developed a repertoire of spelling practices, many of them facilitated by the use of word processing, that helped him construct for himself a theory of spelling that included both the notion of sound–symbol correlation and the use of visual cues.

Production, Composing, and Theories of Writing. The examples above indicate that word processing was a writing tool that allowed Nicky to concentrate increasingly on issues of composing as well as production. With word processing, he could handle enough of the mechanics of handwriting and spelling to attend also to meaning. Over time Nicky began to understand writing as a process of discovering, clarifying, and relaying information to an audience. Nicky's own comments attest to the fact that word processing played a critical role in the evolution of his notions of writing. In an interview during his third grade year, he pointed out that, when he wrote with pencil and paper, his hand got tired and he didn't say as much. He reported that he wrote longer, fuller texts on the computer because "I don't get lazy and leave things out."

What follows is the first draft of Nicky's "How to Make Cars" story, the final draft of which we have already seen in Figure 6.2. Nicky produced this draft in Mrs. Perrone's class during a session where he was not assisted by a coach. It is interesting, but not surprising, that Nicky chose to compose this story with word processing, even though it was for a school-wide contest and, according to entry requirements, had to be submitted in the writer's own hand. Recopying was a laborious process for Nicky, although as we have seen, with enough work time, he was able to produce very attractive papers. But when Nicky created this story in third grade, he realized that, when he wrote stories with word processing, they contained more information and were more complete than those he wrote by hand. Because Nicky's theory of writing had changed from beautiful production to rich content, he chose to compose with a tool he knew would bolster content. The draft below plainly demonstrates that Nicky was interested in content.

How to make cars

> *You will need wood, wires, gears, tools, metle, nails, moters, jenerators, tires l belt. First get a 5 feet peace of wood. Put the moter in the back of the wood. The moter has to be powerful and fast to have a nice ride. If you put the wheels in freewheel, it will be harder, so I suggest you dont do freewheel. Put the wheels about l foot from the moter. Then coneckt the belt the moter and the wheels together. Then get the jenerator and put it next to the wheels. Coneckt the gear to the jenerator. Egeast the gear so it is tight agenst the wheel. Then get one wire and coneckt it from the jenerater to the moter. Get two small peaces of metle. Nail one peace to the 5 feet peace of wood and the other to about a 5 inch peace of wood. Put a spring between the peaces of wood. Coneckt l wire from th peace of metle to the moter and the other to the jenerater. Then get a l foot peace of wood. Nail it to the middle of the wood. Then put the frunt wheels on. Make sure they turn. Coneckt to peaces of string to the wheels and the steringwheel. Make the body and your don. You would havwe to pull it to get the jenerater started.*

Nicky's car story is quite fluent, and its fluency is attributable in part to the nature of word processing and in part to what Nicky learned about writing from the demonstrations of Miss Price, Miss Carlisle, Mrs. Perrone, and Mrs. Kahn. Nicky knew enough about his own writing practices to know that he would write a longer, more detailed story with word processing than with pencil and paper. He knew that writing with word processing made it physically easier to write long pieces. As he explained to us, it was easier to press a button than to handwrite a letter. Further Nicky described with real dislike the difficulty of erasing pencil marks from paper, and celebrated the ability to fix things on the computer screen, thereby avoiding rips and smears. Nicky knew that, when he fixed things, added things, and changed things at the keyboard, his text became clearer and more closely approximated the conventional texts that appeared in books. The letters were always perfectly formed and legible on the screen.

Larson (1986) argues that, historically, the technologies and tools available for writing have played a role in the social options available for its conceptualizations so that there is an interactive relationship between writing technology and theories of composing. She points out that contemporary views of composing as a recursive rather than a discrete, sequential process are intimately related to major 19th- and 20th-century innovations in writing technology.

> As the technologies of writing developed, they directly facilitated certain possibilities inherent in the notion of composing words and controlled what could be done with writing. At the same time, our social needs and uses of writing affected equipment, so that the technology itself responded to human intervention and direction. It is not necessary to privilege the technology of composing in order to suggest that scholars should see it as influential; the possibilities inherent in the mental activity of composing are bound inextricably to our world and cannot be effectively studied in isolation. . . . The physical difficulty of writing has been a major limitation to composing practically since the invention of writing; in the past, only a very few could really use writing primarily as a technology of the intellect. (p. 44)

Larsen's argument makes clear that writing tools make a difference. The assortment of pens, knives, ink wells, blotting materials, and inks necessary for writing until the mid-19th century reinforced the prevailing view that composing ideas was one process and writing them down was another, subsequent process, the focus of which was beauty and first-round accuracy. We are not suggesting here that young children recapitulate the history of composing theory when they have opportunities to write with word processing. But we are suggesting that writing with word processing may make it possible even for beginners, who have not mastered to the point of automaticity the production skills of inscribing and encoding, to use writing as a "technology of the intellect" (Larson, 1986, following Goody, 1968, and Oxenham, 1980; D. Olson, 1985) or, in other words, as a procedure for exploring their ideas. Nicky had evidently realized for himself the implications of tool choice by the time he composed the car story. He chose to use word processing for the initial production of the text because he had learned that, with word processing, he could use writing as a tool for thinking.

Using writing as a technology of the intellect was possible because the interrelationships of tool, task, and teaching/learning processes created a context where mechanics were managed efficiently.

Tackling Communication Problems: Information and Revision. It is clear from the preceding discussion that problems of production and problems of communication were related concerns for Nicky and his coaches. What they did as they tackled problems of production was intimately related to the ways they dealt with information and tackled problems of communication. Hence in the preceding section, in which we have concentrated on the production issues of handwriting and spelling, we have already presented a great deal of information about issues of communication and about the ways Nicky dealt with information and organization. In this section, we add to the previous sections by bringing communication to the foreground.

Nicky's growth in writing was evident in the increasing amount of information he was able to organize and present on a topic. Nicky himself timidly suggested to us at the end of second grade that he wrote longer pieces because he "knew more." Perhaps he meant that he knew more about writing topics when they were drawn from class experiences or from his reading book, or perhaps he meant that he knew more about spelling and about where to get spelling help. His longest handwritten story in second grade, which he identified as his best story, was a reworking of a story he had memorized and read to the class with great success. Certainly his familiarity with the story in the book, as well as with its vocabulary, made it possible for him to render his own version of the story and refer to it with pride. Graves (1983) and Calkins (1986) suggest that children should be encouraged to write on topics of their own choosing, the assumption being that they will choose topics that interest them and about which they have sufficient information. In Nicky's second- and third-grade experiences, he sometimes chose his own topic as he did in the car-making piece. But even when the teacher selected the topic, it was usually one that was familiar to Nicky, drawn from his personal experience, such as "Making Friends Happy" or taken from a story in his reading book, as was the case with "Firefighters." In assigning these writing tasks and topics, Miss Price and Mrs. Perrone consistently demonstrated that writing was about ideas drawn at least in part from the children's literary and actual experiences.

But knowing about the topic was not enough to guarantee that Nicky could get his knowledge onto paper. The amount of information he presented in his writing was clearly connected to his facility in producing print. We argued in Chapter 2 that "more" is not necessarily "better" in writing, and that increased length, which has been cited as an effect when older students write with word processing, sometimes correlates with excessive detail, wordiness, or irrelevant information. This was not the case with Nicky and many of the other beginners whom we observed. When Nicky was seven and eight years old, he was clearly a beginning writer. For him basic fluency—increased length and more extensive information—were quite appropriate goals in writing. Although Nicky confided that he sometimes left things out when he wrote by hand, he certainly did not leave out much in March of second grade when he wrote "The Firefighters" with word processing. The unedited first draft, filled with rich information and detail as well as numerous spelling errors, appears below. The piece makes clear that Nicky's theories of writing were shifting away from emphasis on initial correct mechanical production and toward initial communication of detailed information. Nicky produced this initial draft with word processing and without any adult assistance.

The Firefighters

Firefighters put out fires. Firefighters clam latters to save poeple in the house. Firefighters fight fires. Firefighters save poeple. Sometimes firefighters wear gasmasc to pirtact them slfe from somke. firefighters yus a ax to barc wendos. Firefighters are string. Firefighters are ill. The firefighters tols and aqtmnt are hos gasmasc extingwersh lifenet pocpld latter crbar ax srchlitgh. Some firefighters have dogs. Firefighters have hok an ladder truck. Firefighters have pumpertrucks. And a resctruck. Tose tucks help them to get at fires fast. Firefighters help poeple in the house. Firefighters yus a ax to barc doors.

[Though still not error-free, Nicky's own final draft, which a coach helped him edit for spelling, provides a good translation of the above:

The Firefighters
Firefighters put out fires. Firefighters climb ladders to save people in the house. Firefighter fight fires. Firefighters save people. Sometimes firefighter wear gas masks to protect themselves from smoke. Firefighters use an ax to break windows. Firefighters are strong. Firefighters are tall. The firefighter's tools and equipment are hose gas masks extinguisher lifenet pikepole ladder crowbar as searchlight. Some firefighters have dogs. Firefighters have hook and ladder trucks. Firefighters have pumpertrucks. And a rescuetruck. Those trucks help them to get at fires fast. Firefighters help people in the house. Firefighters use a ax to break doors.]

The language in Nicky's firefighter piece is accurate and technical, as he conveys information about three aspects of firefighting: what firefighters do, what physical attributes enable them to do so, and what types of equipment they use. Further he weaves into his piece a long catalog of the precise names for firefighting tools, including the *pocpld*, or *pike pole*, a piece of equipment used to tear down ceilings in fire-damaged buildings. This language positions Nicky as something of an expert on the topic, and his voice in the piece is strong and certain. In this instance, Nicky's inclusion of so much information was not the result of a coach's prompting, as had largely been the case in his making-friends piece described earlier. Rather, the length and the wealth of information had to do with Nicky' growing facility as a writer. Writing was becoming easier for Nicky because the topic interested him, he had a great deal of information, and he had a writing tool that facilitated the mechanical production of information. Nicky was also becoming a writer who had more resources at his disposal. He used his reading book as a reference for facts and spellings, although he also frequently took his "best guess" at spellings. Willingness to invent or approximate standard spellings was a gradual change for Nicky. When Miss Carlisle had suggested he work with her to put down the sounds he heard during his first word-processing event, he was hesitant, behaving as if he thought spelling was a process of reproducing single words whole, completely unrelated to other words or word parts he might know. Eventually, his reading and spelling skills increased, but so did his willingness to temporarily delay his impulse for correctness. Further, because "Firefighters" was the fifth piece he had either drafted or transcribed with word processing, his keyboarding skill was good. All of these factors combined to help Nicky write at great length. While "Firefighters" is by no means perfect, it marks a considerable improvement in fluency over "Making Friends Happy" and quite a leap from "The Supermarket" or "A Rainy Day."

Increasingly over the period of two years, when he did not have to think about the physical production of text, Nicky could more readily address issues of organization and revision. He began to evaluate his writing from a reader's point of view, revise somewhat so that sentences read more smoothly, and reflect on his own writing processes. Nicky's attention to revision is apparent in his actual composing of "How to Make a Car," the final version of which we contrasted with "A Rainy Day" at the beginning of this chapter. To compose this piece, Nicky brought a list of 10 words with him to the word processor, a prewriting activity Mrs. Perrone commonly used with her third graders. Mrs. Kahn was at the computer, observing and helping other children with word-processing and printing maneuvers. During this writing episode, Nicky talked with her on several occasions but turned to her for help only once, a phenomenon that contrasts dramatically with Nicky's early reliance on coaches. No one was directly demonstrating writing in this example, nor was anyone prompting Nicky to write a longer, more detailed text. It is clear, however, that the past demonstrations of Nicky's coaches and teachers formed the broader learning/teaching context within which Nicky composed the piece.

[Nicky begins typing immediately, referring to his word list often. He seems to have a clear idea of what he wants to say.]

How to make cars

**You will need , wood , wires , tools ,
metle , nails , motors , jenerators ,
tires. First get a 5 feet peace**

[Nicky stops typing, rereads his word list and his piece so far. He looks thoughtfully at the screen, and then moves the cursor up to the end of the word, 'tires.']

Coach: What's happening here? What are you adding? Did you forget something?

Nicky: Yeah. [Inserts "1 belt" after "tires."]

Coach: Belt? What are you trying to say? Can I help?

Nicky: You know those black rubber things in cars?

Coach: That's a belt. You have exactly the right word.
**You will need wood, wires, gears, t
tools, metal, nails, motors, generators,
tires, 1 belt.**

[Nicky moves the cursor to the end of the existing text, types "wood."]

. . . **First get a 5 feet peace wood.**

[Nicky moves the cursor back to the opening lines of his text, a catalog of things one would need to make a car. He pauses. He seems to be considering adding something else, but decides against it. He types 'make,' but changes his mind, erases the word, and continues.]

**Put the moter in the back of the wood.
The motor has to be powerful and fast
to have a nice ride.**

[Nicky continues typing while Alex, the child working at the computer next to Nicky's, engages the coach in an extended discussion about the computer's spelling dictionary and what actually gets 'erased' when the machine is turned off. Nicky types without interruption.]

Coach: You said this (referring to Nicky's list of words) is just your prewriting thing?

Nicky: And this is my rough draft (nodding to computer screen).

Coach: That's your rough draft? What are you supposed to be doing in a rough draft?

Nicky: You transform the prewriting into a draft form.

Coach: Um hum.

[Nicky continues to type.]

**If you put the wheels in freewheel it
will be harder, so I suggest you dont do
freewheel.**

[Session continues until lunch time, when Nicky saves his writing to be continued the next day.]

Nicky's composing strategies, revealed during this episode, are impressive. When he came to the computer to draft the piece, he was very comfortable using a word list as a resource, announcing that his task was to "transform his prewriting list" into story form. He worked steadily at the computer from mid-morning until lunchtime, and, as he wrote, he revised. He inserted new information into the first sentence after he had completed the second sentence, and he began his third sentence by typing in the word *Make*, which he then erased and replaced with *Put*. He used his knowledge about letter–sound relationships as well as visual patterns in spelling to produce approximations of standard spellings that were close enough to allow him to read them. He seemed comfortable knowing that he would correct the spelling later. Nicky himself knew which efforts were appropriate at which points during writing. His third grade teacher, Mrs. Perrone, stressed writing stages and directly taught the children how to work at each stage. She modelled use of process writing language, such as prewriting, transforming prewriting into draft, revising, and editing. She commented to us that Nicky impressed her as a "metathinker" because of his frequent comments about his own composing processes and his goals for various writing tasks.

Unmasking Language Competence. The evolution in Nicky's writing over time indicates that working with word processing helped him to develop new theories of writing and, eventually, to write differently. However, as we pointed out in Chapter 5, word processing also gave Nicky opportunities to demonstrate some of the written-language skills he already had but was not able to make visible when he wrote with paper and pencil. There is evidence in our data, for example, that Nicky was able to think about text revision as early as the beginning of second grade if and when he did not also have to struggle with encoding or inscribing text. As we know, children have experience with the phenomenon of revision long before they begin to write—they revise their verbal utterances, their block structures, and their drawings (Graves, 1979). In writing, however, the ability to revise ideas is frequently masked by the considerable difficulties beginners have inscribing letters and encoding words. Word-processing, or other writing tools that temporarily remove some of the difficulties of these production tasks, often give children opportunities to reveal and practice the composition skills they already have. In this sense, the tool of word processing can function to unmask language competence.

We discovered that Nicky had demonstrated his ability to deal with text revision early in the second-grade year in several sessions with Miss Carlisle, an elementary education student from the university. Miss Carlisle began each session with the low reading group by drawing a picture based on the children's suggestions and then asking the children to compose a story about it, which she either wrote on chart paper or at the word processor. Miss Carlisle then reread the story aloud and invited the group to reorganize and revise it. What is especially noteworthy in the following example is Nicky's demonstration of his ability to think about the sequence of ideas in the text, even with other children talking, and without being able to see well the words on the screen. Despite these distractions, when he suggested that there was an idea he would like to append and Miss Carlisle read the story back to him, Nicky was able to locate the precise point in the text where it belonged.

[Miss Carlisle draws an evergreen tree with a ring around the bottom of it and a sloping line extending away from it. The children immediately take the tree to be a Christmas tree with a train and presents around it and suggest that she add some figures of children sledding down the slope. The story they construct has a winter/ Christmas theme as follows.]

> **We like Christmas because we get toys. There is a choo-choo train running around the Christmas tree. A Christmas tree is in the middle of the tracks. The boy is going down the hill on the sled and the boy is falling off the sled, because it was bumpy and he flew up in the air and got out of balance. He said, 'Aaaagh!' Then the boy went over to his sister. She was flat. His sister is under the snow because her brother**

Nicky: 'The snow went in her mouth when she was buried.'

Coach: OK, where would that go?

Nicky: Where in the story about she's buried.

Coach: You gotta find it for me, Nicky.

Nicky: I don't know. [Nicky can't really see the screen where the words are written.]

Coach: Well, let's read it through. . . . [Reading:] 'We like Christmas because we get toys. There is a choo-choo train running around the Christmas tree. A Christmas tree is in the middle of the tracks . . .' and (more or less to herself) I need to add a word there . . . 'The boy is going down the hill on the sled and the boy is falling off the sled, because it was bumpy and he flew up in the air and got out of balance. He said, 'Aaaagh!' Then the boy went over to his sister. She was flat. His sister is under the snow because her brother . . .

Nicky: [Interrupts.] Right there!

Coach: Where? Ok, back to 'under the snow'?

Nicky: Um-hum.

Coach: Now what am I writing there?

Nicky: 'Snow went in her mouth.'

Coach: [Comments more or less to herself.] We're going to have to do some serious reorganizing on this one. [Types in added sentence as she says it aloud.] 'Snow . . . went . . . in . . . her . . . mouth . . .' Now wait, listen to what we have here. [Reading:] 'We like Christmas because we get toys. There is a choo-choo train running around the Christmas tree.

	A Christmas tree is in the middle of the tracks. There are presents around the Christmas tree and the train goes around the presents—'
Nicky:	[Breaks in.] I want to erase the thing about the choo-choo train and put it where the other sentence is.
Coach:	Ok, so you want this part (pointing) to say choo-choo train and get rid of this sentence. Does that make sense?
Children:	Yeah.
Nicky:	Erase this thing here about the choo-choo train on the first row (pointing toward the screen).
Coach:	But say 'choo-choo train' down here. [Explains to one child who appears confused that Nicky wants to keep the phrase 'choo choo train' in a later sentence but omit the earlier sentence.] He wants to still say choo-choo train but wants to get rid of the sentence. He wants to keep the words 'choo-choo train' but . . . we have two sentences about it. . . [Child still appears not to understand.] You'll see it when it happens, all right? Now we're going to get rid of this whole sentence here. Good-bye.
Paul:	Good-bye.
Annie:	Bye-bye.

Miss Carlisle commented to us that, in sessions where they helped to construct a story and picture, the children often composed easily but contributed sentences about elements of the picture that appealed to them, not always mindful of the sentence that came before theirs and clearly not aware of the need for coherence of the story as a whole. She remarked to the children as they worked that their story would need some "serious reorganizing" later on. Nicky was the child who seemed to understand this idea most clearly. Miss Carlisle reported that Nicky dominated the revision activity in both of the sessions she set up in this way. He knew exactly what sentences should be grouped together and which parts were redundant or unnecessary. He demonstrated his considerable abilities to reconsider the organization of sentences and consider possible alternatives. In this writing event, encoding, inscribing, and rereading were done by someone else. This made it possible for Nicky to think about the sequence of ideas in the piece, with the result that he was able to do some fairly sophisticated reordering of sentences. The contrasts among Nicky's paper-and-pencil writing, his writing with word processing, and his oral composition stress that there are often critical differences between language users' competence and their performance.

THE MORAL OF THE STORY

Nicky's story had a happy ending. By the end of third grade, he had made remarkable strides in reading and writing that surprised even his teachers. His test scores verified that he had made significant progress, and as a result, Mrs. Perrone moved Nicky into a more advanced reading group, just as Miss Price had done the year before. Nicky finished third grade "on grade level," and, we anticipate, "on his way" to success as a reader and writer. As long-term observers, we now believe that Nicky had always had ability and skill as a language user, even at the beginning of second grade when he was placed in the lowest of nine reading groups and considered for end-of-year retention. Miss Price had had insight in this direction when she commented that Nicky seemed to have more ability than others in the low reading group, and hence in a certain sense her estimation of Nicky as "the best of the worst" had been correct. The fact that some adults saw early glimmers of Nicky's language competence notwithstanding, however, his language competence was for the most part masked by his language performance—both by his considerable difficulties encoding and decoding and by his exclusive concentration on perfect letter forms, a preoccupation bolstered by the writing demonstrations of his earliest school years.

It is quite evident that Nicky's development over a 2-year period was influenced by his opportunity to write with the tool of word processing. But it is equally apparent that his progress was not the result of a direct relationship between word processing, as cause, and improved written language skill, as effect. The moral of Nicky's story is not only more complex than linear causality, but also considerably more complex than Weizenbaum's (1976) notion of tools as scripts for the reenactment of skill, or Hubbard's (1985) claim that the ontology of writing processes eventually recapitulates the technology of computer word processing. Over time, Nicky's theories and practices were constructed and reconstructed, and, as we argued above, the reconstruction of each was both *reason for* and *result of* the reconstruction of the other. In addition, however, as we asserted in our framework for understanding beginning writers and word processing (Figure 6.2), the moral of Nicky's story grew out of the dynamic interplay of his theories and practices, on the one hand, and the writing demonstrations in his classrooms on the other.

To conclude and to elaborate on the nature of this dynamic interplay, we revisit the examples of Nicky's writing that we used to open this chapter (see Figure 6.1.)—four sentences describing a boy in raingear, "A Rainy Day," and a full-page essay explaining the process of car-building, "How to Make a Car." Figure 6.4 is an attempt to represent graphically Nicky's progress over two years by juxtaposing as endpoints the apparent theory/practice relationships operating in the production of these two pieces as they were embedded within the context of writing demonstrations in his classrooms.

The figure emphasizes that, when Nicky wrote the rainy day piece early in second grade, his practice consisted of writing with pencil and paper (tool) and expending enormous amounts of time and energy (processes) making his first copy look perfect (task/product). He produced text in an entirely linear fashion, making no changes as he worked (processes). Furthermore, although writing was

Figure 6.4
Nicky's Story: A Shift From Making Letters to Making Meaning

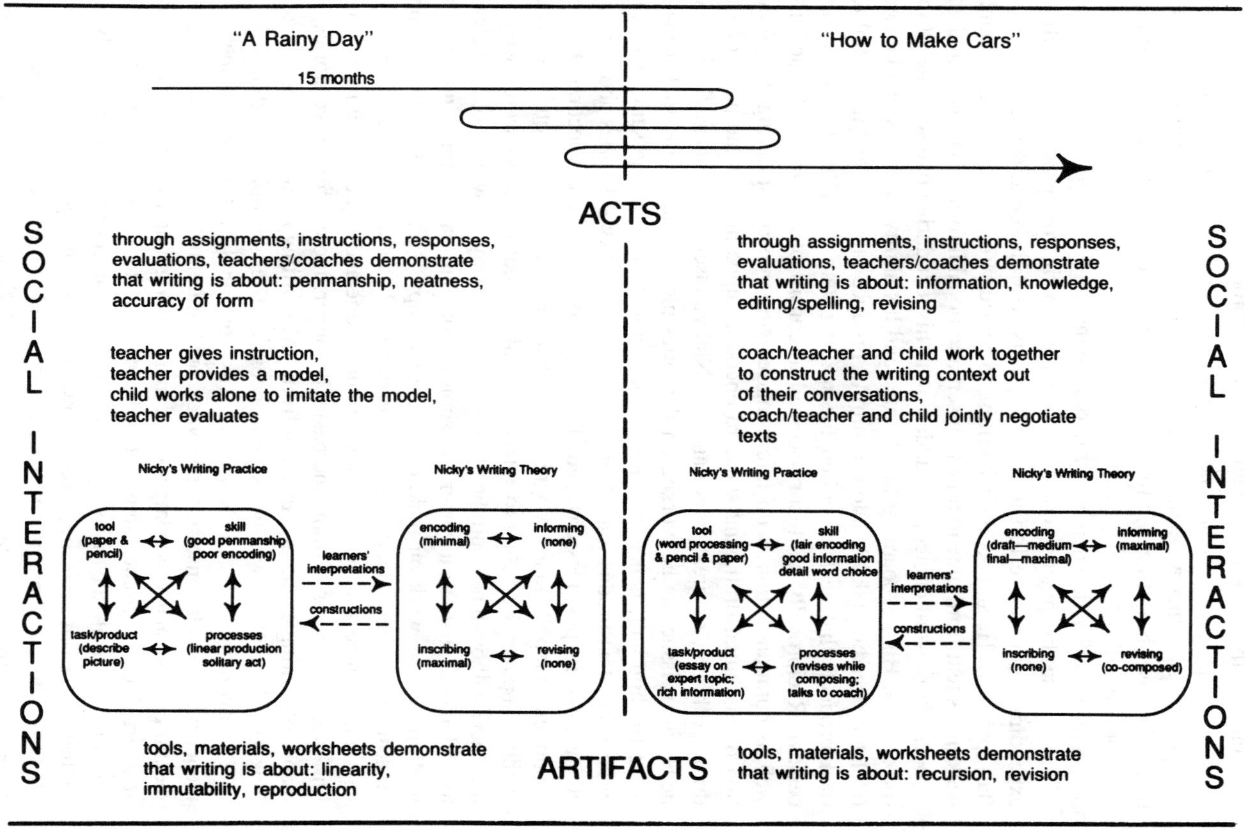

"A Rainy Day"
15 months

"How to Make Cars"

SOCIAL INTERACTIONS

ACTS

ARTIFACTS

"A Rainy Day" (left)

through assignments, instructions, responses, evaluations, teachers/coaches demonstrate that writing is about: penmanship, neatness, accuracy of form

teacher gives instruction, teacher provides a model, child works alone to imitate the model, teacher evaluates

tools, materials, worksheets demonstrate that writing is about: linearity, immutability, reproduction

Nicky's Writing Practice
- tool (paper & pencil)
- skill (good penmanship poor encoding)
- task/product (describe picture)
- processes (linear production solitary act)

learners' interpretations / constructions

Nicky's Writing Theory
- encoding (minimal)
- informing (none)
- inscribing (maximal)
- revising (none)

"How to Make Cars" (right)

through assignments, instructions, responses, evaluations, teachers/coaches demonstrate that writing is about: information, knowledge, editing/spelling, revising

coach/teacher and child work together to construct the writing context out of their conversations, coach/teacher and child jointly negotiate texts

tools, materials, worksheets demonstrate that writing is about: recursion, revision

Nicky's Writing Practice
- tool (word processing & pencil & paper)
- skill (fair encoding good information detail word choice)
- task/product (essay on expert topic; rich information)
- processes (revises while composing; talks to coach)

learners' interpretations / constructions

Nicky's Writing Theory
- encoding (draft—medium final—maximal)
- informing (maximal)
- inscribing (none)
- revising (co-composed)

a solitary act that took him a long time to do (processes), he did not write long pieces (task/product) because he struggled so much with penmanship (skill). Reciprocally, his theory seemed to consist almost entirely of notions of production, with inscribing first and foremost, encoding of little concern, and communication ignored.

On the other hand, when Nicky wrote the making-cars piece during the winter of third grade, his practice consisted of writing with word processing (tool) and expending significant effort to include precise and thorough detail in his essay (task/product). He stopped in his writing to consider/reconsider phrases, doubled back in his text from time to time to insert additional information, consulted with a coach about word choice, and added on to his text during two separate sittings (processes). His keyboarding familiarity, and his ability to encode well enough for later rereading (skill), allowed him to produce rapidly a lengthy initial text (task/product) that he later edited for spelling with the help of a coach (processes). Reciprocally his theory seemed to consist of notions of production as well as communication, with informing/revising uppermost during the production of his initial draft, and standard encoding uppermost at the point of final draft. Although of great importance to Nicky, inscribing and aesthetics were never overt issues as he worked on the latter piece, because the tool managed these for him and, hence, they could be ignored in much the same way adult writers take text production for granted. Clearly, Nicky's theories about writing changed as his practices changed. He began to make the connections between sound and symbol and to recognize word patterns. Based in part on his practices at the computer, he began to internalize rules about the ways words were put together. Although he continued to care about the way his work looked, he came to understand that, as a writer, he should work on making meaning while the machine would work on making the "good copy." Eventually Nicky stopped thinking of writing as tedium and, instead, described it to us as "fun." Over time he made a connection between having knowledge and expressing it in writing, a link that was disclosed in his increasingly longer, more informative stories. His theory of writing eventually evolved from "My writing is good because I make it look good" to "My writing is good because it tells people something."

The evolution of Nicky's writing was not simply a tradeoff of one set of theory/practice relationships for another, but a spiraling, back-and-forth developmental process that was comprised of many configurations impossible to represent graphically. Some attempt has been made to capture the nature of this evolution through the weaving, looping line that connects the two halves in Figure 6.4. Even more important, however, is the notion that the evolution of Nicky's theory and practice was shaped by, and constructed out of, the writing demonstrations in his classrooms. The acts of Nicky's second and third grade teachers generally demonstrated that writing, at least writing initial drafts, was about personal experience, personal knowledge, and detailed, accurate conveying of information, rather than a task intended to produce beautiful printing. As artifact, the computer played a critical role in relationship to the teachers' acts, since it made it possible for Nicky to write in the ways that were demonstrated. Finally, within their social interactions, Nicky and his computer coaches constructed a conversational writing context wherein they could jointly negotiate written texts and eventually Nicky could develop strategies and skills for handling various writing problems.

chapter 7
TEACHERS, BEGINNING WRITERS, AND WORD PROCESSING

We began this study with three goals: (a) to examine the ways word processing might play a role in children's and teachers' opportunities to learn about, demonstrate, and use writing in elementary classrooms; (b) to develop a framework for approaching the study of tool software and classroom learning, or, more specifically, word processing and learning writing; and (c) to explore the implications of our observations for school policy, including professional development programs, classroom implementation procedures, and the development of computer curricula. We conclude this volume by commenting in each of these areas.

LEARNING TO WRITE DIFFERENTLY

This volume has examined both what and how beginning writers learned about word processing, on the one hand, and what and how teachers taught it on the other. Staying close to observations of beginning writers and their teachers, we have argued throughout the volume that uses of word processing interacted with cultures of teaching and learning, the writing tasks and invitations offered by teachers, and the instructional contexts that were constructed out of the talk of teachers and children together. As the title of this volume asserts, the outcome of these interactions over time was that children *learned to write differently* and teachers *learned to teach writing differently*. The semantic ambiguity of the title phrase is intentional. With it, we wish to emphasize each of the overlapping senses in which the phrase may be interpreted.

- When they had opportunities to work with the tool of word processing, beginning writers **wrote differently** from the ways they wrote with paper and pencil.

276

- When they had opportunities to work closely with adults and to use word processing as a writing tool, beginning writers **learned writing differently** from the ways they learned with other writing tools.
- When they introduced and taught beginning writing with word processing, teachers **taught writing differently** from the ways they taught it with other writing tools.
- When teachers taught writing with word processing, they eventually **thought differently about writing**.
- Within the learning and teaching cultures of various classrooms, children's and teachers' **experiences with word processing were different** from one another.

Writing Differently

This book provides a detailed analysis of how 5-to 10-year-old beginning writers learned to write with a tool that was radically different from the marking tools to which they were accustomed. Although beginning writers did not take advantage of the most powerful and touted writing and revising capabilities of word processing, they did learn to enter, edit, and, in some cases, revise text at the computer. Word processing, as pedagogical tool, modeled its own reenactment in a way that precluded narrow concentration on meticulous hand-drawing of letters, penmanship, neatness, or recopying. Because word processing temporarily removed some of the difficulties of print production, it also unmasked some of the writing skills that beginning writers had. They were able to shift their writing efforts from inscribing, recopying, or correcting, on the one hand, to encoding, informing, and revising or editing on the other. The result was a different kind of writing: for some kindergarteners the shift was away from unconnected, isolated words to brief but connected and meaningful prose, while for some third graders the shift was from canned but neat sentences to detailed, informative compositions.

Like much of the word processing and writing literature that we reviewed in Chapter 2, our study points out that part of the reason beginners wrote differently with the tool of word processing is that total writing time was redistributed. Because the time spent producing and correcting attractive text was either reduced or eliminated, beginning writers ended up with additional time to attend to more substantive issues in writing, especially encoding, the conventions of spacing and punctuation, content and information, and editing. Because the physical strain of writing was reduced, beginning writers were willing to spend longer time periods at writing tasks. Further, when they wrote with word processing (and, as we have emphasized throughout, when they wrote with the support of adult coaches), beginning writers often produced more linguistically and substantively advanced texts than they produced with paper and pencil (and, generally, when they worked independently). Hence in several explicit ways, beginners wrote differently with word processing—frequently they attended to developmentally higher order problems of composing, encoding, and revising and consequently produced more complex texts over longer periods of time.

Learning Differently

As we know, beginning writers actively construct and reconstruct their notions of the functions and nature of writing as they interact with others in demonstrations of writing and of language more generally. As we have noted, word processing both temporarily removed some of the problems of print production and foregrounded certain conventions of written language and certain aspects of writing. At the same time, word processing deemphasized and forced to the background other aspects of writing. In this way, word processing not only enabled beginners to write differently, it also enabled them to begin to think differently as they learned about writing. When production occupied the attention of beginning writers, they behaved as if writing were about production, even though this was a theory that significantly interfered with the ability to use writing to communicate. For many beginners, word processing functioned as a powerful interruption and contradiction to their working theories. When coaches helped them develop strategies for handling production, and when they worked with a writing tool that readily helped them do so, many beginners gradually revised their ideas about writing. Over time they began to use writing to make meaning and to explore the power of language. This shift in attention was made possible by opportunities to work closely with adults and to use word processing as a writing tool.

For many of the beginning writers we observed, the most critical difference in learning was the altered instructional context for writing that was constructed by teachers and children as they worked together at the word processor. As we have demonstrated, because teachers initially expected that children would need technological support and supervision in order to use word processing, they arranged for various kinds of adult assistants—teachers, researchers, teachers' aides, university students, parents, and occasionally older children. Almost immediately, however, computer assistants became writing coaches who scaffolded children's attempts to compose and produce written language, and, as we noted above, helped them create texts that were more linguistically and substantively sophisticated than those they could create without help. With word processing, even the least able language users were able to participate in the joint negotiation of text. And the conversations that surrounded word-processing events supported children's efforts in ways that were not possible in the more common but also much more solitary writing contexts of their classrooms.

Coached writing events created different and particularly robust opportunities for beginners to learn procedural and propositional knowledge about language. Together, coaches and children attended to issues of punctuation, spacing, spelling, and capitalization in the course of the joint production of text. Working with a coach provided opportunities for beginning writers to learn some of the composing strategies which coaches implicitly modelled and also made explicit through their questions, prompts, and words of encouragement. As we argued in Chapter 5, coaching and word processing were related synergistically during writing events, each with effects that were greater than, and different from, the effects that either one would have generated independently. These two factors together had a significant impact on opportunities for beginners to learn differently.

Teaching Writing Differently

As we have pointed out, when most teachers introduced word processing into the curriculum, they also set up procedures for beginning writers to receive assistance from coaches. The concurrent introduction of a new tool and a new form of writing assistance significantly altered the participation structures of writing instruction. We have seen that, during coached word-processing events, even the least able, and sometimes most reticent, language users were able to participate in the joint negotiation of texts by pressing keys and composing single-word texts. We have seen that, in coached events, children were writing differently. By the same token, teachers and coaches were teaching writing differently. Coaches were able to participate more actively in children's writing because they were able to concentrate more on their learning as it unfolded and less on the written products they generated. The physical arrangements of the computer screen gave the coach access to some of the children's ongoing composing processes and made visible some of their operational theories of writing. This was a different kind of teaching opportunity for coaches—they could react and respond to children's writing as it unfolded, model some of the composing procedures of more experienced language users, and also instruct directly about writing and word-processing strategies.

The new participation structures constructed within coached word-processing events were not the only changes in the ways writing was taught when teachers used word processing. In addition, some teachers altered the content, focus, and timing of their writing instruction. One teacher eventually allowed children to write stories with word processing at any time during the school day rather than only during the morning period officially designated as language arts time. Several teachers extended word processing beyond the writing curriculum and across several areas, including spelling, math, and social studies. In addition some teachers tightly orchestrated writing instruction and tool instruction, teaching specific word-processing operations on precisely those occasions when they were needed for particular genres of writing.

Thinking Differently about Writing

Closely coupled with different ways of teaching writing were different ways of thinking about writing. Using word processing as a writing tool sometimes revealed to teachers a distinction between a beginning writer's language competence and his or her language performance. The tool helped to unmask writing skills that had previously been invisible to teachers. In many cases, new information about what beginners could do prompted teachers to rethink some of their notions of writing development. One teacher concluded that early experiences with word processing were not just play, as she had assumed initially, but instead part of early literacy development. Another discovered that children could work in pairs at the word processor to edit texts without much teacher supervision and correction of drafts. A third began to doubt her common practice of prearranging the sequence and form of writing opportunities and began to wonder whether or not it was effective to preestablish procedures and tasks without ongoing observation of particular learners. In most cases, thinking differently about writing interacted with other aspects of classroom and school culture to prompt altered instructional practices. In a few cases altered practice was not possible or desired.

As we argued extensively in Chapter 3, the relationship of teachers' theories and practices can in no way be represented as a linear process or even a reciprocally interrelated one. Rather the process was a dynamic one—teaching and learning cultures, the ways teachers interpreted word processing and thought about writing, and the uses teachers made of the tool were interdependent, evolving, and compounded over time. Teachers by no means simply implemented word processing into the curriculum. Rather, devising and revising ways to utilize the capabilities of word processing were ongoing processes for teachers, who continuously reconsidered their instructional and organizational strategies and experimented with new possibilities. Hence our volume emphasizes that it was not only children who were active learners in the word-processing classroom, but also teachers, who functioned as researchers and curriculum creators in their own settings.

Learning Differently Across Classrooms

Closely related to the point above is the final sense in which we intend our title phrase to be interpreted. The tool of word processing was utilized in ways that differed significantly from classroom to classroom, and these ways interacted with the goals and curricula of specific teachers, the ways writing assignments were constructed and interpreted, and the learning conditions of various classrooms. Hence, children's opportunities to learn to write with the identical new writing tool were different depending on the life worlds of their classrooms and the teaching and learning cultures that existed. The difference we are emphasizing here was not simply the result of the different age and developmental levels of the children we observed, although these played a critical role in the opportunities children had. Rather, children's opportunities to learn with word processing depended also, and perhaps more importantly, on their teachers' perceptions of the tool's value in their ongoing writing programs, their decisions about how initially and ultimately to deploy word processing, and their interpretations of what was happening as children used the equipment. Although each classroom in which we observed represented a different grade level, we believe that children would have had different opportunities to learn with word processing even if the grade level across classrooms were the same. Altogether outside of grade level, the cultures of teaching and learning in classrooms are different, the places of individual teachers within the larger cultures of the school and school district are different, and the decisions and interpretations teachers make about tools, tasks, and written texts are different. The dynamic interactions of these factors mean that young children working with word processing simply will not have uniform and stable experiences across classrooms or even within them, but that instead they will learn to write differently.

UNDERSTANDING WORD PROCESSING AND WRITING

This volume has not addressed "how-to" questions about using word processing for writing instruction, nor has it speculated about what might be possible when young children write with a technological tool. Rather it has presented a view of what happened over time when teachers and beginning writers used word processing as part of their daily work within the social and organizational contexts of a working-class, public elementary school. We believe that this information provides a valuable addition to the literature on computers and learning, literacy development, early childhood education, and writing instruction. But another major effort of this volume has been to build an analytic framework for thinking about and talking about teachers, beginning writers, and word processing over time. This framework has the potential to help others understand more clearly some of the issues involved in studying and making decisions about the instructional uses of technology. It is our hope that this work will not simply offer insights into *what* to think about beginning writers and word processing, but also raise questions about *how* to think about them.

As we stated in the introduction to this volume, the analytic framework we have developed is in keeping with the perspectives of ethnography and of sociolinguistics. It is based on the premise that classrooms are interactive and communicative environments, which teachers and children together construct and reconstruct. Central to this perspective is the assumption that language functions as a social context for learning, and that, at the same time, social context influences language use and learning. Also central is the assumption that teaching is an intellectual activity wherein teachers use their knowledge to construct perspectives, interpret and create curricula, make deliberate choices, and to a large extent define their teaching responsibilities. To understand the learning processes that occur with word processing, then, it is assumed that researchers must study the ways teachers interpret and implement technology as well as the interplay of participants' thinking and the social contexts they construct. The aim, in the end, is to make visible the dynamic interrelationships of all of these—classroom cultures, teachers' interpretations and decisions about word processing, the social interactions of teachers and children around word processing and writing, and learners' thinking processes.

In the section that follows we present an analytic framework that accounts for these interrelationships. The framework is discussed and presented schematically as it builds piece by piece. Readers will note that neither the pieces nor the whole of the framework is simple. However, our goal in developing the framework was not simplicity but rich interpretation.

A Framework for Investigation

The framework we have developed locates uses of word processing within the cultures of classrooms and the larger contexts of school and school district, especially the curriculum requirements and professional development programs in place or in the process of changing. It permits examination of the interrelationships of evolving uses of word processing and classroom cultures. Classroom culture is taken to be the interrelationships of teachers' goals, both general and subject specific; teachers' perceptions of children's needs, skills, and capacities; and the ongoing social, language, and literacy processes and instructional activities of the classroom. Hence the foundation of a framework for investigating word processing and writing attends to the cultures of school districts, schools, and classrooms. Figure 7.1 represents this foundation. (See Chapters 1 and 3 for extensive discussion of these ideas.)

When teachers begin to use word processing in their classrooms, it is not a matter of their simply "implementing" it into "the curriculum." *Implementation* implies a static view of both curriculum and teachers' work. Our framework takes a more dynamic view of both, wherein teachers' classroom uses of word processing are mediated by their interpretations of the usefulness of the tool for their current classroom practices, on the one hand, and their decisions about skills instruction, ways and amounts of assistance to offer, access to expertise and equipment, and tasks assigned or invited on the other. These decisions, dynamically related to one another, mediate the ways teachers use word processing. Figure 7.2 builds on the foundation established in the previous figure by adding on to the foundation of the framework the notions of teachers' interpretations and decision making as bases for classroom uses of word processing. (See Chapter 3 and Paris, in press, for more detailed descriptions of these relationships.)

To understand the ways teachers' interpretations and decisions about word processing are instantiated in classroom uses, our framework foregrounds the notion of writing demonstrations (following Smith, 1981, and Harste et al., 1984), which are made up of the acts of individuals, the artifacts they use, and

Figure 7.1
Building An Interpretive Framework: School and Classroom Culture

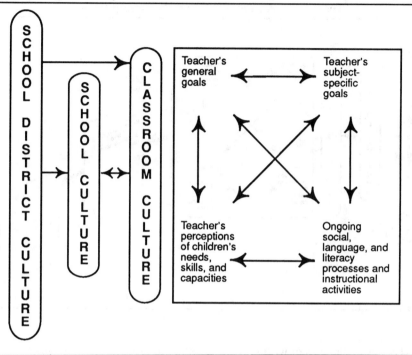

the social interactions of participants in relation to these. Writing demonstrations provide information to beginners about what writing is, how it works in the world, and what tools and other materials are needed. Figure 7.3 displays an inset of Figure 7.2 by enlarging the rectangle representing uses of word processing. This figure shows how writing demonstrations are related to both teachers' interpretations and children's practices. (The notion of writing demonstrations as the interrelationship of acts, artifacts, and social interactions is developed in Chapter 6.)

To look more specifically at writing demonstrations and their relationships to beginners' opportunities to use word processing, our framework provides a way to focus on the experiences of individual beginning writers and/or the individual occasions on which word processing is used. Word processing events, which are structured according to the interrelationships of writing tool, task, writers' skills, and learning/teaching processes, provide a perspective on the writing demonstrations that are salient to individuals. (The concept of a word-processing event is developed in Chapter 5.) Children's participation in word-processing events constitute their practices with word processing. Practices are dynamically related

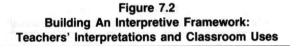

Figure 7.2
Building An Interpretive Framework:
Teachers' Interpretations and Classroom Uses

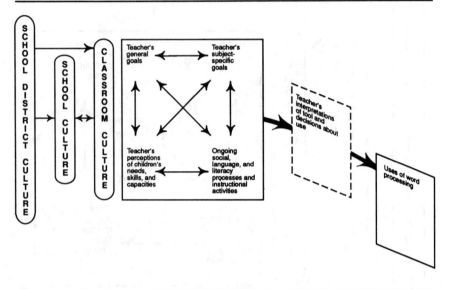

to beginners' theories of writing, which, for our purposes here, are thought of as attention to inscribing, encoding, informing, and revising. Figure 7.4 adds to the inset on writing demonstrations the evolving relationship between a beginning writer's practices and his or her theories of writing. (The evolution of a beginning writer's theories and practices is discussed in Chapter 6.)

Finally, our framework conveys the idea that understanding word processing in elementary classrooms requires attention to the spiraling interrelationships of classroom cultures, teachers' interpretations and decisions, and uses of word processing *as well as* altered classroom cultures, teachers' interpretations and decisions, and altered uses of word processing. We emphasize in this part of the framework that implementing word processing is a process of evolution over time, and that classroom cultures, teachers' interpretations, uses of word processing, and beginners' theories and practices are dynamic and spiraling, rather than static, features of implementation. Only a long-term research design can capture the features that Figure 7.5 adds to the framework. (The long-term evolution of word processing practices and interpretations is discussed in detail in Chapter 3.)

This framework is tailored for the study of beginning writers and word processing. But it is useful as an investigative and analytic framework for classroom uses of other computer technology as well. With some alterations, the framework can be applied to teachers' and children's uses of any software that is

Figure 7.3
Building An Interpretive Framework: Writing Demonstrations

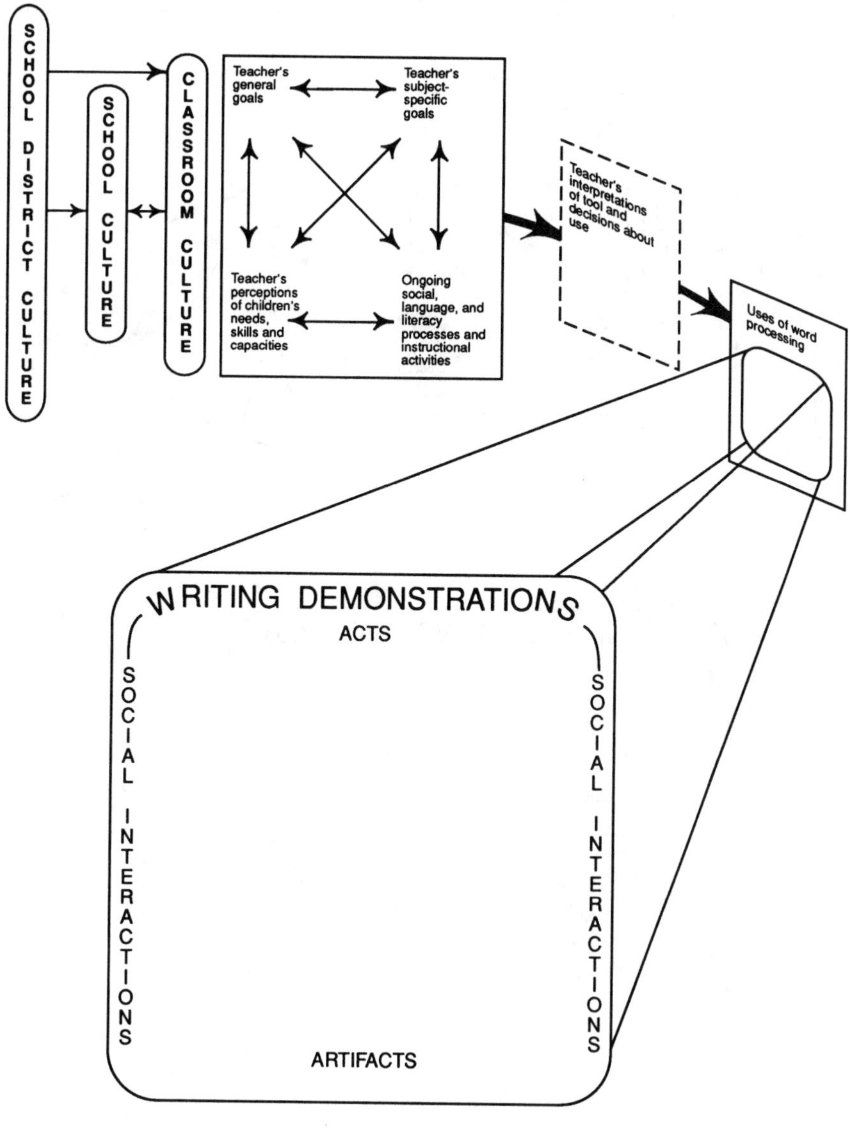

interpretable and open-ended—word processing, data base software, spread sheets, and so on. The interpretable character of tool software necessitates examination of the evolution of teachers' interpretations and decisions, classroom learning demonstrations, and children's theories and practices. In a more general sense, the framework has wider applicability for explorations of the

Figure 7.4
Building An Interpretive Framework:
Word-Processing Events and Writers' Theories

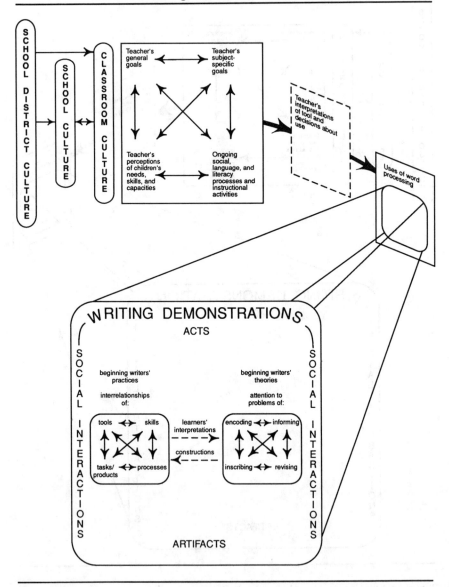

relationships of technology and learning. With modifications to account for the particular tool value of the technology, the framework permits analysis of many critical relationships.

Directions for Research

Our framework uncovers some of the questions that are generally *not* asked about beginning writers and word processing and points instead to alternative questions. It suggests that the most useful questions have little to do with numbers of errors found, lengths of texts created, or numbers of revisions made when children use word processing as a writing tool. More useful questions involve the nature of children's interactions with teachers and coaches as they work with word processing. Close examination of the conversations adults and children have about language and the conventions of print as they jointly negotiate texts can make visible the kinds of opportunities children have to learn about writing within these social contexts. Case studies can explore the development of individual beginners who have opportunities both to write with paper and pencil and to compose with word processing. Over time case studies can document connections between adults' and children's talk about writing and children's independent, as well as coached, writing productions. Finally, the framework suggests that important questions about the implementation of word processing into the curriculum have little to do with whether teachers follow school district guidelines or require children to produce word-processed texts. Rather, teachers interpret word-processing technology for their own programs. As the technology becomes integrated within the ongoing curriculum organization, word processing both shapes and is shaped by the cultures of schools and classrooms. Research that explores the mutual shaping process has important implications.

WORD PROCESSING, BEGINNING WRITERS, AND SCHOOL POLICY

Educators and parents ask a wide range of questions about beginning writers and word processing. These range from queries about space requirements, per-pupil expenditures, and noise levels of printers, to concerns about equity of access, the effects of technology on cognitive processes, and the relationships of writing tools and tasks. Our 2-year study of five teachers and some 200 children provides detailed information that suggests answers to some of these. Of course we do not claim that our answers are generalizable to all settings, nor do we want to imply that it is possible to answer questions about teaching and learning in global or simple ways. To the contrary, the details in the preceding chapters have made a strong case for the complexity of understanding word processing and its varying

Figure 7.5
Word-Processing and Writing In Classrooms:
A Social and Cultural Interpretation

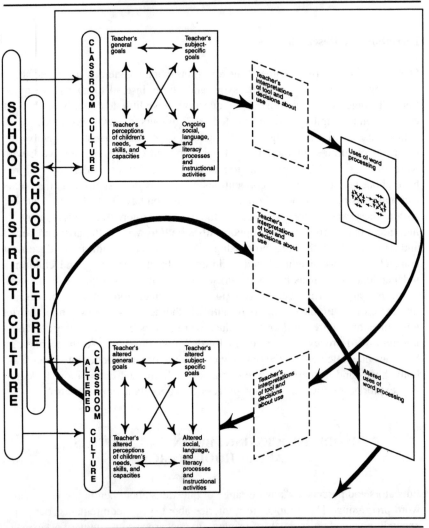

uses in classroom settings. However, we think that it is useful to examine.some of the questions most commonly asked about beginners and word processing and to consider the ways that these might inform policies in curriculum, instruction, and professional development. In order to make decisions about whether and how to utilize word-processing technology at the level of elementary school education, teachers, teacher educators, and policy makers need rich and detailed information about the diversity of ways word processing has functioned in individual classrooms rather than global statements about what works for teachers and children when word processing is introduced.

Asking and Answering Questions

In the section that follows we have posed some of the questions teachers, teacher educators, and parents most frequently ask us about word processing and its uses at the elementary school level. Our answers to those questions make it clear that teaching and learning are complex and context-specific activities, but also recognize the need for policy makers to make pragmatic decisions about the technology that they choose to make available to beginning writers.

QUESTION: *Are beginning writers able to use the computer keyboard and manage the word-processing system?*

ANSWER: Yes, even kindergarten children learned to enter text, erase, space, and capitalize at the keyboard, as well as save and print their texts. But these skills developed during a learning period of two to three word-processing sessions for most children. For older children, who could compose and encode faster than they could locate keys, the initial learning period was sometimes frustrating. At all grade levels children received instruction in word processing, and in most cases, children were coached or assisted by adults as they learned word processing skills.

QUESTION: *How many word-processing systems are needed per classroom to utilize word processing effectively?*

ANSWER: As few as two word-processing systems for a class of 25 children were effective when it was possible for children to use the equipment long enough to take advantage of the capabilities of word processing. The length of time required per session in order to take advantage of word-processing features was relative to the age and writing skill of the children. With the youngest children, who usually completed written pieces in one 20-minute sitting, it was almost always possible to take advantage of the facilitative features of word processing. With the older children, this was the case when individual children could begin and complete a given piece at the computer—by working at the computer for an extended period of time, by working for several days in succession, or by having access during extra periods of the school day (e.g., lunch, recess, before and after school, during other subject periods). Teachers and older children unanimously agreed, however, they would have liked more computer systems in their classrooms.

QUESTION: *Are additional aides needed to supervise children while they work with word processing?*

ANSWER: All classes used additional aides to help children develop keyboarding familiarity and learn to manage the system. Aides included researchers, university students, parent volunteers, teacher assistants, and older children. Children at all grade levels eventually learned to work independently with word processing, and third and fourth graders worked independently most of the time. Although some adults had been concerned about it, no hardware or software was ever damaged due to improper treatment by children working independently. Adults helped kindergarten and first grade children throughout the course of the year to compose their own pieces, but their help focused more on writing tasks than on word-processing tasks.

QUESTION: *Does using word processing take away time the teacher could be spending on other activities?*

ANSWER: Yes, especially during the initial learning period, the teacher's time and attention were required to assist as word-processing skills and procedures for using word processing in the writing program were established. In many cases the situation was alleviated by the presence of additional assistants who helped children get started with word processing. All teachers agreed, however, that the initial time was well spent, and that word processing did not require undue amounts of time once the learning period was completed.

QUESTION: *Do teachers successfully integrate word processing into the curriculum?*

ANSWER: Yes, all five teachers introduced word processing to their children and continued to use it in their reading/language programs. However, all five teachers introduced it differently and initially adapted it to their own goals and ongoing practices. Over time they developed additional ways to use word processing. Using word processing in the writing curriculum did not require that teachers become high-technology experts, and only one of the five teachers had had previous computer experience.

QUESTION: *Do teachers have difficulty working with word processing without curriculum guidelines?*

ANSWER: No, all five teachers revealed that they always experimented and then reconsidered their instructional strategies and their curriculum plans. They worked out ways to utilize word processing through a similar process. Further at group meetings they defined problems and discussed possible solutions with their colleagues, and later tried out various classroom arrangements.

QUESTION: *Do children use the capabilities of word processing to take risks with their writing and to revise their texts in conceptually and organizationally significant ways?*

ANSWER: No, most children did not use the most powerful revision and reorganizational capabilities of word processing. Generally they were not taught these strategies within their writing programs. Most children used the capabilities of word processing to revise, erase, or add on to text at the point of entry, or to edit already created text, or to produce clean-copy final drafts.

QUESTION: *Does using word processing improve children's writing?*

ANSWER: No, in and of itself, word processing did not improve children's writing or teach new composing strategies, but teachers and children working together with word processing did have significant benefits for beginning writers (see discussion below). Teachers and children working together with word processing often created social contexts within which children learned or reviewed writing strategies and learned how to execute those strategies with word processing. Because word-processing capabilities made the execution of those strategies easy, children were willing to complete them.

QUESTION: *What are the most significant benefits of using word processing for beginning writers?*

ANSWER: Two benefits are most significant. First, word processing removed from the writing task some of the difficulties involved with the production of printed language—correct formation and spatial orientation of letters; appropriate spacing, lining, and directionality; trace-free erasures, insertions, and deletions; continuous availability of legible text; and production of multiple clean final copies. The removal of production issues allowed beginning writers to concentrate on other components of the multiple-tasked activity of composing—encoding of individual phonemes and words, spelling and punctuation, word choice, organization and elaboration of ideas, editing, and so on.
Second, beginning writers often worked with word processing

with the help of adults in a "coaching" situation wherein adults and children together jointly produced texts that were more linguistically and substantively sophisticated than the texts children could produce alone. The physical arrangements of word processing made it more possible for adult coaches to see explicitly some of the children's internal writing practices and enter into production of the text with them.

QUESTION: *Does using computer technology for writing significantly alter teachers' roles, their relationships with children, and classroom opportunities for interactions?*

ANSWER: Yes and no—using word-processing technology in no way diminished the instructional roles teachers played in their classrooms or detracted from the warm relationships they established with children. Further, all teachers interpreted the technology of word processing in ways that supported the social and cognitive, as well as the language and literacy learning goals they held for the children in their classrooms. However, over time the technology of word processing made it possible for new learning interactions to occur and for children and teachers to interact around language in additional ways.

Thinking Through the Implications

Preparing teachers to use computers in the curriculum, and/or introducing them to the hardware and software that a school district has purchased, have typically been carried out in top-down fashion. Computers are purchased and installed in schools, software is provided, teachers attend workshops or inservice meetings at which the equipment is displayed and described, and teachers are required to use computers in their classrooms from that time forward. Unfortunately, the results of professional development programs designed in this way are generally unsatisfactory. Because teachers are uncertain about what to do and how to do it, many simply do not use the computers provided or, if pressured to do so, use them for very specific, circumscribed projects that are isolated from the rest of the curriculum and short term in duration (Cuban, 1986). The training is inadequate and far too brief, and, as many professional development studies have demonstrated, top-down curriculum change efforts do not have lasting effects (Berman & McLaughlin, 1974-1978).

Our study traces two of the reasons this approach to professional development does not work and suggests instead two of the ingredients for effective teacher preparation in word processing. First, as we have argued, teachers' ways of using word processing in the classroom are closely related to their interpretations of the software and their assumptions about effective teaching, children as learners, and the nature of language and literacy development. For this reason, it is essential that professional development programs allow time for teachers to sort out their assumptions and then consider them in relation to the capabilities of word processing. For example, teachers need the opportunity to examine what they expect children to learn and accomplish in their writing programs over the course of a school year. They then need time both to learn thoroughly how to use word processing and to consider how and whether word processing might help them meet their goals for children's writing development.

Second, our study indicates that curriculum innovation can be effective when teachers themselves play leadership roles in implementing word processing into the curriculum (see Paris, 1990, in press). Curriculum change in which teachers play a central role is not a quick process. It unfolds over the course of weeks and months. It provides opportunities for teachers to make important decisions about the uses of word processing in their classrooms based on their beliefs about its appropriateness for the children with whom they work and the goals of their writing programs. Staff development of this kind operates on the assumption that the teacher's knowledge is essential in decisions about how and whether to integrate word processing into the curriculum.

Our data demonstrate that the benefits of word processing are derived from the ongoing writing programs that exist in various classrooms. Computer word processing will not, in and of itself, change or improve the nature of children's writing. Children will not revise their writing simply because word processing makes it easy to revise, nor will they use early drafts to discover what they have to say simply because word processing allows for the easy rearrangement of brainstormed ideas. If these writing strategies are not already within beginners' repertoires, word processing will not create them. If, however, these strategies are (or are coming to be) parts of children's expectations for writing, then word processing can enhance them and make it easier for children to use them within their writing. This suggests that teachers and supervisors need to have realistic expectations for the use of word processing in the language curriculum—they cannot expect the tool, by itself, to teach the children.

Albert Einstein once claimed, "Everything should be as simple as possible, but no simpler." There are many ways to look at the complex relationships of classroom cultures, teachers' interpretations of technology, and the interplay of learners' thinking and the social contexts they help to construct. We believe that the perspective we have built in this volume is as simple as possible, but no simpler.

DESIGN OF THE STUDY

During Year 1 of the study reported in this volume, data were collected in three classrooms at Summit Grove Elementary School in the West Brook Public School System—one kindergarten, one second grade, and one fourth grade. During Year 2, data were collected in the same three classrooms, plus one first grade and one third grade.

RESEARCH SITE

Summit Grove School is part of the West Brook School System, a public urban district adjacent to a major northeastern city. Between 1985 and 1987, when data were collected, West Brook served a population of roughly 7,500 students in its seven elementary schools, two middle schools, and one high school. At Summit Grove, the largest and newest elementary school in the district, the population is approximately 600 kindergarten through fifth grade children. This includes children enrolled in a special education program and an English as a Second Language program (ESL), the latter of whom are transported to the school by bus from several neighboring schools in the district. At the time of the study, population increases had produced enrollment figures larger than Summit Grove had been designed to contain, and the school was commonly characterized as "bursting at the seams." In the year following the study, all of the kindergarten classes were shifted to another school to accommodate the growing numbers of children whose families were to be served by the school.

When the study began, Summit Grove was 15 years old, originally constructed during the period when *open-plan* buildings were popular. Several grade-level groups at the school still use the open physical structure for team-taught classes or for jointly planned and/or jointly taught activities, although the school is not thought of by the staff or the community as having an "open education" curriculum. The school serves a working-class, ethnically mixed community, composed primarily of white American families, white Greek families, and Asian families. A very small number of black and other minorities attend the school. Most Greek families actively guard their ethnic and Greek

Orthodox religious identification, and their children regularly attend Greek school for language and religious instruction in addition to their attendance at the local public school. Summit Grove also serves a growing Asian population, most of whom are recent immigrants to this country.

The school faculty and staff enjoy the support of an active and generous parent-teacher organization and generally have very positive relationships with the community. Many mothers volunteer their time in service to the school, especially at the lower grade levels. The composition of the teaching staff at the school is unusually stable, and was especially so during the period preceding the study and during the study itself. Many teachers have worked together since Summit Grove opened, and several have worked together previously within the West Brook district at other school buildings. When the study began, the school had not had the need to hire a new teacher, either for reasons of attrition or added classes, in five years. The large majority of teachers have 15 to 20 years of teaching experience, and most hold master's degrees or an equivalent. The teachers are a close-knit group. They enjoy pleasant and collegial working relationships, and, in a number of cases, social and personal relationships outside of school.

The school principal at the time of the study was a relative newcomer to the building, although an experienced elementary grade teacher of many years. When the study began, she was beginning her third year in the building. The principal and teachers know each other well and demonstrate mutual respect for one another. When there was talk that the principal was to be transferred to another building, many teachers expressed dissatisfaction. The principal is supportive of the teaching staff, encouraging them to undertake new projects, expand their teaching interests, and participate in continuing professional development activities of all kinds. The staff prides itself on being innovative and up-to-date on teaching ideas and events. (Chapter 3 describes the culture of the school in more detail. Also see Paris, in press.)

ACCESS AND RESEARCHER ROLE

The researchers' home university and the West Brook School District had enjoyed a mutually beneficial relationship for a number of years prior to the study. Summit Grove was arranged as the research site through the efforts of the senior researcher, the school principal, and the school district superintendent. The senior researcher, also head of programs in elementary education at the university, regularly places student teachers and teacher assistants (education students completing pre-student-teaching fieldwork assignments) at the school, and in this capacity had worked closely with the principal and superintendent for several years before the study began. In addition, through their work supervising student teachers, the senior researcher and one research associate knew several of the teachers and had worked at Summit Grove prior to the study.

During the first year, the research team was composed of the senior researcher and two research associates, both advanced doctoral students who later completed their doctoral dissertations on separate aspects of the larger study (see Kahn, 1988; Paris, in press). Each of the three served as participant observer in separate classrooms over the course of the first academic year. During the second year, an additional research assistant served as participant observer in one of the classes, and each of the research associates was participant observer in two classes. In addition, the three original researchers participated with the teachers as a researcher/teacher group which met monthly over the 2-year period to share progress, raise questions and concerns, and develop a cross-grade perspective on using word processing with beginning writers.

During the first year, the principal offered the opportunity to participate in the study to teachers at each of the three designated grade levels (K, 2, 4); three teachers agreed to work with researchers. Participation in the study meant that each teacher had the use of at least two IBM Personal Computers in her classroom, ''Bank Street Writer'' software, a teacher assistant from the university's teacher education program 1½ days per week, and the support and assistance of the university research team. (It should be noted that other teachers at Summit Grove who were not in the study also had teacher assistants from the university on a regular basis, so this was not an unusual arrangement for the school.) Teachers were not required to use a particular word-processing curriculum, nor were they required to assign certain writing topics to the children in their classes to be produced with word processing. Rather, they attended a one-week summer workshop designed to let them learn word processing skills and explore ways to use it in the writing curriculum. They were then provided with hardware and software and invited to develop their own ways to use them. During the second year, all three original teachers remained as participants in the project, and two new teachers were added (grades 1, 3). These teachers were also selected by the principal for their appropriate grade levels, their willingness to participate, and their interest in the project.

In each classroom, researchers played several roles. These included observing and noting classroom organization and curriculum, the ways teachers used word processing, and the ways children worked with word processing for writing. Computer-produced pieces of writing and the drafts that preceded or followed them were collected as were other documents related to the language/writing curriculum. Teachers and children were interviewed informally on an ongoing basis. However, the ways duties were carried out, and the ways researchers' classroom/teaching roles were negotiated by the individual teacher-and-researcher pair, were unique within each classroom. In all cases, the researcher followed the teacher's lead in establishing a role and acted in accordance with her preferences about writing instruction and implementation of word processing.

Because researchers' roles were individually negotiated, there was both a great deal of variation of roles from pair to pair of teachers and researchers and a gradual evolution of these roles over time. For example, in some classrooms the researcher was invited to work with children in what came to be a coaching role as children learned to use word processing. In one classroom where the researcher acted as coach, she also consulted with the teacher, shared ideas about young children's writing, and planned some activities for the computer on a joint basis with the teacher. In another classroom where the researcher acted as coach, she served primarily in the role of writing/word processing teacher for individual children as well as informant for the teacher, sharing information with her about how the children were adjusting to word processing and providing insights about both their writing and computing progress. In still another classroom the researcher served primarily as participant-observer and did not take an active part in the children's work with word processing. This was the case because one of the teacher's major goals was for the children to develop independence with word processing and to take risks as they figured out word processing procedures based on their teacher's instruction and their own experimentations. In this classroom the teacher–researcher pair conferred regularly about what each of them saw happening with the children and about ways the curriculum or classroom organization might be revised to accommodate the children's needs and the teacher's goals.

This diversity across classrooms and the explicit avoidance of preestablishing a standardized role for the researchers in their classroom interactions did not present a limitation in the study. Rather, researchers agreed in advance that their approach would be to take their cues from teachers, and that teachers would in fact initiate the structures for researcher/teacher/student relationships that were most comfortable for them and that would facilitate the goals they had established for their language arts programs. Opportunities to see and acknowledge this diversity are strengths of the study. They permit comparative generalizations across idiosynratic cases that enable contrastive analysis among structures and organizational patterns.

COMPUTER HARDWARE
AND WORD PROCESSING SOFTWARE

When the study began, the kindergarten and third grade classes each had one IBM Personal Computer system, including monitor, disk drive, and printer, and the fourth-grade class had two. Within a few months, the second shipment of hardware had arrived, so that kindergarten and third grades each had two, and the fourth grade four, complete systems. In the second year, the kindergarten class used two Apple computer systems supplied by the school district, and all other classes used IBM systems: first through third grade classrooms had two systems, and the fourth grade classroom had four systems.

The IBM PC Keyboard

At the time of this study (1985-1987), the IBM PC keyboard located cursor movement keys on a numeric keypad to the right of the alphabetic keyboard. Cursor movements were as follows: arrow on the #8 key (movement up), arrows on the #4 and #6 keys (movement left and right), and arrow on the #2 key (movement down). The keyboard had two keys for erasing: the "BACKAR-ROW," located in the upper right hand corner of the alphabetic keyboard and identified on the key only by an arrow pointing to the left; and the "DELETE" key, identified by the letters "Del" and located in the lower-right corner of the alphabetic keyboard. The two keys erased in different directions in relation to cursor position. The "BACKARROW" erased the letter just to the left of the cursor and moved the cursor itself to the left. The "DELETE" key erased the letter that the cursor was highlighting and moved the cursor itself to the right. As some excerpts in this volume reveal, the two erasing keys were a source of confusion to children initially. Eventually, however, older children generally used the "BACKARROW" key to erase as they composed and the "DELETE" key to erase when they were editing a previously written piece. Younger children only used the backarrow key. The "RETURN" key on the keyboard was marked by a broken arrow rather than the word *return*. The "TAB" key was marked only with two arrows pointing in opposite directions.

The IBM system had the ability to print an entire screen by pressing a key marked "Prtscr." This operation produced everything that appeared on the screen, including system information printed at the top and bottom of the screen and the boxed frame that surrounded the text entry area. Kindergarten children used this key most of the first year to obtain printouts because adults thought it would be simpler than dealing with the normal print commands.

Bank Street Writer Software

Word-processing software was chosen following a review of programs available in 1984-1985 for use with IBM PCs. "Bank Street Writer" was selected for its user-friendly qualities, such as on-screen menus and prompts, and because it was a well-known, widely used program specifically designed for children and readily available to elementary teachers. When the study began, "Bank Street Writer II" was available and was used. This version, unlike the original, allowed for composing and editing on the same screen. Midway through the second year, the newer version, "Bank Street Writer III," which had a simplified menu on the screen as well as an online spelling checker and thesaurus, was introduced.

The spelling checker located words not in its dictionary and presented several options to the user: choose a correct spelling from a list of possible words, try to spell the word again, or leave the word as it appeared. For instance, if a writer had entered *hopeing*, the program offered both *hopping* and *hoping*, and the user selected the correct spelling. Once the user chose a correct spelling from the list, the program substituted that word for the misspelled word in the text. The list of alternative spellings was generated from the first few letters of the word or from phonetic equivalents, so that a writer who entered *fone* would be offered choices such as *font* as well as *phone*. The spelling checker did not identify incorrect usage of homonyms. If a spelling were so unlike the correct spelling that the program failed to supply any possibilities or failed to supply the correct word, the user was offered the option to try to spell the word again to approximate the correct spelling more closely. The spelling checker also offered the options to leave the word just as it was on the screen or add a word to the dictionary.

DATA SOURCES

The major database for the study included: (a) annotated transcriptions of field notes and audio-recordings of individual word-processing events and narrative profiles of individual children using word processing, (b) narrative descriptions based on field notes of classroom activities and the organization of writing and word-processing programs, (c) transcriptions of audio-recordings of interviews with individual teachers and children, (d) transcriptions of audio-recordings of monthly group meetings of researchers and teachers, and (e) collections of children's writing produced with word processing and, in a few cases, with paper and pencil.

Classroom observations began on the first day of the school year and continued throughout both years of the study. A researcher spent one observation session per week in each of the three classrooms during the first year, and each of the five classrooms during the second year. Lengths of observation sessions depended on class schedules for reading/language arts instruction, children's access to word processing during other periods of the day, and the general school and university calendars. Some observations of word processing and writing were as brief as 45 to 60 minutes, and some as lengthy as 3½ hours. Most weekly observation sessions were between one and two hours in length. Roughly 450 hours of observation were conducted in the five classrooms over the 2-year period. A number of ethnographic methods were combined in order to collect information in each of the areas described below.

Word-Processing Events

Both within and across the five classrooms, word-processing events varied in length due partly to the individual abilities and interests of particular children or the requirements of particular writing tasks, and partly to the organizational arrangements of individual classrooms. In some classrooms children took timed turns at the computer, while in other classrooms children worked until other children who wanted turns had waited what adults considered a "reasonable" amount of time. In still other classrooms children were allowed to work continuously until a given piece of writing was completed. Hence, word-processing events themselves ranged in length from as short as 4 to 5 minutes to as long as 1½ hours. The average length of word-processing events was about 30 minutes.

Almost 400 word-processing events were observed over the 2-year period. Each was recorded in the following ways, which were later combined to produce annotated transcriptions of the events.

Audiotape Recordings of Talk During Text Production. Verbalizations that occurred immediately prior to, during, or immediately following the production of text within word-processing events were audio-recorded with portable cassette recorders. Verbalizations included a writer's talk to himself or herself while composing, or talk that occurred between child and researcher, child and teacher, or child and a peer at the adjacent computer or in some nearby spot in the classroom. Over time, especially with the oldest children in the study, the extent of verbal interaction during composing with word processing decreased. In a number of instances, audio-recordings were discontinued midstream because word processing was no longer accompanied by verbalizations.

Field Notes. For each observed word-processing event, field notes to accompany the audio-recording were kept. Notes included identification of child writer and other participants in the event, time and place information, and details regarding the writing task and instructional events that lead up to or followed the task. Further, the observer noted the child writer's general stance at the computer, his or her keyboarding and composing strategies, and use of paper-and-pencil draft and/or other resources. Most importantly, as the child composed, the researcher used a simple coding system to record each keystroke in sequence and to correlate those keystrokes to ongoing verbal and nonverbal behavior.

Written Products Created with Word Processing. For each word-processing event, the text that appeared on the screen at the end of the sitting was printed out and collected along with any prior and subsequent drafts of that particular piece of writing. What was printed at the end of each sitting could not necessarily be considered a "draft" (although it sometimes was). Younger children did not produce text through a series of drafts, but rather completed their writing within a single sitting. In some situations, older children had not completed the initial composition of their pieces when, for whatever reason, their time at the computer ran out. In these cases, children saved their work and continued to compose later either at the keyboard or with paper and pencil. Copies of texts that appeared on the screen at the end of each session were collected in all of these cases.

Informal Conversations with Teachers about Word-Processing Events.
Fieldnotes were made anytime researchers and teachers discussed particular
word-processing events, writers, and written products. This information provided situational details about given word-processing events.

Annotated Transcriptions of Word-Processing Events. The above information was combined to construct an annotated transcript of each word-processing
event. Each transcript began with a "Word Processing Profile," constructed
from field notes and audio-recordings, which highlighted the keyboarding and
composing strategies of the individual child. Profiles provided comparative
information concerning the individual child writer as well as his or her previous
word processing and writing experiences, previous written products, and available information about reading or writing performance levels in other activities in
the classroom. Following the profile, each transcript was laid out chronologically
in script format, to be read in normal top-to-bottom manner, as follows:

1. Each speaker (e.g., child writer, adult coach or teacher, other child partici-
    pants) is identified by name or title (children and teachers are identified by
    pseudonyms).
2. Actual verbalizations are recorded according to standard print conventions
    and represented in regular print format.
3. Nonverbal actions, including all computer keystrokes as well as composing
    behaviors, are included in brackets.
4. Information about the situational context and the discourse context is en-
    closed in parentheses.
5. The word-processed text is represented in slightly larger, bold-face print.
    When a text unfolded during the child's actual composing event at the word
    processor, the text is embedded bit-by-bit within the dialogue or monologue
    that accompanied it as it was produced. When a text had previously been
    typed into the computer before the event began, or when the event was the
    continuation of an earlier event during which text had been produced, the
    already-existing word-processed text appears intact at the beginning of a
    transcript. Any additional text produced during the event is embedded
    within the dialogue or monologue as it was produced.

In this way each annotated transcript provides four kinds of information about
word-processing events: a narrative profile of the beginning writer, the written
product that was produced with word processing by the end of the event, the
composing and keyboarding strategies the child used as the text gradually
evolved, and the verbal and nonverbal actions that surrounded and supported the
word-processing event.

Instructional Contexts for Word Processing and Writing

This study both assumes and argues that the ways children used word processing for writing are dynamically related to the larger contexts of the teaching culture, the reading/language arts curriculum, the rules and constraints of the school and school system, and individual teachers' perceptions and interpretations. Several kinds of information were collected in order to locate word-processing events within, and in relation to, these teaching/learning contexts. Taken together, these provide a sense of the general classroom environments within which word processing and writing occurred, and especially of the ways these changed and evolved over time.

Field Notes. During each observation session, researchers kept field notes about the general classroom atmosphere, the instructional strategies and routines used by teachers, the physical arrangements of classrooms and organization/uses of time and space, and the materials, decorations, and printed materials available in each classroom.

In addition to general field notes, specific attention was given to the reading/language arts curriculum and especially to the teaching of writing and/or word processing. Field notes included information regarding:

1. How reading/language arts instructional periods were organized and scheduled during the school day/week.
2. What materials/teaching strategies/regular activities teachers used for reading/language arts instruction generally.
3. Whether, and to what extent, reading, writing, and oral language were integrated into other subject areas or to other time periods during the school day.
4. What kinds of instructional groupings were used for reading/language arts instruction (e.g., whole class, small groups by ability or interest, one-on-one conferencing between teacher and child or child and peers).
5. How writing instruction (with word processing and with paper and pencil) was organized, routines, and groupings that were used, and how these related to reading/language arts instruction more generally and/or to the larger curriculum.
6. What kinds of writing tasks (with word processing or with paper and pencil) the teacher assigned/invited children to complete, and what kinds of resources and support were made available for their completion.
7. How teachers introduced word processing to children—the specific tasks assigned for word processing, the language used to talk about computers generally and word processing specifically, the kinds of support and resources used to help children learn to use the computer, the ways teachers grouped children for work with word processing, and the instruction over time that teachers planned and carried out for word processing/writing.

8. Information about reading, writing, and computers that was conveyed to children in classroom decorations, routines, labels, choice of language, kinds of assignments, organizations of time and space, and groupings of children.

Ongoing Conversations/Informal Interviews. Researchers in each classroom regularly talked informally with teachers and children as they worked at writing, word processing, and other classroom activities. These conversations were not recorded verbatim, but information was added to field notes to provide further detail about classroom events and insights about teachers' views. Approximately 100 such conversations between teachers and researchers were noted in field notes.

In addition, second-, third-, and fourth-grade children were interviewed individually at the completion of each of the two school years. Interviews, which were audio-recorded, were open ended, but generally included the following topics:

1. What the child thinks about writing with word processing, how it compares with writing with paper and pencil, which is preferred, and why.
2. Whether the child likes to do certain parts of writing with paper and pencil and other parts with word processing, what these are, and what the child thinks are the best and worst things about writing with word processing.
3. Whether and how the child thinks he or she writes any differently with word processing from the way he or she does with paper and pencil.
4. Whether the child would have computers for writing for children his or her own age if the decision were his or hers.
5. How the child learned to do word processing, what was hardest/easiest at the beginning, and what the child thinks is most important to know about word processing.

Document Collection. In addition to written work produced with word processing (and in some cases, some paper-and-pencil samples of writing), documents were collected that provided additional information about the reading/ language arts curriculum or the general instructional orientation of the classroom. For example, worksheets that outlined the steps of the writing process, written assignments to the students, writing outlines that appeared on the blackboard, computer expert checklists, and so on, were collected.

Cultures of Teaching

This volume makes clear that word processing and writing occurred within complex classroom and school contexts that both shaped, and were shaped by, the introduction of computers. These contexts changed and evolved over time and were influenced by many other factors. These included children's prior and ongoing computer and writing experiences, the social and instructional organization of individual classrooms, the ways teachers interpreted and put into effect school district requirements, and the kinds of assumptions and values they held. Several data sources were collected to provide information about school and teaching cultures.

Interviews with Teachers. Each teacher was regularly interviewed over the 2-year period. Nineteen formal interviews, which were audio-recorded and also noted in handwritten field notes, were conducted. Interviews ranged in length from a half hour to 1½ hours. Interviews conducted early in the study followed an interview schedule geared to teachers' reflections about the implementation of word processing. However, we found that, no matter what questions were asked, teachers talked about their most pressing concerns and told their own stories. Over time, interviews became more unstructured. They centered on the teachers' experiences with word processing as an instance of new curriculum implementation and the ways these related to other experiences with curriculum change and staff development. Over time interviews provided critical information about the meaning perspectives of the teachers as they interpreted the possibilities of word processing, experimented with it in their classrooms, and essentially created curriculum.

Teachers' Journals. Teachers were invited to keep journals over the course of the study to record information researchers missed because they were not present every day, raise questions about the implementation of word processing, and puzzle through issues of children's language and learning. During the first month of the study, all teachers did so, but after the first month, most teachers reported that they preferred to talk with researchers in person or to share their ideas in monthly meetings. Two teachers continued to write throughout the second year of the study. They wrote regularly in journals, approximately two times per month, whenever they had something important to say. One or more researchers responded to their entries so that journals took the form of letters back and forth. The teachers used the journals to chronicle what they did with their classes with word processing and to raise questions about observations and analyses of classroom interactions. Researchers used the journals to provide insights into teachers' changing meaning perspectives.

Discussion Meetings of Researchers and Teachers. Meetings to discuss progress and concerns about word processing and writing were held during most school months, with the exception of those with extended vacation or testing periods. Ten meetings, which lasted approximately 1½ hours each, occurred. Each was audio-recorded and transcribed. The agenda at most meetings was flexible. Researchers shared with teachers the design of the research project, technical information about computer hardware and software, and articles of interest. Teachers shared information about the ways they were deploying computers in their classrooms, children's progress, and problems and solutions. Together teachers and researchers explored using word processing as a tool for beginning writing and discussed curriculum innovation and professional development.

Summer workshops. One-week workshops were held during each of the two summers prior to the two data-collection years. During the first summer, the workshop provided opportunities to learn to operate and manage the word-processing system and opportunities for teachers to explore together ways to use computers in their writing curricula. During the second summer, the workshop was especially geared for the two teachers new to the project. Teachers from the previous year shared their experiences, and the whole group discussed what it had learned from the previous year. Field notes, planning sessions, and documents from the workshops were collected, and selected sessions were audio-recorded and transcribed. Because experienced teachers shared what they had learned about integrating word processing into the writing curriculum, summer sessions provided important insights about the meaning perspectives of the teachers on an overall basis.

DATA ANALYSIS

Our study combines general participant observation with topic-centered observations (Green, 1984). General observations include characteristics of the school and classroom organizations, reading and language curricula, the social and language processes of individual classrooms, and teachers' and children's perceptions of these (Green, 1983). Topic-centered observations include literacy instruction in general, writing specifically, and occasions on which teachers and beginning writers work directly with word processing. Throughout the data collection period and the data examination period, the point of our analysis was to relate "parts" to "wholes" by exploring the ways that topic-centered events reflected, interacted with, and shaped the larger scene.

The most important "parts" in our study were writing instruction and especially word-processing events in which teachers and children worked together at the computer to create, modify, interpret, and/or print texts. While writing instruction and word-processing events are clearly "parts" of the larger culture of teaching, they are also, of course, "wholes" with various parts in and of themselves. For example, word-processing events, which are parts of the larger reading/writing curriculum and the culture of the classroom, are also wholes composed of differentiated elements including participants' utterances, keyboarding actions, composing processes, and written products. Our analysis explores the relationships the differentiated elements of word-processing events have to one another (parts to parts) as well as how these elements interact with and reflect the larger word-processing event (parts to whole) and how all of these interact with and reflect the larger teaching culture (parts to the larger whole).

Throughout this volume, then, our analysis moves between a more comprehensive look at teaching and school cultures and a more focused look at individual elements of those cultures (Zaharlick & Green, in press). Specifically, we move back and forth between classroom culture, teachers' perceptions and interpretations, writing demonstrations and word-processing events, and beginning writers' interpretations. As described in detail in Chapter 6, writing demonstrations were the result of the dynamic interplay of teachers' and children's acts, artifacts, and social interactions that had something to do with writing. Individual word-processing events, described extensively in Chapter 5, were structured and analyzed according to the interplay of task, tool, writer's skills, and learning/teaching processes.

The theoretical framework that combines multiple perspectives and accounts for evolving relationships over time is discussed in some detail in Chapter 7. We argue there that understanding word processing in elementary classrooms requires attention to the spiraling interrelationships of teaching cultures, teachers' interpretations and decisions, and uses of word processing *as well as* altered cultures, teachers' interpretations and decisions, and uses of word processing.

Within this theoretical framework, we used standard methods of qualitative data analysis, including analytic induction and triangulation, during the entire period of the study. Specifically, we generated hypotheses, or propositional assertions (Shimahara, 1988), about the interactions of word-processing events and teaching cultures by testing and retesting them against the growing database and intentionally seeking confirming as well as disconfirming cases (Hutchinson, 1988). Hypotheses were proposed and modified as they were verified or refuted by the emerging database, and discrepant as well as justifying cases were analyzed. Over time, we established the "evidentiary warrant" (Erickson, 1986) for the assertions which comprise this volume by continuous rereading of the corpus of field notes, word-processing transcriptions, documentary materials, and interviews. These allowed us to build a series of interlocking arguments (reviewed in Chapter 7) which explain the "key linkages" (Erickson, 1986) among the various data sources.

References

Amarel, M. (1983). Classrooms and computers as instructional settings. *Theory Into Practice, 22*, 260–266.

Anderson, A., & Stokes, S. (1984). Social and institutional influences on the development and practice of literacy. In H. Goelman, A. Oberg, & F. Smith (Eds.), *Awakening to literacy* (pp. 24–37). Exeter, NH: Heinemann Educational Books.

Andrews, D. (1985). Writers' slump and revision schemes: Effects of computers on the composing process. In T. Martinez (Ed.), *The written word and the word processor* (pp. 243–250). Philadelphia: Delaware Valley Writing Council Spring Conference.

Applebee, A. (1981). *Writing in the secondary school: English in the content areas.* Urbana, IL: National Council of Teachers of English.

Arms, V. (1984). The computer: An aid to collaborative writing. *Technical Writing Teacher, 2*, 750–753.

Baghban, M. (1984). *Our daughter learns to read and write: A case study from birth to three.* Newark, DE: International Reading Association.

Barber, B. (1982). Creating BYTES of language. *Language Arts, 59*, 472–475.

Barrett, E., & Paradis, J. (1988). Teaching writing in an on-line classroom. *Harvard Educational Review, 58*, 154–171.

Bartlett, E. (1982). Learning to revise: Some component processes. In M. Nystrand (Ed.), *What writers know: The language, process and structure of written discourse* (pp. 345–364). Orlando, FL: Academic Press.

Bean, J. (1983). Computerized word processing as an aid to revision. *College Composition and Communication, 34*, 146–155.

Bereiter, C., & Scardamalia, M. (1982). From conversation to composition: The role of instruction in a developmental process. In R. Glaser (Ed.), *Advances in instructional psychology* (Vol. 2, pp. 1–64). Hillsdale, NJ: Erlbaum.

Berliner, D. (1986). In pursuit of the expert pedagogue. *Educational Researcher, 15*, 5–13.

Berman, P., & McLaughlin, M. (1974–1978). *Federal programs supporting educational change* (Vols. I-VIII). Santa Monica, CA: Rand Corporation.

Bickel, L. (1985). Word processing and the integration of reading and writing instruction. In J. Collins & E. Sommers (Eds.), *Writing on-line: Using computers in the teaching of writing* (pp. 39–46). Upper Montclair, NJ: Boynton/Cook.

Bissex, G. (1980). *Gnys at wrk: A child learns to write and read.* Cambridge, MA: Harvard University Press.

Bloome, D. (1987). *Literacy and schooling.* Norwood, NJ: Ablex Publishing Corp.

Bloome, D., & Green, J. (1984). Directions in the sociolinguistic study of reading. In P. Pearson (Ed.), *Handbook of reading research*. New York: Longman.

Borgh, K., & Dickson, N.P. (1986, April). *The effects of computer-generated spoken feedback on children's writing with a word processor.* Paper presented at American Educational Research Association, San Francisco.

Boudrot, T. (1984, Spring). Writing skills and word processing: Eight easy steps to get you started. *Teaching and Computers*, pp. 28–30.

Bradley, V. (1982). Improving students' writing with microcomputers. *Language Arts, 59*, 732.

Bridwell, L., & Ross, D. (1984). Integrating computers into a writing curriculum: Or buying, begging, and building. In W. Wresch (Ed.), *The computer in composition instruction: A writer's tool* (pp. 107–119). Urbana, IL: National Council of Teachers of English.

Bridwell, L., Sirc, G., & Brooke, R. (1985). Case studies of student writers. In S. W. Freedman (Ed.), *The acquisition of written language* (pp. 172–194). Norwood, NJ: Ablex Publishing Corp.

Bridwell-Bowles, L., Johnson, P., & Brehe, S. (1987). Composing and computers: Experienced writers. In A. Matsuahashi (Ed.), *Real time modelling production processes* (pp. 8–107). Norwood, NJ: Ablex Publishing Corp.

Britton, J.N. (1970). *Language and learning*. Baltimore, MD: Penguin Books.

Broderick, C., & Trushell, J. (1985). Word processing in the primary classroom. In J. Ewing (Ed.), *Reading and the new technologies* (pp. 119–128). London: Heinemann Educational Books.

Bruce, B., Michaels, S., & Watson-Gegeo, K. (1985). How computers can change the writing process. *Language Arts, 62*, 143–149.

Bruce, B., & Rubin, A. (1984). *The utilization of technology in the development of basic instruction: Written communications* (Final Report, Contract No. 300–81–00314). Washington, DC: Bolt Beranek & Newman, Inc.

Bruner, J. (1978). The role of dialogue in language acquisition. In A. Sinclair, R. Jarvelle & W. Levelt (Eds.), *The child's conception of language*. New York: Springer-Verlag.

Bussis, A., Chitenden, E., & Amarel, M. (1977). *Beyond surface curriculum*. Boulder, CO: Westview Press.

Butler, D. (1975). *Cushla and her books*. Auckland, New Zealand: Hodder & Stoughton.

Calkins, L. (1983). *Lessons from a child*. Portsmouth, NH: Heinemann Educational Books.

Calkins, L. (1986). *The art of teaching writing*. Portsmouth, NH: Heinemann Educational Books, Inc.

Carroll, J. (1963). A model for school learning. *Teachers College Record, 64*, 723–733.

Catano, J. (1985) Computer-based writing: Navigating the fluid text. *College Composition and Communication, 36*, 309–316.

Cazden, C. (1972). *Child language and education*. New York: Holt, Rinehart and Winston.

Cazden, C, Diamondstone, J., & Naso, P. (1989). Teachers and researchers: Roles and relationships. *The Quarterly of the National Writing Project, 11*, 1–3, 25–27.

Cazden, C., Michaels, S., & Watson-Gegeo, K. (1984). *Microcomputers and literacy project*. National Institute of Education Report Grant # NIE-G-83-0051.

Chomsky, C. (1971). Write first, read later. *Childhood Education, 47,* 296–299.

Cioffi, G. (1984). Observing composing behaviors of primary age children: The interaction of oral and written language. In R. Beach & L. Bridwell (Eds.), *New directions in composing research* (pp. 171–190). New York: The Guilford Press.

Clark, R., & Salomon, G. (1986). Media in teaching. In M. Wittrock (Ed.), *Third handbook of research on teaching.* New York: Macmillan.

Clay, M. (1966). *Emergent reading behavior.* Unpublished doctoral dissertation. University of Auckland, New Zealand.

Clay, M. (1975). *What did I write?: Beginning writing behaviour.* Auckland, New Zealand: Heinemann Educational Books, Inc.

Clements, D. (1987). Computers and young children: A review of research. *Young Children, 43,* 34–44.

Clements, D., & Nastasi, B. (1988). Social and cognitive interactions in educational computer environments. *American Educational Research Journal, 25,* 87–106.

Cochran-Smith, M. (1984). *The making of a reader.* Norwood, NJ: Ablex Publishing Corp.

Cochran-Smith, M. (1988). Mediating: an important role for the reading teacher. In C. Hedley & J. Hicks (Eds.), *Reading and the special learner* (pp. 109–140). Norwood, NJ: Ablex Publishing Corp.

Cochran-Smith, M. Kahn, J., & Paris, C. (1986, March). *Play with it; I'll help you with it; figure it out; here's what it can do for you.* Paper presented to the Literacy Research Center Speaker Series, Graduate School of Education, University of Pennsylvania.

Cochran-Smith, M., Kahn, J., & Paris, C. (1988). When word processors come into the classroom. In J. Hoot & S. Silvern (Eds.), *Writing with computers in the early grades* (pp. 43–74). New York: Teachers College Press.

Cochran-Smith, M., Kahn, J., & Paris, C. (1990). Writing with a felicitous tool. *Theory into Practice, XXIX,* 4.

Cochran-Smith, M., & Lytle, S. (1990). Research on teaching and teacher research: The issues that divide. *Educational Researcher, 19,* 2–11.

Cole, M., Griffin, P., and the Laboratory of Comparative Human Cognition. (1987). *Contextual factors in education: Improving science and mathematics education for minorities and women.* Prepared for Committee on Research in Mathematics, Science, and Technology Education, Commission on Behavioral and Social Sciences and Education, National Research Council. Madison: Wisconsin Center for Education Research.

Collier, R. (1983). Writing processes and revising strategies: Study of effects of computer-based text editors on revising strategies for independent writers. *College Composition and Communication, 34,* 149–155.

Collins, J., & Sommers, E. (Eds.). (1985). *Writing on-line: Using computers in the teaching of writing.* Upper Montclair, NJ: Boynton/Cook.

Crago, H., & Crago, M. (1983). *Prelude to literacy.* Carbondale, IL: Southern Illinois University Press.

Crist, W. (1984). Teaching writing thru word processing and the rhetoric of composition. *Computers in the Schools, 1,* 77–84.

Cuban, L. (1986). *Teachers and machines: The classroom use of technology since 1920.* New York: Teachers College Press.

Daiute, C. (1983a). Writing creativity and change in childhood education. *Childhood Education, 59*, 227–231.

Daiute, C. (1983b). Computer as stylus and audience. *College Composition and Communication, 34*, 134–145.

Daiute, C. (1984). Can the computer stimulate writers' inner dialogues? In W. Wresch (Ed.), *The computer in composition: A writer's tool* (pp. 131–139). Urbana, IL: National Council of Teachers of English.

Daiute, C. (1985a). *Writing and computers.* Reading, MA: Addison-Wesley.

Daiute, C. (1985b). Do writers talk to themselves? In S. W. Freedman (Ed.), *Acquisition of written language responses and revision* (pp.133–159). Norwood, NJ: Ablex Publishing Corp.

Daiute, C. (1986). Physical and cognitive factors in revising: Insights from studies with computers. *Research in the Teaching of English, 20*, 141–159.

Daiute, C., & Kruidenier, J.(n.d.) *A self-questioning strategy to increase young writers' revising processes.* Unpublished manuscript.

Dalton, D., & Hannafin, M. (1987). The effects of word processing on written composition. *Journal of Educational Research, 50*, 338–342.

Davy, J. (1984). Mindstorms in the lamplight. *Teachers College Record, 85*, 549–558.

Dickinson, D. (1986). Integrating computers into a first and second grade writing program. *Research in the Teaching of English, 20*, 357–378.

Edelsky, C. (1984). The content of language arts software: A criticism. *Computers, Reading and Language Arts, 2*, 8–12.

Edelsky, C., Draper, K., & Smith, K. (1983). Hookin' 'em in at the start of school in a whole language classroom. *Anthropology and Education Quarterly, 14*, 257–281.

Emig, J. (1971). *The composing processes of twelfth graders.* Urbana, IL: National Council of Teachers of English.

Emihovich, C. (1989). Learning through sharing: Peer collaboration in Logo instruction. In C. Emihovich (Ed.), *Locating learning: Ethnographic perspectives on classrooms and research* (pp. 289–310). Norwood, NJ: Ablex Publishing Corp.

Emihovich, C., & Miller, G. (1988). Show me the turtle: A discourse analysis of Logo instruction. *Discourse Processes, 11*, 183–201.

Engberg, R. (1983a). Word processing in the English classroom. *Computers, Reading & Language Arts, 1*, 17–19.

Engberg, R. (1983b). I'll write. . . just lead me to my computer. *Classroom Computer Learning, 4*, 68–69.

Erickson, F. (1982). Taught cognitive learning in its immediate environments: A neglected topic in the anthropology of education. *Anthropology and Education Quarterly XIII*, 149–180.

Erickson, F. (1986). Qualitative methods in research on teaching. In M. Wittrock (Ed.), *Third handbook of research on teaching* (pp.119–161). New York: Macmillan.

Evans, B. (1986, April). *The integration of word processing and computer instruction with fifth and sixth graders.* Paper presented at the annual meeting of the American Educational Research Association, San Francisco, CA.

Evans, J. (1985). Teaching literature using word processing. In J. Collins & E. Sommers (Eds.), *Writing on-line: Using computers in the teaching of writing* (pp.83–88). Upper Montclair, NJ: Boynton/Cook.

Evertson, C., & Green, J. (1986). Observation as inquiry and method. In M. Wittrock (Ed.), *Third handbook of research on teaching* (pp.162–213). New York: Macmillan.

Fallows, J. (1982, July). Living with a computer. *The Atlantic Monthly*, pp. 84–91.

Farr, M. (1985). *Advances in writing research, Volume 1: Children's early writing development.* Norwood, NJ: Ablex Publishing Corporation.

Feldman, P. (1985). Using microcomputers for college writing: What students say. In T. Martinez (Ed.), *The written word and the word processor* (pp. 116–124). Philadelphia: Delaware Valley Writing Council Spring Conference.

Fidanque, A., Smith, M., & Sullivan, G. (1986). *Keyboarding: The issues today.* Proceedings of the 5th Annual Extending the Mind Conference. University of Oregon Eugene, OR.

Flinn, J. (1985). *Composing, computers and contents: Case studies of revising among sixth graders in national writing project classrooms.* Unpublished doctoral dissertation, University of Missouri/St. Louis.

Florio-Ruane, S. (1987). Sociolinguistics for educational researchers. *American Educational Research Journal, 24,* 185–187.

Flower, L., & Hayes, J. (1981). A cognitive process theory of writing. *College Composition & Communication, 32,* 365–387.

Genishi, C. (1988). Kindergartners and computers: A case study of six children. *The Elementary School Journal, 89,* 184–201.

Genishi, C. (1989). The worlds of children: What Maisie knew. *Language Arts, 66,* 872–882.

Genishi, C., & Dyson, A. H. (1984). *Language assessment in the early years.* Norwood, NJ: Ablex Publishing Corporation.

Goodman, K. (1986). Basal readers: A call for action. *Language Arts, 63,* 358–363.

Goody, J. (1968). *Literacy in traditional societies.* Cambridge, UK: Cambridge University Press.

Graves, D. (1975). An examination of the writing process of seven year old children. *Research in the Teaching of English, 9,* 227–241.

Graves, D. (1979). What children show us about revision. *Language Arts, 56,* 312–319.

Graves, D. (1983). *Writing: teachers and children at work.* Portsmouth, NH: Heinemann Educational Books.

Graves, D. (1984). *A researcher learns to write.* Portsmouth, NH: Heinemann Educational Books.

Green, J. (1983). Research on teaching as a linguistic process: A state of the art. In M. Wittrock (Ed.), *Review of Research in Education* (Vol. 10). Washington, DC: American Educational Research Association.

Green, J. (1984). Computers, kids and writing: An interview with Donald Graves. *Classroom Computer News, 4,* 20–28.

Green, J., & Weade, R. (1987). In search of meaning: a sociolinguistic perspective on lesson construction and reading. In D. Bloome (Ed.), *Literacy and schooling* (pp. 3–34). Norwood, NJ: Ablex Publishing Corporation.

Griswold, P. (1984). Elementary students' attitudes during two years of computer assisted instruction. *American Educational Research Journal, 21,* 737–754.

Grow, G. (1988). Lessons from the computer writing problems of professional writers. *College Composition and Communication, 39,* 217–223.

Gula, R. (1982). Beyond the typewriter: an English teacher looks at word processing. *Independent School, 42*, 44–46.

Haas, C. (1987, March). *What research with computers can tell us about the uses of reading in writing.* Paper presented to the 1987 Conference on College Composition and Communication, Atlanta, GA.

Haas, C. (1989). How the writing medium shapes the writing process: Effects of word processing on planning. *Research in the Teaching of English, 23*, 181–207.

Haas, C., & Hayes, J. (1986). What did I just say? Reading problems in writing with the machine. *Research in the Teaching of English, 20*, 22–35.

Halliday, M. A. K. (1973). *Explorations in the functions of language.* London: Edward Arnold.

Harris, J. (1985). Student writers and word processing: A preliminary evaluation. *College Composition and Communication, 36*, 323–330.

Harste, J., Woodward, V., & Burke, C. (1984). *Language stories and literacy lessons.* Portsmouth, NH: Heinemann Educational Books.

Hawisher, G. (1987). The effects of word processing on the revision strategies of college freshmen. *Research in the Teaching of English, 21*, 145–159.

Hawisher, G. (1988). Research update: Writing and word processing. *Computers and Composition, 5*, 7–25.

Hawkins, J., & Sheingold, K. (1986). The beginning of a story: Computers and the organization of learning in classrooms. In J. Albertson & L. Cunningham (Eds.), *Microcomputers and education: 85th yearbook of National Society for the Study of Education* (pp. 40–57). Chicago: University of Chicago Press.

Heap, J. (1989a). Collaborative practices during word processing in a first grade classroom. In C. Emihovich (Ed.), *Locating learning: Ethnographic perspectives on classrooms and research* (pp. 263–288). Norwood, NJ: Ablex Publishing Corp.

Heap, J. (1989b). Sociality and cognition in collaborative computer writing. In D. Bloome (Ed.), *Classrooms and literacy* (pp.135–151). Norwood, NJ: Ablex Publishing Corp.

Heath, S.(1983). *Ways with words.* Cambridge, UK: Cambridge University Press.

Herrmann, A. (1987). Ethnographic study of a high school writing class using computers: Marginal, technically proficient, and productive learners. In T. Gerrard (Ed.), *New directions in teaching and research: Writing at century's end: Essays on CAI.* New York: Random House.

Hillocks, G. (1986). *Research on written composition.* Urbana, IL: National Council of Teachers of English.

Hoot, J. (1988). Keyboarding in the writing process: Concerns and Issues. In J. Hoot & S. Silvern (Eds.), *Writing with computers in the early grades* (pp. 181–195). New York: Teachers College Press.

Hubbard, F. (1985). Composing with computers. *National Forum: Phi Kappa Phi Journal, 64*, 25–28.

Hutchinson, S. (1988). Education and grounded theory. In R. Sherman & R. Webb (Eds.), *Qualitative research in education: Focus and methods* (pp. 123–140). London: Falmer Press.

Hymes, D. (1972), Models of the interaction of language and social life. In J. Gumperz & D. Hymes (Eds.), *Directions in sociolinguistics: The ethnography of communication* (pp. 35–71). New York: Holt, Rinehart & Winston.

Hymes, D. (1974). *Foundations in sociolinguistics*. Philadelphia: University of Pennsylvania Press.

Johnson, R., Johnson, D., & Stanne, M. (1986). Comparison of computer assisted cooperative, competitive, and individualistic learning. *American Educational Research Journal, 23,* 382–392.

Kahn, J. (1988). *Learning to write with a new tool: A study of emergent writers using word processing*. Unpublished doctoral dissertation, University of Pennsylvania.

Kahn, J., Avicolli, M., & Lodise, K. (1988). Learning the Keyboard. *Interface, 4,* 4.

Kahn, J., & Fields, A. (n.d.). *How Julia learns to spell: The role of spelling checkers*. Unpublished manuscript. Beaver College, Glenside, PA: Beaver College.

Kahn, J., & Freyd, P. (1990a). On line: A whole language perspective on keyboarding. *Language Arts, 67,* 84–90.

Kahn, J., & Freyd, P. (1990b). Touch typing for young children: Help or hindrance? *Educational Technology, XXX,* 41–46.

Kane, J. (1983). *Computers for composing*. (Tech. Rep. No. 21). New York: Bank Street College of Education.

King, B., Birnbaum, J., & Wagen, J. (1985). Writing processes and the basic college writer. In T. Martinez (Ed.), *The written word and the word processor* (pp. 251–266). Philadelphia: Delaware Valley Writing Council Spring Conference.

Kisner, E. (1984). Keyboarding: a must in tomorrow's world. *The Computing Teacher, 11,* 21–22.

Knapp, L.K. (1986). *The writing process and the writing teacher*. Englewood Cliffs, NJ: Prentice-Hall.

Koenke, K. (1987). Keyboarding: Prelude to composing at the computer. *English Education, 19,* 244–249.

Kurth, R.J. (1987). Using word processing to enhance revision strategies during student writing activities. *Educational Technology, XXVII,* 13–19.

Laboratory of Comparative Human Cognition (1989). Kids and computers: A positive vision of the future. *Harvard Educational Review, 59,* 73–86.

Lafrenz, D., & Friedman, J.E. (1989, May). Children don't change education, teachers do! *Harvard Educational Review, 59,* 222–225.

Lampert, M. (1985). How do teachers manage to teach: perspectives on problems in practice. *Harvard Educational Review, 55,* 178–194.

Larson, E. (1986). The effect of technology on the composing process. *Rhetoric Society Quarterly, 16,* 43–58.

Levin, J., & Boruta, M. (1983). Writing with computers in classrooms: You get EXACTLY the right amount of space! *Theory into Practice, 22,* 291–295.

Levin, J.A., Boruta, J.J., & Vasconcellos, M.T. (1983). Microcomputer-based environments for writing: A writer's assistant. In A. Wilkinson (Ed.), *Classroom computers and cognitive science* (pp.219–232). New York: Academic Press.

Levin, J., Riel, M., Rowe, R., & Boruta, M. (1985). Muktuk meets Jacuzzi: Computer networks and elementary school workers. In S. W. Freedman (Ed.), *The acquisition of written language* (pp. 160–171). Norwood, NJ: Ablex Publishing Corp.

Lindemann, S., & Willert, J. (1986). Word processing in high school writing classes. In J. Collins & E. Sommers (Eds.), *Writing online: Using computers in the teaching of writing* (pp. 47–54). Upper Montclair, NJ: Boynton/Cook.

Lindfors, J. (1987). *Children's language and learning*. Englewood Cliffs, NJ: Prentice-Hall.

Lutz, J.A. (1987). A study of professional and experienced writers revising and editing at the computer. *Research in the Teaching of English, 21,* 398–421.

Lytle, S., & Cochran-Smith, M. (1990). Learning from teacher research: a working typology. *Teachers College Record, 92.*

MacArthur, C.A. (1988). The impact of computers on the writing process. *Exceptional Children, 54,* 536–542.

Martinez, T. (1985a). Apples and pears? Use of Apple computers to aid secondary school writers. In T. Martinez (Ed.), *The written word and the word processor* (pp. 70–87). Philadelphia: Delaware Valley Writing Council Spring Conference.

Martinez, T. (1985b). *The written word and the word processor.* Philadelphia: Delaware Valley Writing Council Spring Conference.

Martlew, M. (1983). *Psychology of written language: A developmental approach.* London: John Wiley and Sons.

McAllister, C. (1985). The word processor: A visual tool for writing teachers. *Journal of Developmental Education, 8,* 12–15.

McAllister, C., & Louth, R. (1988). Effect of word processing on the quality of basic writers' revisions. *Research in the Teaching of English, 22,* 417–427.

McKenzie, J. (1984). Accordion writing: Expository composition with the word processor. *English Journal, 73,* 56–58.

Mehan, H. (1989). Microcomputers in classrooms: Educational technology or social practice? *Anthropology and Education Quarterly, 20,* 4–22.

Michaels, S. (1985, July). Classroom processes and the language of text editing commands. *Quarterly Newsletter of Laboratory of Comparative Human Cognition, 7,* 70–79.

Michaels, S. (1986). *The computer as a dependent variable.* Unpublished manuscript.

Michaels, S., & Bruce, B. (1989). *Classroom contexts and literacy development: How writing systems shape the teaching and learning of composition* (Tech. Rep No. 476). Urbana-Champaign, IL: Center for the Study of Reading.

Moran, C. (1983). Word processing and the teaching of writing. *English Journal, 72,* 113–115.

Morocco, C. (1987). *Final report to U.S. Office of Education.* Special Education Programs. Educational Development Center, Inc, Washington, DC.

Morocco, C., & Neuman, S. (1986). Word processors and the acquisition of writing strategies. *Journal of the Learning Disabled, 19,* 243–247.

Murray, D. (1985). *A writer teaches writing.* Boston, MA: Houghton Mifflin.

O'Brien, G., & Pizzini, E. (1986) Word processing/text editing and the quality of student abstracts. *School Science and Mathematics, 86,* 223–228.

O'Brien, P. (1984). Using microcomputers in the writing classroom. *The Computing Teacher, 11,* 20–21.

Olson, C.P. (1988). Computing environments in elementary classrooms. *Children's Environment Quarterly, 5,* 39–50.

Olson, D. (1985). Computers as tools of the intellect. *Educational Researcher, 14,* 5–8.

Olson, J. (1986, April). *Curriculum change and the classroom order.* Paper presented to the annual meeting of the American Educational Research Association, San Francisco, CA.

Olson, J. (1988). *Schoolworlds/Microworlds: Computers and the culture of the classroom.* Oxford, UK: Pergamon Press.

Oxenham, J. (1980). *Literacy: Writing, reading and social organization.* London: Routledge & Kegan Paul.

Palmer, A., Dowd, T., & James, K. (1984). Changing teacher and student attitudes through word processing. *The Computing Teacher, 11*, 45–47.

Papert, S. (1980). *Mindstorms.* New York: Basic Books.

Paris, C. (1989a, March). *Contexts of curriculum change: Conflict and consonance.* Paper presented to the annual meeting of American Educational Research Association, San Francisco.

Paris, C. (1989b, October). *Quiet resistance: Teachers maintaining integrity in curriculum change.* Paper presented to the Bergamo Conference on Curriculum Theory and Classroom Practice, Dayton.

Paris, C. (1990, April). *Teacher initiative in curriculum change: Altered processes, altered paradigms.* Paper presented to the annual meeting of American Educational Research Association, Boston.

Paris, C. (in press). *Teacher agency in curriculum change: Processes, contexts and meanings.* New York: Teachers College Press.

Paris, C., Barton, N., & Shelow, M. (1988). *Excuse me please, but what was I saying?* Unpublished manuscript. University of Pennsylvania.

Parson, G. (1985). *Hand in hand: Word processing and microcomputers: Two revolutions in the teaching of writing.* Alaska Department of Education.

Pearson, H. (1986). Writing and reading. *Educational Review, 38*, 101–115.

Pearson, H., & Wilkinson, A. (1986). The use of the word processor in assisting children's writing development. *Educational Review, 38*, 169–187.

Phenix, J., & Hannan, E. (1984). Word processing in the grade one classroom. *Language Arts, 61*, 804–812.

Piazza, C., & Riggs, S. (1984). An invitation to play. *Early Childhood Development and Care, 17*, 63–76.

Piper, K. (1983). *Word processing in the classroom: Using microcomputer-delivered sentence combining exercises with elementary students.* Silver Spring, MD: IEEE Computer Society Press.

Piper, K. (1983–1984). The electronic writing machine. Using word processing with students. *The Computing Teacher, 11*, 82–83.

Porter, R. (1986). Writing and word processing in year one. *Australian Educational Computing, 1*, 18–23.

Porter, R., & Sherwood, M. (1987). *Word processing, writing, and revising: A report to the Commonwealth on a project of national significance.* New South Wales, Australia: Macquarie University.

Pufahl, J.P. (1986). Alone on the word processor: Writing and rewriting. *Teaching English in the Two Year College, 13*, 25–29.

Raphael, T., & Reynolds, R. (Eds.). *Contexts of school-based literacy.* New York: Longman, Inc.

Read, C. (1971). Preschool children's knowledge of English phonology. *Harvard Educational Review, 41*, 1–34.

Riel, M. (1985). The computer chronicles newswire: A functional learning environment for acquiring literacy skills. *Journal of Educational Computing Research, 1*, 317–337.

Rosegrant, R.J. (1984). Fostering progress in literacy development: Technology and social interaction. *Seminars in Speech and Language, 5*, 47–57.

Rubin, A., & Bruce, B. (1984.). QUILL: Reading and writing with a microcomputer. In B.A. Hutson (Ed.), *Advances in reading/language research* (Vol. VIII, pp. 97–117). Greenwich, CT: JAI Press.

Rubin, A., & Bruce, B. (1986). Learning with QUILL: Lessons for students, teachers, and software designers. In T. Raphael & R. Reynolds (Eds.), *Contexts of school based literacy* (pp. 217–230). New York: Longman, Inc.

Ryle, G. (1949). *The concept of mind.* Chicago: University of Chicago Press.

Salomon, G., & Gardner, H. (1986). The computer as educator: Lessons from television research. *Educational Researcher, 15*, 13–19.

Scardamalia, M., Bereiter, C., & Goelman, H. (1982). The role of production factors in writing ability. In M. Nystrand (Ed.), *What writers know: The language, process and structure of written discourse* (pp. 173–210). New York: Academic Press.

Scardamalia, M., & Bereiter, C. (1983). The development of evaluative, diagnostic and remedial capabilities in children's composing. In M. Martlew (Ed.), *Psychology of written language: A developmental approach* (pp. 67–95). London: John Wiley and Sons

Schieffelin, B., & Cochran-Smith, M. (1984). Learning to read culturally. In H. Goelman, A. Oberg, & F. Smith (Eds.), *Awakening to literacy.* Exeter, NH: Heinemann Educational Books, Inc.

Schmidt, W., & Buchmann, M. (1983). Six teachers' beliefs and attitudes and their curriculum time allocations. *Elementary School Journal, 84*, 162–171.

Schmidt, W. Porter, A., Floden, R., Freeman, D., & Schwille, J. (1987). Four patterns of teacher content decision making. *Journal of Curriculum Studies, 91*, 439–455.

Schwartz, H. (1982). Monsters or mentors: Computer application for humanistic education. *College English, 44*, 141–152.

Schwille, J., Porter, A., Belli, G., Floden, R., Freeman, D., Knappen, L., Kuhs, T., & Schmidt, W. (1983). Teachers as policy brokers in the content of elementary mathematics. In L. Shulman & G. Sykes (Eds.), *Handbook of teaching and policy.* New York: Longman.

Scollon, R., & Scollon, S. (1981). *Narrative, literacy and face in interethnic communication.* Norwood, NJ: Ablex Publishing Corporation.

Selfe, C. (1985). The electronic pen: Computers and the composing process. In J. Collins & E. Sommers (Eds.), *Writing on-line: Using computers in the teaching of writing* (pp. 55–66). Upper Montclair, NJ: Boynton/Cook.

Seltzer, C. (1986). The word processor—A magical tool for kindergarten writers. *Early Years K-8*, pp. 51–52.

Sheingold, K., Hawkins, J., & Char, C. (1984). *"I'm the thinkist you're the typist." The interaction of technology and the social life of classrooms* (Tech. Rep. No. 27). New York: Bank Street College of Education.

Sheingold, K., Kane, J., & Endreweit, M. (1983). Microcomputer use in schools: Developing a research agenda. *Harvard Educational Review, 55*, 412–432.

Shimahara, N. (1988). Anthroenthnography: A methodological consideration. In R. Sherman & R. Webb (Eds.), *Qualitative research in education: Focus and methods* (pp.76–89). London: Falmer Press.

Skublkowski, K., & Elder, J. (1987). Word processing in a community of writers. *College Composition and Communication, 38*, 198–201.

Sloan, D. (1984). *The computer in education: A critical perspective*. New York: Teachers College Press.

Smith, F. (1981). Demonstrations, engagement and sensitivity: A revised approach to language learning. *Language Arts, 52,* 103–112.

Smith, F. (1986). *Insult to intelligence: The bureaucratic invasion of our classrooms.* New York: Arbor House.

Smye, R. (1984). Computer innovations for teaching the writing process. *English Quarterly, 18,* 27–37.

Snyder, T., & Palmer, J. (1986) *In search of the most amazing thing*. Reading, MA: Addison-Wesley.

Solomon, G., & Gardner, H. (1986). The computer as educator: Lessons from television research. *Educational Researcher, 15,* 13–19.

Stillman, P. (1985). A writer (and teacher of writing) confronts word processing. In J. Collins & E. Sommers (Eds.), *Writing on-line: Using computers in the teaching of writing* (pp. 19–28). Upper Montclair, NJ: Boynton/Cook.

Sudol, R. (1985). Applied word processing: Notes on authority, responsibility, and revision in a workshop model. *College Composition and Communication, 36,* 331–335.

Swinton, S., Amarel, M., & Morgan, J. (1978). *The PLATO elementary demonstration: Educational outcome evaluation* (Final report). Princeton, NJ: Educational Testing Service.

Teale, W., & Sulzby, E. (Eds.). (1986). *Emergent literacy: Writing and reading.* Norwood, NJ: Ablex Publishing Corp.

Tobin, K., & Tobin, B. The one-computer classroom: Applications in language arts. *Australian Journal of Reading, 8,* 158–167.

Turkle, S. (1984). *The second self.* New York: Simon & Schuster.

U.S. Office of Technology Assessment. (1988). *Power on: New tools for teaching and learning.* Washington, DC: (Tech. Rep)

Vygotsky, L. (1978) *Mind in society.* Cambridge, MA: Harvard University Press.

Walker, D. (1983). Reflections on the educational potential and limitations of microcomputers. *Phi Delta Kappan, 65,* 103–107.

Watt, D. (1983). Word processors and writing. *Independent School, 42,* 41–43.

Weade, R., & Evertson, C. (1988). The construction of lessons in effective and less effective classrooms. *Teaching and Teacher Education, 4,* 189–213.

Weick, K. (1976). Educational organizations as loosely coupled systems. *Administrative Science Quarterly, 21,* 1–19.

Weir, S. (1989). The computer in schools: Computer as humanizer. *Harvard Educational Review, 59,* 61–73.

Weizenbaum, J. (1976). *Computer power and human reason.* San Francisco, CA: W. H. Freeman.

Wetzel, K. (1985). Keyboarding skills: Elementary, my dear teacher? *The Computing Teacher, 12,* 15–19.

White, D. (1981). *Books before five.* Portsmouth, NH: Heinemann Educational Books. (Original work published 1954)

Willer, A. (1984). Creative writing with computers: What do elementary students have to say? *Computers, Reading and Language Arts, 2,* 39–42.

Wiske, M.S., Zodhiates, P., Gordon, M., Harvey, W., Krensky, L., Lord, B., Watt, M., Williams, K., & Wilson, B. (1987). *How technology affects teachers.* Cambridge,

MA: Harvard Graduate School of Education Development Center, Office of Educational Research Institute & U.S. Department of Education.

Wolf, D.P. (1985). Flexible texts: Computer editing in the study of writing. In E. Klein (Ed.), *Children and computers* (pp. 37–54). San Francisco, CA: Jossey-Bass.

Womble, G. (1985). Revising and computing. In J. Collins & E. Sommers (Eds.), *Writing on-line: Using computers in the teaching of writing* (pp. 75–82). Upper Montclair, NJ: Boynton/Cook.

Woodruff, E., Bereiter, C., & Scardamalia, M. (1981–1982). On the road to computer assisted compositions. *Journal of Educational Technology Systems, 10,* 133–148.

Wresch, W. (Ed.). (1984). *The computer in composition instruction: A writer's tool.* Urbana, IL: National Council of Teachers of English.

Zaharlick, A., & Green, J. (in press). Ethnographic research. In J. Flood, J. Jensen, D. Lapp, & J. Squire (Eds.), *Handbook of research in teaching the English Language Arts.* New York: MacMillan.

Zinsser, W. (1983). *Writing with a word processor.* New York: Harper & Row.

Zurek, J. (1985). Computers and the writing process: A report of students with two years' experience. In T. Martinez (Ed.), *The written word and the word processor* (pp. 156–164). Philadelphia, PA: Delaware Valley Writing Council Spring Conference.

Author Index

Subject Index